CONSUMER CULTURE

CONSUMER CULTURE

HISTORY, THEORY AND POLITICS

ROBERTA SASSATELLI

Los Angeles | London | New Delhi
Singapore | Washington DC

First published 2007

Reprinted 2010

SAGE Publications Ltd
1 Oliver's Yard
55 City Road
London EC1Y 1SP

SAGE Publications Inc.
2455 Teller Road
Thousand Oaks, California 91320

SAGE Publications India Pvt Ltd
B 1/I 1 Mohan Cooperative Industrial Area
Mathura Road
New Delhi 110 044

SAGE Publications Asia-Pacific Pte Ltd
33 Pekin Street #02-01
Far East Square
Singapore 048763

Library of Congress Control Number: 2006934303

British Library Cataloguing in Publication data

A catalogue record for this book is available from the British Library

ISBN 978-1-4129-1180-1
ISBN 978-1-4129-1181-8 (pbk)

Typeset by C&M Digitals (P) Ltd, Chennai, India
Printed in Great Britain by Ashford Colour Press Ltd, Gosport, Hampshire
Printed on paper from sustainable resources

Contents

Acknowledgements

Because I have learned so much from the friends and colleagues with whom I have exchanged views and experiences about consumption, history, politics and cultural theory in the last decade or so, I cannot imagine a better way to start this book than by thanking them for consuming their time and eyes on various texts of mine, and above all for their enthusiasm, friendship, and intelligence: thanks to Jeffrey Alexander, Adam Arvidsson, Massimo Baldini, Marina Bianchi, John Brewer, Paolo Capuzzo, Tim Dant, Cristina De Maria, Rossella Ghigi, Monica Greco, Yukka Gronow, Shaun Hargreaves Heap, Antoine Hennion, Sandro Mezzadra, Massimo Montanari, Jonathan Morris, Kate Nash, Alessandro Pizzorno, Marco Santoro, Alan Scott, Don Slater, Davide Sparti, Frank Trentmann, Alan Warde, Rick Wilk and to the late Paolo Donati. Most of these friends and colleagues have read early drafts, chapters or parts of this book and offered precious suggestions and comments. To present one's own work in progress is often an exciting and inspiring experience and I am grateful to the following institutions for inviting me to give papers on consumer culture: the History and European Civilization Department at the European University Institute, Florence, the Department of History at Warwick University, the Centre for Nordic Alcohol Studies at Helsinki, the Philosophy and Social Theory Workshop at the University of Exeter, the Department of Sociology at Lancaster University, the Department of Sociology at the University of Cork, the Istituto Gramsci of Rome, the Humanities and Social Sciences Department at the California Institute of Technology, Pasadena, the Social Studies Department at the University of Helsinki. As I have been teaching consumption for a decade, my thoughts have partly taken shape as I attempted to get sharper for my students, both in Italy and the UK: both their enthusiasm and doubts have been constant sources of inspiration, for which I thank them all. Last but not least, I am grateful to Jasper Chalcraft for his graceful help with the intricacies of my second language, Mila Steele and Katherine Haw at Sage for their supportive editorial and production assistance and Chris Rojek for his inspiring appreciation of my work. The book is dedicated to Marco and Riccardo, with deep love.

Introduction

Born to consume

Growing up in most contemporary Western contexts, the average individual will be confronted not only with a cornucopia of commodities and commercialized services but also with a variety of discourses and institutions identifying such a context as 'consumer society' or 'consumer culture'. More or less explicitly, these discourses and institutions will address people as 'consumers'. This book is concerned precisely with the practices, discourses and institutions which have brought about and characterize 'consumer culture'. Although the product of an historical process, the contemporary ways of organizing and understanding the relations between people and objects have several distinctive features.

In all societies objects accompany human beings throughout their existence, offering them support and inspiration and, at the same time, imposing limits and difficulties. In most European countries of today as well as the US or Canada, Australia or Japan, the birth of a child is greeted with a profusion of gifts (booties, bibs, dummies) with which parents, relatives and friends demonstrate their joy, just as the departure of a loved one requires the visible demonstration of pain through the purchase and appropriate use of particular goods (flowers, telegrams, cards of condolence). In so-called 'tribal societies', as in most 'traditional' ones, elaborate public ceremonies are described as making use of different things as numerous and just as specific as these to mark the most significant moments in life. Indeed, we know of ancient civilizations – from the diverse cultures which have succeeded one another in the Mediterranean basin, to pre-Columbian cultures, to early Chinese empires – through the remains of numerous objects which accompanied the everyday lives of their members, and which have often been recovered from rich burials. Even in times and places as profoundly characterized by religious asceticism as medieval Europe, people exchanged and made use of all kinds of things; there was in fact a remarkable circulation of non-essential objects linked to religious devotion in this period, including a blossoming trade in religious relics. More generally, the possibility that every culture could be handed down and become an object of cultural reflection for its members is linked to the spread of supporting materials which fix it (from parchment, to books, to CDs); thus it is through the consumption of cultural objects that a given culture can reach beyond the boundaries of the group which originally created it.

However, there are differences between contemporary Western society and those which preceded it, or those which, through traditions which are presented as marginal or ancestral, still resist it in several parts of the world. These differences often have to do with the processes of consumption. It is frequently claimed, in a tone of regret, that ours is a 'consumer society' or a 'consumer culture'. Such labels – emerging after the Second World War and made famous by authors such as Marcuse, Galbraith, Packard and Baudrillard – were used to suggest that the society which we live in is a particular variant of capitalism characterized by the primacy of consumption. In reality though, underneath the apparent simplicity of the expression 'consumer society' lies profound ambiguity. From its very first appearance, this term has been used more to convey condemnation than to describe; in particular, instead of being deployed to comprehend what characterized actual consumer practices, it served to stigmatize what appeared to be a growing and uncontrolled passion for material things. At that time 'consumer society' constituted an attack on so-called 'consumerism': a continuous and unremitting search for new, fashionable but superfluous things, which social critics have branded as causing personal discontent and public disengagement in advanced capitalism.

With its apocalyptic tones, this moralistic and moralizing connotation masks substantial continuities as well as important differences between our society and other social formations. Even societies radically different from ours can be characterized, at least in part or in certain sectors of the population, as materialist and acquisitive. Thus, people in 'tribal' societies also use objects to distinguish themselves and mark social hierarchy, alliances and conflicts; even in these societies one can find forms of conspicuous consumption which mostly serve to reinforce social and cultural domination by certain members. For their part, the 'new' and 'exotic' have often proved fascinating and alluring even in societies as cautious and traditional as the medieval one – the remarkable diffusion throughout Europe of oriental spices that began in this period being a well-known example. Still, it is evident that these societies are in many ways quite distant from our own. How, then, can we begin to think about the peculiarity of contemporary consumer culture? How can we capture the specificity of our times?

I shall pursue an entry into these issues by borrowing the words which Max Weber (1980, orig. 1923) used to define mature Western capitalism: consumer society is a type of society in which 'the satisfaction of daily needs' is realized 'through the capitalist mode'. This is to say, that daily desires are satisfied through the acquisition and use of 'commodities', goods which are produced for exchange and are on sale on the market. Even if we encounter various forms of capitalism in all historical periods (that is, forms of production characterized by the maximization of profit), according to Weber, it is only in the West, and only from a given moment onwards in the development of modern capitalism, that we can find this type of society. To this, I shall add that in the consumer society we not only satisfy our most elementary daily needs through commodities; we also conceptualize the purchase and use of goods as acts of 'consumption'. Furthermore, we are accustomed to being addressed as 'consumers' by a plethora of scientific disciplines, mundane discourses and social institutions which contribute to circumscribing and delineating what 'consumption' means and what kind of people we are when we act as 'consumers'. Consumption appears to be a world in and of itself, made up of specifically dedicated places and times which are thought of as juxtaposed to, and separate from, those of work. As is evident, consumption gets increasingly coded as leisure, and leisure is increasingly commoditized. Thus, our daily life is typically organized as alternating between times/space of work and times/spaces of consumption: we wake up and 'consume' breakfast at home or in a coffee-shop, we go to work in a factory or office where we spend most of the day, taking a 'break' from 'work' only to 'consume' a sandwich at a pub, in a canteen or food outlet, we return home where a series of instruments help us complete our diverse acts of 'consumption' – from listening to a new CD we bought in the nearest shopping centre to relaxing in a hot bath with a miraculous essential oil recommended by a friend. And, if we still have any energy left, we might go out to other places of consumption (restaurants, cinemas, clubs, gyms, night clubs, etc.) where we can enjoy specific goods and services made available to us through the work of others, who will themselves consume their lot in other spaces and times. Such a structure is associated with the diffusion of waged work, which requires that employees work in a disciplined fashion, concentrating exclusively on their specific job even in an era of increasingly flexible organization of labour. Because it is paid, work-time is precious and is to be purified of every distraction and amusement. Amusement and distractions are important of course, and so they are provided by institutions of consumption which are temporally and spatially bound and by occasions of consumption which are regulated through commoditization. Whilst these institutions and occasions are superfluous to productive organizations, for most individuals they are the most important, representing 'free time', or at least 'freedom' from the discipline of work.

Acting as an intermediary between these two moments of our existence, work and consumption, is the sphere of exchange. In our society this sphere is characterized not so much and not only by its notable size, but also and above all by the dominance of the monetary economy. As Georg Simmel (1990, orig. 1907) revealed, money's infiltration into every aspect of social exchange during the course of modernity facilitated the possibility of purchase and sale of objects thanks to its 'impersonal and abstract nature', making exchange infinitely easier than in economies based on barter and a myriad of specific and personal agreements (a point which is well summarized by the English word 'currency'). The progressive virtualization of exchange with the introduction of chequebooks and cash-points, and the development of financial services for consumption (from credit cards to mortgages) has further facilitated the commercial circulation of goods; this has reduced the inertia inherent in coins and notes which heavily burdened cash exchanges. Conjoined with a situation of flexible exchange is a rather strong and complex system for the commercial promotion of goods. Even in ancient societies, sellers needed to flaunt their goods, and there existed naïve though nonetheless successful forms of advertising, such as was found on the doors of imperial Pompei's brothels. Nevertheless, it is only with modern capitalism that the promotional system has become central, so much so that today's goods are conceived of with a public of consumers in mind: they are, essentially, made to be sold. Coterminous with the unfolding of the historical process in the last three centuries, various media – from newspapers to the radio, from television to the Internet – have been vehicles for commercial culture, hosting and spreading all kinds of advertising.

As we are often reminded, advertising has an important role in contemporary society. It brings new and diverse goods closer to us, goods produced in distant places, through often unknown processes, which may then be consumed in rather unpredictable ways. Our society is characterized by an amazing flowering of material culture. If by 'culture' we intend the ensemble of meaningful practices through which social actors orient themselves in the world, then by 'material culture' we intend the ensemble of objects, man-made or otherwise, which are given meaning by those practices and which, in turn, contribute to giving meaning to those same practices. The concept of material culture goes beyond the material/symbolic distinction, and underlines that objects are part of a system of open meanings which require the intervention of actors to become meaningful. Today, material goods are extremely numerous and each of us makes use of a remarkable variety in the course of a day. The objects available to members of 'tribal' or traditional societies were relatively few as well as less varied and distant. While it is easy to provide stereotypical images of 'tribal' communities in remote places or ancient times, we may safely consider that it was likely that members of such communities would eat food they had procured personally from the richness of their natural environment, eating out of a bowl they had themselves made, sleeping on a mat woven by a member of their family, adorning themselves with beads procured through barter with a neighbouring tribe, amusing themselves with objects exchanged within their clan. Even in traditional societies where the inter-local market had developed a certain importance, this didn't include objects of everyday use, only those luxury goods which weren't always available to everybody. In these subsistence economies where work, consumption and exchange were strongly integrated, people used history-thick objects of closer provenance in ways that were taken for granted and had immediate, straightforward significance. Production and consumption were not specialized and separated spheres of action, held together by an equally specialized sphere of exchange and commercialization: the fundamental cultural dichotomy on which social order rested was that of sacred/profane rather than of production/consumption.

In contemporary Western societies, the hegemonic character of discourses and practices which disentangle production and consumption means that we usually find ourselves confronted with objects whose meaning and use escape us. Mirroring this, advertising and the various aspects of the commercialization of goods (from packaging to branding) are busy constructing meanings around products to make them 'consumable', (i.e. significant for the consumer) by placing them within his or her structure of needs, thus inevitably modifying and expanding his or her desires and needs. The process of commoditization, that is the transformation of a good into a commodity exchangeable on the market at a certain fixed monetary price, extends also to services. The image we hold of economic culture in tribal societies as well as in traditional ones underscores gifts, nepotism or the division of domestic labour by age or gender. Certainly, in our society gifts, nepotism and the sexual division of domestic labour persist; nevertheless, we have more recourse to commodities or commoditized services. Various aspects of domestic work have profoundly changed and, following the decline of domestic service, at least partly been replaced by the wide diffusion, especially after the Second World War, of domestic appliances. An army of laundries, companies dedicated to cleaning, and snack bars have also to some extent, replaced the exchange of unpaid domestic services which took place within the extended family. Even when we want to make a gift, we rarely escape the market, as the crowds which fill shops and malls before Christmas testify.

Corresponding with the inexhaustible commoditization of goods and services, each of us relentlessly tries to preserve personal identities and relations from the logic of the market and price, and we often end up adjusting the second to the first. The logic of personal relations still presides over the exchange of gifts and, at least in part, over commodities. In most Western societies, when we purchase an object as a gift, we have to make sure we remove the price; when we receive one, we can at the most say something like 'it must have cost you a fortune', but we know very well that to ask the actual cost would be extremely impolite. When we receive a gift that we don't like we cannot openly and without good moral cause re-transform it into a commodity or 'recycle' it as a present, and if we dare do so we must act with circumspection, as we are transgressing some of the fundamental rules governing relations between people. But even when we leave a toddler at kindergarten, we demand that the employees look after the little one not only because they are paid but also because the child – which appears as the quintessential human being, unmarked by society, politics, economy – deserves attention and affection. Furthermore, the phenomenon of branding clearly adumbrates the power of loyalty and personal(ized) attachments in the mass market. And, even when we appear to be doing nothing more than engaging in a mechanical impersonal exchange, such as when we grab a snack from a vending machine, in reality we activate a whole series of social mechanisms, like trust, which link us to the product, the channel of sale, technology, etc. well beyond the logic of price. One of the paradoxes of our society is that we actually depend on commodities to complete our daily lives, yet we find it necessary to de-commoditize objects and services if we want our activities to have meaning for us as human beings. If the consumer society is that in which daily needs are satisfied in a capitalist way through the acquisition of commodities, it is also that in which each consumer has to constantly engage in re-evaluating these objects beyond their price, in order to stabilize meanings and social relations.

The so-called consumer society thus appears to be in continuity with, yet different from, other societies which, following an established sociological convention, we can posit as its contrasting 'types'. The differences which characterise it consolidated themselves over the course of at least the last three centuries. If it is true, as Weber maintained, that a general predominance of daily needs being satisfied commercially (including outside of metropolitan areas) occurred only in the second half of the 19th century, it is also the case that other characteristics of a consumer society could be found in earlier periods, above all in England and Holland. For example, already by the end of the 17th century some fairly standardized goods of colonial origin were becoming widely available throughout all social strata: tobacco, tea, coffee and sugar. On the other hand the system of the commercialization of goods began to take a modern shape from the beginning of the 18th century, when techniques of promotion, of advertising, of the presentation of commodities in shops, etc. very similar to those we know today began to be used. At that same time consumption became an important theme of reflection in public discourse, repeatedly debated and interrogated in the diffusion of newspapers which themselves were subsidized by advertising.

As will be apparent in the course of this book, consumption is best considered as a complex economic, social and cultural set of practices, interconnected with all of the most important phenomena which have come to make up contemporary

Western society: the spread of the market economy, a developing globalization, the creation and recreation of national traditions, a succession of technological and media innovations, etc. If it is true that in today's 'consumer society' we are born to consume, it is also true that consumption has cultural and practical implications that go way beyond satisfying our daily needs through commodities, or even symbolically play with them in variously elaborated manners. To consume is also to act as 'consumers', that is to put on a particular, contested kind of identity and to deal with its contradictions. In this light, consumer culture is more than commoditization and affluence, more than conspicuous consumption and the democratization of luxuries. Consumer culture also *produces consumers*. But does so *in a variety of ways* which need further investigation. In a growing variety of activities, growing numbers of people now speak of themselves as consumers, and they are being addressed as consumers by a host of institutions, within and without the market. The centrality of the 'consumer', the lengthy and contested historical processes which led to its formation, the many theoretical portrayals of consumer agency, the political implications of conceiving contemporary culture as consumer culture are the main subjects of this book. The following pages thus elaborate on a fundamental research agenda: adopting a constructivist approach to consumer culture, emphasis is placed on the social, cultural and institutional processes which have made consumption into a contested field of social action and public debate, bringing notions of the consumer to life and promoting it as a major social identity in contemporary societies.

Structure of the book

The book is organized to offer an historically grounded and theoretically informed discussion of contemporary consumer culture as well as a critical understanding of its diversity, reach and ambivalence. Throughout the book a variety of empirical examples illustrate the rich texture of consumer culture(s). The ambivalence of consumption is shown by looking at the various ways in which it can be conceived as an ordinary and yet socially regulated practice of appropriation: people typically remove commodities from their commercial codes and contexts, but do so by negotiating with routines and meanings which are otherwise deemed culturally appropriate, reasonable, fair and even 'normal'. The chapters are thus divided into three parts, organized around three main dichotomies: *production/ consumption*; *rationality/irrationality*; *freedom/oppression*. Both in lay and social scientific discourse, these dichotomies have been applied to understand contemporary consumer culture. Reference to them thus helps in discussing its history, theory and politics, even though much of the book is concerned with showing that consumption challenges dichotomies and involves other, more complex patterns of relation. The first part on *history* maps the multifarious, spatially and temporally articulated historical development of (Western) consumer culture, thus providing a cultural reading of the vast socio-economic and geopolitical transformations this has entailed. The second part on *theory* critically discusses the main theoretical approaches which have tried to model consumer agency from neo-classical economics to sociological classics, from critical theory to communication approaches, up to the recent emphasis on theories of practice and ritual de-commoditization. The third part on *politics* considers the political dimension of consumer culture, looking at the issue of representation and intermediation and in particular the role of advertising; at de-commoditization as a contested terrain where social actors negotiate hegemonic views of identity and choice; and finally the issues of globalization, localization and alternative consumption. While one part naturally leads into the following, each of them can be read separately. The text closes with a brief conclusion that both helps by drawing the book's overarching theses and threads together and offers some analytical tools for further investigation. Finally, at the very end of the book, the reader will find some selected suggestions for further reading. Their purpose is twofold: to mark out key studies related to the arguments proposed, and to point to auxiliary resources to orientate research and writing in the field of consumption.

PART I

THE RISE OF CONSUMER CULTURE

In most conventional descriptions of the birth of capitalism, consumption is rarely portrayed as a crucial phenomenon, let alone one which is capable of being the propulsive force behind historical processes. The birth of modern capitalist society is normally explained through a series of diverse variables, all of them inherent, as it were, to the sphere of production: from the industrial revolution to the spread of an industrious and calculating bourgeois mentality. However, the social sciences have recently begun to recognize that the history of consumption – intended as a bundle of practices, a contested object of moral judgement and a category of analysis – is extremely important in understanding the genesis of the capitalist system as well as its late-modern variant which is strongly characterized by an eye-catching circulation of commodities.

Thus, through changes in consumption we can re-read the history of modernity and of the expansion of Western civilization. By way of example, in *Seeds of Change*, the historian Henry Hobhouse (1985, xi) writes that 'The starting point for the European expansion out of the Mediterranean … had nothing to do with, say, religion or the rise of capitalism – but it had a great deal to do with pepper. The Americas were discovered as a by-product in the search for pepper'. Of course, it was not only desires of consumption that stimulated transoceanic crossings, or that these alone brought new possibilities for consumption. Nevertheless, capitalism was induced not only by the industrial revolution which reached its apogee in the second half of the 19th century, or by the calculating mentality of the petite bourgeoisie of the 17th and 18th centuries (perhaps inspired by the ascetic Calvinism which so fascinated Max Weber), but also by consumption, from the extravagances of the nobility and high finance to the small luxuries of the masses. This, as we shall see, happened from the tail-end of the late Medieval period.

According to Weber (1930, orig. 1904–5), the Protestant mentality – especially in its Calvinist form – promoted an ascetic and calculating attitude which favoured capitalist accumulation, forming through frugality and hard work the financial capital necessary for the development of the capitalist enterprise. However, we should also remind ourselves that contrasting with this asceticism was a hedonistic mentality which saw as much meaning in the comforts and even in the waste of consumption. This mentality was chiefly represented by the nobility, high finance and, in ever increasing numbers, by the lower orders. Thus, hedonism and waste existed – and indeed had re-emerged during the Renaissance – alongside asceticism and prudence. In other words, somebody had to consume those goods which were produced through the industriousness of the first capitalists, and they had to have good reasons for doing so.

As I shall show later on, contemporary economic and cultural history demonstrate that it is impossible to provide a sharp divide between a preceding puritan and Protestant era which gave an initial impulse to accumulation, and a subsequent period of hedonism from which the so-called 'consumer society' sprang forth (Appadurai 1986a; Brewer and Porter 1993; Campbell 1987; Mukerji 1983). From this perspective, the spread of new models of consumption, spurred on by international commerce, the colonies, courtly excess and an increasingly materialistic mentality, gradually favoured the development of a system of credit and debt, and more generally stimulated competition and cross-fertilization between different social groups, other than mere economic exchange. This was accompanied by the speeding up and expansion of the dynamics of taste, freeing them from the constrictions of the medieval period. In medieval society's closed and tight social hierarchy, the tastes and dynamics of consumption were also fairly rigid, tending to reproduce the existing social order. The consolidation of modern society and the relative social mobility which characterizes it have instead brought forth (and been favoured by) continuous – and ever more rapid – changes in lifestyles.

The same *supply/demand* dichotomy which has been so important in the development of economic analysis does not seem to take account of the phenomenon of consumption. Above all, this is because consumption is not only expressed in the *demand* for goods (the purchase of objects or services) but in their *use* (their symbolic associations, the ways in which they are distributed within families, the practices and discourses through which they are managed, etc.) which in ordinary life fills goods with value. The notion of demand in some way isolates consumption from the web of social activities (including production) and reduces processes of consumption to a series of disentangled and re-aggregated acts of purchase, thus making the commercial value of an object appear to be a good proxy for its social and cultural value. Instead, I will show that *economic value* is *culturally constructed* through deep-seated *historical processes*. Obviously, there are events which make a difference and particular places and periods in which the clock of the history of consumption seems to tick more quickly: just think of the precipitating role that the Second World War had in spreading and making legitimate American lifestyles across Western European countries. However, to understand what characterizes today's consumer society, one has to keep in mind a series of phenomena which have developed over a long period at different speeds and in different places. The so-called consumer society is in fact profoundly interconnected with a type of society that sociologists conventionally term 'modern' (Lury 1996, 29 ff.; Slater 1997, 24 ff.) and which has a complex historical genesis. Consumer society can thus be associated with the wide diffusion of a variety of commodities (which occurred, of course, in different waves: for example, colonial goods like sugar in the 17th and 18th centuries, fabrics and clothes in the 19th century, cars and domestic technology in the 20th century). Broadly speaking, it is also coterminous with the process of *commoditization*, so that more and more objects and services are exchanged on the market and are conceived of as commodities.

Furthermore, it develops along with the globalization of commodity and cultural flows; with the increasing role of shopping as entertainment and spectacle; with the increasing democratization of fashion; with the growth in sophisticated advertising; with the spread of credit to consumers; with the proliferation of labels defining a variety of consumer pathologies like kleptomania or compulsive buying; with the organization of associations dealing with consumer rights or calling into being the consumer's political persona ... The list could hardly be closed and perhaps what is most important here is to realize that all these phenomena are linked to broad cultural and political principles which are themselves also considered typically modern; these range from the identification of freedom with private choice to the consolidation of impersonality and universalism as recommendable codes of conduct for social relations; from the idea that human needs are infinite and undefined, to the expectation that each individual can (and must) find 'his/her own way', as personal as possible. The particular cultural politics of value which underpins the development of 'consumer society' is thus not a natural one, it is one which requires a process of learning whereby social actors are practically trained to perform (and enjoy) their roles as consumers.

Capitalism and the Consumer Revolution

1

For a long time sociology and history implicitly followed a dualist position which gave the organization of production the role of the engine of history. Studies of 17th to 18th century material culture have discredited this *productivist* vision which typically presented consumer society as emerging at the beginning of the 20th century as a sudden and mechanical reaction to the industrial revolution, and then gradually penetrating all social classes through the consumption of mass-produced goods. On the basis of the work of the French historian Fernand Braudel (1979), who began to study this problem not as a separate economic phenomenon but as an integral part of culture and the material life of people, historians have begun to give due consideration to the development of material culture, and, in fact, to give it a propulsive role in the historical process. From the 1980s onward the understanding that consumer society is not comprehensible as just a late derivative of capitalism became established; consumption was now seen as having actively participated in the development of the capitalist system.

In this chapter we shall consider some of the most important overall explanations for the rise of the consumer society which have replaced the productivist thesis. These anti-productivist views have foregrounded various aspects of consumer culture – from promotional techniques, to hedonistic ethics, to commercial incentives (Campbell 1987; De Vries 1993; McKendrick et al. 1982). I will then insist on the need to adopt a multi-causal approach, considering economic, cultural and social dimensions and abandoning a linear model of development in favour of an understanding of the multiple geographies and temporalities of different consumer patterns and values. Drawing on Werner Sombart's work on luxury, the consumption of superfluous and refined, colonial and exotic goods, together with the forms of knowledge which accompanied them, are seen as pivotal for a variety of institutions which have worked as engines for the rise of consumer culture, from the court with its competitive merry-go-round of fashions, to the urban environment with its succession of shopping places, to the bourgeois home with its emphasis on decent comfort and polite refinement.

Consumption, production and exchange

As suggested, traditional wisdom has considered consumer culture as the late consequence of the industrial revolution; in this productivist vision the so-called 'consumer society' was but an effect of the capitalist mode of production. Industrialization is thus seen as responsible for the spread of large quantities of standardized commodities, made accessible to ever-larger segments of the population. In other words, the industrial revolution, conceived of as a radical transformation of the economic structure of production, was at the root of the revolution in demand. From this point of view, the consumer society can be conceived of as a *cultural* response which logically follows a more fundamental *economic* transformation. The consumer society therefore coincides with 'consumer culture' or 'consumerism'. Consumer culture is itself defined in reductive and ambiguous terms, mixing and meshing practices with representations, consumer meanings with advertising images – and indeed reducing the former to the latter, thus reducing consumption to mass culture, which is in turn depicted as a mere derivative of industrial mass production. In this way, even when consumption is the subject of analysis, it is both inappropriately and unwillingly taken back to production.

A first important step towards opposing such a position has been taken by historians. Through the use of a variety of quantitative sources (from business profits and taxes, to wills, etc.) and qualitative data (descriptions of stolen objects in police reports, personal diaries, etiquette guides, etc.) historians are now able to indicate that a growth in material culture in Europe began in the early modern period and, thus, before the industrial revolution (Fairchilds 1998). A clear *growth in consumption* was registered above all from the second half of the 17th century and throughout the 18th century in many European nations and in different social classes – from the inhabitants of Paris (Roche 1981), to Dutch peasants (De Vries 1975), to the urban as well as rural English (Shammas 1990; Thrisk 1978; Wetherhill 1988). Of course, given the paucity of adequate sources, it is difficult to identify with certainty the pace of the growth of consumption in this period. It is also evident that the early development of modern consumption has its own particular, uneven and partial geography. Even within a given nation it is difficult to talk of an increase in consumption for the whole population, since consumption could vary massively between social classes, whilst gender and generational differences accounted for the unequal distribution of goods within the same family. Nevertheless, from the second half of the 17th century people of every class and gender began to acquire via the market many more finished goods, in particular household furnishings (paintings, ceramics, textiles) and personal ornaments (umbrellas, gloves, buttons) (Borsay 1989). At the same time the diffusion of sugar and new stimulants like tobacco, coffee, tea and cocoa seems to have played an important role in revolutionizing consumption (Mintz 1985; Schivelbusch 1992). One must not forget either the spread of prints as decorations for domestic space, which paralleled the specialization of rooms in the houses of the nascent bourgeoisie (Perrot 1985; Schama 1987).

These examples are not however due to mass production. Up until the 19th century what was available was the result of flexible production in small units, rather than standardized production in large structures typical of the industrial revolution.[1] In the same way, even though superfluous commodities were widely available, their distribution was through channels of small specialized retailers (Fawcett 1990). Manufactured goods were often retailed directly by the producers, who offered the possibility of various personalized finishings for the goods. The

THESIS (AUTHOR)	HISTORICAL CAUSE	SOCIAL GROUP	CENTURY	PLACE
PRODUCTIONIST	STANDARDIZED AND CHEAP GOODS	WORKING CLASS	XX	ENGLAND
ANTIPRODUCTIONIST				
CONSUMERIST (McKendrick)	COMMERCIALIZATION SYSTEM STATUS DISPLAY	UPPER MIDDLE CLASS	XVIII	ENGLAND
MODERNIST (Campbell)	CULTURAL CONSUMPTION IMAGINATIVE HEDONISM	MIDDLE CLASS WOMEN	XVIII/XIX	ENGLAND
EXCHANGIST (De Vries)	HOUSEHOLD ORGANIZATION MONETARY EXCHANGE	RURAL FAMILIES	XVII/XVIII	HOLLAND

Figure 1.1   The theses on the birth of the consumer society

situation was similar in many European nations, fostered by international commerce and the diffusion of commodities from the colonies.

Taking stock of the studies of the general growth in consumption in early modernity, authors like Neil McKendrick (1982), Colin Campbell (1987) and Jan De Vries (1975), have led the way to what I call the *anti-productivist* turn. In fact, not only do their studies push back the revolution in demand to the 18th century or the second half of the 17th century, but they also present alternative theoretical paradigms, providing an anti-productivist view of the birth of consumer society. They all attempt to show that demand, more than production, became a vital part of the economic and cultural process. In different terms, they all underline that it was the desire for consumption more than processes of work that played an active role in giving shape to modernity. Let us consider them one by one, outlining their main arguments (see Figure 1.1).

McKendrick's observations marked a shift in studies of the history of consumption. McKendrick stresses that the consumer revolution was 'the necessary analogue to the industrial revolution, the necessary convulsion on the demand side of the equation to match convulsion of the supply side' (McKendrick 1982, 9). According to this British historian, the revolution in consumption should be placed in the second half of the 18th century in England, and be seen against the background of a society that was becoming more flexible and less hierarchical as a result of the *status aspirations* of the new bourgeois classes; in McKendrick's view they saw a possibility for social advancement in the conspicuous emulation of the consumption of the class which had until then been the custodians of refinement – the nobility. Furthermore, the desire of the bourgeoisie to consume was stimulated by avaricious entrepreneurs who, despite not yet using industrial techniques of production, knew very well how to use sophisticated modern *sales techniques* to foster these status aspirations.

To this end McKendrick mentions Josiah Wedgwood's porcelain, among the most important of the period and still some of the most appreciated in the world. Wedgwood understood and exploited the pretensions of the nobility and the aspirations of the bourgeoisie, getting his porcelain sponsored by royal families throughout Europe and then benefiting from the aura created by this apparent patronage of the 'great' to sell his wares at a high price to the *nouveaux riches*. This entrepreneur was one of the first to adopt genuine *ante litteram* marketing techniques (that is, the planning of production with the sale in mind) and design (applying sophisticated aesthetics of artistic merit to consumer goods). All this with the intent to produce a large quantity of goods, available at accessible prices, ready to satisfy the ascendant bourgeoisie's desire for taste and refinement. As Andrew Wernick (1991) writes, Wedgwood heralded a 'promotional culture' in which objects are products commercialized with a particular market in mind. For example, he cultivated the growing interest amongst the privileged in archaeology and antiquity, and exploited it by producing 'Etruscan' vases which were exhibited in spectacular fashion in his chain of shops and subsequently achieved even greater prestige through being displayed in the homes of the nobility. From this perspective, the demand for refined goods on the part of the new ascendant middle classes, provoked by shrewd entrepreneurs and artisans, created the market which modern industry needed and soon learned to exploit to its advantage. McKendrick therefore offers us an explanation for the birth of consumer society that I may define as *consumerist*. In this way the process of industrialization is the effect and not the cause of new desires of consumption, and these corresponded with the possibility of displaying one's status and were stimulated through promotional techniques.

In sharp contrast to the productivist thesis, McKendrick treats demand as an active part of the historical process which developed capitalism. However, he does not historicize demand itself. On the contrary, he portrays demand as the result of some 'natural' human inclination to imitate those with power and status, waiting to free itself the moment material conditions permit. The birth of consumer society is thus credited to consumerism, which in turn, is seen as catalysed by the dynamism of fashion fused with social emulation and encouraged by the manipulative sales techniques of wily producers. Therefore, his explanation is not able to take account of the cultural specificity of a social environment in which it was becoming possible, lawful, and even proper (for some) to follow fashion, to spend for their own pleasure, to be attracted by the exotic, to learn to enjoy luxuries and ostentation, etc. The motives and values which pushed the first bourgeoisie to consume more and more are never taken seriously and given the attention they deserve: instead they are reduced to emulation, envy or the demonstration of status.

In an explicit countering of McKendrick's thesis, and in particular of his historically and culturally flat view of the motives for consumption, Campbell offers an explanation I may define as *modernist*. His well-known work *The Romantic Ethic and the Spirit of Consumerism*, (Campbell 1987) is inspired by Weber's (1930, orig. 1904–5) celebrated essay on the Protestant ethic and capitalism, and at the same time wants to complete it, demonstrating that not only production but also consumption contributed to the birth of capitalism. According to his view, conspicuous consumption is only an incidental, and not even a particularly significant, part of a new ethical and aesthetic attachment to novelty and originality which draws heavily on its roots in Romanticism. Romanticism provided people with both the good reasons and a repertoire of justification for their consumer desires (see also Campbell 1994).

Campbell is concerned with trying to pin down what is distinctively 'modern' about the attitude towards material culture that takes hold with the modern era. In his view, the search for novelty appears to be a fundamental characteristic of modernity, along with a particular type of hedonism: the modern consumer is a 'hedonist' who, Campbell (1987, 86–7) writes, continually 'withdraw(s) from reality as fast as he encounters it, ever-casting his day-dreams forward in time, attaching them to objects of desire, and then subsequently "unhooking" them from these objects as and when they are attained and experienced'. What distinguishes modern consumption is its being a private exercise of a particular kind of hedonism, of the mind rather than of the body, and consequently infinite. The body and its desires are no longer sated by the banquets of old: the mind and the myriad meanings it can give to experience and things, extend the possibilities of consumption to infinity. In other words, in living above the level of subsistence, modern consumers have developed a form of modern hedonism which sees objects as ripe for personal creative fantasy. Their interests are concentrated in the meanings and images which can be attributed to a product, something which requires the presence of 'novelty'. Thanks to 'private and imaginary' modern hedonism, consumption becomes not so much the ability to bargain over price, or to use products, but 'the imaginative pleasure-seeking to which the product image lends itself, "real" consumption being largely a resultant of this "mentalistic" hedonism. Viewed in this way, the emphasis upon novelty as well as that upon insatiability both become comprehensible' (*ibid*, 89).

Placing the consumer revolution around the end of the 18th century and the beginning of the 19th century, Campbell maintains that in contrast to what occurred in ancient and traditional societies, modern consumers tend to construct the context of their personal enjoyment through mixing up and manipulating illusions, thus reproducing their 'day-dreams', primarily through objects. Objects are appreciated above all for their meaning and their images, thus making continual 'innovation' both possible and necessary. Social actors are pushed in this direction by the teachings of Romanticism. According to Campbell, the ethic which is derived from these teachings motivates consumption not through some idea of otherworldly salvation, nor through the ostentation of status and social climbing, but in relation to self-improvement and aesthetic enjoyment. The Romantics maintained that, essentially, the goal of human beings was to set oneself in opposition to society: rather than bettering oneself through work, discipline and sacrifice, one should throw oneself into self-expression, in a search for different and meaningful experiences (Campbell 1987; 1994). The constant search for new forms of gratification is not only anti-traditionalist behaviour, but also the opposite of traditional forms of hedonism. The hedonism of the ancients was, as Campbell reminds us, linked to certain specific sensorial practices (eating, drinking, and so on). As mentioned above, modern hedonism is instead defined by the pleasures of imagination and so is linked to the capacity to control emotions, for instance the ability to live situations of risk and fear vicariously as one finds in Romantic literature. In fact it was the novel (from the *feuilleton* to Gothic tales) which, due to its structure and commercial circulation, was at the same time one of the first standardized mass products, one of the first examples of mass circulation (and thus potential universality) of culture, and naturally an important diffuser of the very same Romantic ethic to, above all, women of the middle classes (Bermingham and Brewer 1995).

Campbell has rightly shown how some specific motivations for consumption have been fostered by new ethical and aesthetic orientations and have given rise to new cultures of consumption. He has attempted to explain an apparent contradiction in the development of capitalism, namely the fact that it is the very same English bourgeoisie amongst whom the Protestant ethic was strongest that gave life to a revolution in consumption; he maintains that it is precisely the control of emotions within the Protestant ethic which made the modern conception of pleasure possible, focused as it is on the ability to contemplate objects and manipulate their meanings. If we move just a little bit forward in history, we come across the type of person who best expresses the attachment described by Campbell: the English *dandy*. In fact, the image of the dandy, which became a topic of fervent debate between the 19th and the 20th centuries, was linked to a particular conception of pleasure: a general disposition to new and exotic experiences rather than the enjoyment of this or that particular object. As Rachel Bowlby (1993, 16 and 23) has suggested, Oscar Wilde's *The Picture of Dorian Gray* can be seen as a way of reflecting on pleasure and the price that the life of a dandy bore: Dorian 'exchanges his moral self for the unbounded liberty of the new hedonist', there is no limit to what he can have, 'to the number of personalities he can adopt, to the experiences he can try', he becomes a pure 'container and carrier for sensations'.[2]

Whilst he does demonstrate the cultural character of individual fantasies, Campbell brushes over those social processes which make some fantasies more suited to some individuals, to their attributes of class, race, sexuality, etc. In fact, for at least the 19th and the beginning of the 20th centuries, the negation of the self typical of Protestantism was able to express itself in the gratification of the self typical of Romanticism, mostly because production and consumption had become two (relatively) distinct spheres, organized in different times and places, and linked to different types of people. As we will see more clearly later on, in bourgeois society it is middle-class women who could (and indeed had to) become the consumers *par excellence*. It was they, above all others, who had to 'daydream'.[3] More generally, what Campbell sees as an 18th to 19th century syndrome – that is, the dissatisfaction with purchased goods and continual search for new objects of desire capable of personal stimulation beyond social distinction – could be found in every urban community which was sufficiently large and commercially developed, where at least a certain percentage of the population had the time and money to spend on the construction and presentation of the self through the growing number of goods on the market (Burke 1978; Mukerji 1983). As Peter Burke (1993, 157) recalls, even back in the 1500s the geographer and political theorist Giovanni Botero noted that living in close proximity in cities had made the Italian nobility more inclined to seek personal identity in demonstrative effects obtained through the use of novel and different goods. Thus, in his major work, Campbell doesn't fully account for 'imaginary' hedonism as a long-running cultural tendency privileging materialism, nor does he seem to be interested in a cultural genealogy of why and how it happened that, from the 18th century onward, the use of goods came to be problematized as 'consumption' and social actors were addressed as 'consumers'.

To demonstrate the cultural embeddedness of economics Campbell concentrated exclusively on consumption. Meanwhile, the economic historian Jan de Vries (1975; 1993) attempted to reconcile the history of consumption with that of the modes of production and distribution, focusing on the role of distribution and commercial relationships which have developed in modern markets. I may define the explanation he offers for the birth of consumer society as *exchangist*. Concentrating on Holland, he describesd how, from the end of the 17th century, spending on consumption increased even as disposable real income decreased, explaining this as due to the reallocation of productive resources within the family unit. De Vries notes that as real salaries decreased and available goods grew, families did not behave 'rationally', saving and reducing their commodity consumption. Instead, they consumed more commodities and financed their expenditures by working longer hours to produce for the market, which enabled them to obtain the money they needed to act as consumers. Rural families were as important as urban dwellers in this shift. 'This complex of changes in household behaviour constitutes' – writes De Vries (1993, 107) – 'an "industrious revolution", driven by Smithian, or commercial, incentives, that preceded and prepared the way for the Industrial Revolution.' The consolidation of mechanisms of freer and safer monetary exchange offered both the opportunity and the stimulus to modify traditional economic tendencies, shaped as they were by conservation and the management of scarcity. Thus, from De Vries's perspective, it was the opportunity and necessity to participate in monetary exchanges which heralded the beginning of the consumer society.

De Vries's explanation is particularly useful in demonstrating that production and consumption are just two faces of the same coin. Already in the 17th century, social actors chose to act as producers for the market in order to become consumers of goods, thus reorganizing the relationships and boundaries between production and consumption. However, the hypothesis of the 'industrious revolution' has its limits. The market mechanism and monetary exchange are presented as the real agents of this transformation. In particular, the market is naturalised as a sort of *deus ex machina* thanks to which production and consumption find a new balance, whilst the exchange value of goods appears as a neutral instrument of economic processes whose meaning resides in the private desires of consumers. Instead, in this period there were political and cultural scripts which constructed commodity value, contributing to the structure of prices and, what is more, to making commercial exchange widely legitimate and highly desirable: commodities were not only objects with a price that could be purchased by anybody who could afford them, often they were also exotic objects of colonial origin, especially from Asia (Carrier 1995; Willis 1993; Zahidieh 1994). Commercial exchanges were thus invested with a particular cultural value: to participate in market relations was becoming a fundamental gesture of agency for the citizens of the Low Countries as much as the private acquisition of new commercial goods was related to political visions that were both progressive and nationalist.

Exchange value becomes something more than a neutral instrument when it is intertwined with modern markets. In fact, these are characterized by processes of de-personalization and disentanglement of relations on the one hand, and by an increasingly rapid obsolescence of commodities on the other, with the risk of disorientating rather than encouraging people. That is why one begins to notice a need to promote not only commodities but also a particular vision of consumers. Contested as it might have been, the 'consumer' was called forth and brought into life as an important social 'role' or 'identity', the economic analogue of the 'citizen': someone able to rely on themselves to assume the responsibility for their own choices and tastes (see Chapter 7).

The genesis of consumer capitalism

Whilst extremely important, the explanations offered by McKendrick, Campbell and De Vries have been variously criticized. As suggested, history is abandoning the attempt to offer univocal and overall explanations for the 'consumer revolution'. The most recent economic and cultural historiography has instead adopted a multifaceted approach which insists on multiple trajectories and shows capitalism to be the result of the reciprocal action of elements that were already present and widely spread before capitalism, as it is conventionally understood, fully manifested itself (Glennie 1995; Trentmann 2004). The development of the consumer society is thus increasingly described as a *long-term phenomenon* with *multiple geographies* and a variety of particular *object histories* (see Figure 2.2, p. 44). Importantly, some studies have underlined how, even during the time of the Renaissance cities of Italy, in courts and city markets, commodities began to exert a direct and powerful attraction on a growing part of the population (Burke 1978; Findlen 1998; Mukerji 1983). The notion that there was a definitive historical event has been brought into question by the knowledge that both capitalist forms of production and the phenomena of modern consumption have developed at unequal paces, and differentially according to country and the types of goods. Historians thus try to account for the wide variety of forms, places and times in which different factors have operated: from international commerce to colonialism, from new technologies of transport and communication to new worldly ethics, and so on. Particular attention has been given to the formation of new needs and to new means of attributing value to commodities linked to international commerce (Carrier 1995; Curtin 1984; Lenman 1990; Mukerji 1983), to colonialism (Mintz 1985; Spooner 1986; Thomas 1991; Zahidieh 1994), and to the relationship between gender and consumer practices (De Grazia and Furlough 1996; Roberts 1998).

Phenomena such as these were much in evidence to a contemporary of Max Weber, the sociologist-historian Werner Sombart. Anticipating the current historical debate, Sombart (1928) explained the genesis of capitalism through combining the factors of economic growth relative to production with those relative to consumption. According to Sombart, we can see traces of the development of a new type of society back in the 14th century – above all in Italy and later in Germany, Holland and England. Here the accumulation of capital saw a marked increase, and was no longer based on the feudal economy; instead, it was based on the trade with, and exploitation of, colonies, on the discovery of new reserves of precious metals and money lending. To be sure, the exploitation of the colonies and the needs of armies and international commerce were fundamental to the development of capitalism, since they contributed to the total growth of commodities in circulation and the frequency of their exchange. Nevertheless, Sombart is adamant that we cannot simply explain capitalism through geographical enlargement or through a simple increase in the market transactions. The development of the colonies and international commerce were in fact initially linked to particular commodities: luxury goods. On close examination, a large part of the goods which make up the growth in demand of early modernity are precisely those goods which appeared on the European market for the first time: non-essential goods which took on new and refined roles that had previously been filled by more simple resources – and in particular spices and drugs, perfumes, dyes, silk and linen, precious stones and then, from the late 16th century onwards, sugar, coffee, tea and cocoa.

In his book *Luxus und Kapitalismus*, Sombart (1967, orig. 1913) maintains that luxury has the capacity to create markets, essentially because it concerns goods of high value which promote and require capitalisation and economic rationalization, including a growing availability of credit-providing devices. Thus, it is the very 'nature' of these commodities which favoured capitalist formation: for Sombart, then, it is above all the characteristics of a part of material culture – those refined goods 'of superior class' which go 'beyond the necessary', intended as the 'common currency' in a given 'culture' – which promoted a new capitalist organization within commerce, agriculture and industry. In fact, the desire for luxury goods occupies an important position amongst the genetic factors of capitalism, both materially (supporting consumption and favouring the development of forms of production that are ever more efficient and on a large scale), as well as culturally (as indicator and catalyst of a new configuration of needs which gradually spread from the nobility to the upper bourgeoisie and thus throughout the social fabric). By stimulating commerce and production, the consumption of luxury goods contributed to the accumulation of capital which constituted one of the material prerequisites for the development of modern industry. Furthermore, these forms of consumption also signalled the spread of a hedonistic-aesthetic attitude towards objects. According to Sombart, it is mainly from the 18th century onwards that a hedonistic attitude to shopping developed. Thus, it was those shops selling luxury goods which were the first to arrange themselves as places of elegant entertainment; having reached notable dimensions, they began to differentiate themselves according to the needs they wished to satisfy and to fuel (female *toilette*, soft furnishings, etc.), promoting the diffusion of fixed price, and an increasing depersonalization of the relationship between seller and buyer.

In Sombart's view, economics, culture and politics contribute together to the development of the capitalist way of life. The new models of consumption which stimulate capitalist production thus correspond to a new political model characterized by the advent of the absolutist state. The Renaissance courts of Italy had already developed a lifestyle that anticipated modernity, and had a crucial role in stimulating the consumption of luxury goods and the refining of tastes. These were followed in the 17th century by the absolutist courts, of which the French remains the most important example: here, as Norbert Elias notes in his classic study (1978/82, orig. 1936/9) and thanks also to a new relationship between the sexes, refined material pleasures and their manners became social weapons, genuine status-markers in the courtly game. It is from the court that desires of consumption spread, gradually and then in waves, throughout the rest of society. Initially, Sombart insists, it was mostly the upper bourgeoisie who had rapidly accumulated capital through commerce or finance, who represented the new and most important segment of consumption. They wanted to mix with the nobility and used shrewd strategies of marriage, whilst competing with the noble elite not only with their pecuniary power but also through their use of refined goods to demonstrate their taste and sophistication. In the final analysis, Sombart writes (1967, 80–4), 'the longing for luxury would not have descended to wider strata of Europe within so short a time, nor would luxury expenditures have assumed such gigantic proportions almost overnight, if it had not been for ... the very great need for luxuries on the part of the nouveaux riches' and if the nobility had not participated in the game of emulation, attempting to 'equal the bourgeois parvenus in ostentatious display'. Supported and stimulated by the provision of financial services and credit, this social game gave way to processes of hybridization between a high culture of waste and refinement and a bourgeois one of thrift and prudence.

In the 17th and 18th centuries there were thus important transformations of the *economic culture* as a whole: these are centuries which saw both the development of a new rationalist orientation to production among emergent social groups, and the appearance of a more reflexive and self-sustained culture of consumption among not only the elites but also the upper-middle strata of the population. These observations enable us to take into consideration what, broadly speaking, characterized the *culture of consumption* during the 17th and 18th centuries. They are helpful in correcting Weber's well-known hypothesis which, as already suggested, links the birth of capitalism to Calvinist worldly asceticism and thus to a particular *culture of production*. For example, if we consider consumption among the nascent upper-middle classes of the Low Countries in the 17th century, at the apogee of their economic and cultural splendour, a number of interesting cases demonstrate how production, commerce and consumption were profoundly intertwined, and how most groups participated in new lifestyles which combined asceticism and hedonism. Thus, notwithstanding its being a rigorously Protestant country, it is in the Low Countries that we witness one of the most celebrated booms in demand of early modernity: the so-called 'tulip mania'. This mania reached its apex in 1637 when speculators and enthusiasts were willing to pay the equivalent of a rich and vast agricultural estate for just one tulip bulb (Bianchi 1999; Garber 1989). Such a phenomenon is difficult to understand today if we are unaware of the potent allure of the exotic (tulips came from the Orient), of a new materialist and rationalist attitude which made collecting and the cataloguing of the world a widely approved pastime, and of the commercial and investment opportunity – however risky – offered by such a small and readily transportable good. Similar factors were brought to light in Simon Schama's 1987 well-known study *The Embarrassment of Riches*, which discusses the spread of paintings and prints amongst devout Dutch Protestants. Schama shows how the passion of Dutch artists for detailed representation, through still lifes so rich in detail and so codified and formal that they are almost catalogues, and the corresponding passion of *petite* and *haute* Dutch bourgeoisie for those paintings was a way of invoking their growing material well-being through subduing it to a regime of temperance.

Going back to Sombart and following his observations, we may consider that the enlargement of the market is initially *qualitative*, with the production of objects of high value which stimulate capitalisation and business mentality on the one hand, and a hedonistic-aesthetic attitude on the other; and then *quantitative,* with the democratisation of luxuries. However, the latter does not simply represent the freedom of the masses from need. The intensification of the capitalist spirit pushes, in Sombart's view as well as Weber's, towards a rationalization of the economic system which may have disciplining effects upon people. In contrast to Weber, Sombart concentrates not only on the rationalization of the organization of work (previously observed by Marx), but also on the rationalization of consumption. The rationalization of consumption – its becoming subject to bureaucratic control and instrumental calculation – may be noticed from the end of the 17th century onward. If the desire for new and non-essential goods is one of the driving forces of early capitalism, the management of luxuries through their creation and domestication in the dynamics of fashion is one of the factors which keep the wheels of commerce in constant motion, stabilizing the capitalist economy in its more mature phases. Thus, Sombart insists on the fact that with the progression of capitalist society luxuries will be produced in series for ever-larger groups of people; in this way they are not only democratized but also rationalized, that is they are subjected to the dynamics of 'fashion', becoming largely 'responsive' – to use a term later proposed by Kenneth Galbraith (1958) – not to the needs of the 'rich' so much as to that of programmed large-scale production. It therefore seems that Sombart would agree with Arjun Appadurai's (1986b, 32) argument that '[m]odern consumers are the victims of the velocity of fashion as surely as primitive consumers [or 'traditional' ones] are the victims of the stability of sumptuary law' which selectively forbids the use and possession of numerous non-essential goods according to status, gender, age, etc. The sumptuary laws prescribed which colours, styles and materials could be used by people of different social positions, at least in public, so that it was in fact forbidden by law to dress 'above' one's station. These laws were slowly abolished, and with the division of labour, social mobility and the monetary economy which have come to characterize the modern period, everyone – provided they have sufficient money – has the right to buy whatever good they please on the market. In this situation, the merry-go-round of fashion stimulates people to buy, but it is also independent of individual volition and with its ever more frenetic speed constantly engages them in new acts of consumption.

The circulation of luxuries tended to speed up following the spatial proximity and cultural amalgamation connected to the development of the large cities of modernity, above all the large colonial and commercial capitals like London and Amsterdam which were filled up with industrious great consumers. As suggested by Sombart (1967, 24):

> The large cities of the early capitalistic epoch are basically consumer cities. The most important consumers are familiar with us; the princes, prelates, nobles, who are now joined by a new group, 'haute finance' (which may be regarded as a class of consumer without disparaging its 'productive' function in the politico-economic organization).

In its turn, the consolidation of large modern cities contributes to the growth of the need for luxuries by creating a wealth of occasions for mundane pleasures and cultural exchange. Parties and social gatherings no longer remain confined to princely palaces, spreading instead to other social circles who find a need for public places of entertainment and pleasure like theatres, music-halls, refined restaurants and hotels. Even shops, which had begun to be furnished with care and refinement from the 18th century, change, becoming spaces of leisure, of worldly amusement rather than just mere places for the supply of goods. Elegant shops were important places for the development of a modern culture of consumption. They heralded the spread of a new recreational attitude to purchasing (which is now taken for granted in the phrase 'going shopping'). They became a public space in which women were not only well accepted, but also over which they were said to 'reign' (all this in a period in which two separate and typically gender-segregated spheres of action become delineated, the public and the private). Recent literature on both England and France has shown that the development of elegant shopping places at the heart of urban environments favoured the public visibility and personal autonomy of middle-class women, otherwise confined to the domestic sphere as mothers and wives (Rappaport 2000; Tiersten 2001). Populated by a mostly female workforce (Benson 1986), the department stores became a feature of the 19th century novel, which charged them with anxieties about female desires, but also with visions of respectability and female emancipation (Bowlby 1985 and 2000). To go shopping became a new feminine form of sociability, the germ of a feminine public sphere, which found expression also in a variety of initiatives deploying purchasing power as a political tool (Hilton 2002).

The changing gender order – namely the changing system of relations among men and women and their cultural attributes – and the changing configuration of both the public sphere and the sphere of intimacy are phenomena which have notoriously been associated with the process of commercialization (see Beck and Gernsheim 2001; Giddens 1990). One of Sombart's sharpest intuitions indeed relates to the role of evolving relations between the sexes in promoting and developing modern consumer culture and society. Examining art and literature from medieval Europe, and once again the Italian Renaissance, he suggests that there was a link between the 'secularization of love' – its slow but progressive emancipation from religious institutions and rules – the uses of riches in a luxurious manner and a general hedonistic-aesthetic attitude to things. As love became gradually more justifiable in and of itself as an 'earthly enjoyment' of beauty and the 'emancipation of the flesh', and therefore (in a society still markedly male-dominated) there developed a new 'hedonistic-aesthetic conception of the woman and of love for a woman', the doors to all sensory pleasures and their tireless refinement opened. In this view the development of consumer society was driven not only by men risking huge amounts of capital to arm the large commercial transoceanic trading vessels of the colonies, but also, as Sombart (1967, 39 ff.) writes provocatively, by a specific category of women: the 'courtesans'. These women were not simply lovers, but 'intelligent and beautiful' ladies who incarnated a new female figure, initially intrinsic to the court, but gradually present also in upper-bourgeois society. Expert in refined pleasures and luxury, they ended up creating aspirations throughout society for elegant entertainment and opulence: the gradual social affirmation of the courtesan thus 'contributed to the formation of taste of the honest woman', so much so that bourgeois wives followed the tastes and styles of the courts, bringing new extravagant desires to the whole of society. For Sombart, sexuality as eroticism and sensory delight was intimately linked to personal luxury and materialism, that which excited sight, smell, hearing, etc. in a refined way. Of course, once they were hooked, the mechanism of luxury also nourishes the desire human beings have to compare themselves with others and to demonstrate their status. Therefore Sombart notes that this emulative-competitive thrust, to which Thorstein Veblen (1994, orig. 1899) gives a primary causal role (see Chapter 3), is a universal feeling which can manifest itself in many different and culturally specific ways:[4] it develops through conspicuous consumption and refinement only where materialistic attitudes, 'sensory delight' and 'eroticism' have a certain influence on the values and lifestyles of a relevant part of the population.

From courts to cities, from luxuries to fashion

Sombart's work on luxury has been defined as '[t]he best general treatment of the relationship between demand, the circulation of valuables, and long-term shifts in commodity production' (Appadurai 1986b, 36; see also Mukerji 1983; and for a sociological appraisal Grundmann and Stehr 2001). His reflections on consumption help us to consider the importance of a long process, both cultural and material, in which a new form of consumption linked to non-essential goods and social mobility ended up catalysing industrialization. Many of Sombart's points have been taken up in numerous and important studies which have underlined the role of the *consumption of luxuries* linked to the development of a *new spatiality of consumption*, namely a new social and cultural organization of the spaces where practices of consumption are to be found. Institutions and places such as the courts and their thirst for luxury, the urban environment in which luxury shops spread and the latest fashion was on display, and the development of the bourgeois household in which women were confined and reigned as consumers are prime elements of this new spatiality which put luxury into circulation (see Figure 1.2).

The absolutist *courts* have been indicated by many as fundamental in stimulating the desire for consumption, especially from the Renaissance onward (Burke 1993). For instance, the Canadian scholar Grant McCracken (1988) has maintained that the growth in consumption in the last quarter of the 16th century in England was linked to Elizabeth I's attempt to centralize her kingdom using, amongst other devices, the magnificence of courtly ceremony. To better control the nobility and to legitimize her power, Elizabeth was able not only to promote literary texts which smoothed the contradiction between her gender and her power, but also to attract nobles to court and to send them into a 'spiral of consumption': the nobles, who had previously spent with consideration for their rural communities and for future generations of their family, now became increasingly concerned with themselves and their immediate ability to keep up with the styles and extravagances of the courtly game.

When living in close proximity with their subordinates, the lifestyles and sheer possibilities of consumption of the noble classes had *directly influenced*, through bans and gifts, what the lower classes could consume. With the development of

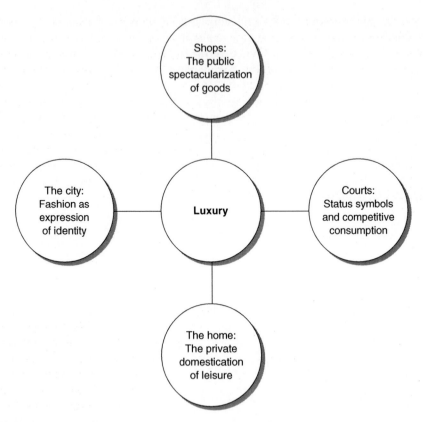

Figure 1.2   Luxury and the new spatiality of consumption

the court, its disentanglement from the wider society and its closure though competitive consumption, the noble classes started to exercise a *mediated influence* on the lower classes, notably through the mediation of an ever-growing industry for the shaping of tastes and fashions. This, in turn, contributed to further disentangle communities which favoured, yet again, the spreading of market-mediated tastes. While courts are now much less relevant, a similar mechanism is to be found in contemporary societies in other social strata. We may see the formation of a relatively close group of people competing for status using lifestyle and consumption in the mass media star system – which includes music, film and TV stars. We may also see that their styles and tastes reverberate outside their circles, influencing a variety of more or less distant social groupings especially through the mediation of a host of cultural goods and professions.

The courts also had a propulsive role because they found themselves at the centre of large modern *cities*, which acted as cultural amplifiers and were also huge concentrations of commerce. The urbanism which developed between the 17th and 19th centuries is undoubtedly connected to the development of capitalism, not only because – as a productivist view would have it – it enabled a high concentration of low-cost labour, but also because it favoured that close proximity and social mobility of different social groups which stimulated processes of imitation, hybridization and opposition coupled with the spread of new non-essential goods. To be sure, the large commercial capitals of the 17th and 18th centuries, London in particular but also Amsterdam, worked as catalysts for consumer culture: here high finance converged with the arrival of masses of colonial riches from all over the world (Schama 1987). These were the cities in which the distribution of goods came to be radically modified, mostly through a liberalization of commerce from the corporations which had limited the types of goods on sale from circulating through generalized shops, keeping them bound to artisan workshops (Miller 1981). From the 18th century, with the introduction of larger and larger glass windows, street-fronts became window displays and began to be used as 'stages' where goods could be arranged in elaborate scenes as advertisements for themselves (Schivelbusch 1988). As Rudi Laermans (1993) observed, goods were no longer squirrelled away at the back of the shop where the seller could control their accessibility to and meaning for the public; they were transformed instead into a spectacle to attract clients. Increasingly, especially from the middle of the 19th century with artificial lighting of interiors and the increase in the size of glass plate, windows offered an opportunity to put goods on display for the public.

Consumers not only bought, but also learned to gain pleasure from the spectacularization of commodities, something which was amplified by the creation of covered commercial galleries or *passages* – from the first one in Paris, *Passage Feydeau* built as early as 1791, to London's famous *Piccadilly Arcade* built in 1810 to Milan's *Galleria Vittorio Emanuele* finished in 1878. Galleries were complemented by visual events of cultural, commercial and political importance such as the great world exhibitions of the second half of the 19th century. Wandering around enjoying the spectacle of the commodities became a celebrated pursuit for the refined sensibility of the *flâneur*, as the French poet Charles Baudelaire puts it in his well-known *Le peintre de la vie moderne*. The department stores of the 19th century – Harrods in London, Macy's in New York, the Bon Marché in Paris, to cite but a few – popularized this tendency, becoming important aspects of the urban environment. In fact, these department stores presented themselves as places to visit, as the apple-in-the-eye of their respective cities. The Bon Marché, for example, which was France's first department store, was constructed as if it was a monument open to tourists, just like a church or museum; thus it quickly established itself as an essential stop on tourist itineraries (Miller 1981). What changed then, beyond the functions of the seller and the mode of sale, was the characterization of commodities. As suggested, commodities were gradually reconfigured as a spectacle, which alone had to communicate to a public made up of increasingly fewer known clients and more and more anonymous consumers. These new forms of retail did not simply replace previous forms – such as farmers' market or high street boutiques – but went alongside them, forcing them to adapt to a new situation. In general, hand in hand with the *de-personalization of the sale relationship* went a *more personalized relationship with objects* and their meanings. This relationship was and still is guided by a host of culturally mediated principles of selection, such as those which can be found in the many magazines which give advice on lifestyles and consumption. Typically tailored to gendered audiences, such magazines help reduce the complexity of individual choice and ironically have become necessary to make appropriate, identity-marking purchases (Breward

1994; Jackson et al. 2001; Winship 1987). All in all, going shopping has increasingly become a playful activity, but to participate in it social actors have to acquire the serious cultural and economic tools which enable them to play suitably with commodities (see also Chapter 8).

As modernity became consolidated we find that even the consumption of luxuries, which had previously been a possibility for only the nobility with their extravagances, became disciplined under the system of *fashion*. In terms borrowed from Georg Simmel's (1971b, orig. 1904) celebrated observations, we may say that luxury consumption was socially regulated by fashion dynamics, and thus ended up reflecting and facilitating the divergent tendencies of capitalist material culture: standardization and diversification.[5] The improvement in the possibilities for consumption of intermediate and lower social strata is accompanied by the standardization of needs, stimulated by urbanization, the development of communications and a huge growth in the availability of commodities, their variety and their rhythms of change. The democratisation of luxuries is thus both an effect *and* a cause of the capitalist organization of production which, as we have seen, can create a market for its products, beyond the unpredictable caprices of the rich, disciplining all consumers through some social mechanisms (fashion, style, design, etc.). These disciplining mechanisms are, as I shall show, ambivalent: as Simmel says, they allowed consumers to feel that they belonged to a particular group, while at the same time distinguishing themselves; they also, I shall add, allowed for individual identity, but provided the toolkit for its expression (see Chapters 3 and 7).

Simmel maintained that fashion is often associated with women and femininity. This association has clear historical and cultural roots: the historical weakness of their social position oriented women towards 'comparatively great uniformity' and fashion was instrumental in enabling them to express themselves through a shared language, becoming 'the valve through which a woman's craving for some measure of conspicuousness and individual prominence finds vent, when its satisfaction is denied her in other fields' (*ibid*, 309). Even more than what Simmel tells us, we shall see that *gender* is a social construction which shapes practices of consumption at the same time as it itself is constructed by such practices. As a gendered process, consumption is a site of power relations.

It was precisely while stressing power relations that Veblen (1994, orig. 1899, Chapters III and IV) pondered on the role given to women in the development of capitalism. In his opinion, the production/consumption divide which characterizes the development of the modern economy corresponds to the harmonization by difference of the sexes in the bourgeois family: the sphere of consumption – conceived of as shops, luxury goods, refined tastes, display and opulence – was reserved for women, confined to the role of consumer within the family and always subject to function as a status symbol for their husbands; the sphere of production with its sobriety was restricted to the male head of the family. Considering the urban industrialized US communities of the late 19th century, Veblen maintains that the display of riches, which had previously manifested itself in employing vast numbers of servants, was now transformed into a division of labour within the family. With the development of the bourgeois family the duties of consumption were to be fulfilled by wives, whereas it fell upon men to bring home as much money as possible. Women of the upper-middle classes became a 'subsidiary leisure class', whose delicate office was to perform 'vicarious' leisure and consumption, in the name of the household and its male head. It is no coincidence that one of the rhetorical critiques used to stigmatize consumer society associated consumption and luxury goods with the feminine, intended as superficiality and effeminacy, using this association to denounce the risks run by traditionally masculine civic virtues.[6] Veblen (1994, 53) thus suggests that commercial culture mingled with the patriarchal tradition:

> In a sense which has been greatly qualified in scope and rigor, but which has by no means lost its meaning even yet, this tradition says that the woman, being a chattel, should consume only what is necessary to her sustenance – except so far as her further consumption contributes to the comfort or the good repute of her master.

In this light, all the ambivalences of the role of upper middle-class women in promoting luxury consumption are revealed: theirs was perhaps a golden cage, which defined quite rigidly the duty and rights of women; a necessary luxury which needed continuous surveillance. Indeed, more broadly, consumption has often been constructed – to reinforce the complementarities of the sexes – as a mirror of the sphere of production, a private rather than public space, feminine rather than masculine, hedonistic rather than ascetic and, finally, frivolous rather than serious (Bordo 1993; Bowlby 1993; De Grazia and Furlough 1996) (see Chapter 8).

Even if women had always undertaken unpaid labour and still were, their efforts had to be masked now more than ever: in the house there were to be no signs of work, less still of the mechanization and bureaucratization which increasingly characterized production (Roberts 1998). The *home* has indeed typically been constructed as a private space where one doesn't work but consumes, even if consumption may take the rather disciplined format of bourgeois comfort (see Chapter 2). Especially from the beginning of the 19th century, the home provided a space for the domestification of consumption, it had to be a comfortable refuge from the pressures of work, a place where a man could at last express himself, comforted by a caring wife who had – above all else – a decorative function. As Adrian Forty (1986) suggests, the home came to be seen as a place of non-work also because of the aesthetic qualities of the goods which were fast becoming a part of the domestic environment. In the design of objects, reference to instrumentality had to be abolished, even if an object was entirely functional. This is the case with the domestic sewing-machines which spread widely between the 19th and 20th centuries and which literally brought work into the home. In order to be widely accepted, they had to be designed in such a way as to remove any industrial connotation. This is why Singer, one of the most well-known brands both then and now, produced light domestic machines, small and extremely refined, 'artistically' decorated in order to make them 'a beautiful ornament' for the boudoir. Only in this way could they remain in tune with the homely atmosphere and seem appropriately feminine. The ideals of respectable comfort and refined practical gentility were not only implicated in the construction of gender identities, but were also important features of the emerging middle-class cultural identity, at least in Great Britain (Kidd and Nicholls 1999). More broadly, the home has both been constructed as a private sphere of consumption as opposed to work, and idealized as a place of intimate, warm non-commercial relations

(Zelizer 2004b, see also Chapter 8). As such, it comes to complement public consumer spaces such as the department store, the café, the theatre, the cinema, the restaurant, etc. Just like these spaces though, the home provides a socially and culturally organized context for consumption (and work) which has been crucial in stabilizing the boundaries of economic rationalities such as gift-giving and gratuitous care, ostensibly expelled by commercial relations but strictly intertwined with commercialism in both the private and the public sphere. The spread of luxury goods and refined comforts was thus organized by a number of different spaces and institutions which, as I shall show in the next chapter, offered a complex architecture for the construction of economic value.

Summary

Contemporary historical research has revised the traditional wisdom which considered consumer culture as the late consequence of the industrial revolution emerging at the beginning of the 20th century. This *productivist* vision typically presented consumer culture and society as a sudden and mechanical reaction to the industrial revolution, reaching all social classes through the consumption of mass-produced goods. Recent literature considers that *consumption has had an active role* in the development of capitalism. Authors such as **Neil McKendrick, Colin Campbell** and **Jan De Vries** have proposed *anti-productivist explanations* foregrounding factors such as *promotional techniques*, *hedonistic ethics* and *commerce*. Looking at 18th century England and 17th century Holland, these authors show that there were significant historical trends contributing to the development of new patterns of consumption and new attitudes towards the use and enjoyment of goods well before the advent of the industrial revolution. Today historians, sociologists and anthropologists tend to favour *multi-factor explanations* of the genesis and development of the so-called consumer society. They have abandoned a linear model of development in favour of an understanding of the *multiple geographies and temporalities* of a variety of consumer goods and values. The classic work of sociologist **Werner Sombart** has anticipated this perspective, providing a study of the rise of luxury consumption since the late medieval period. He considered the *luxury goods* and the *colonial commodities* which, together with new *values* and *social relations*, contributed to the emergence of a new way of life. These goods and relations were pivotal for a variety of *spaces and institutions* which have worked, since at least the 17th century, as engines for the rise of consumer culture. These spaces range from the absolutist *court* with its competitive merry-go-round of fashions, to large commercial *cities* with their capacity to spread and make visible elite lifestyles, to the development of pleasurable and refined *shopping places*, to the bourgeois *home* with its emphasis on decent comfort and polite refinement.

Notes

1 This may be derived also from studies of proto-industrialization: see, for example, Jones (1968) and Mendels (1981).

2 Mike Featherstone (1991) has suggested that what characterizes post-modern society is the fact that not only the artistic elite but also consumers are *hedonistic experimenters* who have learned to aestheticise consumption. In fact, forms of controlled hedonism (through aestheticisation, irony, etc.) have developed as one of the key rhetorical codes for the legitimation of a number of practices of consumption (see Chapter 7).

3 This can also have perverse effects. For instance, kleptomania is a phenomenon which mostly concerns middle-class women (Abelson 1989) and its whose social roots have recently been underlined even by psychotherapeutic studies (Baker 2000).

4 More recently Colin Campbell (1994) developed a critique of Veblen similar to that which can be derived from Sombart's views. Comparing Veblen's theory of motivations with that of Weber, Campbell draws on Wright Mills's views of agency and maintains that subjective motives should not be seen as universal psychological drives, but as vocabularies which allow people to claim that what they do is not only their desire, but also a fair and moral desire.

5 Simmel's analysis appeared in *The American Review of Sociology* and circulated widely among contemporary scholars. It differs from Sombart's: Simmel was preoccupied with considering the relationship between fashion, modern identity, the attribution of value and processes of identification/dis-identification, brushing over the means of production and of commercialization that Sombart, in a more Marxian fashion, puts centre stage. On Simmel's observations on fashion see, amongst others, Gronow (1997); Nedelmann (1991); McCracken (1988) and Sassatelli (2000b).

6 Some studies, including those by Frank Mort (1996) and Sean Nixon (1996), have shown that today masculine identity is constantly engaged and challenged by 'superfluous' and 'frivolous' commodities, by shopping as entertainment and by visual codes that cross genders. Furthermore, the model of the 'female' 'glossy' magazine covering consumption, health and beauty, which had a key role in linking femininity with luxury consumption, has now been extended to the male public, as the success of magazines like *Men's Health* demonstrates (Jackson et al. 2001). On the other hand masculinity is increasingly represented as an 'object' of desire in commercial images (Savage 1997). See also Chapter 6.

The Cultural Production of Economic Value

2

The rise in material standards and the increase in consumer spending in the West was accompanied by the development of particular attitudes and mentalities which need to be considered in their own right if we are to appreciate the development of consumer culture and society. The history of consumer society is also the history of the formation of new cultural orientations towards the economy, goods and material culture. It is also the history of how the category of 'consumption' has become more and more significant in public discourses and, in parallel, of the ways in which social actors have progressively become referred to and called forth as 'consumers' as well as 'citizens', 'workers' or indeed 'housewives'. Consumer society entails a tacit 'contract', to paraphrase Carole Pateman's (1988) famous book, not only between the sexes, or among citizens, but also among producers, sellers and consumers. Such a contract assumes the form of a promise of self to the self, with each individual actor having to learn – according to his or her particular social position – to appropriately accomplish and possibly enjoy the role of the consumer as much as that of the producer. In other words, the consumer society blooms as consumption begins to be problematized as an activity that is relevant in and of itself as well as crucial in defining social relations and identities. And it reigns when it successfully produces the 'consumer' as a dominant, if constantly contested and variously nuanced, social identity.

In this chapter I shall initially consider the work of authors like Arjun Appadurai (1986b) and Chandra Mukerji (1983) who have attempted to offer not only historical reconstructions but also theoretical paradigms addressing the cultural trajectories which created needs and classified commodities. I shall then consider the way in which the notions of 'consumption' and the 'consumer' have become important in defining the social order and personal identity. In this light, I shall re-examine some selected phenomena which, following the shift which happened from the late 17th to the 18th century, accompanied the development of Western consumer culture in the 19th and 20th centuries.

Commodity flows, knowledge flows

As suggested, to understand contemporary consumer society one needs to consider a long historical process in which new forms of consumption disentangle themselves bit by bit from rigid social stratification, and end up being governed by fashion and by experts who supply advice on good taste. This amounts to a focus on what Appadurai (1986b, 38) has defined as a new '*register of consumption*', identified with the consumption of luxuries and therefore of goods 'whose principal use is *rhetorical* and *social*'. Following on from this, Appadurai shows how a materialist consumer culture is to be considered the prerequisite for the technological revolution of capitalism and not its result: this new register of consumption is in fact connected to a new configuration of flows of culture and material objects. Material objects always implicate forms of social knowledge: as the *flows of commodities* became more *complex*, *global* and above all *long distance*, they brought with them *flows of more articulate yet unequal knowledge* which provided new arenas for the construction of value that engaged producers, traders and consumers.

As Appadurai writes (*ibid*, 41–4), 'as distances increase, so the negotiation of the tension between knowledge and ignorance becomes itself a critical determinant of the flow of commodities'. Stress is thus put on the ability of the consumer to recognize the value of things and it is by instructing them on the value of things that consumption can be governed. In this new situation the emphasis passes from the *exclusivity* to the *authenticity* of goods, expert knowledge becomes crucial and social actors have to measure themselves more and more through discourses which connect their identities with their desires of consumption (see Chapter 7). The increasing role of knowledge in the processes of consumption made knowledge itself into a commodity. This, in turn, resulted in a cultural emphasis on authenticity and the spread of expert discourses about taste. Expert discourse on taste, commoditization of knowledge and a cultural emphasis on authenticity can all be found, for example, in a significant phenomenon such as the diffusion of cookbooks, which reconstruct national, regional and local traditions, and thus shape the consumption of foodstuffs. In Europe this process was coeval with the consolidation of capitalism – let us think for example of the widespread success of French cookbooks from the beginning of the 18th century (Mennell 1996). In those countries which had long been European colonial dominions, like India, colonization and de-colonization have given way to the construction of a repertory of national recipes which has reclaimed authenticity and originality by portraying certain ingredients and their combinations as culturally valuable in opposition to what appears as exclusively Western (Appadurai 1988).

Mukerji (1983) also considers modern attitudes towards consumption as part of wide-reaching '*materialist values*' (including rationalism, calculative mentality, worldliness, related to innovations in the means of production, transport and communications). She maintains that the culture and practice of modern consumption have a necessary precursor in the 'commercial revolution' of the 16th and 17th centuries. It was in this period, thanks to enormous progress in transport and communications, that many new and unknown products became available on the Western European market; these provoked people into cultivating their *capacity for cultural classification*, pushing them to develop materialist cultural attitudes. Mukerji documents a shift to a materialist culture of consumption through an analysis of the appearance and diffusion of print designed for a mass public, showing that printing and books contributed to two apparently distinct markets (mass and elite); through studying the diffusion of Indian printed cotton cloth in England which contributed to the symbolic relationship between the two countries; and, finally, through considering the advancement of materialist and scientific thought. This materialist culture went hand in hand with expanding social mobility, an attitude to change, and with the transformation of cultural categories of time and space. Furthermore, it is seen as joined with the Protestant ethic and rationalistic entrepreneurial orientation, thus bringing about the capitalist system.

Emphasis is thus placed on the emergence of a *new economic culture*, the diffusion of worldly cultural attitudes through which people were able to look with different eyes at a huge array of new objects brought from the colonies. Only through attributing new meanings (from the exotic to the dietetic, from the technological to the gastronomic) could these objects become commodities of economic value. This culture was favoured by the new technologies of communication and representation, from the printing press and cartography to technical navigational instruments, which made possible the circulation of cultural values and, with these, a system of cultural innovation. As Mukerji (*ibid*, 4) nicely puts it:

> Hedonism and asceticism seem, on the surface, contradictory, but they share one feature: an interest in material accumulation. The pure ascetic rationalist of Weberian theory accumulates capital goods, while the hedonist consumer revels in amassing consumer goods. The two types can be envisioned as extremes on a continuum of materialist tendencies ... hedonistic consumers and ascetic investors have been, in fact, quite difficult to distinguish. Both acted as economic innovators in the early modern period replacing a traditional pattern of hoarding wealth with new ways to use it, to make it a more active part of social and economic life.

Indeed, amongst Protestants there was no lack of materialist attitude or expenditure for consumption; rather there was a greater sobriety in the goods produced *and* consumed. The ambiguity of the cut-off point between hedonism and asceticism is evident in the number of goods that could be used as forms of capitalization. As we saw earlier, for example, in the second half of the 17th century Dutch merchants used to purchase paintings not only for decorating their houses, but also as a form of investment in an economy in which the scarcity of land made investing in it difficult (Schama 1987).

We may read Mukerji and Appadurai's works as intending to underline that *economic value is a cultural product* shaped by consumers and traders, producers and cultural intermediaries. Both these authors stress the distinctive material and cultural circuits which define different commodities, and highlight the way in which practices of consumption are socially and culturally entwined with those of production and exchange in a complex non-deterministic web of interdependencies (see also Chapter 4). They both focus on the way in which objects become defined, perceived and socially governed. Commodity flows were accompanied and sustained by knowledge flows: as complex configurations of goods-with-thought they gave way to cultural and economic changes. Following from this perspective, it is crucial to analyse the *cultural processes of commodity classification* which accompanied the beginnings of modernity and the new patterns of consumption – and still today define the shifting boundaries of consumer culture. These are processes which gain visibility in moral and moralistic discourses on the relationship between people and objects, but which can also be seen in artistic representations and, with the establishment of scientific economics, in the analysis of economists.

The normative discourses surrounding the relationship between objects and people are a fundamental dimension of all social action, including consumption. Because of this we cannot easily read back from increased consumer spending the rise and dominance of consumer culture (Trentmann 2004). Labelling some goods as national, others as exotic, some as tasteful, others as tasteless, some as natural, others as artificial and so on, these discourses offer a moral picture of consumption. It is through similar classificatory processes, which are reflected in daily practices and sustained by social institutions, that notions such as necessity, luxury, fashion and good taste are continually defined. These notions in turn structure the cultural space where consumption acquires meaning and the social figure of the consumer starts to move; in other terms, they contribute to the repertoires of motives and reasons which people may draw upon in order to understand and justify their consuming desires and practices.

The invention of the consumer and the cultural trajectories of goods

In all cultures and societies we may find a variety of discourses and practices through which material culture and our modalities of relation to goods are classified. Nevertheless, these classificatory processes were becoming markedly visible as a contested terrain from the end of the 17th century, when the need to take account of new forms of consumption based on the growth and diversity of objects on sale, the predominance of monetary exchange and competitive display, became strongly felt (see Hirschman 1977 and 1982b, Horowitz 1985; Lears 1983; Searle 1998; Williams 1982; see also Cohen 2003 and Cross 2000 for more recent developments in the US). Starting from this period we may witness not only the consolidation of the first modern forms of capitalism, but also a flourishing of discourses which tried to provide legitimate grounds for the ways of consuming and the goods which were such an important part of the emerging bourgeois way of life. It is from this period that *consumption* started to be identified as a *meaningful category*, supplanting the notion of luxury in moral discourse and becoming ever more central to public debate, especially in Great Britain.

'Luxury' has been the classic category used to distinguish between 'good' and 'bad' uses of objects in Western thinking, providing the tool to establish whether people's relationships with material culture were right or wrong. The notion of luxury had in fact been a fundamental category in both Classical and Renaissance moral discourse: in pre-modern Western morality – from Aristotle to Thomas Aquinas – luxury was usually associated with subversion of universal natural needs which defined human beings, a vision that we find again in Locke and in civic humanists like James Harrington (Berry 1994). However, right at the end of the 17th century, luxury began to be discussed also within economics and politics, rather than only in moral terms. In Nicholas Barbon's 1690 *Discourses of Trade* or Dudley North's 1691 *Discourses on Trade* we already have the idea that luxury and excessive materialistic desires represent the best incentive for commerce and economic growth (Appleby 1978; Berry 1994; Sekora 1985).[1] It was

Bernard Mandeville's *Fable of the Bees*, published in 1714, which represented a kind of parting of the waters not only for its ironic and iconoclastic style, but also because it established a new vision of luxury consumption: luxury may be a 'private vice' but, Mandeville wrote, is a 'public benefit', employing 'a Million of the Poor' and drawing the 'World's Conveniences' and 'all the most elegant Comforts of Life' to 'an industrious, wealthy and powerful Nation' (Mandeville 1924, 4 and 54, orig. 1714).[2] Such a position opened the way to a new politico-economic perspective centred on the apparently obvious duo of the Nation and the Citizen, whereby the Nation indicated Western, developed, civilized or colonial powers and the Citizens could express their sovereign power also and above all by economic freedom, and in particular by the freedom to consume. It is this particular framework of values which, in time, provided new grounds on which to pass judgement on practices of consumption. In so far as value was placed on the prosperity of the Nation, from Mandeville onward luxury was, so to speak, *demoralized*: it was possible to conceive of it as something which simply favours commerce and productivity and which cannot be easily judged on transcendental moral grounds. This indeed marks a shift from Aristotelian ideas of human nature based on finite desires to modernity proper, which sees man as a social animal of infinite desires; whilst the latter never managed to totally displace the former, it nonetheless assumed a dominant position. For Mandeville, in particular, desires are not objective or given, but mutable and undefined, always linked to the relative social position of who is doing the desiring. It is for this reason that, in his view, objectively and universally defining luxury would be impossible, and every definition would instead be hiding a moral vision of the world. Clearly, however, whatever might have been Mandeville's intentions, the moral implication of such a position was that there was little merit in frugality, and that there was no reason to be satisfied with one's own lot in life.

Just when luxury goods began to spread and to interest wider strata of the population (see Chapter 1), the notion of luxury lost its discriminatory moral force. In the midst of the Enlightenment, for instance, the well-known Scottish philosopher David Hume felt the need to qualify 'innocent' and 'blameable' forms of luxury according to period, country and the person's social standing, but these qualifications were so specific that in abstract terms luxury could only be defined as the 'refinement in the gratification of the senses'. As refinement, luxury could only enrich humans and society and favour sociality and sympathy: 'to imagine, that the grafting of any sense, or the indulging of any delicacy in meat, drink, or apparel, is of itself a vice, can never enter into a head, that is not disordered by the frenzies of enthusiasm' (Hume 1993, 167, orig. 1760). Innocent luxury is associated with both private and public 'benefits' which are larger than material welfare and include an idea of refinement and culture. This de-moralization was based on the idea that luxury was no longer the gauge of the unhealthy conflict between commercial and political activity (and in particular civic virtue). Commercial activity itself had come to appear more beneficial and legitimate, and so luxury had come to be valued mainly on the basis of the effects it had on economic and commercial life.

This process mirrors another, that is the *privatization of a separate sphere of consumption*. As we saw in the case of luxury goods, consumption became disentangled from the kind of *legal-political* regime provided by sumptuary laws, and instead became caught up in the *cultural-economic* regime found in the dynamics of fashion. In the fashion regime, aesthetic judgements such as 'tasteful' and 'tasteless' may work as political and moral tools, to justify social inclusion or exclusion (see Bourdieu 1984). The de-moralization of luxury does not mean that the cultural repertoires which were deployed in the 18th century luxury debate were lost; on the contrary, they were often reworked upon and reframed in new ways – and they have indeed left an important legacy for the moral appraisal of consumption till the present day (Hilton 2004).[3] All in all, the de-moralization of luxury gives way to a moralization of the new configuration of economic value consonant with the entrenchment of capitalist modernity. This is a configuration which, amongst other things, separates consumption and production between the private and public spheres. The social system comes to be described as the interaction of two distinct and different *modes of relation* with the material world – consumption and production – and this distinction, itself value laden, is overlain with an ascription of primary value to production. The characterization of life as a continuous dynamic merry-go-round of production and consumption becomes dominant, with consumption typically in an ancillary position, at least morally. If work and enrichment become freed of any moral restraint, consumption (which, as suggested, is construed as the reciprocal of production) takes on ambiguous connotations: unequivocally positive as a stimulus of growth in production and commercial exchange, rather dubious where it appears as non productive – i.e. when not directly linked to accepted forms of capitalization or personal enhancement. Amongst the recommended forms of capitalization we find those linked to self-improvement, referred to as refinement of the self and of taste, which Hume, amongst others, recommended as an exercise in personal freedom for the gentleman. Indeed, refinement was a delicate issue, which re-introduced social hierarchies (class, gender, ethnicity, etc.) from the back door both in the proclaimed indifference sported by Mandeville and the refined relativism favoured by Hume.

This is the cultural climate in which not only the notion of consumption took shape, but also that of a new social role: the 'consumer'. The consolidation of scientific economics and of modern market institutions has *naturalized* notions of consumption and the consumer to the extent that their prescriptive values may go unnoticed. Of course, in *An Enquiry into the Nature and Causes of the Wealth of Nations* (1981, orig. 1776) Adam Smith, the founder of economic liberalism, sees even excessive and luxurious consumption through mercantile lenses as a factor in economic development: in his view, the expenditure of the 'great' aided the birth of a class of merchants and bourgeois who drove society towards modern capitalism and who, freed from all personal dependence, guided the entire population to civil liberty. Smith does, however, emphasize production, and it is by modelling consumption onto production that he defines *correct* and *incorrect* forms of consumption. Merchants, as we all become under market conditions, are not pictured as ascetic monks, they do not disdain the decencies of life, they are indeed good, well-behaved, rational consumers as opposed to the immoral, irrational, whimsical wasters impersonated by the old, declining nobility. To discriminate among goods, Smith thus uses the notions of *convenience* and *decency*. Decencies indicate those goods which can be used for non-ostentatious comfort. They are neither needs nor luxuries, and incarnate a type of consumption which brings both order and rationality. These are bourgeois comforts: a category of 'durable goods' which make a genuine capitalization possible, as they are 'more favourable' than others 'to private frugality and, consequently, to the increase of publick capital', responding to the 'calm and dispassionate desire' to better one's own condition, while diverting from 'profusion' or the 'passion for present enjoyment' (Smith 1981: 341–9; see also De Marchi 1999 and Muller 1993). These are also 'necessary ornaments' (Smith 1982: 84, orig. 1762–66) brought about by the very nature of human beings, by their 'delicate frame and a more feeble constitution' which 'meets with nothing so adapted to … use that it does not stand in need of improvement and preparation' (*ibid.*, 334). The 'same temper and inclination' which prompted the 'savage' to construct his hut, 'push him to still greater refinement'; thus a contemporary ordinary day-labourer, with his 'blue wollen coat', his 'linnen shirt', his 'tanned and dressed-leather shoes', his 'knives and forks', his 'plates of pewter of earthen ware', all the products of the modern division of labour, 'enjoys far greater convenience than an Indian prince' (ibid., 335–9). As I shall show, Smith's thinking, naturalizing (some) goods and their uses as part of an evolutionary process situated in a particular colonial geopolitics, acts as a normative background for contemporary consumer culture, placing value on the search for personal gratification while emphasizing self-control and individual autonomy. Under these conditions, the consumer-merchant becomes the foundation of a new social and political order: the sovereign whose desires the market shall respond to and the sovereign of his own desires (see Chapter 7).

The web of value relations between commodities is part of an ongoing classificatory game which has contributed – through attributing value to objects and through defining the boundaries of morality in consumption practices – to the emergence and stabilization of a consumer culture we came to consider as modern. The 18th century debates over luxury not only underline the importance of new models of consumption, but they provide indications of *moral compromises* which were reached to integrate the values of asceticism and rationality with the production of new commodities which initially appeared as superfluous, and with the consumption of luxuries. The new *cultural configuration of economic value* presents new lifestyles, some of them compromising and unstable, which seem to accommodate the needs of consumption and production, and also, as suggested before, the gender division of labour within the family. This combination of extreme contradictions expresses itself in a lifestyle which favours commercial exchanges, and which makes a linchpin of them: and so it is Mandeville himself who celebrates in the pages of *The Female Tatler* – an early 18th century magazine – the lifestyle of Urbano, a fictitious character who incarnates the worldly and civic bourgeois in his combination of industrial rationality and refined hedonism. Urbano is described as a man who 'is employed in heaping up more Wealth the greatest part of the Day; the rest he devotes to his Pleasures', a rational bon vivant who knows both how to invest and also how to 'live in Splendour', a pragmatic materialist who 'minds only himself, and lets every body do as they please' (see Sassatelli 1997). This style of life requires a capacity to gauge different attachments, emotions and behaviour, and thus is found mostly in well-favoured emergent social groups. However, the whole population also has to take account of the new relationship between production and consumption, which sees the latter as a sort of liberated enjoyable space where hard-working characters can finally relax from (and prepare for) the discipline of work.

Of course, there is a relevant cultural geography to this, and to the compromises between entrepreneurial asceticism and hedonistic consumption. This is in fact one of the ideas expressed by, amongst others, Wolfgang Schivelbusch, in his fascinating essay on the history of luxury goods. In considering the diffusion of coffee from the end of the 17th century to the first half of the 18th, Schivelbusch (1992, orig. 1980) shows that this drink quickly took on a meaning different from the search for refinement driven by courtly consumption. For the nascent bourgeois, coffee was above all counterposed to alcoholic drinks and associated with puritan virtues such as sobriety, reason and industriousness. English puritans, and more generally the Protestant ethic, made it their drink of choice. Medical and commercial discourses alike contended that coffee could help the masses lost in the fumes of alcohol to regain their 'capacity to work': 'with coffee, the principle of rationality entered human physiology, transforming it to conform with its own requirements. The result was a body which functioned in accord with the new demands – a rationalistic, middle-class, forward- looking body' (*ibid*, 39).

This 'heroic phase' coincided with the development of public consumption in coffeehouses, which, as Jürgen Habermas (1992, orig. 1962) revealed in *The Structural Transformation of the Public Sphere*, were fundamental to the development of a truly bourgeois and liberal culture. There the consumption of coffee mixed with and catalysed new attitudes well beyond lifestyle and consumption. Coffee then infiltrated the private sphere as a domestic beverage and it was in this second 'conformist phase', continues Schivelbusch, that it no longer exclusively symbolized the 'public dynamism' of the first bourgeoisie, politics, literature and the world of business, but increasingly came to represent the 'warmth of the home', and thus acted as a 'stabilizing force' for an already well-formed culture.

Meanwhile, if coffee represented a Nordic and Protestant drink, chocolate was considered its Catholic and Southern counterpart. In a world which was still profoundly marked by fasting and Lent, chocolate served as a food surrogate, but more importantly it was also a fashionable drink of the Catholic courts; first the Spanish court and then Versailles made it a symbol of the nobility's lifestyle, sensual and idle. As Schivelbusch demonstrates, a breakfast of chocolate in a luxurious boudoir is one of the most recurrent themes in rococo painting: in these images bodies are reclining lasciviously 'between lying and sitting', recalling carnal pleasures and representing 'Baroque-Catholic embodiment against Protestant asceticism'. Obviously chocolate, like coffee, has its own historic trajectory: from powdered cocoa mixed with milk as a drink for children, to chocolate pralines which represent a luxury to be given as gifts to (stereotypically) women. Thus, by the 19th century, that which once represented power and splendour belonged to those excluded from power and responsibility: 'bourgeois society as the historical victor over the old society, made a mockery of the status symbols once so important to the aristocracy' (*ibid*, 101).[4]

This example shows how even the consumption of what are today banal everyday goods is always linked to processes of value construction which are deeply rooted and have numerous cultural and social, economic and material ramifications. Significantly, coffee, cocoa and tea were accompanied in all European countries by another revolution in foodstuffs: the consumption of sugar. This revolution also carried with it profound cultural changes. In his famous study on the spread of sugar Sidney Mintz (1985; 1993) shows how the rapid spread of sugar in the 18th century (in 1775 the English consumed twenty times more sugar than just a century before) was not only due to the increasing availability of sugar at decreasing cost; instead he implicates a kind of cultural idiosyncrasy in consumption. Sugar and sweetened bitter drinks became the first democratic luxuries: they were not necessary for nutrition and yet were used daily by everyone, including the working masses, and were ritually codified in complex ways. Connecting the South and the North of the world, sugar also epitomized the two faces of the global division of labour: gradually European workers who had never had access to products of distant provenance became habitual consumers of these colonial commodities which were the product of slave labour on tropical plantations. Reiterating a dynamic which we encountered earlier (Appadurai 1986b), Mintz maintains that consumers became dependent on markets that extended way beyond their vision of the world, and thus they began to recognize systems of cultural value different from those of their local communities. To be sure, there is a class dimension to this, as much of what is sometimes called 18th and 19th century mass consumption is in fact middle-class consumption, reflecting the expansion of the lower-middle classes in particular (see De Grazia and Cohen 1999; Kidd and Nicholls 1999). Still, thanks also to the increasingly professionalized provision of mediated systems for the representation of consumption and its values, more and more people began to conceive of themselves primarily as individuals who had (more or less) capacity and will to meet the new ideals of consumption.

In general then, the diffusion of sugar marks and reinforces a particular vision of social actors: they were becoming 'consumers' and as such they had to be capable, beyond their specific social position, of procuring their own satisfaction in disciplined ways. In societies such as those of England and Holland at the end of the 17th century and beginning of the 18th a kind of *individualist materialism of the masses* developed, with its roots in international commodity flows and in the idea that the satisfaction of individual desires of consumption is the principal source of the social order and a vital characteristic of any life worth living. In William Reddy's (1984) words, this marks the rise of 'market culture'. The *individual desires* of Western consumers – constructed through an international division of labour that made the colonies distant reservoirs of new exotic and mysterious commodities – are described as *inexhaustible* and come to appear as the origin of the social world and as the *source of the value of things* (Sahlins 2000, part 3). Thus, it is through the diffusion of goods which today appear banal, but which often brought with them new meanings and values, that the fervent debate around the role of the consumer was born, a figure who soldered together the links between identity and consumption characterizing Western contemporary culture.

Analysing the discourses addressing the consumer, contemporary historiography, anthropology and sociology are starting to engage with the precise cultural and political dynamics which have transformed the consumer into a powerful and compelling cultural code displayed by a variety of social institutions to mobilize people's desires and govern their practices, and indeed by people themselves to understand and manage their aspirations (Cohen 2003; Daunton and Hilton 2001; Strasser et al. 1998; Trentmann, ed. 2006; Brewer and Trentmann 2006). As suggested, the legitimizing rhetoric which emerged in the 18th century to justify market societies and modern cultures of consumption epitomized not so much the supposed de-moralization of luxury as the entrenchment of a new sphere of action and 'order of justification' (Boltanski and Thévenot 1991) for the enjoyment of goods. Consumption was defined as a private matter, constructed as opportunely opposed to production, and envisaged as the pursuit of private happiness indirectly but firmly linked to virtuous mechanisms in the public sphere – as Mandeville's famous motto states. Within this framework consumers were thus constructed as private economic hedonists, preoccupied with individual pleasures and doing all right – for the common good and themselves – provided they behaved in disciplined ways within the rules of the market (see Chapter 7). Still, as suggested, market rules themselves contained a vision of moral order, and the purification of the consumer identity from political and moral repertoires was never fully accomplished. As a contested identity the consumer became an important device for social and cultural change. Indeed, Frank Trentmann (2006a, 6) puts this well:

> consumers did not arise effortlessly as an automatic response to the spread of the markets but had to be made. And this process of making occurred through mobilization in civil society and the state as well as the commercial domain, under conditions of deprivation, war and constraint as well as affluence or choice, and articulated through traditions of political ideas and ethics.

It is especially from the late 19th century that a number of economic, cultural and political agencies increasingly claimed for themselves the right and duty to address consumers and to speak for them (see Cohen 2003; Daunton and Hilton 2001; Trentman and Brewer 2006; see also Chapters 6 and 8). Social scientific discourses, advertising and marketing, state welfare agencies, consumer defence organizations, women's groups, consumer boycotts and, more recently, the European Union, environmental groups, and new global movements have all contributed to situate the 'consumer' as a fundamental subject-category within public discourse. Of course, different collective actors and institutions have called forth different, often conflicting, images of the consumer, defining it as a sovereign of the market or a slave of commodities, a snob or a *flâneur*, a rebel or an imitator, a private collector or an entrepreneur with a sense of social duty, and encoding these images as belonging to a separate economic sphere or as moral and political figures in their own right (see Figure 2.1). They have thus contributed to naturalizing recourse to the consumer as a key social persona, and to consolidate consumer culture as a culture both *for* consumers and *of* consumers: both a set of commodities for people to consume in certain ways, and a set of representations of people as consumers, with the latter working as an intrinsically normative way of encoding the varieties of meanings associated with consumption practices.

Consumer society as historical type

It has been argued that the historical process behind the development of modern consumption is so varied and contested, and current cultures of consumption are

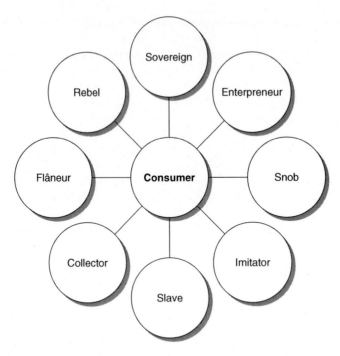

Figure 2.1   Some key identities attributed to the consumer

so multifaceted and contradictory that '"consumerism" and "modern consumer society" ... are concepts with diminishing analytical and conceptual usefulness' (Trentmann 2004, 376). Still, we must be wary of throwing away a notion which has generated such a wider public debate and we should continue to ask ourselves genealogical questions about the specificity of contemporary consumer culture as developed in the West. Whilst anthropological studies have made it clearer that humans have always used goods symbolically – mainly for marking social boundaries, demonstrating status, developing and defining social relationships, etc. – it is also true that different and specific commodities, consumption places and consumer practices have come to characterize the development of Western consumer culture (Clunas 1999). To be sure, the 'West' is internally differentiated. All in all, as a recent critical survey by Heinz-Gehard Haupt (2002) has shown, throughout the 19th and the 20th centuries access to consumer culture was markedly different in different European regions, as well as differentiated across gender, generation and profession. Well into the 20th century, important distinctions could still be detected between what Victoria De Grazia (1998) calls a European 'consumption regime', where participation in consumption was more clearly mediated by various forms of social participation and economic redistribution via the state, and an American one largely based on individual market choice. Likewise, while Eastern cultures of consumption might have been important in their own right also in the early modern period, in recent decades they have appeared to be increasingly present, both in academic consumer literature and in everyday culture, as providing powerful alternatives to westernized versions of consumer culture (Beng-Huat 2000; Garon 2006; Pomeranz 2000; Watson 1997; see also Chapter 8).

With these cautionary tales in mind, and drawing on a variety of historical studies which nuance its Western context and revise its linear picture of development, we can consider 'consumer society' an historical type of society which gradually became prevalent in the West from the dawn of modernity to the present. Different waves of consumer goods, social identities, places and practices were instrumental in defining different periods from early modernity onward. To account for these, we do not need to build a stage theory of development (see Stearns 2001). Instead we can resort to an imagery of *increasing but uneven stratification*, whereby a variety of ongoing processes, among different sections of the population in different places and times, are piled one on another, partly displacing previous trends, partly resuming them. To outline the phenomenon of modern consumption, historiography has traditionally focused not only on the commercial cities of the Renaissance and the consumption of colonial produce of the 17th-18th centuries, but also, and especially, on a much more recent period which runs, approximately, from the second half of the 19th century to after the Second World War. Studies on the end of the 19th century overwhelmingly focus on the spread of department stores and the modern system of advertising; those on the post-war period are mostly concerned with the spread of mass-produced durable goods for domestic use, from fridges to televisions. To these we can add various sociological studies on contemporary society which underline the shift to a post-Fordist model of production and the subsequent diffusion, thanks also to new technologies, of ever more individualized flexible models of consumption. These different studies of the changes in the practices of consumption may be read via a focus on how consumption has been framed and which features have been ascribed to consumers as social actors.

In the next few pages I shall briefly run through a selection of the crucial shifts which have characterized the consolidation of modern patterns of consumption in the last two centuries, suggesting an initial picture of the most important factors behind the historical formation of the consumer society (see Figure 2.2). The vast majority of studies which concentrate on the end of the 19th and first years of the 20th centuries consider the immense and rapid development of commercial space in cities, and the spread of mass media which radically changed the conditions of the commercialization of goods through ever more sophisticated advertising. Following in the footsteps of classic studies such as Simmel's on the metropolis (1971a, orig. 1903) or Benjamin's on the commercial galleries of Paris (1999, orig. 1981), these works tend to concentrate on the metropolitan cultures of consumption, focusing for example on the development of the great European capitals of the late 19th century (Williams 1982) and the enormous cultural impact of the world exhibitions between the 19th and the 20th centuries (Greenhalgh 1988). While we should also notice the persistence of more traditional retailing practices such as farmers' markets and the development of alternative forms of retail such as consumer cooperatives, second-hand shops and car-boot sales (Trentmann 2004), the transformation of retailing is often described as the engine of the transition to a mature consumer society. Important studies have thus focused on the development of department stores and the spread of modern forms of retail, both in France (Miller 1981; Tiersten 2001) and in the United States (Benson 1986; Fraser 1981; Leach 1993; Zukin 2004).

	Sec.	XIV	XV	XVI	XVII	XVIII	XIX	XX	XXI
INTERNATIONAL COMMERCE			spices	colonial goods/stimulants/sugar	cotton/porcelain			consumer durables	franchising chains
MODES OF PRODUCTION				rationalized colonial plantations	entrepreneurial spirit/worldly ascetism			Fordist production line	post-Fordist flexible production
FINANCIAL SYSTEM		monetary economy		credit				consumer credit	
NATION STATES			military provisioning				public education	welfare	
LUXURIES			nobles			urban financial bourgeoisie		petite bourgeoisie	lower-middle class
WORLDLY ETHICS			materialism			romanticism		therepeutic ethic of self-realization	
FASHION			courts		cities			celebrities	youth subcultures
COMMERCIALIZATION SYSTEM					promotional culture		department stores/world exhibitions	marketing, design, advertising professionalization	malls
LEISURE INDUSTRY						newspapers/books	female magazines	cinema/radio — TV	theme parks mass tourism
PUBLIC DISCOURSE						luxury & the wealth of nations — bourgeois household	citizen as consumers	consumer protection	critical consumption

Figure 2.2 Chronology and factors in the development of consumer society (XIV–XXI centuries)

Dream Worlds, Rosalynd Williams's (1982) seminal work on 19th century France, provides a good demonstration of how the birth of department stores and the various discourses associated with it marked the way we consume. It was thanks to the development of places which made a large quantity of goods visible to the whole population that the connection between personal identity, commerce and objects became central to a growing number of people, and it was thanks to a thematization of consumption as a meaningful social activity that the changing patterns of consumption gave way to consumer society as such. This was accompanied by the rise of the 'consumer' as a powerful social identity, called into life and engaged by a host of discourses and situated strategies of enticement which both democratized desires and standardized them. Market actors, and in particular retail entrepreneurs, were pivotal in such development; still, commercial processes were embedded in a conducive social environment, which, in the case of the department stores of New York and Philadelphia studied by William Leach (1993), amounted to the urban circuits of power, including universities and art museums. This should not surprise us, as shopping in the department store was indeed often portrayed as the quintessentially urban and civilized leisure activity. If the invention of leisure time for the masses can be traced to the end of the 19th century (Corbin 1995), mass leisure was immediately and strongly connected to commercialization and shopping. From the 19th century someone walking the streets of a large metropolis could be considered, and consider themselves, a 'consumer', an actor who could buy objects for sale in the department stores and who gained part of the meaning and significance of their walks from the display of commodities. Presenting themselves as potential buyers, everyone could enter and leave the shopping place when they desired, looking at commodities, imagining using or purchasing them, mixing the new and the old: shopping became a typically bourgeois leisure activity, a socially approved way of spending time, like going to the theatre or visiting a museum. In the same way the discourse surrounding commerce stopped insisting on the immediate acquisition of particular goods, and attempted to provoke a state of constant desire (Williams 1982).

Social actors were in fact increasingly referred to as 'consumers'. This came about thanks to, among other things, *market actors* such as the advertising and marketing agencies which, especially in the United States, developed significantly between the 19th and 20th centuries. Such development was accompanied, particularly between the two world wars, by the consolidation of new professional forms of knowledge and the institutionalization of various professional figures: advertising executives, marketing experts, shop assistants, etc. (Benson 1986; Cochoy 1997; Ewen 1976; Frank 1997; Lears 1994; Marchand 1985; Strasser 1989) (see Chapter 6). On the whole, these studies show that, especially from the beginning of the 20th century, advertising contains an increasing emphasis on self-realization, self-presentation and impression management, stressing the self-creating potentialities of the choosing self. Marketing and advertising were complemented by a number of other increasingly professionalized figures such as designers (see Forty 1986; Molotch 2003) or fashion journalists (Blumer 1969). These different figures, the so-called 'cultural intermediaries' (Bourdieu 1984), partook of a broad process of institutionalization, which gave way to a variety of diverse collective actors (professional organizations, market watchdogs, consumer movements, etc.) that were all busily engaged in providing a picture of consumers, of their wants and capacities. Recent scholarship has shown that *political actors* were also involved in shaping the image of the consumer and in designing a more explicitly public role for consumption (Cohen 2003; Daunton and Hilton 2001; Furlough and Strikwenda 1999; Kroen 2004; Hilton 2004; Micheletti 2003 see also Chapters 7 and 8). Political ideologies and movements which dealt with consumption range from the late 18th century movements against the slave trade, to 19th century movements concerned with the welfare and moralization of the lower orders, to early 20th century consumer cooperatives and consumerist movements underscoring the agency and rationality of consumers. They not only responded to changes brought about by the consolidation of modern consumer society, they also imagined, theorized and mobilized people as consumers – and did so in a variety of distinctive ways according to different national traditions.[5]

The studies on the period around the Second World War have generally focused on the structural changes in daily life stimulated by technological innovations which were brought to the masses by Fordist production. In particular, they have dealt with the effects of the diffusion of mass-produced goods in the United States, for example the spread of the motorcar and how this revolutionized the lifestyles of Americans (Flink 1988), or the diffusion of consumer durables like fridges and washing machines and how, ironically, this perpetuated gender divisions in the home both in the US and Canada (Cowan 1983; Parr 1999). These changes are often portrayed as the epitome of progress and freedom. Yet they drew together moral, practical and economic concerns and were not simply driven by consumer demand: for example, from the 1930s to the 1950s, companies changed refrigerator models every year and copied masculine automobile styles, despite the fact that their largely female target desired more feminine touches and longer lasting designs and products (Parr 1999). The American model has often been taken as a touchstone for post-war Europe, so much so that the marked changes in daily life in Italy, Germany and France, and also in England, have been seen as forms of *Americanization* of technologies (De Grazia 2005; Zeitlin and Herrigel 2000). In her *Irresistible Empire*, Victoria de Grazia (2005) focuses on a series of interlinked stories – ranging from the Hollywood star system, to modern advertising, to the supermarket, and to ideals of the housewife – to chart the 'rise of a great imperium with the outlook of a great emporium'. She reconstructs the political agenda of US market expansion, implying that the US-led rise of international commodity flows was intended also as a 'global traffic in values'. Indeed, as early as 1916 President Wilson infused contemporary US statecraft with a distinct consumer sensibility, on the assumption that the 'greater barrier in this world is not the barrier of principles, but the barrier of taste' and that US firms could spread peace and American principles by 'study(ing) the tastes and needs of the countries where the markets were being sought and suit (their) goods to those tastes and needs' (quoted *ibid.*, 1–2).[6]

The *geopolitics of global consumer culture* is definitely a crucial aspect of the modern and contemporary history of consumption. Still, we should be wary of providing a linear, American-driven picture of globalization. This is not only because, as De Grazia claims, the rise of a global consumer culture did not bring forth global concord, but also because, as she tends to omit, the great powers to promote consumer democracies marshalled by the US did not mean that national or local cultures of consumption were simply subsumed in the American way of life. As we will see more clearly later on (see Chapter 8), the anthropology and sociology of consumption do underline the determinant role of diverse *local and national cultures* in metabolizing mass-marketed consumer goods and global commodities (Brewer and Trentmann 2006; Howes 1996). Local circumstances and interests have filtered dominant American lifestyles, constructing new versions of them. For instance, in Italy the years following the Second World War were not only those of mass distribution, consumer durables and supermarkets, but also those of an economic transition from a rural economy to an urban culture (as recently as the post-war years nearly half of the population lived on the land and most farmers did not produce for the market) and of a political transition from monarchy and Fascism to a welfarist Republic (with increasing numbers of state employees on limited but reliable disposable income ready to buy on credit) (Crainz 1996; see also Haupt 2002; Zamagni 1992). In a nation in transition such as post-war Italy, consumer goods and practices acted as a battlefield where new visions of nationhood could emerge. Food habits which united tastes and created a new sense of belonging to the nation became widespread – examples including typical regional dishes such as pizza which spread along with migration flows and pizza restaurants from the South to the northern regions and panettone, which, originally from the northern city of Milan, came to take on the role of a national symbol and quickly established itself as a must on Italian Christmas tables (Helstosky 2004). Taking the case of clothes, we may well see that Italian fashion and American politics, industry and culture were powerfully linked after the Second World War, but they were so in rather intricate and bi-directional ways. America provided some technology and some funding through the Marshall Plan, but also lots of consumers for the rising fashion industry in Italy which, in its turn, benefited from a strong local tradition in craftsmanship coupled with a rather sophisticated internal demand (White 2000).[7] With all their differences, similar considerations apply regarding the shift from socialist to market economy in Eastern Europe and Russia (Caldwell 2004; Merkel 2006). It would be a mistake to maintain that both transitions to consumer capitalism – that of Italy after the Second World War and that of ex-Communist East European countries at the end of the 20th century – represent, as it were, a fast track to consumer culture which simply reproduces in an accelerated, condensed format what has happened in Great Britain or the US. Certainly there are historical parallels (for example, urbanization for Italy and the ideological and legal shift in Russia), but each of these countries has come to confront global commodities, commercial processes and consumerist discourses in a particular moment and from a particular position, concocting its own culture of consumption.

As much as we need to emphasize the varied topography of consumer culture(s), it is especially after the Second World War that certain important transnational phenomena such as *youth culture* became visible. Youth cultures in fact consolidated around particular commodities and practices of consumption.[8] These goods and practices – such as the growth in private transport and the diffusion of the legendary Vespa (Arvidsson 2001; Hebdige 1988) or the massive sales of records and cassettes and the spread of rock (Cohen 1972) – which would have been luxuries only a few years before, may be read as clues to wider social phenomena (Capuzzo 2001). Enabled through geographical mobility and mass education as well as nuanced by gender and social origin, the sharing of certain styles of consumption between teenagers and youth was linked to the development of an increasingly global media and a mass motorization which gave youth autonomy and the possibility of leaving the confines of villages and urban neighbourhoods to become an ever more visible social identity. In the 1970s the so-called 'bedroom cultures' of American adolescents became reality in most West European countries, even if this was mostly restricted to the middle classes: in their bedrooms teenagers found a space in which to express themselves, and they did it through consumption. Youth cultures thus helped to change the home as much as they changed public spaces. As suggested, from the early modern period we saw the rise of a functional specialization of domestic space which offered a material and symbolic base for associating the house with consumption. From the post-war period not only did houses function as places for family consumption, they also became enriched with technology and, what is more, became an aggregate of spaces in which various members of the family were able to consume as individuals.

Contemporary social and cultural theory has underscored the processes of *individualization* and *rationalization* and stressed their link with consumer culture, seen alternatively as an arena where individuals construct their identities via lifestyle projects facing increased anxiety and risk, or as a mass-produced dehumanized apparatus which provides rather stiff standards and blind security (Beck 1992; Giddens 1990; Ritzer 1993). Many of these works turn to consumption in order to question modernity or its disappearance and transition to late-modernity. As specialized studies in consumption developed and addressed it as a subject of analysis in its own right, the theoretical engagement with modernity has finally been replaced or complemented by an empirical assessment of the situated dynamics of consumption. These studies do provide a much more nuanced picture of consumer culture(s). Still, there is by now a degree of consensus that we have entered a post-industrial or post-Fordist era in which the tendency is to distance oneself from standardized products and to serially produce infinite varieties of finish (Lash and Urry 1987 and 1994; see Tomlinson 2003 for a critical empirically grounded discussion). This is the case, for example, with the sports shoe industry. The world's largest manufacturers of sports shoes have already reached such levels of global sales that they can serialize variety, producing hundreds of thousands of shoes for each of the many different models they sell; at the same time, thanks to a segmentation of production, companies like Nike are able to obtain economies of scale even with small quantities of commodities (Goldman and Papson 1998). Of course, shoes are no longer made-to-measure, but the variety and the attempt to attract consumers with products 'made for them' and 'their differences' is increasingly becoming the norm. In the Fordist phase the economy was dominated by mass production, commodities were little different and the phenomenon of consumption was characterized by the spread and, to quite an extent, the appreciation of standardized consumer durables. Today's post-Fordist economy is instead characterized by *customization*: a generalized emphasis on individual style as well as specialized and flexible production, a greater variety of commodities changing rapidly, and niche models of consumption that are proudly hybridized, eclectic and fluid.

Studies on late modernity, postmodernism or post-Fordism have shown that during the last two decades of the 20th century new and complex models of consumption were met and stimulated by niche marketing, reflexive advertising, new media, new spaces for leisure, new forms of tourism, and so on. It is in this post-Fordist phase that, as Pierre Bourdieu (1984) and Mike Featherstone (1991) have claimed, the 'cultural intermediaries' have acquired more power and have become agents of change, promoting new styles of consumption which potentially cut across traditional social divisions. In particular, according to Bourdieu (1984, 310):

> The new bourgeoisie is the initiator of the ethical retooling required by the new economy from which it draws its power and profits, whose functioning depends as much on the production of needs and consumers as on the production of goods ... the new logic of the economy rejects the ascetic ethic of production and accumulation, based on abstinence, sobriety, saving and calculation in favour of a hedonistic morality of consumption based on credit, spending and enjoyment.

Bourdieu rightly captures the mediating cultural role of some of the fractions of the middle classes. However, he proposes a far too dichotomous argument which should be historically and geographically qualified. As suggested, hedonism and asceticism are mixed together throughout the history of the modern economy, and hedonistic ethics emerged well before the second post-war period.[9] The American historian Thomas Jackson Lears (1983; 1994) has documented that during the last two decades of the 19th century commercial messages promoted the secularization of the Protestant ethic. He considers that a social climate particularly favourable to consumption developed in the United States with the emergence of a new type of ethic blending hedonism and asceticism: the 'therapeutic ethic of self-realization' which pushed actors to try and develop themselves through goods and services dealing with health and physical appearance. As we have already seen, Mukerji (1983) has pushed back the dates of the materialistic mixture of hedonism and asceticism to at least the Italian cities of the Renaissance.

Notwithstanding this, we can consider hedonistic ethics of consumption to have found a new impulse in the post-war period, also thanks to the civilizing character which was yet again attributed to the development of the market economy (De Grazia 2005; Kroen 2004). In such a cultural and political climate, and also thanks to the massive development of the media, the reach of the cultural intermediaries became wider, stretching its influence well beyond the upper and middle classes. Still, the growing visibility of cultural intermediaries or tastemakers can be placed in a series of broader dynamics. The post-Fordist era is in fact one of mass design and the aestheticization of ordinary objects: we only have to think of the huge commercial success of businesses like Ikea or Habitat which offer furnishings and household goods created by innovative designers at prices accessible to the mass of Western consumers. Furthermore, it is a period of marked standardization of the consumer experience, through strategies of 'thematization' not only in theme parks, but also in a general thematic organization of restaurants, shops, and spaces within shopping centres (Gottdiener 1997; Kowinski 1985; see also Chapter 8). Aestheticization and standardization are aspects of a consumer culture predominantly characterized by the symbolic elaboration of commodities, whose diffusion is also linked to financial phenomena like the development of credit services for consumption (i.e. monthly rate payments for the credit cards of department stores) which have lowered the material and cognitive barriers to acquisition (Zelizer 1994). Finally, it is also a period of increased global visibility of consumer culture and of its politicization: just think of the cultural and political dynamism generated by consumption in societies in transition from Communist to capitalist systems (Caldwell 2004; Merkel 2006); or the crucial intercultural function that global brands have in contemporary culture, providing a contested terrain for social mobilization and protest as well as dispersed, ordinary and perhaps banal forms of cosmopolitanism (Lury 2004).

As suggested both in this and in the preceding chapter, to account for the genesis and advance of consumer society historians place emphasis on different times, places and phenomena. Taken together, history underscores certain key moments of transformation, utilizing metaphors of transition which tend to counterpose modern forms of consumption with pre-modern ones in which people were the 'users of things', bogged down in a 'natural activity oriented to use values' rather than 'consumers' who purchase 'commodities' (Glennie 1995, 165). Running through five centuries of history, from the Renaissance to today, we have seen that it is very difficult to establish a date of birth, even a rough one, for the consumer society. Rather, the consumer society emerged *gradually* through a progressive, but not linear or uniform, *coming together* of a variety of factors which have varied from time to time in their sometimes profoundly innovative forms (see Figure 2.2, p. 44). Consumer society or culture has been created by both broad social phenomena (like the growth in social mobility, the evolution of the relationship between the sexes, urbanization, etc.) and more specific economic phenomena (the growth in consumption of luxury goods per capita, the development of standardized production, the reinforcing of a complex commercial system, the spread of consumer credit services, etc.), which in turn have been accompanied and mediated by new economic ethics of production and use and new cultural views of social identity. This has been a transformation of massive importance, which has given way to a form of life characterized by the centrality of the social figure of the 'consumer'.

Summary

This chapter has suggested that the history of consumer society is both the history of a great *material and institutional transformation* and the history of the formation of *new cultural orientations* towards the economy, commodities and material culture. Especially from the 18th century, consumption begins to be problematized as an activity that is relevant in and of itself as well as crucial in defining social relations and identities. Since then, both *market actors* and *political actors* contributed to produce the 'consumer' as a dominant, if constantly contested and variously nuanced, social identity. The works of **Arjun Appadurai** and **Chandra Mukerji** show that global *commodity flows* and *knowledge flows*, and in particular *colonial goods* and *materialist values*, have played an important role in the development of consumer culture in the West. While in contemporary public discourse

(Continued)

consumption has replaced *luxury* as a central category, the cultural repertoires which informed the 18th century luxury debate were reframed in new ways during the 19th and 20th centuries. An ongoing moralization thus accompanied the different historical waves of consumer goods, social identities, places and practices which appear to define different periods in the history of consumption from early modernity to the present – from the rise of the *department store* and modern *advertising*, to the spread of *mass-produced durable goods*, to the transition to a *post-Fordist economy* and the emphasis on *individualization* and *customization*. The chapter thus identifies some of the processes which contributed to the development of consumer culture. It addresses the *privatization* of the sphere of consumption which was caught up in the dynamics of fashion while continuing to underscore *class* and *gender* differences. It looks at the *geopolitics* of consumer culture, in particular at the role of Americanization in spreading a free market ideology and at the importance of diverse *national cultures* in metabolizing global commodities. It also focuses on transnational phenomena such as *youth culture* and the growing influence of *cultural intermediaries*.

Notes

1 On this debate in France, which is also extremely rich, see Williams (1982).

2 The *Fable* is a satire of classical and civic-humanist positions against luxury: if we examine the 'Nature of Man' we will see that 'what renders him a Sociable Animal' are 'his vile and most hateful Qualities': they are 'the most necessary Accomplishments to fit him for the largest, and, according to the World, the happiest and most flourishing Society' (Mandeville 1924, 4). The clause 'according to the World' is crucial: it underlines secularization, the idea that 'civilization' is something different and distinct from 'morality' based on religion. See Berry (1994); Hundert (1994); Sassatelli (1997).

3 In Victorian times, for example, as Matthew Hilton (2002, 106) shows, liberalism not only advocated 'laissez-faire free trade and the rights of the individual to be left alone in the marketplace', but also spoke of 'the duty to consume with as much of a concern for others as for oneself', promoting an 'ethic of respectability' which recommended consumption according to criteria such as beauty and appreciation instead of vanity and ostentation (see also Searle 1998). This repertoire, which follows from the 18th century luxury debate, is complemented in the late 19th and early 20th by the preoccupation with the diffusion of cheap, standardized and petty luxuries and with allegedly herd-like, indiscriminate behaviour of the masses. In more recent times, the medical framework has markedly shaped the cultural frames for the moralization of consumption as evident in the moral panics over alcohol, cigarettes and drugs (see Chapters 6 and 7).

4 The associations that Schivelbusch makes between religion and consumption have drawn important criticisms, i.e. Camporesi (1994).

5 For example, in post-war America consumer politics separated the consumer from the producer and, to a large extent, the citizen (Cohen 2003), whereas the post-war Japanese consumer movement embedded consumption within civic values that blended ideals of citizenship, national identity and production (Maclachlan and Trentmann 2004).

6 De Grazia (2005, 6 ff.) indicates five features of the American 'market empire': the US recognized that its trade could be a cultural infringement, but found numerous ways to justify it, regarding 'other nations as having limited sovereignty over their public space'; exported its civil society which was 'responsive to the ethos of a modern consumer-oriented economy'; deployed the 'power of norm-making' such as the codes of best practice as spelled out by enterprising businessmen, civic leaders, conscientious bureaucrats, etc.; promoted 'consumer democracy' as 'espousing equality in the face of commonly known standards' and a 'sociability' organized around mass consumption; presented its apparent 'peaceableness' as an alterative to European militarism, making the 'soft power' of consumer democracy appear as a distant alternative to 'hard power' of totalitarian nations.

7 See Ellwood (2001) on the propaganda of the Marshall Plan in Italy. See also Kroen (2004) on the negotiation of the American way of life and the disputes over the Marshall Plan in Germany, Britain and France.

8 This phenomenon is also partly linked to the development of international marketing which with its promotions of toys began to consider children as a 'category' of consumers separate from adults (Kline 1995). See also Cook (2004) for the creation of a market for children's clothes and the rise of the child as a consumer.

9 Featherstone (1991, 27) differs from Bourdieu precisely because he maintains that, in so far as it is pushed by the hegemonic lifestyle of new middle classes, contemporary consumer culture needs to consider goods both as conventional signposts, which 'can be read and used to classify the status of their bearer' and as catalysts for the mixing of 'images, signs and symbolic goods which summon up dreams, desires and fantasies', suggesting a search for 'romantic authenticity' and 'emotional fulfilment'.

PART II

Theories of Consumer Agency

In order to understand contemporary cultures and practices of consumption it is crucial to bring into focus the way in which social actors define, perceive and govern their relationship with commodities. As we have seen, from the beginnings of modernity people have progressively learned to satisfy their needs through commodities; they have thus become more capable and willing to act not only as producers but also as consumers, purchasing goods on the market at their discretion, combining them with other objects in everyday practices. But how do these actors behave when they act as consumers? How do they make sense of what they do? What kind of action is consumption? Such questions have accompanied the development of social and cultural theories dealing with consumer agency. In spite of being quite different, these theories tend to account for the phenomenon of consumption by concentrating on the rationalities that guide consumer behaviour.

From their beginnings the social and cultural theories of consumer agency have opposed the atomistic vision typically proposed by economics. Back in the second half of the 19th century economics had already conceived of consumption as an act of purchase performed by a consumer by calculating what was most convenient to buy entirely on the basis of personal need and independently of the choices of others. The first sociological reflections on consumption tried to show that the alternative to such an individualistic, instrumental rationality was not irrationality so much as social rationality. In other words, consumption cannot be simply reduced to one of two extremes of the *rational/irrational* dichotomy: it cannot be held up as the prototype of cost-benefit calculations which actors make in trying to satisfy their own inner-directed desires, nor can it be liquidated as an example of irrational action, impulsive, other-directed or without purpose. Rather, consumption practices are social phenomena, and as such they display internal forms of order and are organized according to a variety of logics.

The first sociologists to concern themselves with consumption identified the *positional* logic as its main rationale. From this point of view, consumers are interested in getting and using objects which can serve as symbols of status, demonstrating and possibly bettering their stranding in the social structure, marking social hierarchies and boundaries. Fashion, a phenomenon that became ever more important in the great metropolises at the end of the 19th century, seemed to be an exemplar of modern consumption practices. It was indicated as an efficient – and only superficially innocuous – device to constantly

mark the boundaries between those who know and can afford the latest thing
and those who are destined to follow the changes in the tastes of others. In the
post-war period – a period years of great economic expansion which saw the
spread of cultural goods via the market – a different idea emerged that took less
account of the conflicts amongst consumer tastes, and instead concentrated on
the power exercised by mass communication, by the cultural industry and
advertising, and on their capacity to *manipulate* tastes. According to this critical perspective, people are not always able to act on the basis of their own sense
of distinction; they are victims of the variety of images and the speed of innovation, so much so that it appears everything changes even though in fact it
remains the same. More recently some important anthropological studies have
attempted to round out this pessimist view which once again negates any rationality within acts of consumption. Cultural anthropology has delved deeper
into the relationships amongst consumers, and their capacity to use goods not
only according to a positional logic, but also in ways that are broadly speaking
communicative, adumbrating the creation, maintenance and modification of
social ties. Even today, in the face of a growing advertising system which
undoubtedly traffics in meanings and lifestyles, consumption practices can con-
figure themselves in various ways: as actions which express and consolidate
social bonds and personal relationships, according to a logic that we can define
as relational; or as actions oriented towards values, towards whatever is considered good taste or correct, according to a logic that we can call normative;
or as ways of presenting oneself in interaction and obtaining deference, according to a ceremonial logic; or yet again, as aimed at the construction of a world
of pleasure, according to a hedonistic logic.

Reviewing the various theories of consumption and consumer agency, I shall
show that the reasons behind consumption are many and anything but univocal
or coherent. Practices of consumption happen through modalities that are far
more open and situated and much less structural and linear than the idea of
instrumental rationality suggests. Therefore, they appear to need a different model
of action which is radically social. The classic dimensions of social analysis –
social stratification, cultural classification, power, institutions, rituals, interaction,
identity, collective action, professions, etc. – are all crucial in understanding the
phenomenon of consumption. To account for such complexity contemporary
sociology increasingly tends to view these phenomena as *social practices*. That is,
it recognizes that, on the whole, the acts of consumption are informed by a variety of *different logics*, that each of these acts may contain more than one moti-
vating factor, and that each can be lived and presented, read and justified
differently according to context. Consequently contemporary sociology concentrates on the *contexts* in which consumption practices take place. The times,
places and institutions of consumption, the rhetorical tropes which actors may use
to justify tastes, the social dynamics that these tastes embody, the lifestyle models
which underlie particular preferences, the identity which is bestowed on the figure
of the consumer: these are the social dimensions of consumption which make
it such an important object of study for contemporary sociology. Through a
growing corpus of empirical studies, the sociology of consumption not only
opposes itself to the atomistic vision of economics in showing that tastes and

preferences can only be understood as social phenomena, it has also begun to document the richness and complexity of taste. Thus, it is increasingly aware of the thousand and one ways in which consumption practices work as a mirror of our relationships and of the larger social structure and its ideologies, while offering a terrain where models of relations, social structures and ideologies are played out, transformed and brought into question.

Utility and Social Competition

3

Of all the social sciences, economics has had a pivotal role in portraying what consumption is and is not, in representing the relationship between production and consumption, and in defining the place of consumption within society at large. Economics has indeed occupied a hegemonic role in public policy and public discourse concerning consumption. However, in this chapter I shall show that the science of economics has encountered some significant difficulties in its attempt to model consumption as purely an instrumentally rational decision.

Notwithstanding a few attempts to include the social dimension, the economic view has in the main remained bound to a business and individualistic conception of the sphere of consumption. Meanwhile, from its very beginnings, sociology has conceived of consumption as a fully social phenomenon, and thus one that is understandable only when it is borne in mind that, along with the instrumental logic of utility maximization and cost minimization, there are others; these are linked to the symbolic and ceremonial function of goods, to their role in marking relationships between people and in demonstrating their different social standing and cultural views. The first properly sociological reflections on consumption emerged at the end of the 19th century and brought into focus some of those aspects rejected by economics. In particular, use became tightly linked to the capacity of goods to demarcate and underscore social boundaries and cultural differences. Thus consumption came to be seen as an important space of social competition, rather than a mere realization of individual preferences.

The sovereign consumer

Consumption began to be addressed and recognized as an economic phenomenon with Adam Smith and the emergence of classic economics in the 18th century (see Chapter 2). This coincided with a particular representation of the economy as the intersection and interaction of two opposed and distinct spheres: production and, of course, consumption. To the first economists, Ricardo and Malthus in particular, who lived in a society where scarcity of resources was the order of the day, consumption appeared by and large as an obvious end in itself: it was thus seen not as an object worthy of specific study, but as a natural outcome of productive processes. More production meant more riches for a nation, whereas being able to consume, if not luxuries then life's comforts, appeared as the longed-for and well-deserved outcome of work.

Thus in classical economics consumption was seen as a given end and, at the same time, as a structural need: to create the riches of a nation someone had to be consuming enough to stimulate production. This is the meaning of Malthus's (1820) famous hypothesis of 'effective demand': production depends on the existence of effective demand which enables the producer to cover the cost of production plus profit. Effective demand cannot only be generated by the capitalists (who have a strong propensity to save and invest rather than consume), or by labourers (whose salaries are often less than the prices of their products). To possess a strong productive capacity a nation also needs to have servants, statesmen, judges, soldiers, doctors, priests, etc.: that is, a group of 'unproductive consumers'.

As we will see later on, Marxist political economy takes the idea that consumption develops as a structural consequence of the capitalist economy to extremes, so that it ends up seeing consumption as a totally other-directed act – this inspired a number of important critical reflections in the second half of the 20th century (see Chapter 4). However, with the *marginalist* or *neoclassical* revolution in the last quarter of the 19th century, economics has in the main taken a different path and has constructed its analytical models through considering *all* consumers as *sovereigns* of the market. Each consumer makes self-directed choices which, put together with those of other consumers, create a 'demand' to which production can do little else but respond. Within marginalist or neoclassical economics, the social actor was made to coincide with the economic agent known as the 'consumer'; and in turn, he became the essential element of the model: his purchase decisions were in fact the motor of a system, the market, in which the two separate but interrelated domains of demand and supply were kept in equilibrium (Schumpeter 1955).

Having postulated the idea that consumers are sovereigns of the market, the science of economics hasn't often questioned the reasons for their choices, how they were taken, or the subjective and social meanings they might have. Its interest hangs on the possibility of modelling those mechanisms which balance demand and supply. Consumers are indicated as actors who know how to act instrumentally, and do so, purchasing only what is useful independently of the judgement and persuasion of others, and carefully considering their choice against the various options offered by the market (Hargreaves Heap 1989). Their choices will thus be aimed at *maximizing the utility* derived from objects. Utility is itself conceived, on the one hand, as individual pleasure and, on the other, as subject to interpersonal comparison inasmuch as numerically quantifiable and in inverse proportion to the quantity consumed of a given commodity.

This viewpoint was not substantially altered in the attempt to purify marginal utility theory of its psychological and utilitarian origins with the notion of *revealed preferences*.[1] In fact, the model of action is still the same: the neoclassic consumer is conceived of as a kind of atomized black box whose preferences and tastes, as well as their genesis, are not studied in and of themselves (Hargreaves Heap 1989; Hirschmann 1985). Rather, they are studied as if realized in purchases which are in turn identified through numeric variables like the quantity of bought objects and the money spent: in other words, preferences and choices (or purchases and tastes) have become synonymous. The choices made are limited and structured only by budgetary limits, and are conceived of as instrumentally rational decisions, aimed at realizing a given, ordered and stable field of preferences at the lowest possible cost. The utility that the consumer derives from each good remains negatively correlated with the quantity of the same good consumed, and independent of the preferences of other consumers.

In this neoclassical vision the dynamic aspects of the system are entrusted to a stimulus-response mechanism, so that rather than economics purified of psychological variables we can instead talk of economics founded on mechanistic psychology (Katona 1960). At least three problems are thus neglected: the process of preference formation, especially inasmuch as it is linked to their social and cultural interdependence and to their standardization across time and space; the qualitative characteristics of goods, or rather the subject/object relationship in its socio-cultural details; and the question of power, especially in its symbolic aspects. These are also the shortcomings which, as we shall see, fuelled the development of a sociology of consumption.

Still, the precise status of the consumer in orthodox economic theory is a matter of dispute (Winch 2006). To be sure, contemporary economics has tried to introduce a limited social characterization of the consumer, essentially by considering that the positive correlation between growth in income and growth in consumer expenditure is mediated by social position. Duesenberry's work (1949) has undoubtedly been fundamental in macroeconomics (that part of economics which considers aggregate economic phenomena, in this specific case the determinants of total expenditure for consumption). Duesenberry put forward the idea that it was relative income (that is, mediated by social position and demonstrative effects) that influenced demand: in a society with strong social mobility, the expansion of goods of higher quality gives place to status display which is stronger amongst the weaker classes and stimulates demand even when real income doesn't grow. A similar idea was proposed in microeconomics (that part of economics which tries to model individual behaviour, and thus in this specific case, the act of consumption) by Leibenstein (1950). In an attempt to model the purchasing decisions of consumers with more attention to social aspects, Leibenstein introduced refinements to the relevance of motives of emulation and status display, labelling them 'Veblen effect', 'Bandwagon effect' and 'Snob effect' (Adams and McCormick 1992). The Veblen effect comes into play when the function of consuming an object is to demonstrate the acquisitive power of the consumer so that – in open opposition to the utilitarian logic and the minimization of cost – the higher the cost of a product, the greater its display value. The Bandwagon and Snob effects indicate situations in which the demand for a good or service respectively grows or diminishes as other consumers show interest and consume that good or service.

Both Leibenstein and Duesenberry have not been without their critics, however. They tend not to consider the complexity of the symbolic significance of goods, failing to examine other cultural meanings like style or taste which are central to the dynamics of demand, nor the situational and institutional character of consumption. To this end we just have to recall the importance not only of the different characteristics of goods, but also of the places in which they are purchased, or of the practices that follow purchase and which are often highly structured by institutions, such as the family or other cohabitation units, explained with difficulty by the logic of economics alone.

Of course, even in economics there has been an increasing attempt to overcome the conception of the actor as an isolated utility maximizer who knows very well how to get satisfaction from the market. Particularly influential is the work of Amartya Sen (1977; 1985) who has tried to include both altruistic motivations, power structures and cooperative/conflictual forms of interaction (Hargreaves Heap 1989; Hirschman 1985). The work of heterodox economist Tibor Scitovsky (1992) should also be mentioned here, although it remains at the margin of prevailing wisdom. Scitovsky stresses that revealed preferences and tastes are not simply coterminous and points to social and structural factors that can trigger their divorce. He considers that the economy has been organized so as to boost a trade-off between comfort (i.e. goods that save time, effort and skill) and pleasure (i.e. goods that promote creativity, require time and enrich one's own faculties); he envisages a possible conflict between standardized goods which provide novelty by obsolescence and individualized pleasure which may grow slowly as consumption competences develop in a free, non-commercialized fashion; and, finally he posits an insidious gap between generalized knowledge which is needed for everyday consumption and specialized skills which are required in the work environment (see Bianchi 2003).

Notwithstanding a number of attempts to broaden its scope, dominant economic theory is still characterized by atomistic and instrumental approaches, equating revealed preferences with taste.[2] This is the case for Gary Becker's *Accounting for Tastes* (1996), which proclaims the need to relocate economic actors in their society and culture, recognizing that tastes are important for consumption and cannot simply be left outside of economic modelling. Becker holds firm to the assumption that individuals behave so as to maximize utility. However, he also proposes that we consider the utility that a person gets from a good as a function not only of the goods consumed, but also of their 'human capital', a variable which is in turn constituted of two basic 'capital stocks': 'personal capital' which 'includes the relevant past consumption and other personal experiences that affect current and future utilities', and 'social capital' which 'incorporates the influence of past actions by peers and others in an individual's social network and control system' (Becker 1996: 4). Thus Becker proposes a new extended utility function in which personal biography (as the effect of past consumption on present consumption), ethics and culture become numeric variables which influence consumption in the same way as other classic economic determinants such as prices and salaries. Despite his attempt to socialize consumption and taste, Becker has simply moved a step further in *economicizing* what a social action is. 'Current choices' – he writes – 'are made partly with an eye to their influences on future capital stocks, and hence on future utilities and choices' (*ibid*, 6). He thus continues to depict consumers according to strongly individualistic premises, such as the maximization of future utility where they know very well what they want and choose through comparison, acting through a precise calculation of probability which separates the means and ends of that action, but also negates its creative and processual character (Sassatelli 2001b).

The limits of economic rationality

In spite of the language used and the labels chosen, mainstream neoclassical economic theory exemplified by Gary Becker's work once again contrasts with the most recent sociological, anthropological and historical studies of consumption.

Today, these disciplines start not with individual choice or a pre-determined vision of the consumer, but with the contexts of consumption in which practices take place. Becker's work is an excellent example of the *imperialist tendencies* of neoclassical economics (Fine 1999) which, having recognized the difficulties of leaving the social aspects of consumption out of their model as exogenous elements, has made them endogenous only to filter and encode them into its own logic. Thus, Becker has translated preferences which are rooted in culture, situation-dependent and process-like into the vocabulary of abstract instrumentalism. Consumption itself is *reduced* and *taken back to* an *abstract* act of acquisition seen essentially as an *instrumental decision* of what to buy according to the utility of available goods, no matter how much this might be filtered through the variables of personal and social capital. Lost are the myriad different and even contradictory relationships which people can build with objects and among themselves through objects – from eating out to celebrate a friend, to listening to a record bought from a second-hand shop recommended by a colleague, from dashing through the aisles of a supermarket to find one's own usual brand of pasta, to trying to decide which new lipstick will go with an outdated but treasured dress, to imagining oneself at the wheel of a new car, then test-driving it, buying it, and finally using and sharing it with friends and family, and so on. In sum, economics has mainly refined its model of consumption from a *technical* point of view, but it has altered little its way of conceiving action and the actor. As suggested, the rise in material standards or the purchase of commodities may be accompanied by different attitudes: we cannot easily read back tastes from revealed preferences, just as we saw it was problematic to read back from increased consumer spending the historical rise and dominance of consumerist mentalities (see Chapter 2). What is more, within economics there is very little awareness of the fact that the proposed atomistic and instrumental model of the consumer, while inaccurate as a description of practice, may well work as a normative device: it orientates the construction of economic institutions and policies and may also be adopted by individuals to work out possible routes of behaviour as well as to justify or criticize their own and other people's practices (see Callon 1998; Carrier and Miller 1998).[3]

Social sciences other than economics should be wary of transforming it into a whipping-boy. We should acknowledge situations where action is institutionally modelled to resemble neoclassical logics. Also, prices and budget constraints are important social conditions for consumers, and consumers often find it appropriate to try and work out some kind of cost-benefit calculation. Sharon Zukin's (2004) recent work on American shoppers shows for example that there is a more rational core to people's shopping than the image provided by notions such as conspicuous consumption or compulsive purchase. However, her interview data show that there are many conflicts within families as well as within each individual shopper's soul which a neoclassical view would not pin down: working-class mothers agonizing over buying clothes for themselves or for their children, conflicts between these mothers and their partners over buying branded or unbranded items; family conflicts between shopping for necessity and shopping for status. By and large, the neoclassical view of the consumer is inadequate to understand consumer practices because it superimposes its model onto reality without considering its normative effects; because it pretends to portray a neat view of individual reasons whereas we may have only aggregate correlations (i.e. we know that in contemporary societies demand grows as income grows, but many different micro-explanations would fit this), because too much is left out of the picture and underestimated (i.e. power relations and the negotiational nature of shopping, namely conflicts among different family members and within each individual consumer over the appropriate purchase rationale) (see also Chapters 5 and 8). Furthermore, the temptation to make an equation between embedded prudential action reasonable within a specific context and abstract calculating instrumentality obliterates the role of ex-post rationalization, mutual recognition, contingency, institutions, and so on.

There is certainly much evidence that, despite prices and budgets and even the apparent functionality of certain goods, consumers do not simply consider price and convenience, nor do they follow the logic of informed instrumental purchase. For example, casting a eye on class differences in clothing among 19th century French men, Diane Crane (2000) shows that working-class folks would not buy fashion-able items such as cloves, canes and top hats even when they could easily afford them, as these items embodied a middle-class etiquette which was at odds with their identity and cultural capital (see also Galilee 2002 on contemporary middle-class British men and their clothes choices). If price is not (always) what makes us buy, it is not what makes us cry either: research conducted in contemporary Britain on people who are robbed shows that they seem most affected by the loss of items which are neither the most expensive nor the most necessary, but those rich in iden-tity value, having being individualized as markers of social relationships and per-sonal attachments (Leonini 1988). Also, if we consider objects which are out of fashion, from the past, superseded – an old radio or scratchy gramophone – should we negate their value, seeing as their functionality is almost non-existent? On the contrary, the main function of the superseded object is that of signifying the past, a very important task in a world made of new objects which are increasingly built to be modern, functional and disposable (Baudrillard 1996). Even for those objects which seem not to be particularly evocative, consumer durables for instance, we can see an 'aesthetic' effect in action, such as the so-called 'Diderot effect' (McCracken 1988). Grant McCracken coined the term 'Diderot effect' inspired by a story in which the French philosopher spoke of a luxurious dressing-gown given to him by a friend which made him modify his modest study to adapt it to this new presence, that is to recreate coherence and harmony with a new centre of cultural classifica-tion represented by the dressing-gown. Thus, McCracken uses this term to indicate the tendency of deploying goods to create coherent cultural and aesthetic unities. Together with authors as diverse as Jean Baudrillard (1996; 1998), Mary Douglas and Baron Isherwood (1979), he shows that goods can only communicate their meanings if they are supported by other goods, whereas when isolated from others they remain muted. In other words, each good derives much of its symbolic func-tion from the system of objects in which it is inserted and which is the expression of a particular unity or cultural principle. From this point of view neoclassical eco-nomics is not only atomistic as regards the subject of consumption, but also as regards commodities: it doesn't consider that the world of things is culturally orga-nized according to principles which link objects together into a genuine semantics. Nor, indeed, does it consider that qualitative differences between commodities exist which prefigure different contexts and uses, and cannot be simply reduced to a numerical indication.[4]

Even when we do our shopping in a supermarket for small daily needs, it is difficult to reduce our preferences and acquisitions to a series of single and punctual purchase decisions entirely reducible to instrumental calculation. This is because we rarely have the time, capacity or, frankly, the will to arm ourselves with all the information necessary to perfectly weigh one commodity against the other, as mainstream economics itself has recognized since Akerlof's (1970) famous article on the uncertainties of the second-hand car market. To go back to the supermarket, just think of how little we actually read the labels which regulations in favour of the consumer insist upon, or of the advantage that products placed at our eye level on the shelves have. This is also because, especially in times of food scares, 'mad-cow disease' and the genetically modified, situations of choice are clearly far removed, even in our own consciousness, from decisions between alternatives with definite outcomes (Sassatelli 2001b). Furthermore, even in an activity which seems banal and routine, like shopping in the supermarket, we bring into play a variety of far-reaching symbolic meanings (Falk and Campbell 1997). Daniel Miller's (1998) ethnographic research amongst families of different classes, ethnicities and cultural levels in one area of London demonstrated that shopping in a supermarket is above all a form of *ritual*. Thus, it is an action filled with shared meanings which enables the renewal of meanings and relationships (see Chapter 5). In this case, shopping at the supermarket was revealed as stressing the bond that the person responsible for it (typically a woman/mother) has with the other members of the family, and their relationship with respect to ideals of family, kinship, femininity, parenthood, and so on. By and large, market transactions and social relationships are indeed much more intimately and creatively intertwined than neoclassical wisdom postulates (Biggart and Castanis 2001; see also Chapter 7).

Moreover, the neoclassical emphasis on the equilibrium between demand and supply paints a rather abstract picture of consumption. This has been redressed by neo-Marxist views which consider how different 'systems of provisions' in different market sectors organize contexts of consumption which consumers must actively engage with (Fine 2002b, see also Chapter 4). More broadly, a number of studies from different perspectives have underlined the importance of the specific contexts, situations and places in which consumption is carried out, stressing the role of the interactions that are conceived as normal and natural in such places. For instance, to understand the choice of a restaurant it is necessary to consider not only the price and taste of the food served or the demonstrative value associated with some dishes and venues. Rather than quantify the utility or satisfaction that each participant obtains from a meal, one should understand how participants learn to feel satisfied by looking at how interaction is locally organized and what are the associated cultural meanings, as it is evident that eating out is not a response to a definite individual or universal need, but to needs and desires that make sense only in certain cultures and for some social actors. Going out for lunch or dinner should thus be considered as a social practice both *situated* and *processual*: the choice of certain food is in fact mediated by a process of learning that is locally upheld by a series of specific and highly codified manners that give eating out most of its meaning. As is well demonstrated by Alan Warde (1997; see also Lupton 1996; Warde and Martens 2001), learning to be at the table, thus acquiring the proper manners, learning to manage them and finally getting to like them, is as much part of consumption as eyeing the menu for the prices of given dishes. As much a part of the consumption, and of the satisfaction or utility that each actor can derive from it, is the knowledge (gastronomic or social) that derives from having eaten out, tasted this or that dish, having used a given type of cutlery, and having managed well the phases of the meal, that is tasting, commenting on the dishes, chatting and exchanging information.

Fashion, style and conspicuous consumption

The close link between consumption and social relations so well illustrated by studies of conviviality has been one of the starting points of the sociology of consumption. In this early sociology of consumption individual actors are still the essential source of economic value, just as they are in neoclassical economics. Nevertheless, in contrast to economics, the focus is on how actors come to make their value judgements, and under which structural and social conditions tastes and preferences emerge and get standardized. In his *Philosophy of Money* (1990, orig. 1907) Georg Simmel maintains that the value of things depends on the value they are given by the subject, rather than being founded on absolutes such as the intrinsic value of their material properties, or the amount of work necessary to produce them, which they embody. However, this subjective valuation is itself conditioned by the historical and cultural context in which it takes place.[5] To be sure, the inhabitants of large modern cities are increasingly able to translate the value of things in numeric and monetary terms, to consider lengthy chains of cause and effect and to perform some kind of cost-benefit calculation, but they never reach the calculative instrumentality which neoclassical economics holds to be the basis of action. Instead, according to Simmel (1971a), it is social and cultural repertoires of action – and above all the possibility of self-recognition within a group and distinction from others – which are of utmost importance in large urban environments where one is all too easily lost in the anonymous crowd.

Consumption thus appears to Simmel as a culturally ordered field of action, rather than a threat to social order, as his French contemporary Emile Durkheim would have it (Slater 1997). For example, it is precisely in the chaotic and overcrowded metropolis that more and more people need to dress themselves in clothes which signal their identity to others, both as a members of a group and as individuals. Fashion appears to Simmel to be an excellent means of achieving both these effects. In his well-known work *Fashion*, the German scholar presents this phenomenon as the typical outcome of two fundamental principles of social logic: the need for *cohesion* or union and the need for *differentiation* or isolation (Simmel 1971b, orig. 1904) (see also Chapter 1). In following fashion we align ourselves with some people and differentiate ourselves from others, but at the same time we can enjoy expressing ourselves in a common language that is widely understood.

For Simmel, fashion is also a metaphor for the allure that the *new* exerts on the modern subject in general, and on the bourgeoisie and the middle classes in particular. Indeed, the social position of the middle classes predisposes them to fashion: in contrast to the nobility, the bourgeoisie cannot rely on tradition and established, long-standing styles and, unlike less well-to-do classes, they hope to better their social position and to find their own style (Simmel 1971a; 1971b). More recently the anthropologist Grant McCracken (1988, 13 ff.) has maintained that whilst in traditional societies the guiding principle in attributing value to goods was the *patina* of time (that is the appearance that objects gain through use over generations), in modernity it is fashion, intended as the search for the new. However, for McCracken this also occurs with the nobility which, as the royal courts developed at the beginning of modernity, had become the foremost inspiration of fashion: courtly nobles could no longer allow objects to accumulate value and prestige through age, so that value became increasingly connected with appearing new, original and modern (see Chapter 1). Today however, some centuries on, we are able to see that fashion and patina coexist. In fact, patina has been recuperated, perhaps in a simulated form, by fashion itself in the trends for second-hand and vintage dresses or in the furniture market, where antique, early modern or simply 'old' items, as well as new ones which are purposively built in retro styles and perhaps artificially aged, are mixed and matched with the latest designs (Gregson and Crewe 2003; Molotch 2003).

While periodical switches in dresses and aesthetic forms are as old as history, according to Simmel fashion characteristically holds to the modern spirit. This is not only because it proposes novelty, but also because it propagates it; that is, it makes change normal:

> We can discover one of the reasons why in these latter days fashion exercises such a powerful influence on our consciousness in the circumstances that the great, permanent, unquestionable convictions are continually losing strength, as a consequence of which the transitory and vacillating elements of life acquire more room for the display of their activity. (Simmel 1971b, 303)

The propensity for newness, as it is changeable and transitory, corresponds to the 'impatient time' of modern life which implies the desire for a 'rapid change of life's contents' and is attracted by 'the charm of novelty coupled with that of transitoriness'. Being ephemeral and destined to disappear, fashion enables novelty to seem unlimited and at the same time allows for the 'absolutely unnatural' to exist at least in this ephemeral form. Still, Simmel's vision presents fashion and style as providing individuals with a 'temporary anchor', which enables them to approach things whilst maintaining a certain distance, allowing them to underline that they are not reducible to any exterior image or form.

Modern individuals, epitomized by the bourgeois, have to learn to govern themselves as original subjects, as suggested when we looked at Campbell's (1987) work on the Romantic ethic and consumerism (see Chapter 1). This is an irksome task indeed and, for Simmel, *style* might be very helpful here: 'as the manifestation of our inner feelings', style 'indicates that these feelings no longer immediately gush out but take on a disguise the moment they are revealed' (Simmel 1990, 473). Through adopting a certain style, especially if it has been acceptable for a while, we free ourselves from the 'absolute responsibility' for ourselves, we can experiment in indirect ways, as if through a 'veil', demonstrating our taste without having to keep steady 'on the narrowness of mere individuality' (Simmel 1991, 68). Furthermore, the variety of different styles that characterizes the material environment of the modern subject provides again a space for individual originality, allowing for objects to be mixed and mingled to 'receive a new centre which is not located in any of them alone' (*ibid*, 69), but coincides with the specific combination contrived by the subject. In other words, by choosing to combine different styles in the same home, for example, the individual creates new meaning for those things; they thus acquire value together, as a mishmash, and underline the capacity for self-expression for a particular taste (see Chapter 8).

Simmel offers a rich reading of the phenomena of style and of fashion which, as I have suggested, doesn't reduce the dynamics of fashion to a positional logic i.e. the establishment of social hierarchies and boundaries through the display of goods. Notwithstanding this, he does tend to describe the social dynamics of fashion as functioning only through imitation, with a top-down descending movement. Indeed, according to Simmel (1971b, 299), the latest fashion:

> affects only the upper classes. As soon as the lower classes begin to copy their style, thereby crossing the line of the demarcation the upper classes have drawn and destroying the uniformity of their coherence, the upper classes turn away from this style and adopt a new one, which in turn differentiated them from the masses; and thus the game goes merrily on.

Less favoured social groups would not be able to create their own fashions, and they would limit themselves to imitating the more fortunate. Simmel thus seems to propose what would later come to be codified in the 1950s by American marketing as *trickle-down*, a mechanism through which fashion spreads by dripping from the top to the bottom.

Simmel and Sombart (see Chapter 1) were amongst the first to make a significant contribution to developing a sociology of consumption. We must also add, though, the American Thorstein Veblen who in *The Theory of the Leisure Class* (1994, orig. 1899) clearly engages with neoclassical thinking. In fact, Veblen created the concept of *'conspicuous consumption'* to indicate those phenomena of consumption which escaped the logic of utility maximization at minimal cost. He observed that, alongside necessity and calculating acts of consumption explainable by the use value of commodities, there also operated ceremonial forms of consumption linked to status and honour: 'no class of society, not even the most abjectly poor, forgoes all customary conspicuous consumption' (*ibid*, 62). In his view, the value of *some* goods was exclusively determined by their capacity to make a given social position visible. Conspicuous consumption and waste thus served as demonstration/recognition of elevated social position, founded on the knowledge that 'wealth or power must be put in evidence, for esteem is granted only in evidence' (*ibid*, 30). Indeed, as we may still see quite often, a costly object may be sought out precisely because of its high cost, because through displaying it social actors can visibly demonstrate what Veblen called 'pecuniary strength', thus obtaining 'good repute' and showing their good chances of controlling the future course of the social and symbolic processes.

In Veblen's theory, the display of wealth is essentially a form of luxury which serves to flag distance from the world of practical necessity. Writing in the United States between the 19th and 20th centuries Veblen had in mind, in particular, the social and cultural dynamics between the *nouveaux riches* and the leisured elite; the former being a social group who had the money to finance their rise to more exclusive circles and who needed, at the same time, to legitimize their recently acquired social positions through visible demonstration of their success. In this context taste, that is 'good taste', appears to have been associated with displaying distance from work and practicality, and thus whatever appeared to be too

PATINA	CONSPICUOUS CONSUMPTION	FASHION	STYLE
Families/Clan	Families/Individuals	Individuals	Individuals
Closed competition	Open competition	Virtual competition	Self competition
Emphasis on the past	Emphasis on the future	Emphasis on the present	Emphasis on the past
Emphasis on stability	Emphasis on exclusivity	Emphasis on novelty	Emphasis on originality

Figure 3.1 Techniques for identity construction and social distinction through objects

'economic' was seen as opposed to the 'cultured'. Whilst in societies which preceded the industrial era, a 'life of pure leisure is the most definitive proof of one's own supremacy', in the industrial cities where all were strangers to one another goods multiplied and appearances were of the essence; the most effective demonstration of status happens through the display of certain commodities which embody leisure and refinement. The dominant groups were thus pushed to obtain not only expensive goods, but also increasingly refined ones, whose use demanded a continual 'cultivation of the aesthetic faculty', which itself required time as well as money, sophisticated manners of consumption as well as 'arduous application to the business of learning a life of ostensible leisure in a becoming way' (*ibid*, 55).

All in all, conspicuous consumption, fashion and style can each be considered as modern and individualist versions of that technique of identity construction and social distinction which in traditional societies was found in the accumulation of precious objects whose value increased with the patina of time (see Figure 3.1). While patina was typical of societies where status competition was limited to the elite and managed within clans, conspicuous consumption, fashion and style involve individuals belonging to wider and wider social strata. Functioning through the democratization of competitive consumption, conspicuous consumption, fashion and style were all catalysed by the modern urban environment, but entail different temporal emphases: as suggested, fashion emphasises 'newness' as an absolute present; style and conspicuous consumption draw on the relative stability of some cultural codifications to emphasize, respectively, past and future.

According to Veblen, in industrial metropolises conspicuous consumption extended to the entire population: inferior groups did nothing but imitate the superior ones, buying the same commodities (or, we can add, cheaper versions of these) as soon as it was possible; these then lost their power for social distinction and were abandoned by superior groups, who rushed to find new objects that could demonstrate their social and cultural primacy. This is why, thanks to the trickle-down effect that Simmel notes in his work on fashion, consumption as status display became fundamental in all social strata. Thus, in Veblen's view it is through the mechanism of emulation, conceived of as competition for status and as envy, that new goods serve, often only fleetingly, as goalposts in the game of social distinction and the reproduction of hierarchies of taste.

Veblen's analysis of conspicuous consumption remains extremely important, helping to bridge economics and sociology (Tilman 1996, Trigg 2001). Yet it has been widely criticized. For mainstream economists Veblen hasn't provided a clear enough analytical framework, and many historians have accused him of making generalizations which are too formal. The identification of conspicuous and competitive consumption with the display of magnificence is tricky. For instance, in certain socio-historical moments the display of austerity has been the best way to make oneself visible, sobriety could be used as a highly elaborated way of presenting oneself, and demonstrative consumption occurs through the most subtle understatement or even staged carelessness – examples include the eminently modest collars or *golillas* adopted by Philip IV of Spain in the 17th century (Burke 1993), the embracing of 'inconspicuous consumption' by British gentlemen starting in the 18th century (Kutcha 1996), the severe but nonetheless costly clothes of the Protestant bourgeoisie in France during the 19th century (Perrot 1987) and, more recently, the 1970s fashion of anti-fashion, and the late 1990s minimal chic of Armani or Prada (Steele 1997; 2003). Largely due to Veblenesque echoes, reference to envy, imitation and status symbols has become a default explanation and indeed a straitjacket for the reading of all and every act of consumption. In this way, as Campbell (1987) has underlined, what is commonly described as 'consumerism' has often been explained on the basis of mere social stratification, as the effect of the continual ephemeral strivings of subaltern groups to reach the upper class by imitation, and of the latter's defensive strategies. This is inappropriate as it elevates emulation to the decisive role, so that the meaning of novelty is bound to aspirations of a culturally empty social differentiation. In other words, attention is placed on the fact that certain goods mark difference, not on *what* differences are signalled, or on *how* this comes about.

Thus, Veblen's theory may prevent us from understanding the specific objectives of those who use fashion, and the reasons that they choose particular objects and reject others. It is not only the *existence* of a difference, but also the *nature* and *character* of the difference between cultural categories that fashion signals. Even when imitation is a factor, it is always selective, and it is the selection that matters. Women did not simply imitate men: when at the end of the 19th century women started to wear bloomers, they used them both to ride bicycles and to make a statement about their right to full citizenship; they did not want to be men, but women were entitled to certain liberties, and it is no coincidence that the women of the suffrage movement largely used them (Finnegan 1999). Much later, especially in the last three decades of the 20th century, working women have used male dress codes in clothing to appropriate those expressive qualities normally attributed to men and to become accepted as competent work colleagues. This has required a complex negotiation of male and female connotations: the selective adoption of male codes which convey authoritative images at work, so-called "power dressing", has been a way in which women have eased their access to professional environments, maintaining some femininity but also restricting sexual connotations. The structured jacket in sombre colours is thus combined with skirts and high-heels, creating an unstable hybrid between masculine connotations (authority/detachedness) and feminine ones (sexuality/emotiveness) which women are sometimes able to work in their favour, but which force them to be constantly more self-aware than their male colleagues (Entwistle 2000).[6]

Beyond emulation

From a sociological perspective, the model of emulation, epitomized by Veblen's considerations, has the limit of reducing consumption to one social logic alone. In Veblen's case, in particular, emulation is also brought back to 'envy' seen as a universal psychological foundation. Considering emulation as a universal impulse or instinct like envy, Veblen doesn't allow for a modern culture of consumption also being expressed in the historical construction of a distinctive cognitive, emotional and moral outlook (see Chapter 2). Also, in a Veblenesque model we can't easily conceive of imitation as mimesis and identification on the one hand, and as a necessarily creative and selective process, on the other. Furthermore, the social dimension seems to have a pleonastic character, because only public practices of consumption may appear as social, whereas private ones may be presented as having some sort of pre-cultural function. Even if he recognizes that there are forms of leisure (i.e. 'non productive consumption of time') which are cultivated in the private sphere only to endow people with distinctively useless capacities (i.e. 'the knowledge of the dead languages') or superfluously refined manners (Veblen 1994, 34 ff.), Veblen tends to provide only a partial socialization of consumption, whereas there seems to be no reason to suppose that private consumption is any less culturally shaped or expressive of values. As Pierre Bourdieu (1979) (see also Chapter 5) has shown in a refined version of Veblenesque reasoning, social differences are *reproduced* and not only affirmed through consumption, and so even those tastes which are so intimate that they appear to be ours alone are in fact traceable to social maps. Indeed, the social psychology of consumption has shown that the personal dimension of the relationship with things is important (Csikszentmihalyi and Rochberg-Halton 1981; Dittmar 1992). The smallest of things can function as support for the formation of personal identity, and as a refuge from the pressure of the thousand and one upsets that we are faced with when acting in public. These intimate modalities of relations between objects and subjects, however, develop according to specific cultural codes and in specific institutional contexts. It is thus important not to represent the world of consumption as split in two: a rational or positional public world and an irrational or emotional intimate reality (see Chapters 6 and 8).

The meaning of objects, even the most hidden and private – from the small things we use for daily personal care to those which structure our domestic spaces (from washing machines to stereos) – is not in fact determined once and for all by their form and function, but is shaped by gender, sexuality and the life course, these being in turn socially structured by material culture and a variety of domestic and commercial environments (Csikszentmihalyi and Rochberg-Halton 1981; Dittmar 1992; Kirkham 1996; Riggins 1990). If we take objects which seem to be purely functional and which are presented and seen as private, hearing-aids for instance, we can clearly see that there is a social history behind their use and their meanings which stresses gender differences (Schwartz 1996). During the 19th century hearing-trumpets were used only by men even if deafness was also found amongst women; instead, during the early 20th century, hearing-aids, which had become far less visible, were used by both men and women; however, the virtues of the two sexes and the defects that the hearing-aids were seen to correct were gender-specific. Through using these objects, advertisements maintained, women could once again become 'good listeners', whereas men would 'be more able to interact'; women would be able to recuperate 'closeness with their husband and family', men could confront their 'lack of authority' or the trials and tribulations of 'work'.

Veblen's analysis, and to some extent Simmel's observations, also run the risk of reducing fashion dynamics to hierarchical and pyramidal structures in which subaltern groups follow higher status groups without ever reaching them, and without ever building a culture of their own. However, the idea of a creative centre of fashion (or of 'good taste' as Bourdieu puts it, see Chapter 5) situated at the top of a simple social scale contrasts with the complexity and the strong functional differentiation of a socio-cultural fabric, such as today's, which is not reducible to a hierarchical model (Crane 2000; Frow 1995; Lamont 1992; Lash and Urry 1987). In a similar context the spread of fashions sometimes may *trickle-across* social groups or indeed may *trickle-up*, moving from the bottom to the top. In a society that is increasingly fragmented, in which consumption itself is an important catalyst of social recognition, every social grouping seems to be guided by its own innovators or tastemakers rather than by a unique fashion elite (Davis 1992; König 1973). Still more evident is the fact that weak social groups, far from adopting purely imitative strategies, tend to develop fashions which can be considered genuine and original. Even working-class styles or the so called 'street-styles' often end up being adopted far outside these social circles (Polhemus 1994).

This is the case with punk styles and the piercing that the first punks adopted with clearly transgressive intent, using everyday objects (safety-pins for instance) and transforming them into decorations which appeared unattractive to those outside the group (Hebdige 1979; see also Chapter 4). Subsequently, piercing has become a more widespread and even normal way of marking the body, emerging from marginality and even becoming chic. Adopted by famous people within the music industry as well as the world of high fashion, made more elegant with the addition of jewels conventionally thought of as elegant, spread by piercing studios that are increasingly fashionable and also conform to health regulations, piercing has lost part of its transgressive character and has become, at least in some forms, a widespread, normal practice amongst youth of all social classes (Le Breton 2002b).

The emphasis on emulation and trickle-down also tends to obscure the role of the *fashion industry*, *fashion journalists*, and *stars* of the big screen, music and sport who act as *fashion leaders*, often on a global scale. Spun by the global circulation of images, fashion leaders may operate as a socially distant reference group promoting the creation of virtual communities for both young Western consumers – in post-war Italy televised consumer lifestyles have been considered a means of 'anticipatory socialization' for the masses migrating from the south to the north of the country (Alberoni and Baglioni 1965) – as well as non-Western ones – as research on the penetration of Adidas sneakers in developing markets has shown (Arnould and Wilk 1984). If Simmel and Veblen pass over these aspects, Herbert Blumer (1969) was amongst the first authors to underline the importance of the fashion industry and its mediating role. According to Blumer a style becomes fashion not when the privileged groups wear it, but when it corresponds to the 'incipient taste of the fashion consuming public'. In his view (*ibid*, 281):

> The efforts of an elite class to set itself apart in appearance takes place inside of the movement of fashion instead of being its cause...The fashion mechanism appears not in response to a need of class differentiation and class emulation, but in response to a wish to be in fashion, to be abreast of what has good standing, to express new tastes which are emerging in a changing world.

Thus, the privileged classes can of course influence the direction of taste but they cannot control it; the 'incipient taste' is highly elusive and tortuously interconnected with the fashion industry. While he assigns an important role to consumers, in Blumer's eyes fashions are also, at least in part, the product of selective choices made by stylists, fashion journalists and even by stockists and shopkeepers. The stylists know that their creations will be filtered through these actors who work as cultural intermediaries. In noting the strong similarities between the preferences of journalists and stockists, and tracing this to their common root in the fashion world and an orientation to new trends, Blumer anticipates Bourdieu's emphasis on the driving force that the new middle classes and cultural intermediaries constitute for consumer culture (see Chapters 2 and 5). However, underplaying the conflicts and negotiations that mould the world of fashion, he is at odds with Bourdieu, who considers *haute couture* as a pivotal field of power and competition (see Bourdieu and Delsaut 1975).

To follow on in this direction one has to keep in mind that fashion is not only an aesthetic phenomenon involving consumption, but also a composite cultural industry (Braham 1997; Crane 2000). We may consider that 'what is distinctive about the fashion code is that it must pass through the filter of the fashion industry. Thus the suggested code modifications displayed on the catwalks of Paris stand to be rejected, toned down or embraced not only by a host of publicists, critics, journalists and fashion leaders, but also by garment manufacturers and store buyers' (Braham 1997, 134). Consumers, of course, contribute to the ongoing negotiation of the fashion code, responding both to the fashion industry and to wider cultural circumstances. Lise Skov's (2005) research on the return of the fur coat shows, for example, that the renewed fashion for furs in recent years has been the result of combined changes in production, distribution and consumption, partly in response to animal welfare protests. Changes in production of furs (from wild to farmed) and in their marketing (increased use of promotional techniques), in the manufacture of fur garments (from craft to ready-to-wear) and their distribution (from specialized shops to fashion boutiques), and in consumers' outlook (a new generation of women exploring new images of femininity) have contributed to reposition the fur coat. Now furs may be coded as a young, sexy and rebellious fashion statement for the assertive woman in her thirties as opposed to a life investment for the middle-aged, middle-class traditional woman. All in all, directing our attention at the role of cultural intermediaries and the fashion industry doesn't mean that we should fall yet again into the trap of a productivist model or the temptation to obscure the active role of consumers, as ultimately has happened to critical theory (see next chapter). Instead, it should help us to keep in mind that the intricate non-deterministic interrelation between the spheres of production, promotion and consumption is also the result of their internal differentiation.

Summary

In this chapter we have looked at the rise of the social scientific study of consumption, describing the modelling of the consumer within *mainstream economic theory*, neoclassical theory in particular. Economics has had a pivotal role in portraying consumption, focusing on consumer *demand* as an aggregate of individual *purchase decisions* based on an individualistic cost-benefit analysis. The consumer is portrayed as an *instrumentally rational actor* who maximizes utility and minimizes costs. In the course of the 20th century, neoclassical economics has encountered some significant difficulties in its attempt to model consumption as a purely instrumentally rational decision and has tried to open up to social variables, introducing the social under the limited rubrics of, for example, *Veblen, Bandwagon* and *Snob effects*. More recently, mainstream neoclassical economics, as epitomized by the work of economist **Gary Becker**, has tried to broaden its model of decision-making but has remained bound to instrumental rationality. Issues such as power, institutions, emotions and values are still largely eschewed. On the contrary, the social dimension of consumption has been central to its sociological study. Classic sociology has brought into focus some of those aspects rejected by economics concentrating on the *ceremonial* function of goods, stressing their role in *marking social relationships* and in demonstrating *social position* and, to a lesser extent, cultural views. **Thorstein Veblen**'s seminal work on the American 'leisure class' has proposed the notion of *conspicuous consumption*, while **Georg Simmel**'s celebrated essay on fashion has stressed both the role of *status competition* among classes, and the centrality of *novelty* as a modern, bourgeois cultural value. Consumption thus comes to be seen as an important space of social competition, rather than a mere realization of individual preferences. More contemporary research on *fashion* has further nuanced this picture, showing that competition occurs not only via *emulation* and the *trickling-down* of elite taste, but also through the formation of subcultural styles and the *trickling-up* of marginal tastes which are increasingly appropriated by the fashion industry.

Notes

1 Whilst Pareto had proposed a formal notion of utility with his 'ordinal utility' which organized consumers' gratifications in a purely numerical scale, it is with Samuelson that tastes became substituted with the numeric representation of 'revealed preferences': see Schumpeter (1955) and Hargreaves Heap (1989).

2 Recent developments in economics, from game theory to behavioural economics, have recognized the temporal dimension and have tried to factor in a processual view of action: see Steedman (2001). For a recent review of those trends and aspects in the economic theory of consumption which may go beyond utility maximization, see Swann (2002). For an institutionalist perspective on consumer preferences see also Dolfsma (2002).

3 Callon and Miller offer differently accented positions: Callon considers that markets are indeed disentangled realities, disciplined by economics' expert discourse; Miller considers that neoclassical wisdom offers only a virtual picture of consumption, its ideological function being resisted in practice. See also Barry and Slater (2002); Fine (2002a) and Miller (2002).

4 The qualitative innovation of goods is a phenomenon of particular relevance within contemporary society where goods develop and multiply also and above all through the continual refinement of pre-existing variants. To introduce qualitative aspects into the neoclassical model, Kelvin Lancaster (1991) proposed that we consider that it is not only the goods, but also their characteristics, which are desired. However, in this case consumption also remains modelled as an instrumentally rational action, uprooted from practice, history and social structure.

5 On Simmel's complex theory of value see Sassatelli (2001b).

6 Susan Bordo (1993) prefers a different accent, maintaining that at work women mix male dress with female accessories to recall their decorative role and to appear less dangerous in the career market. The ambivalence of fashion for women has been underscored by Elisabeth Wilson (1985), who critically discusses the rejection that feminist thought has traditionally reserved for this phenomenon and shows how dress can also be a source of rebellion and a catalyst for reformist groups, including feminists (see also Evans and Thornton 1989; Nava 1991).

Needs, Manipulation and Simulation

4

The first sociological analyses saw different forms of consumption as social and cultural phenomena, but rarely did they bring into focus the role of the media or of the cultural industry, concentrating instead on fashion as a means of social distinction. When a renewed interest in the processes of consumption appeared after the Second World War, the perspective had totally changed. Calling on the development of the advertising industry the new theoretical approaches underlined the growing disorientation of consumers, who now found themselves afloat amongst thousands of messages trying to sell them products of every kind.

A large part of post-war sociological reflection was aimed at unmasking the manipulative character of the symbolic dimension of goods, and in this way tended to conceptualize consumption as the ultimate domain of deceitful domination. The first sociological analyses had, as it were, socialized the neoclassical idea of consumer sovereignty, showing that consumption was aimed at marking differences and affinities between social actors, contributing to the reproduction of the social structure, and with this to rather serious forms of exclusion. Critical approaches of the post-war period instead were entirely opposed to the idea of consumer sovereignty: the market was not an instrument to satisfy needs, but the mirror of relationships of domination seen as characterizing late-capitalist society. In other words, if the neoclassical consumer is sovereign in the market, the critical theory consumer is a slave of commodities: consumers buy more because they are induced to do so, not because they really want to. Facing increasing wealth, the average consumer is represented as a kind of anomaly, a passive and heteronomous degeneration of autonomous, active and self-determined forms of subjectivity, typical of a less prosperous past. Critical theory, and later the pessimistic postmodernism embodied by Jean Baudrillard, end up denying consumers the ability to respond creatively, or at least actively, to the siren-songs of contemporary consumer culture.

From commodity fetishism to critical theory

We can hardly address the relationships between economics and power without some of the ideas introduced by Karl Marx. In those parts of his renowned *Das Kapital* which deal with consumption, Marx (1974, vol. I, 103–15, orig. 1867) considers that, in order to get capitalism working, human needs have to be shaped to the needs of the production system. Individuals' capacity to consume cannot be a barrier to economic development: the capitalist system must therefore *induce* ever-new needs in the human spirit, manipulating desires for commodities and increasing them incessantly.[1] According to Marx, in capitalist societies consumers no longer understand what is and isn't of use to them and they end up consuming commodities whose only utility is to enrich those who organized their production and circulation through the exploitation of labour at low cost.[2] As people are alienated from the fruits of their work, they are unable to realize that commodities incorporate a certain amount of work and that their prices are an abstract and structurally biased calculation of work-time. Market value is therefore nothing but a relation between people; nevertheless it is 'a relationship that is hidden behind things'. Commodities therefore become *fetishes*, they appear to have their own life, being almost metaphysical, distant, divorced from people: 'surrounded by magic and necromancy', they are only the shadow of the social relations of which they are expressions (see also Chapter 7).

Marx only assigned any real importance to the material structure (intended as the organization of production) in the historical process, and he considered the cultural superstructure (or 'ideology') as but a derivative of this, and therefore not worthy of deeper study. Instead, the cultural sphere is the space in which the Frankfurt School's critical theory took up, in a new form, the notion of alienation and of commodity fetishism (Jay 1973; Wiggerhaus 1995). Closer to the interests of the Italian Marxist, Antonio Gramsci, the Frankfurt School analysed in particular the development of what is defined as the 'culture industry'. The sharp awareness of the development of the culture industry as a system in and of itself geared to the production of meaning and of advertising as a final mechanism for transferring these meanings to the world of everyday life makes the arbitrariness of symbolic associations evident. The Frankfurt School stigmatized, above all, the birth of a mass culture in which the differences between *high* and *low culture* were shaded over. In their well-known book, *The Dialectic of Enlightenment* (1973, orig. 1947) Max Horkheimer and Theodor Adorno maintain that whilst the former reduces itself to the latter, the arts and other 'manifestations of the spirit' adapt to the perhaps civilizing but certainly homogenizing logic of the market. Thus, in so far as they are commodities, the products of the culture industry have two basic characteristics: on one side they are 'homogeneous', just the same under an appearance of variety, and on the other they are 'predictable'. Taking up Weber's idea that modern society is characterized by the progressive affirmation of instrumental rationality according to which all can be weighed up and treated as calculable objects, including persons and their needs, Horkheimer and Adorno maintain that the culture of consumption is the result of a world that is increasingly 'administered', in which people are not considered as such, but matter as functional elements of the system.

From this point of view, productivist imperatives orient and determine people's consumption practices: the spread of instrumental rationality from the sphere of production to that of consumption and the substitution of use value with exchange-value create the conditions under which a large number of symbolic associations can be easily exploited by the culture industry. To attract the largest number of buyers, these symbolic forms are increasingly geared to the lowest common denominator, simple and conformist. In this way, someone who watches

a film can fairly quickly imagine how it is going to end, and someone who regu-
larly enjoys 'easy listening' knows what to expect after the first note and will even
feel gratified when he or she is proved right. In his study of popular music,
Adorno (1941) maintains that music produced by the culture industry is stan-
dardised, promotes passive listening and works as 'social cement', so that dominant powers can be reproduced. In being produced as a commodity to be sold to
as wide a public as possible, and as such undifferentiated, music loses its artistic
quality, it becomes a non-authentic pre-digested commercial product which promotes passivity and escapism masking its actual pseudo-individualized character.

From these theoretical musings Herbert Marcuse (1964) took inspiration for
his famous criticism of the pervasiveness of the capitalist market. The theoretician
of 'one-dimensional man' conceptualized the growth in capitalist production as a
refined means of domination which subordinates culture to the creation of new
demand, and which menaces individuality and creativity through the *manipulation* of 'real needs'. In Marcuse's view, late capitalism, through the entertainment
and information industry, promotes an ideology of consumption which generates
false needs which function as control mechanisms over consumers. The attachments, the habits and emotions pre-written by the culture industry through
the promotion of goods become a way of life which imposes itself on all possible
alternatives, and does so even through the management of cultural change. The
same search for novelty is thus the product of techniques of manipulation whose
expressive potential conditions not only the masses of consumers, but also the
operators of the market themselves, the presumed tastemakers, who are likewise
taken by the charm of the goods and the messages that they themselves create
(Featherstone 1991; Lears 1983).

Similar ideas are echoed in the critical thinking coming from the United States,
in a different theoretical tradition which extends from the economist John K.
Galbraith (1958; 1971) to the polemicist Vance Packard (1958) to more contemporary authors such as Christopher Lasch (1991, orig. 1979). Some of Galbraith's
reflections are particularly well known, and underline how, with the development
of large commercial businesses, the consumer loses power in favour of the technical-productive apparatus. Thus, the market is transformed from a consumer-
driven mechanism to a sphere where the producers assimilate consumers' needs to
their own through commercial activity. In Galbraith's terminology it was with the
development of the large oligarchic businesses that the 'accepted sequence', which
gave consumers primacy in the market, was substituted with the 'revised
sequence', in which the technical-productive apparatus gives the market its
rhythm and content. Advertising and marketing are thus extremely effective in
their powers of persuasion, and this is also because consumers are 'so far removed
from physical want that they do not already know what they want' (Galbraith
1958, 131; see also Galbraith 1971).

These theories have several merits. They underscore that consumption is an
activity with important political implications. Furthermore, they also remind us
that the link between production and consumption cannot be fully understood if
we do not give due consideration to the role of the promotional system, as indeed
the anthropological tradition tends to do (see Chapter 5). In fact, marketing and
advertising have a crucial role in linking production and consumption, and taken
together they are a highly specialized industrial sector with its own norms and

functional principles predominantly dedicated to symbolic elaboration and the diffusion of images aimed at winning the largest possible number of consumers. Nevertheless, the power relations which are in built in the link between production and consumption are less deterministic and more fragmented than those envisaged by manipulation theories. Indeed, conceived as an arena of power, the link between production and consumption is essentially a complex, ongoing *interaction* meditated through various institutions and embedded in a wider social environment (see Figure 4.1; see also Chapter 6).

As proposed by Paul Hirsch's (1972) well-known model of the 'cultural industry system', mass-marketed cultural goods are the result of a collective process of production which entails various different actors (artists, gatekeepers, talent scouts, managers, journalists) responding to different institutional and personal interests and, what is more, involves considerable feedback from consumers.[3] Also, the cultural and fashion industries are set against the background of a political economy which typically entails some kind of direct state intervention contributing to specify the national/local conditions of appropriation which partly determine the degree of product transferability across countries. Furthermore, the cultural industries try to accommodate the views of consumers, both individual consumers and families, by getting a variety of information about their wants and desires (Leiss et al. 1991). Both producers and consumers respond to *institutionally embedded cultural principles and hierarchies* (cultures of production and cultures of consumption), which cannot be reduced one to the other. Yet, they are involved in a continuous process of interaction, a 'cultural circuit' whereby commodities both reflect and transform consumers' practices (du Gay et al. 1997). As suggested in the previous chapter, for example, the world of fashion with its many and different institutions and actors – from professional organizations to individual designers, from retailers to fashion leaders – contributes to the orientation of consumers, but it is likewise nourished by those innovative tendencies which emerge from street styles.

Street styles are often the result of the crystallization of needs of consumers in a host of *subcultures* of consumption which variously act as relatively autonomous communities of meanings. While subcultures have helped destabilize the boundaries between highbrow and lowbrow culture,[4] they evidently mediate between production and consumption. This is well illustrated in Dick Hebdige's (1988) study on the spread of the Vespa scooter throughout England. Vespa was a success in post-war Italy: indeed it was the symbol of Italian reconstruction, associated with modernization, urbanization and the new possibility for young adults of travelling freely around the city epitomized by such Hollywood films as *Roman Holiday* (Arvidsson 2001; Mazzanti 2004). While one of the most recognizable global cultural icons of the 20th century, as a commodity Vespa was not immediately transferable across countries and its uneven distribution worldwide both reflects a variety of social environments (characterized by different political arrangements, cultural repertoires, family structures, etc.), and stresses the active roles played by specific channels of appropriation such as youth cultures. In particular, Hebdige demonstrates that in England this spread followed unpredictable routes that were uncontrolled by the advertising executives who were trying to promote Vespa. Publicized as an elegant and comfortable female vehicle, it became a cult object of the mod youth subculture, mostly composed of young

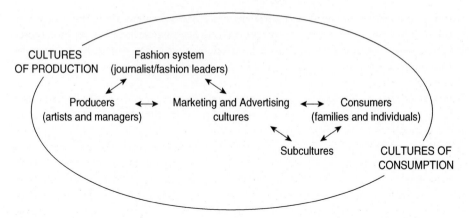

Figure 4.1   The interaction between producers and consumers as a field of power

men who were social climbers. Industries have to try to read the market so as to differentiate objects in line with emergent social divisions, but they cannot predict through which processes of consumption the new social groups will effectively create themselves. Of course, once a subcultural movement is established, the objects it has made its own can be newly placed within commercial circles, such as in the fashion industry which recuperates even the most off-beat trends, often incorporating social changes into the existing cultural frame and diluting their destabilizing potential. However, taken together these processes of interaction generate opportunities both for social reproduction and for change, divergent tendencies which may even be mixed together in the same phenomenon. In the case studied by Hebdige, for example, we may see that through the Vespa scooter, Mods were able to oppose their refined and aestheticized masculinity to the more traditional one of the motorcyclist Rockers. Therefore their consumption represented a challenge to hegemonic forms of masculinity and, at the same time, tended to reproduce, and even reinforce, dominant class distinctions.[5]

Nature, authenticity and resistance

Critical approaches are often founded on a dualistic and essentialist view which opposes *nature* and *culture*. For example, Galbraith doesn't exclude the possibility that there are consumers able to perceive their own needs autonomously and respond to them rationally, but he relegates these figures to a mythological period: '(w)hen goods were less abundant, when they served urgent physical need and their acquisition received close thought and attention, purchases were much less subject to management' (Galbraith 1971, 217). In this way he posits the idea of a natural way of consuming guided by the use value of things, to be opposed to a situation in which the artificial attribution of symbolic value becomes just manipulation.

The distinction between original needs (to some extent biologically determined) and induced needs (produced through cultural manipulation) has been a potent rhetorical device to show that economic exchange is anything but devoid of power relations. Still, such distinction is tricky, to say the least. In theories which adopt such distinction we can avoid being slaves of the commodity only if we remain slaves of nature; we can only be ourselves as long as our desires remain simple and based on necessities. Relegating symbolization to being the product of manipulation or the expression of irrationality, such a position thus obscures a fact that anthropological studies have long revealed (Douglas 1992; Sahlins 1972), namely that concepts such as functionality, necessity or scarcity are culturally and historically constructed, and that this process of symbolic construction is ingrained in the genesis and the satisfaction of human needs.[6] Modern people have of course been fascinated by the idea of stripping the subject of material possessions to uncover the true essence of human existence: thus the trope of the shipwreck survivor, starting with Defoe's famous *Robinson Crusoe*, is articulated as a battle to liberate us from our habits of consumption (Cruise 1999). Even for those needs which appear fundamental, such as shelter from the cold, food and drink, we cannot turn back to a supposed state of nature: even in prehistoric societies what counts isn't survival but *how* people protected themselves from the elements, *what* they ate and *with whom* they drank. Thus, even in what are considered the most simple societies, humans are social beings, relating to nature and things through their culture and the power relations structuring it: the animism of a prehistoric hunter is no more natural than the cynicism of a yuppie of the third millennium; instead it marks different cultural constructions of the relationship between what is perceived as human and what as natural. It is therefore no coincidence that much contemporary sociology holds that it is impossible to abstract human needs from social interaction, and thus from the interpretations and discourses which define it often through opposition to notions such as luxury, fashion or even art.

Today, in particular, art is not that which is difficult, unique or opposite to commodities. Even an author within the critical tradition, like Baudrillard, clearly distances himself from the overly normative vision of a decline in artistic authenticity in advanced capitalist society, such as that proposed by the Frankfurt School. For Baudrillard (1997) the aura of authenticity of modern art doesn't rest in the singularity of the original image which precedes its mechanical reproduction (Benjamin 1968; Horkheimer and Adorno 1973). There can be an 'authentic form of simulation' where copying and the commodity aesthetic have been incorporated into modern art, as in Andy Warhol's legendary Pop Art for example (Baudrillard 1997; see also Dant 1999). What counts is that the art object appears as the intentional product of a single creator. The author's signature and the existence of a corpus of works which legitimize an individual as the 'author' are thus two main principles on which the recognition of artistic value is granted, where technical reproduction has replaced the uniqueness of craftsmanship. In other words, art and commodity exchange are not necessarily antithetical, even if specific, more singularized and less predictable forms of exchange like auctions often serve to underline the differences between artistic and everyday objects (Smith 1989).

In particular, if we consider popular music we cannot ignore that Adorno's critical observations were focused mostly on swing music of the 1930s and 40s, which was nothing but a commercialized form of jazz, the latter being a genre which today is generally classified as cultured, having gone through a process of aestheticization of listening. But above all we have to consider that the attraction of authenticity is not simply the antithesis of commercialization, and that in fact there are different ways of putting together the logic of commodities with that of the authentic. For instance, work on the celebrated singer-songwriter genre in Italy, the so-called *canzone d'autore*, shows how authenticity, intended above all as the singer-songwriter's need to dwell on his or her life experiences as opposed to the shallowness of commercial music, has been one of the cultural logics through which this type of music has been able not only to establish itself, but also, paradoxically, to carve itself notable commercial success (Santoro 2002). On the other hand, Sarah Thornton's (1995) well-known study of the world of dance music in the UK has shown how even in a genre which is otherwise conceived of as commercial and artificial, there is space for opposition to the mainstream, this time however through a problematization of the traditional notion of authenticity – which required authorship and the live performance of music – and the proposal of a new form of authenticity which extends to the user and embraces the whole embodied experience of dancing in discos or at raves (on art and commoditization see also Chapter 7).

In a more general sense, the authenticity of artefacts derives, as Daniel Miller (1987, 215) puts it , 'not from their relationship to some historical style or manufacturing process – in other words, there is no truth or falsity immanent in them – but rather from their active participation in a process of social self-creation in which they are directly constitutive of our understanding of ourselves and others'. A similar process obviously has ambivalent uses, as is shown by the music industry's recuperating of ethnic and traditional music under the "world music" label, which even includes the songs of the Calabrian Mafia, a criminal association called *'ndrangheta* (Santoro and Sassatelli 2001). When songs whose content and sound evoke the world of the bonds and daily cruelties of the Mafia are put in circulation, it becomes clear that the continual interplay between commercialization and authenticity implies the exploration of increasingly subcultural, marginal or even deviant worlds. Thus, in the case of the songs of the *'ndrangheta* the reference to authenticity seems particularly pregnant because it is accompanied by another register which underscores its supposed truthfulness: the grotesque, the extreme, the excluded. One can then easily discern the duplicity of the symbolic world which is brought to life by this commercial operation: the criminal and Mafia associations can be exorcized but also legitimized, their symbols read with voyeuristic curiosity and thus repudiated in life, or experienced nostalgically as the reflection of a reality that is hard but more intense and genuine.

A plethora of voices from a variety of perspectives have recently underlined that to better understand our relationship with the world of commodities it is necessary to overcome the monolithic conception of power which characterizes the critical theory of the Frankfurt School and American radicalism and to conceive of consumption as an active and even creative practice (Campbell 1987; Douglas and Isherwood 1979; Featherstone 1991; Miller 1987; Slater 1997). The inadequacy of an emphasis on alienation as homogenization is evident in the vast array of products which appear to be progressively stylized by increasingly particular and varied types of consumers (Lash and Urry 1987). Likewise, the view of power as manipulative domination masks the fact that the current social context seems to be characterized by strategic interrelations of power rather than vertical ones (Foucault 1978; 1983) and that consumers respond, and often do so in creative ways, to the solicitations of consumer culture. It is certainly true that there is a massive disproportion between the resources invested by producers to control the market, and those invested by consumers as a group. Nevertheless, as Frederick Hayek (1961) underlined back in the 1960s in criticizing Galbraith, consumers are 'armed' with a series of customary practices to manage the unknown which enables them to actively oppose producers' strategies, though perhaps not quite as successfully as the Austrian economist believed. So, as the historian and social theorist Michel de Certeau (1984, orig. 1980) says, consumers manage to use commodities and their meanings in personal ways, sometimes even subversively, operating as *bricoleurs* in the gaps and the contradictions of dominant consumer culture (see Chapter 5). Consumers 'assimilate' goods, not necessarily in the sense that they become similar to that which they consume; rather, they make goods similar to themselves, they appropriate and re-appropriate goods. To do so they use 'tactics' which are 'ingenious ways in which the weak make use of the strong thus lending a political dimension to everyday practices' (*ibid*, xvii). In this view, the practices of consumption appear as unconscious forms of *resistance*. To remove this resistance from analysis is to eliminate the complexity of the emotive, hedonistic and communicative aspects of goods as well as the theoretical space where we can address the various rituals through which goods can be re-elaborated, de-codified and personalised (see Chapters 7 and 8).

Individual consumers and to a much greater extent social groups (from youth subcultures to environmental and feminist movements) *can* use goods in a *subversive* way, as an aid to exploring alternative ways of seeing oneself and the word. Critical theory has correctly brought into focus that consumption is the ideal place in which to construct cultural hegemony, namely a form of dominion based on consensus and the manipulation of symbolic resources. Still, numerous more recent studies have underlined that, even if to a lesser degree, consumer practices can be important occasions for popular resistance, acting as catalysts as well as vehicles of expression of innovation and counterculture. Studying youth cultures, Paul Willis (1978; 1990) has shed light on the "symbolic creativity" which characterizes the consumption of cultural goods in everyday life as a "realm of necessary symbolic production within the undiscovered continent of the informal" (1990: 18). Mostly it has been those authors who take Gramscian views, and in particular those from the British Cultural Studies tradition, who have emphasised that commodities and their images are not only *polysemic* (that is, have many meanings) but also *multiaccented* (they can be read and articulated with different accents). It is for this reason that goods can be read and used in ways that are not homologous, and do not serve to reproduce the dominant structure.

Of course, as noted by Stuart Hall (1980) with regard to television discourse, there are different positions from which 'de-coding' can take place: a 'dominant-hegemonic' position (which adopts the dominant frames encoded in the text); a 'negotiated' position (which acknowledges the legitimacy of the encoded dominant frames in the main but adapts them to local meaning in the detail); and an 'oppositional' position (which tries to read the message through the lenses of an alternative, subversive frame of reference). As marginal as it may be in numerical terms, 'oppositional' de-coding is a significant phenomenon in cultural terms and it is crucial for subcultures. As Stuart Hall and Tony Jefferson (1976, 56) write in their important edited volume on youth subcultures in Britain, *Resistance through Rituals*, goods can be 'appropriated' by a group and made 'homologous' with their problems, with their existence, with their self-image. In fact, a large part of youth culture, even in its most radical forms, revolves around consumption. Youth subcultures in particular, as Dick Hebdige (1979, 103) puts it, are 'cultures of conspicuous consumption – even when, as with the skinheads and the punks, certain types of consumption are conspicuously refused – and it is through the distinctive rituals of consumption, through style, that the subculture at once reveals its 'secret' identity and communicates its forbidden meanings', and it 'is basically the way in which commodities are *used* in subculture which marks the subculture off from more orthodox cultural formations'. Also in the culture of the motorbike boys studied by Paul Willis (1978), goods were attributed distinctive meanings through which the group constituted itself: the classic rock'n'roll of Elvis Presley and Buddy Holly was a 'deliberate choice' designed to give members an excuse to channel their aggressive masculinity which valued the ability to respond physically to a hostile and hard world. The styles of consumption of the motorbike boys thus demonstrate the 'profane' power of subordinate and marginal groups 'to select, develop and creatively make some objects their own, to express their own meanings' (*ibid*, 166).

Postmodern pessimism

The cultural pessimism of critical theory and the Frankfurt School led, at the end of the 1970s and early 80s, to the first postmodern theorisations, many of which shared a marked distrust of consumer culture.[7] These were works that tended to emphasize the central role taken by consumer culture and the symbolic dimension of goods; in fact they emphasized that the distinction between material and symbolic was so blurred that actors could hardly from orientate themselves genuinely in the world. Consumption no longer referred to the bettering of the human condition; on the contrary, with the era of mass consumption reality had been transformed into a *pastiche* of images and pseudo-events empty of meaning (Baudrillard 1996 and 1998; Jameson 1989).

The author who most clearly represents this position is the French theorist Jean Baudrillard. In his early work, *La société de consommation*, Baudrillard (1998, orig. 1970) maintained that in contemporary societies the sphere of consumption has triumphed over that of production. Baudrillard deliberately sought to remove the concept of production from the position of primacy which Marxist theory in particular gave it, thus trying to overcome the idea that objects had an original and natural use value, falsely obscured by price and by the symbolic meanings which were assigned to them in capitalist society. For the French theorist, the value of an object is bound to its meanings, so there is no pure, material or natural use value (Baudrillard 1981). Post-industrial societies are, however, different from preceding ones because these meanings – or more precisely 'signifiers' as signs which indicate a meaning – gain autonomy through the manipulation of mass media and advertising and are able to fluctuate free from objects. Thus, in this point of view the symbolic no longer exists: in its place is a continual cross-referencing between different signs, between multicoloured images which no longer symbolize a social reality but refer back to themselves to such a degree that they themselves constitute reality.

Baudrillard's semiotic-structuralist approach takes forward a number of themes developed by Roland Barthes (1972) and sprinkles them with a post-Marxist flavour, so that he maintains that objects become configured as a separated 'system'. Altogether they form a 'global, arbitrary and coherent' system of signs: thus we can no longer understand consumption through considering the relationship between the consumer and the particular good he or she purchases because needs are 'produced as *system elements*, not as *a relationship of an individual to an object*' (Baudrillard 1998, 75; emphasis in original). Thus, consumers do not consume specific objects because of concrete and specific needs, but signs which are part of an abstract system that replaces a contingent world of needs and pleasures with a social order of values and classifications. Baudrillard thus concludes that in advanced capitalism, where not only production but also consumption is disciplined and rationalized to favour the reproduction of the economic structure, the subject powerlessly faces the system of objects, so much so that all that is left is a world of 'self-referential signs' based on the recurrent generation of 'simulated' differences, a 'hyper-reality' which is placed beyond the distinction between the real and imaginary (Baudrillard 1983). The media and the frenetic multiplication of commodities are thereby the vehicles through which a *simulated* world characterized by the supremacy of the signifier is created, a world wherein individuals are nothing but predetermined patterns of consumption: 'we are living the period of the objects: that is, we live their rhythm, according to their incessant cycles' (Baudrillard 1970 in Poster, ed. 1988, 29). In this perspective objects do not signify anything outside themselves, they develop as totally interchangeable signs, becoming the causes of a nihilistic removal of all content. The desolate implications of a similar argument are revealed as it is 'objects which quite tyrannically induce categories of persons. They undertake the policing of social meanings, and the significations they engender are controlled' (*ibid*, 17). Thus people exist merely as the vehicles for expressing the differences between objects, their identity becoming synonymous with patterns of consumption which are determined elsewhere.

Baudrillard's analysis has the sure merit of conceiving of material culture as a system of signs which refer to each other and gain their meanings only in relation to each other, and which must be used by consumers, even involuntarily. This same notion of hyper-reality is useful in understanding some contemporary phenomena: visiting Disneyland or one of the many different theme parks which have sprung up throughout developed societies amounts to an experience based on our capacity to enjoy not the real, but an extreme and typified sign or trace of reality which often ends up being itself reduced to a typified sign when it is captured in a photograph or home video. As John Urry (1990, 3) says in his study on mass tourism, '(w)hen tourists see two people kissing in Paris what they capture in the gaze is "timeless romantic Paris"': it is a canonical and stereotypical image. Indeed, as suggested by Susan Steward (1993, 134–5), the souvenir 'both offers a measurement of the normal and authenticates the experience of the viewer'; we desire souvenirs of events that 'thereby exist only through the invention of narrative. Through narrative the souvenir substitutes a context of perpetual consumption to its context of origin'.

However, Baudrillard's theory takes directions which are merely polemical. Alongside the unmasking of the fictitious character of the difference between real and symbolic which aptly works on a critique of the biological foundation of use value, there is also the presumption of a world of objects *per se*.[8] Objects are 'the only reality' and they dance to their own tune; they are not constituted together with the subject, rather they constitute the subject and they cancel out any capacity for meaning (Baudrillard 1998 and 1983; Jameson 1989). Thus the individual is no longer a social actor, a subject who makes meaningful symbolic distinctions through action and interpretation. Sociology and anthropology however have taught us that we cannot properly conceive of a world of objects unless in relation to social actors and their practices. A world of objects in which, in the final analysis, there is no space for agency, is based on the assumption of a metaphysical ontology which cannot be further investigated. In fact, it is only through metaphysics that commodities can form a world of images that is autonomous, separate and *a priori* (Kellner 1989). The postmodern idea of a social sphere 'liquidated' into pseudo-images is indeed sustained by a dubious theoretical operation which conceals the social relations realized and embodied in consumer practices. In other words, it seems to me that the abstraction of the symbolic dimension of goods from social interaction which leads to a hyper-real system of object-signs is the fruit of postmodern theorising which polemically and arbitrarily obscured the different forms of relationship implicit in the practices of consumption.

Social relations and consumption

The paradigm of simulation put forward by Baudrillard, even more than that of manipulation proposed by critical theorists, doesn't account for the great variety of subjects who act as consumers. It is extremely difficult to describe consumers, all consumers, as a homogeneous 'mass' enthralled by the strategies of publicity. It may be true that in contemporary Western societies we are all consumers, but it is also true that we all consume in different ways. When we operate as consumers we deploy cognitive and normative frameworks which we have developed throughout our lives, starting from the particular position we occupy in the social structure, negotiating with a variety of roles which are not reducible to our experiences as consumers. Our identity as consumer interacts, as it were, with other social identities and relations. In particular, through our purchase decisions and through the way we use goods we not only shape ourselves as particular consumers but also express and stabilize our different identities and cultural orientations linked to gender (Jackson and Moores 1995; Nixon 1996), to sexuality (Badgett 2001; Kates and Belk 2001; Wardlow 1996), to age (Chin 2001; Cook 2004; Gunter 1998; Gunter and Furnham 1998; Kline 2006), to ethnicity (Davila 2001; Halter 2000; Lamont and Molnar 2001; Pleck 2000; Waters 1990), and to class and education (Burrows and Marsh 1992; Casey 2003; Crompton 1996; De Grazia and Cohen 1999; Galilee 2002; Tomlinson 2003). As Pierre Bourdieu (1984) has demonstrated, our tastes, standardized according to our social position, amount to a flexible selection device which reproduces and underlines our differences as social actors. For example, if we consider the health market, we can clearly see that there are very different attitudes to the body and its state of health which correspond to different forms of health service consumption. The middle classes tend to operate around the idea that they can and must control themselves, their body and their state of health, and so they generally have more medical check-ups, with the result that they effectively have a longer life-span. Instead, the working class tend to adopt a fatalist attitude, not worrying about small illnesses or discomforts, and they only reluctantly visit the doctor in cases of emergency, with the result that their life-span is less, and they are more prone to serious disease, therefore almost enacting their fatalistic prophecy at its worst (Boltanski 1971; see Bourdieu 1984). These observations are grounded on empirical data collected in France in the late 1960s; however, similar evidence has been gathered for Great Britain in the 1980s and early 1990s. Considering a number of consumption habits as reported in national surveys which stretch along the healthy–unhealthy dimension (such as smoking, alcohol intake, frequency of eating chips, frequency of eating fresh fruit, taking vitamins, practising sport, etc.), it appears that the average professional – especially if female, relatively young and living alone – is much more likely to adopt a healthy lifestyle, as are managers and white-collar workers, than are the working classes – with young, unskilled male manual workers having the most unhealthy combinations (Tomlinson 2003).

In maintaining that humans are 'surrounded not by people but by objects', Baudrillard (1996) presupposes an alternative between social relationships and consumption as a relation with objects which isn't verified by empirical studies. Contrary to critical and postmodern pessimism, quite often consumption functions as *relational work*, not only being embedded in social relations but also being used to maintain, negotiate and modify interpersonal connections, especially those related to family and household life, their hierarchies and power structure (see Chapter 8). Consumption may be seen as expression of kinship and other social and personal relationships, and the density of a consumer's purchases may reflect the density of his or her social networks (Douglas 1992; Miller 1998). And this is true for adults as well as for children: a recent study conducted on low-income black children in the US shows, for example, that they are tempted but do not always succumb to brand-name logos and that their purchase decisions are meant to affirm specific relations with other members of their household (Chin 2001). Moreover, looking into the household as a site of consumption, we may clearly see that what is often classified as just consumption in fact hides forms of unpaid work which bear out a web of social inequalities. A collection of studies considering amateur practices, hobbies and cultural self-production in France – from gardening to photography, from music playing to do-it-yourself – shows that these 'ordinary passions', which defy the boundary between production and consumption and partly derive their very meaning from the transgression of such a boundary, occupy a large share of practitioners' time and are variously coded by class, gender and generation (Bromberger 1998). Even more striking is the case of domestic practices – from sewing to cooking – which are mostly carried out by women. In a study on contemporary American families, the feminist Marjorie DeVault (1991) showed the amount of preparation work that women have to do as housewives, or as those who effectively fill that role even despite their professional careers, so that what was bought as a necessity for the family can effectively be consumed; she also showed the huge capacity for negotiation and conflict management that they frequently have to bring to bear so that the needs of all the family members come to be accommodated in some way. As we saw earlier (see Chapter 2) gender relations, like class, have important effects on our consumption preferences. There are not only 'masculine' and 'feminine' objects, objects appropriate for one or the other sex according to the degree to which they convey femininity or masculinity (Ames and Martinez 1996; Kirkham 1996), but men and women consume things in different ways, and it is also through the accomplishment of such differences that masculinity and femininity are continuously reciprocally constructed, altered and reproduced. A number of studies have shown, for example, that the diffusion of home appliances and plastic ware in postwar Italy, France and Great Britain promoted new visions of femininity defined by a search of autonomy and self-realization which contrasted with traditional visions of the housewife while anchoring women to traditionally female roles within the family (Arvidsson 2002; Clark 1997; Frost 1983). A number of studies on food preferences have documented that meat is a male food (associated with hunting, force, violence, wilderness, etc.) and is, at the same time, actively chosen, refused or distributed within the family to signal gender boundaries (Lupton 1996). Other studies have shown that men and women participate differently in sport (Guttman 1991). If we consider that modern sport developed in the Anglo-American world mainly as an arena for the production and reproduction of the male elite (Bourdieu 1978) it becomes easier to understand why, even today, women are still generally less prone to spend time and money on sport and, when they do so, they tend to prefer non-competitive sports which can be undertaken with other members of the family, rather than competitive or contact sports.[9] Finally, we know very well that toys are strongly gendered and that often, as in the case of Barbie dolls, they can be instruments of socialization to particular visions of gender relations, femininity and masculinity (Rogers 1999).

Studies of material culture, in both contemporary Western societies and tribal ones, underline above all the *diversity among objects* and thus the existence of different types of objects, produced on the basis of different conditions, distributed according to different principles, enjoyed and used in different contexts (Appadurai 1986b; Miller 1987) (see Chapters 2 and 5). Commodities may have rich histories which render them dissimilar and certainly not interchangeable or equivalent as, ironically, both neoclassical economics and Baudrillard's postmodernism would like them to be. As suggested, within neo-Marxist approaches Ben Fine and Ellen Leopold have developed a 'system of provision' approach, showing that notions such as demand, market and retailing are meaningless when applied across all economic sectors (Fine 2002b, see also Chapter 3). A focus on different systems of vertical integration between production and consumption – food system, fashion system, furniture system, etc. – each characterized by a particular set of structures and practices consolidated through time allows a deeper understanding of consumer choices. To be sure, for some commodities in some circumstances we are more likely to surrender ourselves to the siren-songs of seductive marketing, while for other goods and in different circumstances we are socially conditioned to keep our distance, calculate or gather information from relatives and friends. Baudrillard (1996) though, by way of example, maintains that the practical uses of a washing machine are insignificant and that it is basically exchangeable with any other good which can be presented in the same way, as it is essentially 'prestige' value that counts. He thus has very little to say on how objects are used in daily life, since the meanings attributed to the object are entirely reduced to those attributed to them by advertising executives.

This perspective tends to offer a rather flat view of consumption, reducing it to one, and only one way of facing commercial communication. In fact, rather than conceiving consumers as embodied social actors, postmodern theorists often speak of them as *spectators*. As spectators, consumers are typified and removed from everyday life, so that they navigate between different images without wanting to make any sense of them or being able to do so, simply enjoying the sensations provided by images and the surface of goods. The supposition that reality is experienced as a succession of images devoid of meaning holds up the idea of the 'schizophrenic' subject (Jameson 1989) who acts in order to fill his or her interior emptiness through the momentary emotional intensity of continually buying new things. Postmodern analyses seem therefore to take to their extreme an apocalyptic vision which has individuated a correspondence between the culture of consumption, reduced to the totality of promotional images, and a de-centred self which, seeking self-realization through commodities instead of developing interpersonal relationships and solidarity, degrades itself and others to an object (Lasch 1991) (see Chapter 6). Nevertheless, the consumer is so hyperbolically passive that these analyses appear motivated more by a utopian and polemical desire to condemn the present life conditions than by a real commitment to understand consumption.

As Elihu Katz (1959) would lament about communication research in the 1950s, attention should concentrate more on what people do to the media than on what the media do to people. Indeed, recent studies of audiences and media consumption show that spectators actively de-codify messages and images, referring them to the context in which they are experienced, to their own social position, gender, life course, and so on (Moores 1993) (see Chapter 8). In particular, today advertising is often patently artificial, that is it increasingly plays with complex symbolic associations constructing articulate worlds of meaning around objects. However, it is not necessarily more effective (see Chapter 6). Contemporary consumers are in fact much more distant and critical than postmodern pessimism and critical theory would have us believe: surveys conducted in the United States, for example, show that on average less than 25 per cent of spectators can remember a television advert even if asked the day after its screening, and more than 80 per cent of spectators consider at least part of television advertising quite misleading (Schudson 1984) (see Chapter 6). To be sure, particular audiences, such as children and teenagers, may be 'weaker' than others. Still, while they happily absorb certain elements of advertising language into their forms of self-expression, adolescents appear on the whole quite selective in reinterpreting the meanings that advertising associates with goods (Ritson and Elliot 1999). Even when we consider popular programmes which have been roundly criticized for their vacuous content, such as soap operas, we can clearly see that the spectators make distinctions which enable them to 'enjoy themselves' whilst maintaining a 'sense of reality': even if at the connotative level (and thus in relation to the capacity to let oneself get emotionally involved) they maintain that the situations onscreen are 'recognizable', at the denotative level they consider them plainly absurd (Ang 1985). In other words, as I shall show later on, contemporary consumer culture doesn't require consumers to lose themselves in pleasure and futility; rather it requires subjects to have a well-disciplined capacity to get into places and emotional states in which one can let oneself go through following rules that manage spontaneity, informality and even superficiality.

Summary

This chapter has charted the development of a critique of consumer culture which is grounded in the perception that *mass-production* and *commoditization* have transformed material culture *manipulating* consumers' needs. Critical approaches of the post-war period were aimed at unmasking the idea of consumer sovereignty: in the work of authors such as **Adorno** and **Galbraith** the market was not an instrument to satisfy needs, but the mirror of relationships of *domination* seen to characterize late-capitalist society. The transformation of art and cultural goods into commodities is criticized as resulting in *standardization* and *pseudo-individualization*. Facing increasing wealth, consumers are conceived as passive, other-directed and superficial, their civic qualities being lost in the vain search for material comfort. More recently, the *pessimistic postmodernism* of **Jean Baudrillard** has stressed that, through the manipulation of mass-media and advertising, meanings gain autonomy and are able to fluctuate free from objects. Reality becomes a *simulated hyper-reality* removed from social relationships: a continual cross-referencing between different images which determine people's choices. While critical approaches aptly point to cultural and fashion industries and stress power dynamics, Baudrillard rightly shows that commodities are linked into a system of meanings. Still, all these approaches end up denying consumers the ability to respond creatively, or at least actively, to contemporary consumer culture. Recent scholarship, on the contrary, has emphasized the activity of the consumer as well as the importance of social relationships (families, subcultures) and social identities (gender, class, ethnicity) in shaping consumer practices. Commodities and their images are not only *polysemic* (that is, have many meanings) but also *multiaccented* (they can be read in different ways). As a result, the *power relations* which develop through the link between production and consumption are less deterministic and more fragmented than those envisaged by manipulation-based theories.

Notes

1 George Bataille (1988) partly follows in Marx's footsteps by considering that what characterizes production is not scarcity but 'excess' and that, therefore, the aim of production becomes destruction or management of the 'accused share', the excess of energy

translated into an excess of products which, if not controlled, may bring the whole system to anomie and stasis.

2 According to Marxist labour theory of value, the true value of objects is use-value as value 'conditioned by the physical properties of the commodity and has no existence apart from the latter' (Marx 1974). As it derives then from their material relation with the body, the value of goods can really grow only through human labour (Rubin 1972). The primacy assigned to human labour as the universal and objective foundation of value opens a theoretical space for the notion of alienation. Postulating a particular notion of what is and what ought to be a person, the labour theory of value considers that within the capitalist system people are alienated from their own humanity expressed in their creative labour (Geras 1983). From this point of view, capitalism does nothing else but produce anomalies of personality, given that it distorts the natural relationship between people and objects, a relationship that exists only when it is mediated by the creativity that may be expressed, according to Marx, only through work.

3 Cultural industries are a case of cultural production which is clearly oriented towards the market. Art production as studied by Bourdieu (1993) is a more self-directed form. In both cases there appears to be a productive dialectic between commercial and anti-commercial values (see Chapter 7). For a discussion see Hesmondhalgh (2006).

4 The boundaries between high and low culture are historically shifting, institutionally supported and often dialectically linked with the process of commercialization. For example, in the US, Shakespeare was played mainly in short scenes inserted in variety spectacles including music-hall up to the end of the 19th century (Levine 1988). Likewise, opera and museums became legitimate as high culture during the 19th century via a process of detachment from market forces and the institutionalization of non-commercial circuits and expert discourses (Di Maggio 1982). On the interplay between popular and high culture see the classic work of Gans (1974).

5 The interplay between resistance and reproduction, class and gender has also been detected in a recent study of fashion choices among middle-class young men (see Galilee 2002).

6 Most objects have a functional purpose, but there is only a 'vague relationship' between the form objects take and their suitability for a particular function: even if 'functional purpose must impose a certain constraint on the shape and form of an object, that constraint is generally a very loose one for everyday forms' (Miller 1987, 116). This is not only true for contemporary societies, which have been accused of privileging excessive aesthetic variety that has no meaning, but also for tribal ones where the decoration of objects, their aesthetic elaboration, is so evident that it constitutes a significant part of anthropological research. Furthermore, every artefact can be used not so much for its efficiency of use as for its idealized function and, what is more, for an ideal of efficiency. A good example here is the 17th to 18th century fascination with clocks which were seen as the symbol of efficient social order and regulation, or today's fascination with high-tech items which symbolizes the clean sweep of a technological future that many desire as soon as possible.

7 Not all self-proclaimed postmodern writing is pessimist; on the contrary, we may discover an oscillation between optimistic celebration and pessimistic deprecation in such forms of theorizing, which all in all emphasizes the fall of grand narratives, superficiality and fragmentation of culture (see Featherstone 1991; Slater 1997).

8 The theme of the transformation of reality into pseudo-events can be found in a simplified form also in a variety of studies which call upon a plurality of traditions. By way of example, Haug (1986) maintains that late capitalism is characterized by an advertising-induced commodity aesthetics in which the appearance of commodities becomes detached from the objects themselves and Ewen (1988) contaminates postmodernism with a Galbraithian spirit in maintaining that the intentional manipulation of large

enterprises is successful because, with post-industrialization, the world has dematerialized into a collection of signs and is no longer under the reign of Weber's 'disenchantment', but is taken (back) to a state of 'simulated enchantment'. Also in this case we see that little attention has been given to how in practice subjects appropriate different goods and which form of knowledge (other than ads) they thus deploy.

9 Certainly, sporting and fitness activities can transform the opposition between male and female, placing emphasis on the gender-neutral theme of self-competition in controlled conditions of equality (Sassatelli 2000a). Still, even in unisex sporting cultures such as windsurfing, women not only have the opportunity to reinforce capacities defined as masculine like strength and courage, but they also encounter difficulty in overcoming gender distinctions and remain anchored to traditional sexual dichotomies, above all with respect to the personal sphere (Wheaton and Tomlinson 1998).

Taste, Identity and Practices

5

Trying to leave behind dichotomous thinking, an approach towards consumption which brings it back down to earth has developed showing that goods work as a system of non-verbal *communication* and are put to use to mark *social* and *cultural boundaries*. The communication approach, which no differently from Marxism pops up periodically throughout the history of reflection on consumption, has found fertile ground in contemporary anthropology and cultural sociology. It saw its apogee in the late 1970s and the early 1980s, after some years of economic stagnation which brought back to light the activities that consumers had to perform in order to use commodities appropriately. In this period, two seminal studies on consumption were published: Pierre Bourdieu's *Distinction* (1984, orig. 1979) and *The World of Goods* by Mary Douglas and Baron Isherwood (1979). These rich and complex works both start by considering that objects serve as a material support for interaction as well as symbolic indicators in making the world intelligible. Goods are conceived as material elements through which social actors reproduce the cultural meanings which structure social space. In turn, social actors learn to prefer certain objects according to their particular socio-cultural location and, through their choices, testify to and reproduce their socio-cultural location.

We may consider that it is largely in response to Bourdieu and Douglas's studies that a sociology of consumption as a specialized branch of sociological knowledge has consolidated. The broad and rich literature which has been produced in the last two decades now accounts for the diversity of the processes collected under the banner of consumption. Thanks to an increasing awareness of such diversity, we have moved from goods being recognised as a *language,* to considering *how* such a language is *spoken in practice*. Of course, a tie or a pearl necklace communicate, they call to mind various universes of commodities and meanings. We associate the male suit and perhaps some formal work occasion like a business meeting with the former, whereas for the latter the female cleavage springs to mind and perhaps a special leisure occasion like a ball or prom. However, these symbolic associations only exist because commodities have histories which have become established over time through social practices: it is social actors who, operating in different social capacities and contexts, have made them variously significant. Consumer *agency* – namely the room for manoeuvre which social actors have when they act as consumers – has therefore become one of the key issues in current studies of consumption.

Taste and distinction

In Bourdieu's view consumers operate according to a logic of distinction, and they have *embodied* this in their own taste. In contrast to Veblen's ideas (see Chapter 3), consumers all do distinguish between goods in order to distinguish themselves. They also cannot do anything but distinguish goods and themselves: that is, they are placed in different categories, included or excluded, according to their capacity for distinction. In clear opposition to Baudrillard's approach (see Chapter 4), Bourdieu proposes a theory of practice in which human action can be constructed as something material and concrete, something different from representation, or the exchange of signs and symbols.

From this perspective human experience shouldn't be understood through cognitive or linguistic models, but in terms of *mimesis* and *embodiment*. To this end Bourdieu (1990, orig. 1980) proposes the notion of *'habitus'*, which enables us to conceive of embodiment as something preceding consciousness without having to resort to biological essentialism. According to Bourdieu (*ibid*, 53) *habitus* is a:

> system of durable, transposable dispositions, structured structures predisposed to function as structuring structures, that is, as principles which generate and organize practices and representations that can be objectively adapted to their goals without presupposing a conscious aiming at ends or an express mastery of the operations necessary in order to attain them.

Habitus is written in the body through past experiences, it is established in the first years of life and is an unconscious but extremely adaptable mechanism which determines the attachment of actors to objects, themselves and others. Tastes are conceptualised as subjective realizations of the mechanism of *habitus* which organize consumption and lifestyles. Although it is expressed in the apparently neutral and innocuous language of individual preference, taste 'marries colours and also people, who make "well-matched couples", initially in regard to taste' (Bourdieu 1984, 243, orig. 1979, see Figure 5.1). Thus it is a generative and classificatory mechanism which, at the same time, classifies the classifier and contributes to stabilizing his or her social position.

To this complex and finely calibrated description of *habitus*, Bourdieu juxtaposes a hierarchical and linear vision of the social structure and the relationship that runs between this and the structuring of taste. In fact, the individual *habitus* is always in a relationship of homology – that is, of 'diversity within homogeneity' (Bourdieu 1990) – with respect to the class *habitus* defined by two main forms of *capital*: *economic* and *cultural* capital. Inasmuch as it is a creative classificatory instrument applicable to infinity, the individual *habitus* thus helps reproduce these forms of capital. In their turn, consumption practices *reflect* the cultural genesis of tastes from the specific point of the social space they originate from. Tastes are thereby implicated in 'classificatory systems' which freeze 'a state of social struggle', or rather 'a given state of the distribution of advantages and obligations', and are 'not so much means of knowledge as means of power' (Bourdieu 1984, 471). Thus taste establishes itself as a form of 'symbolic power', through which 'objective classifications' come to coincide with 'subjective' ones,

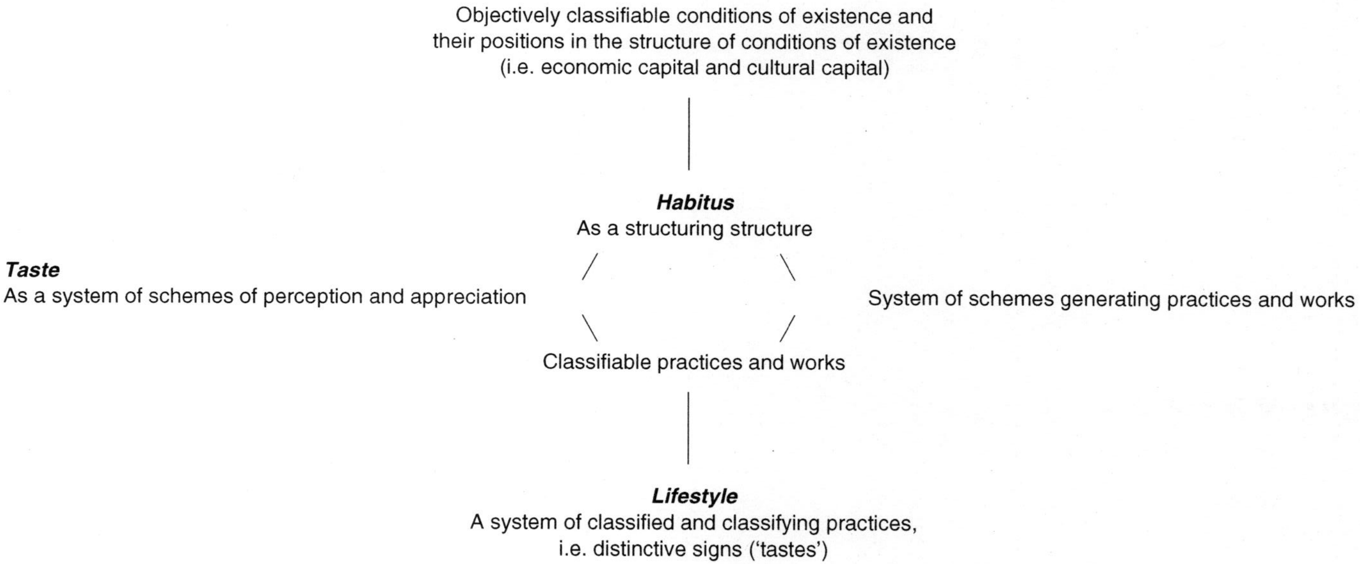

Habitus
As a structuring structure

Objectively classifiable conditions of existence and
their positions in the structure of conditions of existence
(i.e. economic capital and cultural capital)

System of schemes generating practices and works

Classifiable practices and works

Taste
As a system of schemes of perception and appreciation

Lifestyle
A system of classified and classifying practices,
i.e. distinctive signs ('tastes')

Figure 5.1   *Habitus* in Bourdieu's theory. Adapted from Bourdieu (1984, orig 1979)

allowing for the 'naturalization' of social and cultural order. Indeed, the '(s)ystems of classification which reproduce, in their own specific logic the objective classes, i.e. the divisions by sex, age or position in the relations of production, make their specific contribution to the reproduction of the power relations of which they are the product'. This occurs through a type of experience which Bourdieu has defined as 'doxa', that is 'the misrecognition of the arbitrariness' on which social divisions are based (Bourdieu 1977, 164, orig. 1972; see also Harker et al. 1990).

In *Distinction*, based on a huge amount of empirical data gathered in France at the beginning of the 1960s, Bourdieu tries to take account of the social roots of what he considers the 'dominant' Kantian aesthetic judgement. The French scholar traces the 'Kantian aesthetics', typically characterized by a distanced and formal contemplation which privileges the mind and transcends the immediacy of experience and the body, back to the perspective or *habitus* of superior social groups, and places it against the 'aesthetics of popular culture' which, with its preference for immediacy, pleasure, sensuality and the concrete, is instead typical of lower social groups. Bourdieu thus elaborates a *cartography of taste* not only for the arts and culture, but also for certain areas of mass consumption such as food or cosmetics, and he superimposes these on a *map of social positions* determined by the different combinations of economic and cultural capital. In analysing the correspondences between the two maps Bourdieu is able to individuate different *lifestyles* which characterise different social groups. For example, in clear opposition to the subordinate classes with little cultural and economic capital, the dominated fractions of the dominant class (that is, those who have high cultural capital and reasonable economic capital) prefer *Le Monde* to a tabloid, Chinese cuisine to picnics, going to avant-garde music festivals rather than listening to traditional popular music, Andy Warhol's Pop Art instead of the virtuosity of the Impressionists. The lifestyles thus identified show once again that goods have links to each other and, even though they can be chosen one by one, they group together in rather coherent universes of meaning.

Bourdieu's work is fundamental in many ways. It conjoined an ambitious theoretical project with a variety of empirical studies, showing that consumption is essential to social stratification and participates in the consolidation of various 'fields' of social practice – from fashion to photography, from cuisine to sport. Furthermore, the notion of *habitus* attempts to overcome those dichotomies – structure/action, liberty/necessity, rationality/irrationality – which have so profoundly marked approaches to consumer agency. Nevertheless, in his book on taste, Bourdieu himself tends to offer a too hierarchical and determinist picture of social stratification and to fall into dualistic reasoning. On closer reading, we may see that he tends to propose on the one hand a structural and causal explanation regarding the standardization of taste and, on the other, a voluntarist one at the level of individual action. Bourdieu has been accused of dualist structuralism (Margolis 1999) and even of determinism (Garnham and Williams 1980): in fact, whilst being a creative mechanism which generates behaviours that are both relatively unpredictable yet limited in their variety (McNay 1999), *habitus* often appears as a causal mechanism, stable, finished and all-inclusive, which produces action. The advantages of an approach which stresses that goods are at the same time symbolic markers and practical tools, are partially lost where Bourdieu insists on adopting a unidirectional argument. For example, the thesis that differences in style are always representative of, and reducible to, intimate dispositions of taste rooted in material situations, masks what Daniel Miller has defined as 'material ideology' (Miller 1987, 161 ff.; see also Slater 1997). These are circumstances in which the representations of a particular group deny alternative perspectives access to a given aspect of culture and portray the forced preferences so constructed as belonging exclusively to those excluded – such as when dominant classes attribute degrading hygienic preferences to subordinate classes, which are in fact the result of a state of necessity.

All in all, Bourdieu boils down all consumption to a logic of distinction which reproduces the social positions of actors, these being individuated through the generalization and abstraction of real social differences in various forms of capital (Campbell 1995; Miller 1987).[1] Tastes are in fact structured once and forever on the basis of relative social position, so much so that the choices of consumption are always, even if only unconsciously, expressive of a *positional* and *hierarchical logic*. In Bourdieu's view, although other variables are taken into consideration, economic and cultural capital play a fundamental role, converging or competing for the determination of the dominant taste, the so-called 'good taste'. Thus those who possess both large stocks of money and education become the arbiters of taste: they are able to promote their *habitus*, to naturalize it as a cultural benchmark. The *nouveaux riches* only seem to be capable of imitative strategies, whereas lower social strata are condemned to a residual and marginal role. Despite their increasingly relevant role in the development of fashion, those who principally possess cultural capital, in particular the 'new cultural intermediaries', are considered an emergent but subaltern fraction of the elite. The insistence on social distinction and its reproduction seems therefore to propose yet again a trickle-down effect (see Chapter 3) which, as refined as it might be, poorly explains the very rapid style changes and quest for novelty in contemporary markets (Gronow 1997). Such a position ends up denying the sphere of consumption the relative autonomy which makes a field capable of generating classifications and styles (see Chapters 7 and 8).

Whilst they are far from being the direct expression of a natural individuality or of self-interested calculation, not all styles of consumption are easily reducible, even with the mediation of *habitus*, to the economic, cultural or social capital of those who adopt them. In particular, it may be useful to consider whether there is a relatively autonomous *consumer capital* and that, at least in some cases, it is the practices of consumption itself which create a structure for the standardization of taste. As I see it, consumer capital may be conceived of as the result of previous consumer experiences which are themselves linked, but irreducible, to class and formal education, involving the workings of large mass-oriented institutions both within the market (such as global brands or mass media) and without it (such as social movements).[2] Without going so far as to maintain that 'lifestyles' have displaced class, education, gender and the like, configuring themselves as social groupings typical of advanced industrial or postmodern societies (i.e. see Featherstone 1991), it is possible to conceive of some tastes as a particular dimension of social identity which establishes itself in consumer practices. This obviously tends to happen with the mediation of different 'experts' (from fashion journalists to architects, from chefs to environmentalists) who try to orient our choices in particular socially recognisable and relevant directions.[3] Thus conceived, consumer capital may be seen as a form of generalized knowledge, which is increasingly recognized by all society. More often, consumer capital appears to be fragmented and, following Sarah Thornton (1995), may be conceived of as *'subcultural capital'*, i.e. capital in the eye of the relevant, more or less marginal, social group. Indeed, youth and subcultural styles are constituted precisely through the choices of consumption, they do not always reflect the other social belongings of the individual, their class, gender or age, and they are increasingly practised even by actors who are well past adolescence (see Chapter 4). A particular case which might be placed under the rubric of consumer capital as subcultural capital is that of collectors or amateur circles, which effectively work so as to create relatively separated 'small worlds' sustaining specialized tastes, meanings and hierarchies (Bromberger 1998; Fine 1998; Hennion and Teil 2004).

These considerations are not to deny that class and education are still important determinants in understanding lifestyles. Yet they do not explain all, and not only because they have to be integrated with other social determinants such as gender, generation and the life course, ethnicity, sexuality, nationality, etc. For example, we know that while fitness training in the gym is a predominantly female, white-collar activity, only a small part of the variance in the purchase of fitness services and loyalty to a programme is explained by the combined facts of gender, class and age (Sassatelli 1999). Likewise, a study on culinary habits in the United Kingdom where vegetarians represent 6 per cent of the population, has shown that this style of consumption is spread throughout most families, with gender, age or education explaining only a fraction of the variance (Warde 1997). In both cases the experiences of involvement, the interpersonal relationships and the emotional codes which are marshalled by institutions of consumption as diverse as the gym, the family and the vegetarian societies must be taken into consideration. To understand both the meanings of fitness programmes and of vegetarianism, and thus to consider their potential for social change in matters of bodily regimes, health and diet, we should look more deeply into their cultural history, their institutional embeddedness, and their emotional significance for consumers. The personal histories of vegetarians, for example, are long and complicated, often signalled by a genuine conversion (Beardsworth and Keil 1992; Tester 1999), which seems to be supported not only by health and animal rights campaigns, but also and above all by habits, rules and opportunities rooted in the relations (peer group, family) and institutions (restaurants, shops) of consumption.

The general validity of Bourdieu's schema has been brought into question by new empirical studies which set out to test its robustness (Bennett et al. 1999; Lamont 1992). In particular, comparing American and French middle classes and their attitudes towards consumption and money, Michèle Lamont has shown that Bourdieu forgot the importance of *national traditions* in providing and organizing a cultural repertoire: the cultural boundaries traced by education, cosmopolitanism and refinement are indeed weaker and less defined in the United States than in

France.[4] This is not the result of a simple variation on a theme: if in the United States cultural equality reinforces anti-intellectualism and favours a more open culture, in France low geographical mobility limits materialistic attachments which are far more portable in a globalized material culture. Lamont's research contradicts the hierarchical image of taste offered by Bourdieu. As we have seen, Bourdieu assumes that the differences in taste inevitably give way to hierarchies and this is because he starts from the idea that meanings are structured in relation to one another within defined, stable and largely coherent fields. Instead, Lamont underlines that contemporary societies are dynamic, that the various *fields of power*, including those of taste and consumer preference, are *open* and *unstable*. Above all, they intersect in increasingly complex ways with other fields, not least that of mass communication, rendering cultural distinctions more fluid, subtle and multifaceted.

On these premises, the analysis of taste in many contemporary societies should acknowledge the coexistence of many tastes appropriate for different contexts and the difficulty in establishing once and for all the connotations of 'good taste'. Rather than disregarding social boundaries, today such a perspective seems more suitable to understanding how social differences are both maintained and contested through consumption. The studies on the *omnivorous consumer* conducted by Richard Peterson show that for goods as different as food and music, strategies of consumption are developing which instead of being expressed by just one genre, style or taste, are expressed by an assorted mixing of different genres, forms and products (Peterson 1992; see also Peterson and Kern 1996; Van Eijck 2000 and Warde et al. 1998). Indeed, the omnivorous style values *variety* in and of itself, making refinement and cultural sophistication the experience of the widest possible variety of things. This allows people to choose between different commodities in the market where the infinitesimal differentiation of options makes it particularly difficult to create a coherent aesthetic style. Furthermore, it enables individuals to keep up with as large a number of social groupings as possible, thus increasing their chances of being recognised as aesthetically competent (see Di Maggio 1987). In this situation the working classes are culturally disadvantaged not because they are excluded from so-called 'high culture', but because they consume a smaller and less varied basket of cultural goods, as some recent research on Australian consumers has revealed (Bennett et al. 1999). Furthermore, at least as suggested by Bernard Lahire in the case of France (2004), the most eclectic individuals largely maintain a sense of hierarchy in their varied practices by a form of reflexive second-order distinction. They do consume all sorts of culture, but they are very careful in constructing elaborated topographies of where, when and with whom they consume different cultural goods. In particular they tend to prefer 'cultured' genres for public, formal occasions and 'popular' ones for private settings. All in all, these studies clearly show that consumption is an ambivalent phenomenon even when established cultural hierarchies are called into question and blow up in a myriad fragments: if the opening up of variety may likewise open up unexpected spaces of tolerance and cultural exchange, what appears to be the control of variety by variety functions to fabricate symbolic capital which may very well reproduce social boundaries.

Cultural classification and identity

Sticking to an anthropological angle, the British anthropologist Mary Douglas, whose concern with consumption is best expressed in her well-known book *The World of Goods* written in collaboration with the economist Baron Isherwood, provides a perspective that is partly similar to Bourdieu's. As with Bourdieu, goods function as sorting devices: they 'can be used as fences or bridges' to regulate social access and belonging (Douglas and Isherwood 1979, 12). In contrast with Bourdieu, Douglas doesn't put together a complex theory of practice and embodiment.[5] However, her view of the link between consumption and social structure is predicated less on a hierarchical representation of social differences. This is partly because Douglas is determined to show how *active* the consumer is, the main target of her critique being the portrayal of the consumer as an 'incoherent and fragmented being, a person divided in her purposes and barely responsible for her decisions, dominated by reaction to prices on the one hand and to fashionable swings on the other' (Douglas 1996, 81). In Douglas's approach the emphasis is on identity and classification: following Lévi-Strauss, she considers that goods 'are good to think': they can be treated as symbolic means of classifying the world, as the tools of a particular form of non-verbal communication. The subject would be unable to act rationally were the surrounding world not characterized by a certain coherence and regularity. Thus the social actor requires an intelligible reality of visible signs, and goods serve this function by providing the material basis for stabilizing cultural categories.

Considering that humans cannot avoid continually reading the world that surrounds them, the 'main problem of social life is to pin down meanings so that they stay still for a little time'; the acquisition and use of objects is therefore a way of 'mak(ing) firm and visible a particular set of judgements in the fluid processes of classifying persons and events' (Douglas and Isherwood 1979, 65 and 67). We choose these goods over others precisely because they are not neutral, because they are culturally incompatible and even in opposition to those perspectives on the organization of society and identity which we want to refute. In this sense consumption is 'the very arena in which culture is fought over and licked into shape' (*ibid*, 57) – that is, it reflects fundamental choices of the type of society which we want to live in and the type of person we wish to be, and obviously of what we do not accept and do not want to be. Indeed, it is *refusals* that most clearly underline both subjective preferences and the cultural role of consumption. In fact, for Douglas (1996, 81) 'consumption is governed by protest': 'protest is a fundamental cultural stance' and 'consumption behaviour is continuously and pervasively inspired by cultural hostility'.

For the social actor the act of consumption responds to a logic of affirmation of one's interpretations not only as socially *acceptable*, but also as *dominant*. Every individual aims, in competition with others, to occupy a dominant position in the creation of meanings. Consumption is fundamental since it permits a continual marking and re-marking of the surrounding world and a constant confrontation with others, and thus a control of respective interpretations and roles. The adoption of a new commodity, or the innovative use of an existing one, is seen as a way of controlling precious bits of information. This analytical frame

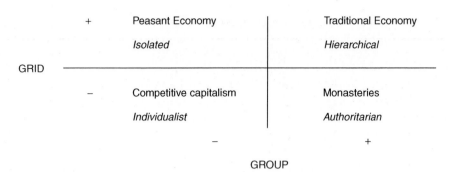

Figure 5.2   Cultural biases in Douglas's theory. Adapted from Douglas and Isherwood (1979)

enables Douglas to maintain that shopping is not simply determined by the market or by fashion. The consumer is neither reactive, nor passive nor irrational; on the contrary 'the consumer wandering round the shops is actualizing a philosophy of life' (*ibid*, 86), communicating his or her own identity both to him/herself and to others.

Even if consumption is 'part of a live information system' (Douglas and Isherwood 1979, 10), consumers' philosophy can be located in one of four fundamental *cultural biases* which are present in *all* forms of social organization (Douglas 1978; 1982). These cultural orientations or biases correspond with the intersection of two dimensions of social organization: the social structure or 'grid' can be strong and hierarchical or weak and egalitarian, the 'groups' can be strongly integrated or weak (see Figure 5.2). Forms of life defined by strong and hierarchical social structures and by integrated groups give way to the 'hierarchical' bias; on the contrary, weak structures and groups support the 'individualist' bias; strong and egalitarian groups within a weak structure give way to the 'authoritarian' bias; finally, individuals outside groups but within hierarchical and strong structures follow the 'isolated' bias. These biases represent the prevailing orientations of different societies: the hierarchical corresponds with traditional societies, the individualist with competitive capitalist economy, the authoritarian with the life of monks in monasteries, and the isolated with that of peasant economies (Douglas and Isherwood, 1979, 41–2). In each society these biases are connected, even if not in deterministic fashion, to different structural conditions of life. In Western capitalist societies Douglas thus identifies four lifestyles: a 'competitive' and 'individualist' style, 'driving in the fast lane, as the advertisements say', which implies 'enjoying high-tech instruments, sporty, arty, risky styles of entertainment, and freedom to change commitments'; a style which is 'hierarchical', 'formal' and 'thriftier', 'adhering to the established traditions and established institutions' and centred on 'the family'; a style which is 'egalitarian, enclavist, against formality, pomp and artifice' and prefers 'simplicity', 'frankness' and 'spiritual values'; and finally the 'eclectic, withdrawn but unpredictable lifestyle of the isolate' which runs away from whatever other styles embrace (Douglas 1996, 83–4).

Douglas's work has done much to consolidate a cultural reading of consumption, providing a communicative approach that considers commodities as a *semantics* with consumption working as a language. Still, Douglas's theory is not beyond criticism. Various doubts have been raised over her grid/group analysis: one asks what happens at the borders between different cultural orientations, if these orientations are individual or social, how exactly are they connected to structural social conditions, and above all if are they really universal (Thompson and Ellis 1997)? In fact, coming as she does from the anthropological tradition, Douglas aims to offer an analytical tool which can be used in different societies and periods and tends, just like Bourdieu, to undervalue the question of long-term historical and cultural changes. As suggested, even though Bourdieu proposes a dynamic approach (tastes change continually in response to the field of cultural production), he doesn't consider the massive changes to class structure which have occurred with modernity, or the cultural ones from the new media of mass communication. For her part, Douglas concedes that modern consumption is a result of the industrial revolution. In *The World of Goods* the development of a consumer society is traced back to the development of industrialization described as a factor which has 'complicated the life of the consumer' (Douglas and Isherwood 1979). To keep up to speed with the process of classification and identification necessitated by the growth of material culture the consumer, active and rational, must run faster only to stay in the same place. Douglas and Isherwood acknowledge the development of 'tertiary' goods (that is, those goods which substitute for domestic work, thus freeing up time for more consumption). Yet, they do not consider that the meanings of novelty and luxury should be seen in the context of the historical establishment of the 'consumer' as a particular kind of social figure with normative force (see Chapters 2 and 7).

All in all, in Douglas's analysis the active consumer is an anthropological universal: it emerges as an ahistorical subject who actualizes a unitary worldview, proceeding according to steps which are universally defined both in terms of formal strategy (i.e. cultural opposition) and in terms of possible contents or meanings of action (i.e. the four cultural biases). Because it also tends to confine the actor to a cognitive dimension instead of a more practical one which would situate them in time and space, Douglas's approach often portrays consumers as engaged in maximizing the expression of their socio-cultural position. It thus runs the risk of re-proposing a version of instrumental rationality which, splitting means and ends of action and considering them as somehow given, empties (consumer) action itself of its processual and creative features. Furthermore, as suggested, when looking at today's Western societies, (many) consumers do not simply apply some given cultural logic of consumption 'on a larger scale', as Douglas seems to maintain, they produce new cultural forms, and may even embrace cultural de-classification to the point that, as we have seen, styles of consumption can be quite eclectic.

This is related to the fact that material culture has not only increased, but has also become enormously differentiated. Simmel (1890) was probably the first to notice that in modern societies the growing social differentiation and specialization of relatively separated social and cultural spheres was accompanied by a corresponding differentiation of objects, defined by different process of production, access, use, distribution and enjoyment (see also Miller 1987). Functional differentiation allows and obliges the subject to engage with different role expectations and institutional demands. It asks consumers to learn and follow a variety of locally specific logics of self-presentation. Corresponding with this are the different modalities through which social actors use goods, not only in the course of their life, but also in a variety of different social environments where they are asked to manage different emotional outlooks: of control and sobriety, of release and hedonism. To some extent, in contemporary consumer culture fragmentation is being turned into a value and provides a unitary perspective which consists in accommodating to the principles which govern the various occasions of consumption. The same practice can, thus, take on different and even contradictory meanings: for example, the weekly shop at the supermarket may be organized so as to save money, but also to provide a special treat (Falk and Campbell 1997; Miller 1998); the purchase of a fur coat may work as middle-age middle-class status display but also enhance young fashionable feminine sensuality (Entwistle 2000; Skov 2005); reading a romantic novel may be seen as fantasy-pursuit and relaxation, but also as education and social bonding (Radway 1987). Of the rest, as Mike Featherstone (1991) has noted, the cultural intermediaries, advertising executives in pole position, do not seek to promote just one lifestyle, they work to expand the range of styles available, with the result that there is a tendency to present lifestyles as no longer needing internal coherence.

Bourdieu and Douglas help us consider that it is not enough to postulate a relationship between taste and the world of things, since the second doesn't generate the first, or vice versa. Still, the mediation of the social structure occurs through places, situations and institutions that an abstract map of cultural orientations or social positions, no matter how complicated, simply cannot reflect. Understanding how tastes and material culture find correspondences, and are indeed mutually shaped, requires more attention to the *contexts of consumption*, and in particular to the institutions which mediate acquisition and use, organizing identities, interaction and manners in ways we consider appropriate. There are local and institutional logics, linked to the particular historical contingencies and different institutions in which consumption practices occur, which orientate consumption practices on a daily basis, and which cannot be attributed to an individual actor-consumer seeking coherence without making consumption appear a more reflexive and rational activity than it actually is. The distinction between *local logics* which inform consumer practices, and a *reflexive logic* which consumers can reconstruct *a posteriori* through seeking to attribute coherence to their choices, is not an academic gimmick. Rather, this distinction corresponds with the need to give adequate attention to the places and manners of consumption – aspects which remain largely unexplored both by Douglas and Bourdieu (see Chapter 8). Such distinction becomes especially crucial in a situation of social complexity and strong cultural de-classification where individuals acting as consumers must face a plurality of relatively separated and institutionally embedded spheres of meanings while, at the same time, engaging with a plethora of discourses and practices which propose a particular version of 'consumption' as master narrative.

Appropriating commodities

The sociology of consumption has set great store by Bourdieu and Douglas's works and, at the same time, is trying to obviate their limits. By and large, the communication approach today appears, paradoxically, still to be linked to a productivist vision of the social, in so far as it surreptitiously gives priority to the standardization of tastes in the sphere of production. On the contrary, consumption as a whole should be portrayed as a *relatively autonomous sphere of action*, different from but loosely interrelated with that of production, of sales promotion, of formal education, and so on. Therefore, not only are tastes and consumer practices internally complex, but the different contexts and cultures of consumption are key mediators in the formation of taste. As a relatively autonomous sphere of action, consumption has come to be defined as a practice of *appropriation* which occurs on a variety of socially organized occasions (Appadurai, ed. 1986b; De Certeau 1984; McCracken 1988; Miller 1987; for an early formulation see Simmel 1990, orig. 1907). Each of these occasions is relatively self-governing and translates in its own terms what has been inscribed in commodities by the circuits of production and distribution. In particular, in contemporary societies consumption engages with the nature of objects as commodities at various levels. The moment of purchase is clearly only the beginning of a complex process in which the consumer works on a commodity to recontextualize it, so that it may eventually end up no longer having any recognisable relation with the world of monetary exchange. In fact, even the most simple article of trade doesn't inevitably and constantly have the character of a commodity: it may start off as such, but it often ends up being something different, at least for those who consume or possess it. Therefore, one of the key objectives of the sociology of consumption today is to focus on the concrete, active, fluid and different ways in which people transform and make their own those resources that they have acquired on the market.

It is in this context that we can read Grant McCracken's work. McCracken (1988) has tried to provide a culturalist perspective which sees consumption as part of a process of meaning attribution. There are two stages in this process: advertising and fashion move meaning from the culturally and historically constituted world into the goods; the meaning of things is thereby practically re-elaborated by consumers through a series of *ritual activities*. Following the lessons of anthropologist Victor Turner (1969), rituals are actions saturated in shared symbolic meanings which fix, in turn, other meanings.[6] If ritual is defined as an 'opportunity to affirm, evoke, assign or revise the conventional symbols and meanings of the social order' (McCracken 1988, 84) which is carried out by a community or a group gathered together, in contemporary Western society individualist rituals are blossoming. Individualist rituals are carried out by individuals with reference to a relevant community as opposed to in the presence of this community, and rituals of consumption are often of this type. McCracken (1988, 83–7) has identified four principal types of *consumption ritual*: exchange, possession, maintenance and divestment. Rituals of exchange are often encoded by the logic of the gift which links together objects and people; gift elements – such as some form of personal trust or ceremonial propriety which goes beyond mere instrumental calculation – are widely present also in most cash transactions. Rituals of possession are undoubtedly the most diverse: taken together, they imply some form of symbolic and material appropriation of objects and a personalization of things and their meaning. To these, we add rituals of maintenance which help to maintain the personal meanings of objects over time, refreshing their symbolic value for the owner and those close to him/her. Finally, even when social actors just want to throw a good away, they practise rituals of divestment which empty it of its attributed value.[7]

McCracken demonstrates that these rituals require work and a certain amount of commitment on the part of the social actors; the work that is invested 'produces' the object anew and binds it to the person 'in a living relationship'. According to McCracken (*ibid*, 100), this enables the cultivation of utopias that may not be realizable in ordinary life.[8] Thus objects represent bridges stretching not only towards others, as Douglas and Bourdieu tend to emphasize, but also towards ideals that normally escape us, and which we don't want to renounce. It is from this perspective that we can interpret the growing enthusiasm, especially amongst certain sectors of the middle classes, for green and environmental products (Halkier 2001; James 1993): even if a style of consumption that is genuinely environmentally friendly remains difficult, through buying and using green products, recycling some of the commodities they use, taking eco-tourism holidays, these consumers can gain proof of the importance of environmental aspirations, feel as if they have the capacity to contribute, and claim a new kind of identity for themselves. In other words, they can express an ideal of the world and of themselves and assert its legitimacy, even if this will not change the world as such.

The idea that *consumption is a form of production*, because in using commodities in countless ways consumers transform their cultural meanings, was pointed out by the French historian and cultural theorist Michel de Certeau in *The Practice of Everyday Life* (1984). In line with Umberto Eco's (1994, orig. 1964) emphasis on reading as 'interpretive cooperation' between the reader and the writer, and with Stanley Fish's (1980) emphasis on the inscription of the reader within everyday 'interpretive communities' which orientate meaning, De Certeau opposes Barthes's structural semiotics which portrayed reading practices as the actualization by the reader of the meanings intended by the text. Arguing that objects just like texts are not charged with constrictive power, he extends these observations to the whole of everyday consumption. Just as the reader of a novel finds herself facing a text written and marketed according to a well-defined rationale and still in her 'drift across the page' introduces her world of meanings and her experiences into the author's space, pulling out something altogether different from that originally intended; in the same way the consumer interprets commodities in a personal way, assembling them in an ever-changing '*bricolage*', which gives way to 'innumerable and infinitesimal transformations' of the dominant cultural order. De Certeau thus proposes that consumption is a form of value production opposed to that of organized commodity production. The latter is 'rationalized, expansionist and at the same time centralized, clamorous and spectacular'; instead, consumption is an *ordinary 'poaching'* with which subjects re-appropriate, sometimes subversively, goods officially intended for other uses: it is 'devious, it is dispersed, but insinuates itself everywhere, silently and almost invisibly, because it does not manifest itself through its own products, but rather through its ways of using the products imposed by a dominant economic order' (*ibid*, xii).

A similar position is held by the British anthropologist Daniel Miller. Considering consumption as a 'relatively autonomous and plural process of cultural self-construction', Miller lucidly suggests that:

there is no single or proper way to consume. The imperatives of consumption may be as varied as the cultural contexts from which consumers act. Consumption stands for the diversity of 'local' social networks that maintain their differences in the face of the homogenization of institutions and mechanisms of production and distribution. (Miller 1995, 41)

Because of its polymorphous nature, Miller therefore insists, consumption can be seen as the 'vanguard of history', the attempt by social actors to 'extract their own humanity through the use of consumption as the creation of a specificity, which is held to negate the generality and alienatory scale of the institutions from which they receive goods and services' (*ibid*, 31). In his earlier, influential book *Material Culture and Mass Consumption* (1987), Miller reaches this diagnosis by a wide-ranging theoretical discussion of the notion of material culture. He stresses that material culture cannot be intended as a collection of objects to be judged as good and authentic or bad and false, as the Frankfurt School would have it. Material culture is instead a *process* which implies – in terms that Miller draws from Hegel's notion of objectification – a 'dual' movement of externalization first, followed by internalization. Objects are not quite culture until they have been both produced and consumed, both placed outside subjects by production and internalized by subjects in their use and consumption. Miller (*ibid*, 17) thus maintains that consumption can be considered as a form of *sublation* or assimilation – that is, 'the movement by which society re-appropriates its own external form' and the way in which a subject 'assimilates its own culture and uses it to develop itself as a social subject'. If for Hegel this was an activity of the spirit, for Miller it is a practice which organizes consumption as a material and cultural activity at once: commodities don't work as culture, they remain dead and unfinished, until they are used and consumed.[9]

Miller (*ibid*, 192) has thus rightly insisted on the fact that consumption too contains the potential to realize the human being which Marx tended to attribute only to work: '(i)n consumption, quite as fully as in production, it is possible ... to emerge through a process of re-appropriation towards the full project of objectification in which the subject becomes at home with itself'. The term 're-appropriation' is eloquent: obviously it implies the capacity to make an object properly *for* and *of* oneself. Goods that are anonymous, identical or fungible at the moment of purchase can be re-contextualized in numerous different ways by consumers, so that practices of consumption tend to generate diversity rather than homogenization. However, in Miller's view, appropriation also implies feedback effects on identity, thus by absorbing or appropriating, the subject expands and modifies him or herself. It is in this process of renegotiation of one's identity that a space opens up in which the advertising industry intervenes, trying to manage and modify our needs. But it is thanks to this process that consumption can also be a creative act and produce something truly 'authentic' – that is, something which actors not only may use in a personal way, but which can also become part of them (Friedman 1991; 1994).

These approaches are motivated by the need to take what consumers do seriously, stressing their *active* role in the cultural process. They rightly show that consumption should not be dismissed as merely the end point of the process of capitalist production, nor as its logical consequence, but should be seen as a meaningful sphere of action with subversive as well as integrative potential. Still, De Certeau's and Miller's works can be read as running the risk of placing a disproportionate emphasis on a defiant consumer (see Frow 1991; Gell 1988). For example, in a recent contribution Miller (2001, 234) maintains that 'far from expressing capitalism, consumption is most commonly used by people to negate it': it is the 'very means that people use to try and create the identity they feel they have lost as labourers', 'confront(ing), on a day-to-day basis, their sense of alienation'. Indeed, while both De Certeau and Miller clearly put forward dialectical theories of consumption and are well aware that consumption and production are not simply symmetrical spheres of action, they do not fully appreciate the *systemic effects* of such *asymmetry*. Perhaps a telling illustration of the asymmetry between consumption and production is that the notion of demand does not describe what consumers are about, but does capture much of what producers are after: for consumers consumption is ultimately much more than the money they spend, but for producers and retailers sales volumes and revenues remain the nut and kernel of consumption. Furthermore, if it is true that consumption is subjectively more important than production for many people, it is also true that, at the systemic level, producers and distributors are more powerful than consumers. In other words, private rebels may not become public revolutionaries. If they do, the meanings originally associated with rebellion may be altered and subversive results are by no means guaranteed.

Looking at everyday consumption, we must also acknowledge that, at the *subjective level*, consumers are not always able to complete their rituals of consumption, appropriating commodities successfully. As Simmel (1990) suggested, '*sterile ownership*' is a typical disease of modern society, fuelled by the growth in material culture, the diversity of objects and their continual innovation. Thus, consumers may find themselves with objects which are useless and meaningless or even alienating, and they may be upset by having discarded an object which still represented them. McCracken (1988, 85) concedes that the process of appropriation doesn't always end well: '(o)ccasionally a consumer will claim that a possession such as a car, house, article of clothing, or other meaning-carrying good "never really seemed to belong to me". ... The good becomes a paradox: the consumer owns it without possessing it. Its symbolic properties remain immovable'. Paradoxically enough, as consumption requires time, some forms of sterile ownership may be a feature of economies where leisure time is the shortest for the moneyed elite. A recent study of consumption patterns in contemporary 'liberal market' societies indeed shows that expensive leisure goods (sophisticated cameras, camping equipment, sport accessories, etc.) are purchased by time-pressured high-income earners and are often left unused, remaining in storage at home as symbols of a potential future and a wished-for self-identity (Sullivan and Gershuny 2004). While these 'inconspicuous' luxuries are only *virtually consumed*, being as much bearers of frustration as offering symbolic support in daily life, they do contribute to consumption expenditure at the macroeconomic level. The idea of sterile ownership thus adumbrates the gap between consumer practices as the use of goods and demand as the purchase of commodities. It also hints at the lack of reciprocity between consumption as subjective culture and consumer culture as objective or material culture. This lack of reciprocity means that even successful appropriation in ordinary life may have *perverse effects*. Indeed, following Simmel,

Miller himself suggests that the increased pressure on individual consumer choice may have unintended cultural effects. In a recent paper he illustrates this by setting a puzzle (Miller 2004): why do Western women dream of colourful dresses and increasingly buy black, grey and plainly unadorned clothing? His reply points to the fact that choice has become so overwhelming that it might be given up altogether or indeed strictly regimented by resorting to hegemonic codifications: the 'little black dress' is seen as an anxiety-reducing response to the variety of clothing available and the de-classificatory trends in the fashion system.

Ambivalence and practice

Consumption increasingly appears to be a terrain of *ambivalence*. By this I am referring to the dual character of many social phenomena whereby they are able to emancipate subjects, but bind them to specific conditions; to offer significant capacities which may become heavy burdens; and to solve certain problems, but create others. Consumption is likewise a disputed territory which does not always herald freedom, but which is nonetheless a potential carrier of social change, creativity and satisfaction. If at the historical and systemic level the development of a 'consumer society' shouldn't simply be disparaged as an outcome of the process of industrialization, at the subjective level it is true that consumption can be one of the ways in which global brands can be successfully confronted as well as passively taken up. Thus, while the ideological function of advertising and marketing deserves critical attention (see Chapter 6), we must also keep in mind that it is through certain kinds of consumption (green, alternative, local, traditional, etc.) that people can oppose the homogenization promoted by capitalist production and global business (see Chapter 8). In other words, that same fear of consumerism and materialism which is often found in sociological reflection on consumption can also be found in many consumers all over the world, precisely when they buy, use and organize goods in everyday life (Ger and Belk 1999). All in all, it is precisely as consumers that people may try to face the anti-social potential of their investments in objects; this has been shown, for example, by a number of studies which have revealed the effort consumers put into organizing an important place of consumption like the home in such a way that its furnishing, decoration and technologies underline and facilitate those relationships they consider constructive (Gell 1986; Miller 1997b; Shove 2003; Wilk 1989).

Clearly, individual creativity is limited even when acting in a practical sphere like consumption which appears to be less rigidly prescriptive than the sphere of paid work. Consumption establishes itself as a *gratuitous and creative activity* inasmuch as people reinterpret and reorganize things they have bought according to a particular style which they are continuously engaged in accomplishing (a style of dress, living, listening to music and so on). This doesn't imply, however, that these acts are totally consequential, purely rational or absolutely free, that they are acts of sovereignty over the world and things. Rather consumption is a *socially and culturally standardized activity*, inasmuch as the ongoing constitution of a personal style draws on commodities whose trajectories consumers can never fully control and it is negotiated within various contexts, institutions and relations which both habilitate and constrain subjects. Arguably, contemporary studies of consumption are now sufficiently mature to overcome that moralistic swing of the pendulum which, as I shall show in the next chapter, either celebrates consumption as a free and liberating act, or denigrates it as a dominated and subjugated act. Just as the sphere of consumption appears more meaningful in itself even though it remains firmly interrelated with the spheres of production, retail and promotion, so practices of consumption are meaningful for people even if they are not entirely free or always consequential; they are enclosed in mechanisms of power even if these are not deterministic. Being both less preoccupied with defining modernity, and more focused on the empirical, contested and ambivalent unfolding of social practices, studies of consumption can thus start to ask sharper questions, such as how practices of consumption really occur and under which conditions they are advantageous, to whom, and to what effect.

To proceed in this direction it may be useful to rethink the act of consumption according to a *theory of practice*, as Bourdieu and De Certeau anticipated. As it has been variously developed in the last decade (Schatzki 2001), the model of practice tries to respond to the urgency in contemporary social theory to reformulate traditional theories of action in a new direction. Alan Warde's (2005) recent contribution to the application of the notion of practice to consumption shows that it may provide a middle ground, neither holistic nor individualist which, by focusing on relatively organized and situated contexts for action, addresses agency without relying on presumptions about the primacy of individual choice. Furthermore, in contrast to Bourdieu, a focus on the organization of practices, allows us to consider their internal differentiation without imputing differences to external, transposable dispositions or structural determinants such as class. The 'principal implication of a theory of practice is that the sources of changed behaviour lie in the development of practices themselves' (*ibid*, 140). In other words, the effect of production and retail on consumption is mediated through the nexus of practices: '(b)ecause practices have their own distinct, institutionalized, and collectively regulated conventions, they *partly* insulate people, qua consumers, from the blandishments of producers and promotional agencies' (*ibid*, 141, my emphasis). This may be seen as in line with some classic ethnographies – from Becker's (1963) to Willis' (1978) – which considers that different degrees of involvement within a relatively separated social world (fan cultures, subcultures, sports cultures, music cultures, etc.) are as important as external determinants in understanding meanings and differentiation in a given field. Indeed, the works which have conceived of consumption as a form of appropriation looking at rituals of consumption or at subcultural styles have largely responded to a similar research agenda. In this vein, and by sensitizing Bourdieu's approach to local realities, recruitment to specific consumer activities may be given its due. Levels of involvement, hierarchies and differences which are generated by the activity itself rather than by external dispositions may also be considered. Of course, questions arise as to how relevant this may be outside the specific rituals of consumption (see Chapters 7 and 8).

As I shall argue, practices should be viewed as creative acts, irreducible to, but not entirely outside of, the structural principles of a given culture. Rather than strategic action (and thus the product of a fully defined, autonomous and accomplished self), consumption is best represented as a series of improvisational acts undertaken by social actors who have to move through a variety of worlds systematized by collective routines and imaginaries. For all their diversity, theories of practice try to replace the image of the actor as a cognitive operator, communicator or interpreter of texts, with that of the *embodied subject* who is *situated* in space and time, interacting with objects within social contexts which participants continuously stabilize through practice. This way of thinking may be sensitized to issues of power by integrating Harold Garfinkel's (1967) eth-nomethodology and Erving Goffman's (1961; 1967; 1974) microsociology with French poststructuralist theory such as Michel Foucault's late works (1978; 1988). Emphasizing embodiment and the situated nature of consumption, it brings down to earth the Gramscian notion of de-codification proposed by British Cultural Studies to show that, following the codification enacted by television, spectators have to reinterpret the messages using ideologies that are typically dif-ferent from those operating during the codification by the culture industry itself (Hall 1980). The shaping of *experiences* is emphasized: the actor-consumer expe-riences consumption as situated in spatially and temporally specific institutional contexts and, on the basis of these experiences, contributes to reproducing both such contexts and the wider cultural meanings of objects (Sassatelli 2001a; 2001b). The same emotions of the actor-consumer take shape through certain specific forms of expression and manners that are mediated, and thus partly shaped, by the contexts of consumption and their ways of metabolizing material culture and the various *discourses* about the consumer as a social type.[10] Discourses especially as they have been associated with a variety of movements (from the temperance movement at the turn of the 19th century to green consumerism today), should be considered as utopias and dystopias which both discipline and are negotiated by people as they self-constitute themselves as consumers (see Chapter 7).

In the model I propose, the relationship between actors and consumption is an intimate one, even if it cannot be thought of as fully reflexive (Ilmonen 2001; Warde 1994). Routines indeed have been shown to be important in understand-ing ordinary consumer practices – from eating to cleaning to supermarket shop-ping (Gronow and Warde 2001; Shove 2003). To be sure, in ordinary life we hardly address the nature of many of our consumption habits. *Entrenched con-sumption routines* are part of a taken-for-granted background and are often expe-rienced as having nothing to do with choice or, indeed, with 'consumption'. In most cases they are certainly not questioned. Yet, in the face of a fast-changing market, with the increasing fragmentation of society, and the increased relevance of a discourse about 'consumer culture' some of these routines may lose their self-evidence, and become questionable and questioned. Within cultural theory, much emphasis has been placed on purposive individual stylization. Theories of late modernity have stressed cultural de-classification and individual lifestyles (Lash and Urry 1994) as well as reflexive individualization and the purposive construc-tion of identity through commodities (Bauman 1992; Beck 1992; Giddens 1990). Still, empirical studies continue to show that reflexivity, routines and the taken-for-granted are all mixed up in consumer practices. When we consume, precisely because we act in practical ways, we do not reflect on everything; on the contrary, the meanings we attribute to our actions and the accounts through which we reflexively represent our trajectory of consumption partly reflect, and thus blindly build upon, the specific conditions in which we find ourselves. The *bounded reflexivity* of consumption corresponds to the fact that people act through the nexus of practical activity which is organized in relatively autonomous, self-evident and well-ordered contexts. In this light, the notion of practice enables us to emphasize that consumption is not only *expressive* but also *performative action*, it constitutes identities: through making objects or the experience of consumption their own, social actors create themselves, both as consumers and as selves with specific and different roles linked to their ethnicity, sexuality, gender, social status, etc., which combine with specific styles of consumption.

Through consumption then, social actors not only contribute to the fixing of a series of cultural classifications, not only express themselves through symbols or communicate their social positions, but also constitute themselves and their social identities – as women and men, mothers and fathers, lovers and professionals, friends and enemies, and, of course, with the increasing visibility of consumer culture, citizens and consumers. In so doing, social actors reorganize the surrounding world while being shaped by it. Having reconceptualized consumption through the model of practice, it becomes clearer that commodities are produced by the system of production in some characteristically rigid ways, but are experienced and utilized by consumers in different ways according to context and circumstance; and that by consuming, social actors elaborate the meanings and uses of goods, articulating their symbolic and material qualities with various degrees of reflexivity and in ways that are sometimes functional to the reproduction of the existing structures of power, sometimes not.

Summary

Within the social sciences, emphasis has been placed on the *symbolic function* of consumption: goods are conceived as material elements through which social actors reproduce the cultural meanings which structure social space. This leads to the *marking of social boundaries*. People's tastes reflect their particular socio-cultural location which, through their choices, they demonstrate and reproduce. The seminal works of **Pierre Bourdieu** and **Mary Douglas** have greatly contributed to this perspective. Bourdieu considers taste as an expression of *habitus*, namely an embodied, transposable individual disposition which is defined by *economic capital* and *cultural capital*. As means of distinction, tastes are thereby implicated in social hierarchies and contribute to reproducing them. Douglas also maintains that goods can be used as bridges and fences to mark social boundaries. She insists that the link between taste and social position is not deterministic, and concentrates on different *cultural biases* which provide the larger structural framework for the standardization of taste in all societies. Partly revising these approaches, the rich literature which has been produced in the last two decades within sociology and anthropology has focused on the organization of consumption in a variety of spaces and occasions, stressing their

(Continued)

diversity. Such diversity adumbrates the *relative autonomy of consumer practices*. Authors such as **De Certeau, McCracken** and **Miller** have conceived of consumption as an *active process of appropriation* which occurs according to different *rituals*. Miller in particular has shown that consumption may contain subversive potential and that it may even be used to question capitalism and commoditization. Consumer *agency*, namely the room for manoeuvre which social actors have when they act as consumers, has become a key issue in current studies of consumption. Reference to a theory of practice may provide a perspective on the *ambivalence* of consumption, by focusing on relatively organized and situated contexts for action and by addressing agency without giving priority to individual choice.

Notes

1 The data gathered for *Distinction* came mainly from a questionnaire with multiple-choice answers which obviously imposed a field of preferences on respondents and was therefore better suited to supplying a relatively abstract map of lifestyles, rather than analysing the concrete ways in which tastes are acquired or objects utilized in daily life. For example, musical taste was measured by asking respondents to indicate the composers of 16 given pieces of music and to express three preferences, a simplistic operation if compared with the theoretical apparatus which Bourdieu constructed with the *habitus* (see Dant 1999; Miller 1987).

2 While adopting a vocabulary which could easily be subsumed within an economic instrumental model such as that proposed by Gary Becker, this notion shall not be understood as consumers rationally investing in 'consumer knowledge' nor as consumers possessing discrete quantities of knowledge, but as people being differently positioned within relatively separated and institutionally defined fields of practices of consumption.

3 All in all the concept of 'lifestyle' is far from rigorous and takes on a variety of meanings according to disciplinary boundaries. In sociology it has been put to use to indicate the fact that in contemporary Western societies choices of consumption are at the core of personal identity (Giddens 1990). Placing emphasis more on the aesthetic characteristics of objects than on relationships of power among people using them, the notion of lifestyle has been associated with the idea that we have already reached a post-Fordist phase characterized by cultural de-classification and social complexity and the difficulty of individuating boundaries between groups as well as hierarchical differences between styles (Chaney 1996). This perspective risks presenting lifestyle as superficial, something that can both be chosen and abandoned by individuals at will. In marketing, the notion of lifestyle has long been the main theoretical tool to account for the differences between consumers and is used to formulate targeted sales strategies, typically created through psychographic techniques which mix individual psychological factors with actual purchasing behaviour (see Belk 1995a). Thus defined, lifestyles are lumped together into general groups and provide only vague understandings which marketing executives typically have to integrate, individuating more specific market segments, perhaps starting from styles of consumption which revolve around the use of a particular object. Whilst providing a map of the distribution of purchases within a given population, psychographics doesn't account for the contexts

in which commodities are consumed, the way in which social actors consume them, and thus the meanings attributed to objects and their use (Holt 1997).

4 On this subject see also the work by Tony Bennett, Michael Emmison and John Frow (1999) on cultural consumption in Australia which, whilst being more faithful to Bourdieu's theoretical position, reveals a plurality of value scales signalled by differences of gender, age or geography, thanks also to the greater cosmopolitanism of Australian culture.

5 Indeed, in her studies on the body Douglas (1966) also tends to privilege semantic aspects.

6 The 'classical' form of ritual is that of the rite of passage from infancy to adulthood in tribal societies (Turner 1969); but also, in modern societies, from a superior social status to an inferior one, as in degradation rituals which accompany criminal sentencing. Other forms of ritual are used to give 'experiential reality' to certain principles or concepts and in particular to signal a political contract or social bond. Some typologies of rituals of consumption have been provided by Dennis Rook (1985) and by Douglas Holt (1995).

7 An extreme example of this is offered by research conducted in Montreal, Canada on older people who have to move from their home to a care environment; here divestment rituals entail distributing possessions among the kin, thus trying to construct the self through emptying the home and establishing/reinforcing one's own network (Marcoux 2001).

8 According to McCracken (1988) it is mostly luxury objects that function in this way: buying a hugely expensive perfume when we have a low wage may offer us some emotional relief which is greater than the extent to which in fact it changes our life. Consumption in this guise may be seen as having a consolatory function: it enables people to carry on living in an imperfect world, believing that perfection can eventually be reached in a distant future.

9 Following Simmel's footsteps, Miller (1987, 32) starts from the hypothesis that objects and subjects are not *a priori* separate, but that they are in 'a process of mutual construction which always takes place in history, proposing a refiguring of the notion of material culture which favours neither objectivism nor subjectivism. Similar views are also to be found in Sahlins's seminal works on culture and utility (1974; 2000).

10 Sociology can thus engage directly with some of those themes which have traditionally been of central interest to marketing and social psychology (see Belk 1995a; Lunt 1995) while placing much more emphasis on socio-cultural circumstances (from the organization of the spaces of consumption to the histories of use and diffusion of different goods) which have made certain experiences possible.

PART III

THE POLITICS OF CONSUMPTION

In contemporary Western society there's an obvious tendency to read consumption through a series of antinomies. As we have seen, acts of consumption are not only understood through an opposition between rational and irrational action, but also through a *freedom/oppression* dichotomy. When not being considered as a sphere of self-interested gratification, consumption appears instead as a place of the loss of self, illusory self-realization and compulsive imitation. It is conceived of either as the kingdom of a strong autonomous sovereign, or as a trap for the weak, heteronomous dupe. Thus, discourses on consumption present diametrically opposed imageries which oscillate between the two poles of control or abandon, of full information or total determination. However, as we shall see, consumption happens within ordinary social practices and it has uncertain and indefinite outcomes: it neither frees subjects nor is it the expression of absolute freedom, outside of social norms. Likewise, it is not totally determined by advertising and the culture industry, by commodities, shopping centres, theme parks, fast-food chains, and suchlike.

It is because of this *ambivalence* that consumption is essentially a site of *politics*. For a long time consumption was mainly described as a private act, untouched by power: aligned with the market, commerce, the family and pushed into the private sphere, consumption was opposed to the public and political spheres of the state, of citizenship and rights. However, it is becoming increasingly evident that both the ways in which consumption is represented and the ways in which it is carried out are deeply intertwined with power relationships. It is for this reason that we can speak of a genuine *politics of consumption*, since the manifold ways of getting and using goods may be occasions for self-realization and emancipation as well as for frustration and subjugation. As I shall show, power works through consumption in complex ways. For the sake of analysis, they may be seen as amounting to four intertwined dimensions: they concern *social differences* in everyday life as well as *cultural representations*; they work through consumers' identities and their engagement with visions of *normality* as well as through the *systemic effects* of consumption on other spheres of life.

Firstly, as I have widely documented in the preceding chapters, choices of consumption function as a *politics of difference*: they are means of social inclusion as well as exclusion. The *de gustibus non disputandum est* which seems to make of consumption a space where subjects can, and must, freely express themselves, is more wishful thinking than social reality. In reality tastes are anything but indisputable. Judgements are made on the basis of taste. People are preferred and celebrated, or despised and marginalized, because of their own tastes and those of others. I may add to this intrinsic politics of difference, linked as it is to the distinctive function of consumer practices themselves, a *politics of representation*, which has to do with the way consumer goods, practices and identities are represented via symbolic means and images. Representation, through commercial advertising as well as through a variety of collective actors, from consumer movements to fairtrade organizations, is a powerful means of mobilizing people as consumers (see Trentmann, ed. 2006b). The imagery which surrounds consumption provides people with a repertoire for self-representation and self-understanding which may be selectively taken up and challenged in everyday life.

Furthermore, related to these two dimensions there are other, perhaps more subtle, relations of power which have to do mostly with the 'normality', 'legitimacy', 'fairness' or otherwise of certain goods and practices and with the identity ascribed to the consumer. There is thus a *politics of normality*. That which we today consider 'normal' consumption is in fact a social construct which has become established through time, varies across places and applies to different subjects and objects in different ways. We only have to think of the history of tobacco, a colonial commodity which early on, at the beginning of the 17th century, became one of the first global mass luxuries. To spread to the West as a consumer good, tobacco had to distance itself from the ritual intoxication which was its normal use amongst the indigenous American cultures from which it came, and re-make itself on the model of bourgeois sobriety and efficient individualism which epitomized the diffusion of pre-packaged cigarettes (Hughes 2003; Schudson 1984). If today tobacco consumption is seen, mostly in the Anglo-American world, as an unhealthy vice and even as a genuine disease of will for women and young people in particular, we have to remember that back in the 1940s it was being recommended by doctors and was seen as an indisputable sign of masculine power which women began to use to signal their social progress. The knowledge of the geographical and historical boundaries of normality should not make us forget that, in our own culture, there still exists a hegemonic vision of what is 'wrong' and what is 'right' to consume, and how this is to be 'normally' done. The very linguistic choice which is expressed in the label 'consumer society' or 'consumer culture' implies at once a subjectivity, which is then open to dispute. This normative vision is the expression of dominant cultural forces, even though it can be articulated by disadvantaged groups; it is interconnected with the legal configuration of the market, even though it is not reducible to it. Its normative quality is apparent in that it stresses consumer choice while defining manners and boundaries of choice. In particular, it portrays consumers as looking for personal satisfaction but doesn't allow them to fall into excess or dependency. Scratching under the surface of that universalistic abstraction which the label 'consumer' adumbrates, we may notice that the demonstration of autonomy and self-control appears more or less credible according not only to the goods and the context of consumption, but also to the social attributes (of class, gender, age, sexuality, ethnicity, etc.) of the subject who consumes. And all this is mediated by various forms of representation which provide symbolic support to the association of 'normality' with certain consumer identities. In other words, in consumer culture, as in most other social phenomena, the politics of normality, the politics of difference and the politics of representation intersect, reinforcing marginality but also opening contradictory spaces for change.

A fourth dimension of power has to do with the systemic and often unintended effects produced by consumer practices in other spheres of action. I may call this dimension the *politics of effects*. Of course, when they consume an object, people in contemporary Western societies essentially engage with the process of commoditization (i.e. with the translation of objects and services into commodities, exchangeable on the market through money), and they make use of meanings produced and reverberated by the promotional industry, advertising in particular. Nevertheless, consumption may work as a process of *de-commoditization* (see Appadurai, ed. 1986a; De Certeau 1984; Miller 1987). By de-commoditization I indicate the re-translation of the meanings and uses of commodities through daily life, on the basis of needs that are not directly reducible to those of production, retail or promotion even if they are not entirely free and are anything but individual. Conceived as de-commoditization, consumption is however not only different from and irreducible to production and retail, but also *asymmetrical* to these other spheres of action. This opens the space for power effects, techniques and strategies of different sorts, including the global division of labour (with consumerist nations consuming a disproportionate share of global produce) and environmental effects.

In this last part of the book, consumption is considered as a *context of reframing* (Goffman 1974) whereby goods are '*keyed*' as other than commodities: through a variety of de-commoditization practices social actors enter into a dialogue with the market, and even battle against it, to appropriate standardized commodities and to transform them into goods with personal meaning. Only in this way can consumers use commodities to construct their identities, without themselves being reduced to a commodity. For example, the pervasive allure of connoisseurship may be seen as having to do with mastering objects and demonstrating aestheticized detachment from them: by piling up a complex repertoire of knowledge, the connoisseur finds a way to get close to commodities while distancing him or herself from their immediate hold. Similar paradoxical constructions may be found on a rather larger scale in consumer culture: for example, the globalization of commodities has brought forth a contrary movement of the localization of consumption. In contrast to standard belief, there are in fact few really global commodities because businesses adapt products, often with slight variations, to different sales conditions. Furthermore, even with global commodities like Barbie, Coca-Cola and the Big Mac, it is the local context of consumption which, so to speak, finishes up commodities and their meanings. Still, the creation of authentic experiences by consumers in local contexts is not simply a process of liberation. Resistance in the face of the standardization and globalization of commodities often causes people to rely on other forms of social control: gender differences rooted in intimate relationships, ethnic differences reproduced by local traditions, generational conflicts established by youth subcultures, and so forth. What is more, the local appropriation of global commodities may alter their meanings and usages, but may leave the global commodity flows which sustain them somewhat unchanged. A growing demand for 'ethical' products in the form of fairtrade goods, an awareness of ecological side-effects testified by the spread of green produce, a desire for transparency in the commodity chain met by the growth of protocols for responsible business, all seem to respond to this. As we shall see, these phenomena bestow a distinctively political function on consumers, yet it is still arguable to what extent they can work as perfect substitutes for political action as such and indeed how challenging this may be for the present socio-economic order.

Representations and
Consumerism

6

Consumption has usually been envisioned through extreme rhetorical tropes, both *anti-consumerist* and *pro-consumerist*. Newspapers frequently carry critiques against 'consumerism', peppered with hyperbolic images and passionate moralism. Consumption is criticized as the incarnation of the vices of our era fuelled by the advertising industry: materialism, superficiality, hedonism, dissatisfaction, massification, bad taste, and even personality disorders. Indeed, often it is what consumption does to individual identity which is criticized and it is the fear that the self might become simply a 'consumer' anxiously seeking refuge in superfluous objects which is dreaded. This, it is said, would destroy society, culture, refinement: all collective goods would be swallowed up by illusory private gratification. However, a chorus of voices has countered this rhetoric, not least the advertising industry itself, which celebrates commodities and consumption as opportunities for self-realization and happiness for all.

Advertising industries occupy an important mediating position between consumption and production, art and commodities, materiality and symbolic forms. Commercial advertisements can indeed be considered one of the dominant cultural forms of contemporary capitalist societies. Even if it is up to consumers to de-codify, select, and translate into their realities the meanings promoted by advertising, it is difficult for them to ignore advertising's messages, including those they may consider embarrassing or offending. If the public is fascinated or offended, it is because, in trying to accomplish its commercial function, advertising often finds itself performing an ideological function. For instance, advertising uses different visions of masculinity and femininity only to make its products more attractive, but in this way it serves to propagate – involuntarily as this might be – those different visions. The ideological function of advertising shows its ambivalence: indeed, advertising images not only promote visions of identity, the family, gender, race, etc. which serve to reproduce cultural hierarchies and consolidate social differences, but also, especially with the development of increasingly diverse niche markets, they provide a space for minority, marginal and even subversive images to circulate widely. Likewise, advertising overall promotes consumption as a way of life, but it also accommodates a plurality of images of what consumption is and does to people and the world. These images may come to reflect the contested nature of commercialization and new visions of the consumer.

The anti-consumerist rhetoric and the apology of consumption

Voices from a range of quarters have rallied to stigmatize consumption, casting it as a source of moral disorder, a soul-corrupting mirage. Given the role of consumption in American history, it might not be surprising that American intellectuals have often been particularly vocal supporters of the *anti-consumerist rhetoric*.[1] According to this rhetoric, consumption – depreciated in its modern guise as 'consumerism' or 'consumer culture' – gave birth to spiritual impoverishment for which people sought comfort in material goods, a surrogate for traditional forms of satisfaction, self-realization and identification through work and political participation. Daniel Bell (1976) in *The Cultural Contradictions of Capitalism*, and Christopher Lasch (1979) in his famous book, *The Culture of Narcissism*, considered that the sphere of consumption was organized according to principles radically opposed to those of production, and gave way to the formation of a series of unhealthy and profoundly pathological cultural contradictions.

Through a pessimistic reading of David Riesman's (1961) observations on the other-directed personality, Lasch (1991, orig. 1979) maintains that the collapse of the public sphere and the bureaucratization of work combined to form a 'consumer culture' which promoted a 'narcissist personality type'. The *narcissist* is so obsessed by his or her own needs that he only sees others in relation to himself. In consumer culture, identity formation is no longer based on stable ideals maintained by the traditional family, but on the possibility of 'presenting' a convincing 'saleable' image of the self. In this perspective, where the ascetic culture of production favours the development of strong personalities attached to duties and to the family, consumer culture favours the development of weak and isolated personalities, who continually search for gratification in objects and who are fated to be continually deluded: the pleasures which they are desperately seeking out to fill their 'empty interior' are in fact a form of 'aggression' which holds nothing sacred but reduces all to a commodity, an object interchangeable with other objects. According to Lasch, the culture of commodities that enters the home and transforms everyone into isolated consumers is a constant source of dissatisfaction. In his view, '[t]he best defences against the terrors of existence are the homely comforts of love, work, and family life, which connect us to a world that is independent of our wishes yet responsive to our needs' (*ibid*, 248). Thus, consumption is positive only if it is functional to production; otherwise it becomes a threat where it turns in on itself and away from the rules of the traditional family.

The identification of a schizoid splitting of culture within modern capitalism is a recurrent theme in academic literature and public discourse, and it has been taken up again by the American feminist Susan Bordo (1993). Bordo maintains that the contemporary self is constructed around *contradictory demands*: to incorporate the discipline of the work ethic and to consume as many goods as possible, surrendering oneself to immediate enjoyment. In her view, the regulation of desire becomes a constant problem because subjects find themselves besieged by temptation and condemned if they indulge:

On the one hand, as producers of goods and services we must sublimate, delay, repress desires for immediate gratification; we must cultivate the work ethic. On the other hand, as consumers we must display a boundless capacity to capitulate to desire and indulge in impulse; we must hunger for constant and immediate satisfaction. (1993, 199)

For Bordo, eating disorders are a prime example of the chaos and contradiction in the regulation of desires caused by consumption, something which is much harder on young women pressured to demonstrate their independence and power. She maintains that anorexia and obesity are to be seen as opposed attempts to overcome and resolve the contradictions induced by the development of a hedonistic 'consumer culture': anorexia is thus 'an extreme development of the capacity for self-denial and repression of desire (the work ethic in absolute control)'; instead, obesity is 'an extreme capacity to capitulate to desire (consumerism in control)'. As such, anorexia and obesity 'can never be tolerated by a consumer system' which is however intimately connected to pathological forms of consumption. Postulating a radical split between production and consumption, Bordo in fact ends up maintaining that 'the "correct" management of desire' requires 'a contradictory double-bind construction of personality' and produces 'an *unstable bulimic personality type* as its norm' (*ibid*, 201–2 and 187, my emphasis).

Analyses like these take seriously the idea that consumer culture produces consumers, but offer a polemical view of consumer subjectivity which does not account for the plurality and contested nature of consumption. Rather than producing a pathological consumer as its norm, consumer culture offers visions of normality and deviance which people are asked to engage with (see Chapter 7). Furthermore, they rest on a drastic opposition between the sphere of consumption and that of work and tend to affirm the functional priority and superior moral standing of production. Such a value-laden opposition spreads its roots far off in time (see Chapters 2 and 4). Indeed, whenever economic growth has opened up the availability of new consumer goods to upwardly mobile social groups or has threatened the traditional gender order, strong hostile sentiments towards material riches have emerged. These sentiments may well have a disciplining function. If it is true, as Veblen (1994, 53) insisted, that 'consumption of luxuries in the true sense is a consumption directed to the comfort of the consumer itself and it is therefore a mark of the master' then, when those who consume are all but 'masters', consumption may well elicit moral panic and social control. So it is not surprising that consumption has often been seen as a negative expression of the triumph of the modern market which weakens men, turning them into useless citizens incapable of defending their own country or participating in politics, while making women superficial and idle, unfit as wives and mothers (De Grazia and Furlough 1996; Hilton 2002; Hirschman 1977 and 1982b; Horowitz 1985; Nava 1997; Searle 1998).

As an example, let us take the first female magazine edited by a woman, *The Female Spectator*, which was published in England by Elizabeth Haywood between 1744 and 1746 with great success (Sassatelli 1997). Haywood, a writer of fairly popular novels at the time and in some ways a proto-feminist, proposed 'to check the enormous growth of luxury' for the expanding female public using examples from a female world. Whilst her magazine did not adopt a position of puritan negation of consumption, it is clear in her pages that the new possibilities of consumption introduced in England by the already booming colonial commerce appeared to be a potential danger for the wise management of business and the domestic economy. A curious example clearly demonstrates the barriers that new commodities encountered: in an edition of *The Female Spectator*, under the guise of a vexed husband, Haywood (quoted in Sassatelli 1997) denounces the immoderate use of tea as 'Debauchery no less expensive and perhaps even more pernicious...than those which the Men are generally accused of':

> the Tea-Table, as manag'd in some Families, costs more to support than would maintain two Children at Nurse. – Yet is this much the least Part of the Evil; – it is the utter Destruction of all Oeconomy, – the Bane of good Housewifry – and the source of Idleness, by engrossing those Hours which ought to be employed in an honest and prudent Endeavour to add to, and preserve what Fortune or former Industry has bestowed.

Unexpectedly perhaps, given that today we associate tea with English culture, Haywood uses the occasion to promote what at the time seemed the more traditional and more sincerely national infusions (of mint, for example), and to make this point she opposes production to consumption. Tea and its ceremony are an 'indulgence' which implies a 'loss of time and hindrance to Business'. In other words, Haywood strives to remind her readers that consumption can take the place of production, thus putting at risk the traditional forms of constructing gender and class identities.

More recently, the disgust for the voracity of the modern consumer has been articulated in a critique of the processes of *bureaucratization*, *rationalization* and *standardization*: the consumer has been depicted as someone who undergoes a senseless work routine only to get the money necessary to acquire more commodities (see the discussion of the Frankfurt School in Chapter 4). The huge growth in material culture is thus criticized as a source of disorientation and a threat to the authenticity of the self, which should be strong and autonomous, able to realize itself through its works and not through its possessions. In the words of the well-known Marxist György Lukács (1971), the growth of material culture coincides with a relentless process of 'reification' in which even people become quantifiable and fungible objects like commodities. In this way they measure themselves, and are measured, less for that which they do – or, as Erich Fromm says in his famous *To Have or to Be?* (1976), less for what they are than for what they have. This is why for authors like Lasch (1991) the consumer becomes imprisoned in a perverse circle of consumption and production. Together with Bordo (1993) and many other authors of a critical persuasion, Lasch gives advertising a propulsive role: advertising is, so to speak, the ideological engine of a system in which work has lost its meaning, to which people nevertheless remain attached because they cannot give up the dreams of well-being associated with advertised goods, dreams which will still remain a possibility for a few only.

Of course, consumption, the market and commercialization have also had their apologists. Generally, in contemporary Western societies the 'consumer', as the one who buys goods, has a positive political economic role: especially in moments of recession he or she is the last resort to keep the economy turning. That commerce and consumption are the 'wheels of the market' is an idea that extends back to the origins of modernity: attempting to account for and legitimize the new modern, capitalist and bourgeois lifestyles, liberal theories have indeed opposed critical ones and in so doing have even taken on a genuine *pro-consumerist* character (see Appleby 1978; Boltanski and Thévenot 1991; Hirschman 1977 and 1982b; Pocock 1985; see also Chapter 2). From the end of the 17th century able apologists of the free market began to claim that it was essentially a *civilizing* force which pacifies societies. The gratification of human desires through growth in personal consumption was seen as dangerous neither for the nation nor the individual. Consumption was in fact defined by its first apologists, much as it is by dominant contemporary economic theory, as 'the active seeking of personal gratification through material goods' (Appleby 1993, 164). Since humans are essentially defined as rational animals with infinite and undefined desires who have been able to guide the economy of nations to unimagined levels of prosperity, great care must be taken in ensuring that this gratification is authentic. This generates pressure to stress the autonomy of the consumer which, as shown in discussing economic theory (see Chapter 3), culminates in a somewhat acritical notion of consumer sovereignty. The idea of the sovereignty of the consumer has found numerous supporters far outside the science of economics, above all in marketing and commercial advertising, institutions which have had an important role in promoting consumption as an arena of meaningful and legitimate action.

Whatever its social effects, advertising surely has a privileged role in articulating messages which, for all their different contents, call upon consumers as sovereign actors, free to express themselves through consumption. Commercial advertising associates a series of positive individual aspirations with consumption: happiness, sociability, youthfulness, enjoyment, friendship, eroticism, etc. A large number of products – even the most banal and ordinary, from electric razors to cornflakes, from sanitary pads to washing powder – are associated with (sometimes extravagant) images of self-realization. Advertising often tries to relieve the consumer of that residual sense of guilt that flickers every now and then when the image of consumption is darkened by vanity and egoism. This is why a multinational cosmetics producer like L'Oréal puts out a series of television adverts in which celebrities use increasingly sophisticated hair products while pronouncing a claim which has been extraordinarily successful: 'because I'm worth it'. If sometimes consumption is still represented as functional to work discipline (for instance, just think of advertising for food supplements), more often it has reached such cultural legitimacy as to be portrayed as a meaningful behaviour in and of itself. As a result the emphasis may even switch from production to consumption. For example, in some adverts which reproduce scenes of office life, the moment of consumption is represented as a possible escape from the boredom and tiredness of work: it is a distraction and an amusement that people rightly allow themselves not so that they can work better, but to compensate themselves for the routine of work. And in this moment of subversion, all of those connotations (eroticism, excitement, fantasy, etc.) that have been forcefully banished from working life are allowed back in. This is the case, to give just one example, in a successful Coca-Cola television advert shot in an office entirely peopled with young women anxiously waiting for their break when, from the window, their eyes fall upon the rippling muscles of a young builder who is finally able, in his own break, to enjoy his can.

Advertising discourse is, in its tones, styles and objectives, incommensurable with the discourses of economic theory, moral philosophy or social criticism. Yet,

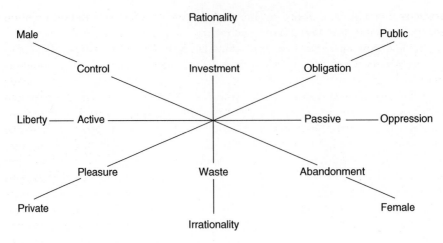

Figure 6.1   The order of discourse about consumption

to various degrees all of the discourses on consumption, even those providing a considered scientific view, run the risk of falling into celebration or censorship, yielding to a series of *binary oppositions* which trap us in dichotomous thought (see Figure 6.1). Primary binary oppositions such as public/private, rational/ irrational, male/female, and of course freedom/oppression are all laminated with further dualities and form chains of meanings which solidify into a compelling order.

These chains of oppositions have also been supported by a number of *metaphors* that have been used across time to express anxieties about consumption, or more simply to describe it.[2] For example, the concerns generated by the growth of the female presence on the public scene at the turn of the 19th century have led to likening women with the 'mob', with women portrayed as an irrational, sexually aggressive and voracious mass taking the public sphere of the department store by storm (Hilton 2002; Huyssen 1986; Kutcha 1996; Nava 1997). The eating metaphor is still crucial today in the representation of women as 'irrational' consumers needing tutelage of some kind lest their desires be overwhelming (Bordo 1993). The main metaphorical systems which currently help people visualize, figure and judge their consumer practices as well as the place of consumption in contemporary culture have recently been discussed by Richard Wilk (2004). The 'life-cycle' metaphor which is widely used in economics invites us to think that consumption is 'like senility, loss of energy, decline of value'; the 'consumption-as-burning' metaphor suggests that consumption is like 'fire' and that 'the rich consume more than the poor because they have more fuel'; the 'consumption-as-eating metaphor' considers the human being as 'driven by desires' and puts it at the centre of the world 'with the impersonal forces of the economy and nature providing the fuel and carting away the waste' (*ibid*, 14–17). Insisting that the eating metaphor works as a 'prototype' so that 'the more an act is like eating the more it seems like real consumption', Wilk shows that the often implicit association between consumption and eating is misleading. It may be detrimental to both an understanding of consumer practices (especially those involving durables, collective and cultural goods) and the pursuit of innovative ideals of consumption (of the environmental variety, for example).

All in all, contemporary scholars of consumption should be aware of the binary oppositions implicit in their language and metaphors, to avoid that evaluative pendulum which makes consumer culture into a 'fetish concept', a ready-made jargon rather than an object of study. In his *Apocalypse Postponed*, Umberto Eco (1994, 17 and 20, orig. 1964), defines a 'fetish concept' as a 'generic concept', utilized either as 'targets for fruitless polemic' or 'for commercial operations which we ourselves consume on a daily basis'; an instrument which has 'a particular ability to obstruct argument, strait-jacketing discussion in emotional reaction', being either a total rejection or an unconditional apology. Eco reproaches both apocalyptic and celebratory attitudes for 'never really attempting a concrete study of products and how they are actually consumed' (*ibid*, 25). Both offer a totalitarian position, which has the attraction of denying ground to alternative visions. Brought back to our concerns, pessimistic and apocalyptic approaches as well as optimistic and apologetic ones can indeed be seen as two different but complementary ways of consoling consumers, letting them catch a glimpse of worlds where absolute liberty exists and can be delivered through prescriptions as apparently simple as total rejection or total acceptance.

Apocalyptic views remove consumption from the web of social relations to criticize its social impact. Let us take Bordo's (1993) observations on the relationship between consumer culture and eating disorders as an example. It is undoubtedly true that contemporary culture as a whole contains contradictory demands, and it is also true that eating disorders emerge as a typical female problem in opulent societies.[3] It is also true that production and consumption have been normatively constructed as separated and different spheres of action. Nevertheless, it is rather misleading to consider contemporary consumer culture as the carrier of contradictions previously non-existent. What is more, in Bordo's book, as in many others whose focus ultimately lies elsewhere, the notion of consumer culture itself is extremely vague. When qualified, it is reduced to advertising images and marked by a host of negative associations which rarely account for what consumers do on a daily basis: it is precisely in such fetishized form that it works as a rhetorical artifice. However, the characterization of consumer culture as totally opposed to work, as ruled by a 'consuming passion' from which 'all inclinations towards balance, moderation, rationality, and foresight have been excluded', so much so that the subjects find themselves 'conditioned to lose control at the mere sight of desirable products' (*ibid*, 201), is a caricature. Such a 'consuming passion' should make people into rather dangerous consumers – just think of the very places of consumption like department stores, supermarkets or shopping centres which are constructed to invite purchase rather than robbery. To consume is not to abandon oneself to desire, but to accomplish some kind of value attribution, demonstrating a certain dose of self-discipline. Even when it is expressed in forms where emotions appear to run free and bodily desires appear to take over, it still involves the learning of certain meanings and the respect of certain rules – as demonstrated by the long learning process by which young people succeed together in gaining pleasure from marijuana smoking (Becker 1963), the elaborate rituals of emotional de-controlling which football fans celebrate in the stadium (Elias and Dunning

1986), or the close social managing of space and personal identity which even the wildest nights in a disco require (Malbon 1997).

If instead, with contemporary eyes, we try and examine Eliza Haywood's pre-occupations with the consumption of tea, we cannot help but be surprised: how could one think that tea was 'pernicious'? And, is this not the English beverage *par excellence*? Undoubtedly it is, now. But this is so because the process of commodity appropriation took a particular path over history: tea was adopted by all sorts of English men and women, its oriental provenance was transfigured by the consolidation of a colonial order and, through elaborated rituals of courteous sociability, it became an integral part of British culture uniting amongst others the mother country with her colonial possessions, India in particular. Certainly, while they do not provide an accurate diagnosis of tea consumption, Haywood's words testify to the fact that the historical sedimentation of tea in English culture was a contested matter, with stiff ritual discipline and the policy of meaning still being at the forefront in Victorian times (Rappaport 2006). On the whole, this example enables us to temper those critical views which lament that traditional values and customs have been slowly disappearing as ever growing portions of daily life have been drawn into the orbit of the market and have to face commercial processes. Yet the example of tea shows very well that national traditions are – to borrow Hobsbawm's phrase (Hobsbawm and Ranger 1983) – invented. Many of these traditions involve consumption, and the market, as well as the state, can give them a hand. In the specific case of tea, this became a constitutive part of the British bourgeois family's drawing room, furnishing a series of practical means and occasions that were useful in the small daily battles which defined what was appropriate for a family, and what role men and women, rest and work, etc., should have in it (Mennell 1996; Rappaport 2006).

On the other side of the fence, *apologetic views* of consumption are surprisingly blind to the social limits of consumption. Taking for granted that consumption is a sphere of self-realization as such, they divert attention from the fact that, in contrast to liberal and neo-liberal slogans, the common good doesn't automatically spring forth from the pursuit of individual interests (see also Chapter 8). Against such a celebratory stance, in his well-known work *The Social Limits of Growth* (1977) Fred Hirsch showed that the democratization of luxuries and superfluous goods which mark status may become a dangerous and pointless game. Only recently has the great majority of the population had access to this 'positional' kind of consumption which was previously reserved only for privileged groups. The opening up of the possibility of competition within the field of consumption for the majority of the population has not, however, cancelled out social differences: for whilst the least favoured groups now consume to display, their relative positions have yet to change. This also has the complex effect of heating up demand, leading to strong social and economic instability, as well as dangerous effects on the environment. In other words, if not tempered by egalitarian views or checked by redistributive policies, the opening up of the competition in consumption does not bring forth a real democratization of luxuries, while producing a number of unwanted externalities.

Indeed, the emphasis on consumer sovereignty, on private consumption and individual satisfaction has tended to blind us to the role of what Manuel Castells (1977) has called 'collective consumption', that is consumption of public services provided by the state or political institutions to the whole population. Of course, after the crisis of the welfare system, it is easy to fall into the illusion that everything can be privatized with excellent results in terms of economic efficiency. Nevertheless there are many who still emphasize that certain goods, those which amount to the perceived minimum necessities in a given society (from water and roads, to education and health), cannot be efficiently produced, distributed and consumed through the mechanisms of the market alone, which in the long term generate strong economic inefficiencies (Sen 1977; 1985). Indeed, as noticed when criticizing neoclassical consumer sovereignty, the differences in economic, social and cultural resources between the members of the West's populations, and even more so between Western and developing countries, are so marked that they may put the efficiency and legitimacy of the free market under stress. To be sure, market relations thrive among equals, and indeed the market requires a heavily pacified social space to realize itself. The idea that everyone in consumer societies is much freer to acquire the lifestyle and identity he or she desires runs the risk of painting an imaginary world, made of equal opportunity and free self-realization. Instead, it is clear, even through observing advertisements which celebrate consumption as a sphere of human realization, that only a certain type of identity, a certain type of look, a particular way of being in the world and, obviously, only certain commodities are acknowledged as plainly positive, and that they all demand growing shares of economic and cultural capital.

A final note may be added on the all too direct relationship between consumption and happiness postulated by neo-liberals in particular. A growing number of voices both without and within the academy – from Tibor Scitovsky's *The Joyless Economy* (1992) to Gary Cross's *An All-Consuming Century* (2000) – are stressing that the growth of material culture does not automatically translate into more happiness. In particular, as early as the late 1950s Scitovsky asked what was the price of economic progress, suggesting that economic growth in the West has provided genuine gains in living standards, but these have not translated into leisure time; on the contrary it is especially the pursuit of creative activities – which is at once time intensive and less dependent on standardized commodities – that appears to be squeezed by the logic of market expansion (Bianchi 2003). Today, there is a growing body of literature in philosophy and the social sciences which pinpoints that people's well-being could be reformulated on grounds other than increasing expenditure, starting from notions of 'quality of life' which will often thicken up a short-term, individualist and private vision of individual choice with environmental or communitarian content (Nussbaum and Sen 1993). This may imply, as in the case of a small but increasing section of the American middle class, some form of 'voluntary simplicity' or 'downshifting' in consumption (Etzioni 1998; Schor 1999): the rejection of upscale spending and long working hours in order to live a simpler, more relaxed life and to enhance personal satisfaction, socio-economic equality and environmental awareness.

Advertising cultures and their languages

The swing of the pendulum between apology and criticism appears to have a *generative role* within consumer culture, as may be noticed in relation to the *ambivalence of advertising*. Both advertising *position* and *functions* are ambivalent.

The advertising world and professions occupy an *intermediate position*, between production and consumption, commodities and art, materiality and symbolic forms. The way this intermediate position is lived out by advertising people is crucial in defining their professional cultures which, in turn, shape the image of consumption and of consumers they propose. Marketing and advertising operators filter the opportunities of the market and construct promotional strategies through a variety of 'cultures of production' (Du Gay et al. 1997). A number of studies help to overcome the image of the advertiser as an all-powerful 'brainwasher' or creative 'genius', showing that the world of ads is socially and culturally embedded in wider cultures of consumption and in specific professional cultures (Cronin 2004; Kawashima 2006; Nava et al. 1997; Nixon 2003; Soar 2000). Advertising worlds may function as melting pots and resonance boxes for complex flows of knowledge, including academic, expert and folk discourses on consumption. For example, it may be suggested that the *emphasis on the active consumer* paramount in contemporary academic theories of consumption partly *reflects* and *is generated* by new consumer identities. The latter both emerge from grassroots social processes, and are mobilized by the need of 'creative' advertising for equally 'creative' consumers. The vision of creativity promoted by this industry is 'inclusivist' rather than 'exclusivist': it broadens the semantic reach of creativity to claim it for both itself and a larger set of activities, which include consumption and consumers' reading of ads (Nixon 2003).

As suggested, advertising has occupied an important place within the accounts of the emergence of consumer culture as it appears coterminous with the rise of a 'promotional culture' which focuses on sales (see Wernick 1991; Chapters 1 and 2). Even though it is just a part of the culture of market societies, commercial advertising[4] has often been identified as its most characteristic trait. The mutual specialization of institutions of both production and consumption implies that the agencies devoted to the commercialization and promotion of goods must also intensify and specialize their activities, thus becoming more visible (Jhally 1987; Leiss et al 1991; McCracken 1988). In particular the spread of commercial messages that are increasingly less *factual* and ever more *evocative* is often seen as at the root of the diffusion of consumerism. The advertising industry is now considerable, but in the cities of the second half of the 17th century, especially in England, there were already newspapers entirely dedicated to advertisements. In this period, when the producer and consumer were no longer in direct contact and the press was beginning to establish itself as the first vehicle for large-scale dissemination of promotional images and texts, advertisements typically had a factual tone. They invited the public to consider the existence of a given product, without specifying exactly what purpose it served, which needs it might satisfy, in which contexts it could be used and for whom it was most suitable. Adverts didn't construct articulated and complex universes of meaning to present products: the products were, so to speak, naked. As Marshall McLuhan (1967) suggests, the tendency in the development of advertising has been to show the product as an integral part of wider social and cultural processes. In this way advertising has moved from a referential form, focused principally on the product, to a contextual one in which the product is symbolically charged and inserted in wider lifestyles (Hennion and Méadel 1989; Leiss et al. 1991). These represented lifestyles can act as 'totems' to consumers, so that the visual sign or picture stands as representing the collective understanding of oneself and society and acts as a call to join an affective, imaginary community.

Despite the different products advertised, the different media used, and the different cultures these companies work in, contemporary advertising appears to have its own particular language. By and large contemporary advertisements oscillate between the openly persuasive promotion of sales and the exploitation of the *metaphoric* possibilities in visual and verbal language, associating symbols and translating their meaning. The latter is particularly evident in branding-advertising which has acquired salience in certain periods and cultural contexts, such as Britain and the US in the 1990s. To consider the language of ads, in his *Mythologies* (1972) Roland Barthes adopted a semiotic approach deriving from the linguistics of Ferdinand de Saussure and considered elements of culture as if they were elements in a language, showing that advertising works by using the logic of the 'myth': a particular 'signifier' is transliterated to signify something different from its literal meaning. The image of a rose, which above all signifies the whole of the 'rose' flower, can allude to other things such as 'love', 'passion', 'desire', etc. One or more of these 'mythic' meanings is used in the formation of advertisements, in association with other signs which will benefit from that association, 'stealing' a little of its evocative capacity: that is why a box of chocolates cunningly presented with a rose can easily connote a perfect gift for a lover on Valentine's Day. To this end Judith Williamson (1978, 20–39) proposed a particularly clear example: a print advert of the famous French perfume Chanel No. 5 next to Catherine Deneuve. Even if there is no inherent connection between the perfume and the French actress, the simple fact that they find themselves juxtaposed in the same image pushes one to imagine that they are in some way connected. And the characteristics of Deneuve, who according to the dominant canon of female beauty represents a classic and elegant French beauty, are thus ceded to the perfume. This simple juxtaposition gives the perfume's image a new emotive cast; it becomes saturated with the famous actress's Parisian charm to the extent that over time the product itself evokes these very meanings.

By and large, symbolic associations are primary resources for the process of commercialization. The phenomenon of *brands*, for example, functions in a similar way to the 'myth': the brand is not only the name of a product or a company, it is a symbol which evokes a series of meanings which serve as an interpretive and emotional frame (Goldman and Papson 1998; Holt 2002; Lury 2004). Some brand-symbols have become self-referential signs, a good example being the fashion of tattooing oneself with the Nike swoosh; others have in some ways taken the place of the product, such as Sony and Tampax being synonymous with the Walkman and with tampons.[5] This doesn't necessarily mean that brands replace products; yet they may become quite independent from products. Just as today there is a healthy market in old biscuit tins of long-dead brands, we can imagine a future in which some of today's dominant brands will no longer correspond with actual products, but only with images that will be sold and put back into circulation for their decorative or nostalgic value. Thus, brands have become a global language as Naomi Klein (2001) has polemically put it in her likewise global bestseller, but consumers continue to buy products and services, and the ways these are consumed are, as we shall see more clearly in the last chapter, always mediated by a variety of different socially embedded local realities. More generally, symbolic associations tell us that the various parts of an advertisement function together as a language, but this doesn't explain why advertising executives have chosen these particular associations, nor how consumers read the advert and why they may do so (Campbell 1997a). In order to do this we need to bear in mind the contexts of both production and consumption of adverts (Cronin 2004; Kawashima 2006; Leiss et al. 1991; Leslie 1995; Nava et al. 1997; Nixon 2003; Soar 2000).

In considering the *advertising industry* we should emphasize that, while the process of advertising production is highly structured, the various professionals within an agency negotiate between each other a complex set of tasks. In doing so they deploy different types of formal knowledge as well as personal cultural resources. Their professional aim is to create the most convincing message for the manufacturing company as much as the public. All in all, no matter how much effort is put into constructing an image of the targeted audience, the manufacturing company is indeed the real client of an advertising agency. Recent works on the organization of advertising agencies in Britain and the US show that advertisers' self-understanding, expertise and practices are geared to the agencies' *imperative for self-promotion* in competitive markets (Cronin 2004; Soar 2000). Drawing on Bourdieu's observations on 'cultural intermediaries', Matthew Soar's (2000) research also shows that the *first audience* which advertising 'creatives' have in mind is *themselves* (see also Nixon 2003). This finding needs to be qualified as the structure of the advertising market may have an effect on the degree of autonomy of advertising agencies, which in turn has an impact on their products (the advertising texts). A recent comparative study of advertising agencies in the UK and Japan shows that the 'creativity' attributed to British ads is to be traced back to the variety of small agencies which populate the industry and the fact that competition among agencies for clients happens mostly through 'branding' messages and creative ideas rather than control of media buying (Kawashima 2006). On the contrary, the organization of the advertising market in Japan, which is heavily dependent on monopolistic control of media space by a few advertising agencies, seems to favour more direct and blunt 'sales' messages and the use of famous testimonials.

To be sure, the metaphoric potential of advertising language is realized in different ways according to the institutional context of advertising production, the specific professional cultures of advertisers, and the wider cultures of consumption which are mobilized. Flows of knowledge are important factors in the process. Looking into the workings of the Tavistock Institute in post-war England, Peter Miller and Nicholas Rose (1997) have shown how market researchers were influenced (both enabled and constrained) by psychological views of the subject-consumer which entailed a meticulous charting of the consuming passions using new techniques of group discussion, interviewing and testing. On the basis of such knowledge, they attempted to mobilize consumers' purchases by negotiating a view of the rational consumer and forging, via advertising, intimate symbolic connections between specific product attributes and human passions and identities (like the texture of a softer toilet paper and the desire for middle-class comfort, or the flavour of a sweeter chocolate and the female longing for more pleasing family relationships). Sean Nixon's (2003) study of the experiences, attributes and cultures of 'creative' people (art directors and copywriters) working for

London-based agencies shows that not only formal knowledge of the target groups influences the construction of ads, but also informal knowledge possessed by practitioners. This knowledge is often related to 'creatives' themselves being consumers of certain goods and services and, more broadly, being *culturally close* to the target consumer. Nixon deals with the 'new lad' and the 'new man' portrayed by much recent British commercial advertising, and respectively characterized by an openness to pleasures previously marked as taboo for men, and by a partial loosening of the binary codes that regulate the relationships between the sexes as well as heterosexual and homosexual masculinities. These new masculinities matched the gender identities of the advertising people analysed. Also through the mediation of advertising gender cultures, 'style and lifestyle products aimed at young men offered the scope for the development of a more image-led form of advertising, upon which the industry's reputation for "creativity" often rested' (*ibid*, 8). While Nixon's work does not come full circle, exploring the advertising texts and their reception, in a different context, the deep interplay between advertising cultures and consumer cultures has been addressed by Arlene Davila's (2001) study of the commercial construction of Latino identities in the US. Based on interviews with Latino marketing professionals and focus groups with a cross-section of Latino consumers, Davila shows that both Latino consumers and professionals respond to the attitudes they encounter in the larger American society, partly resisting ethnic stereotyping, partly contributing to it.

Advertising and marketing have a history which is intertwined with the history of consumer cultures. Advertising and marketing can be seen both as expert discourses which have contested disciplining effects on people, and as institutionally embedded professional cultures which dynamically respond to larger cultural trends. Rachel Bowlby has suggested that a large part of early marketing had its roots in Freudian psychoanalysis in its attention to conscious and unconscious impulses towards life, pleasure and death (Bolwby 1993, 5 ff., see also Cochoy 1999; Miller and Rose 1997). More prosaically, when marketing was born in the United States at the beginning of the 20th century, the model of the consumer was that of someone trying to keep up with the neighbours or the stereotypical Joneses, and who considered 'first impressions' of utmost importance (Ewen 1976; Lears 1983; 1994; Marchand 1985). In his *Captains of Consciousness* Stuart Ewen (1976) has maintained that in order to create demand, advertising made the most of the feelings of inadequacy that characterized many American citizens, people who were often social climbers, uprooted from their culture of origin, recently urbanized and feeling the weight of judgement more keenly than others. Ewen gives us some examples of the terms used to make consumers feel 'inadequate' and, at the same time, to suggest how those 'inadequacies' could be 'overcome' by particular goods: 'ashtray breath' could be masked by a tasty mint, a 'pungent armpit' by a perfumed deodorant. Whilst Ewen's aim was that of unmasking a sales strategy founded on an attempt to instil insecurity, it is clear that the emphasis on conformity and belonging was justified at the time by the necessity of creating a population of consumers corresponding to mass production, flattening the cultural heterogeneity typical of a country founded on the continuous immigration of different populations. The adverts of the time were thus both heralds and examples of that 'American Way of Life' which created banal forms of nationalism above all through a style of consumption (Lears 1983; 1994; Marchand 1985).

Today, whilst on the one hand advertising rarely promotes an idea of conformity, on the other it implies that competitive emulation of film stars and the wealthiest is possible. Indeed, as Thomas Frank (1997) has suggested, considering the links between the advertising industry and the 1960s counterculture in the US, fantasy and creativity, rebellion and non-conformity have become essential elements of the American culture of advertising production. Difference and eccentricity feature prominently in contemporary ads all around the world. For example in Italy, Chinotto – Italy's indigenous soft drink that has largely been supplanted by Coca-Cola and Pepsi – has gradually been regaining mass popularity through exploiting its marginality and attempting, in a period in which local gastronomic traditions are being recuperated, to build itself an original and eccentric image with the slogan: 'Drink out of the mob'. Even when it milks feelings of national belonging, contemporary advertising rarely falls in love with militant nationalism, and when it exploits people's insecurities it rarely points the finger at the consumer, and if it does so this is almost always tongue-in-cheek. The general tendency is to attract attention through presenting positive and joyful images: thus, rather than allude to the potential failings of the consumer, advertising exalts his or her potential. Even this, though, is typically done using allusive, elusive and ironic tones, indirectly evoking a lifestyle, an identity, an attachment (Goldman and Papson 1996). These advertising modes of address call forth and respond to new aesthetic sensibilities and intellectual capacities among consumers, in particular the cultured middle classes. Indeed, contrary to most catastrophic expectations, growing segments of the public have become more critical and more aware of the media's powers of persuasion. Marketing and advertising are thus trying to respond to such sensibilities – which includes making the most of critical or alternative orientations such as green lifestyles, the critique of branding, the recycling phenomenon, or that of the voluntary reduction of consumption (Drumright 1994; Leonard-Barton 1981; Zinkhan and Carlson 1995).

Indeed, provided the relationship between production and consumption through the promotional system is best conceived of as interactive, advertising has to attempt to take account of, and still seduce, a consumer who is well aware of the critique of mass society and consumption, as Ien Ang (1985) has shown in her well-known study on the public of *Dallas*, the famous American series of the 1970s. The spectators studied by Ang appeared rather conscious of the elitist rhetoric stigmatizing their preferences.[6] They felt it necessary to justify themselves, either choosing a 'populist' rhetoric (claiming that the pleasure offered by the programme was equal to more refined pleasures), or more often an 'ironic' attitude (claiming that they viewed the programme as a comedy rather than a melodrama) and even a 'knowing' one (affirming that they were aware of both its dangers and pleasures). Similar forms of reflexivity can be pre-empted by advertising (Littler 2005; Sassatelli 2001a). This is what occurred with the cosmetics firm the Body Shop. The Body Shop advertisements have counted on three factors dissonant with the meanings that normally characterize cosmetics ads. While conventional cosmetic ads sell 'hope in a jar' (Peiss 1998), the Body Shop has relied on irony, the moralization of consumption through a concern for animal rights and a critique of mass consumption, de-fetishization through reference to fair trade, natural ingredients and a *mise-en-scène* of the productive process.[7] In a well-known campaign, the Body Shop invited all women to consider that only a few of them might ever resemble the standard supermodel of contemporary advertising. However, each woman could allow herself the pleasure of a cream, even if she was a little tubby, and regardless of the fact that no cream could or would remove the signs of age-ing from her face. In insisting on a relaxed authenticity, on the ability to reason with one's own head, on the possibility of having a more transparent and fair rela-tionship with the productive process, the Body Shop captured the feelings of those women who, while being socially aware, critical and perhaps feminist, did not want to renounce taking care of themselves. Thus, it put consumers' feelings and increased awareness to work to sell its products.

These observations lead us to consider how advertisements are consumed, and here I offer some broad considerations. Clearly by purchasing and using a given commodity consumers do not simply realize the symbolic associations suggested by advertisers. *Textual determinism* – that is, the idea that a text (or an object which is considered like a text by a scholar) locates readers in a given position and thus determines how it is read or used – has been heavily criticized, and rightly so. In deriving consumers' meanings from the academic interpretation of advertising texts and in treating the structures of these texts as objective, part of the semiotic theories of advertising rests on textual determinism and falls into the same manip-ulationist bias that vexed critical theory (Slater 1997) (see Chapter 4). In this view, it is worth starting from the idea that commercial advertising sells commodities to which it has juxtaposed certain meanings; it doesn't determine consumption. The advert always presents an idealized and stylized image of an object, drawing some meanings from the real world and codifying them in particular ways; it is up to the consumer then to bring these meanings back down to earth. Consumption requires that social actors bestow meanings on goods, and they do so by drawing on a vari-ety of symbolic repertoires besides those proposed by ads. Furthermore, after pur-chase consumers should use the goods, and this will involve a number of socially defined occasions and negotiations which remove commodities from their context of commercialization. Certainly advertisements can be consumed as such, in so far as they are bits of popular culture. More often, though, consumers' reading of ads is unfocused, and only loosely linked to the modes of use of the real products in daily life. In other words, I want to stress that that *reading ads* and *using goods* adumbrate quite different planes of reality, which cannot simply be inferred one from another. As suggested (see Chapter 5), consumption may be conceived as an embodied practice of appropriation: consumers not only cognitively de-codify (and thus re-interpret) the meanings of the advert relative to the objects they use; they also use the objects relative to a myriad situated practices which are structured through habits, social relationships, institutions, etc.

Ideology, social differences and consumerism

The explicit *function* of advertising is that of *selling and promoting commodities*, yet it is not quite so simple to isolate them and measure their *commercial effectiveness*. Advertising can help to consolidate the prestige of a brand and, to a lesser degree, it can initially help a new category of product penetrate the market (see Figure 6.2). Nevertheless, advertising finds it difficult to perpetuate the demand for a product that doesn't meet, at least in part, consumers' expectations. If this wasn't the case, the percentage of failed new products would not be around 40 per cent, sometimes reaching 60 per cent (Schudson 1984). The very directors of large commercial agencies underline that advertising is not a panacea for sales, and they are more prepared to sustain the high advertising costs for articles which have already proved popular. Thus, it has been suggested that the relationship between advertising and sales is anything but clear, that it is in fact difficult to determine once and for all whether it is advertising that causes sales, or vice versa (Aaker and Karman 1982; Broadbent and Coleman 1986).

The difficulty in measuring advertising's commercial effectiveness is largely down to the fact that products and services not only have to be *symbolically presented* to the public through a message, but they also have to be *materially present* for the public. They must and will, as it were, speak for themselves. The cost of advertising has grown enormously throughout the 20th century, but alongside this so have all the relative costs of the commercialization of goods, of direct marketing, packaging, promotional sales, etc.[8] In the complex promotional web that today surrounds a product, the services of an advertising agency for direct advertising campaigns are just one part, which varies greatly according to the category of product. In some cases, the success of a product may have much to do with the deployment of promotional techniques targeting producers or cultural intermediaries, such as when the Scandinavia fur breeders' organization Saga has contributed to the return of the fur-coat by persuading fashion designers of the creative potentialities of furs (Skov 2005). Often, commercial success does not appear to be down to advertising slogans alone, but to a lucky combination of various marketing ingredients along the whole chain of production and the innovative use of less explicit forms of promotion such as packaging (Cochoy 2002). Thanks to a particular retail and packaging strategy, for example, Pepsi-Cola was able to establish itself as a leading brand in Mexico, a country with a deep affection for that most American of brands, Coca-Cola: Pepsi increased its sales by 36 per cent by using coloured display units to be positioned in sales outlets, containing both the drink itself and snacks (Arnould et al. 2002). Sales promotions thus pass through some forms of advertising, but advertising is itself inserted in complex and different contexts (of production, retail and consumption) which condition its effectiveness.

Still, it is obvious that commercial advertising is not, and only occasionally pretends to be, a neutral instrument of communication. Of course, there may be no intrinsic political intent behind advertising. As Andrew Wernick (1991, 25–6) has suggested, in contrast to other institutions with similar functions of meaning circulation (churches, schools, legal and state ceremonies) the *raison d'être* of the advertising system is not that of 'socialising masses to values'; in other words, as an industry advertising may not have intrinsic interest in what the material it promotes may mean ideologically: 'it promotes to sell'. Yet, while we should be wary of assigning advertising executives themselves such a value-neutral agency, we should also be alerted to the fact that advertisements, as Wernick has illustrated, have an *ideological function*. By this, Wernick means that ads transmit ideas and circulate cultural classifications, and they do so through their own modes of speech. The *instrumental mission* of commercial communication tends to render it standardized. For all its gloss, advertising carries meanings which are widely

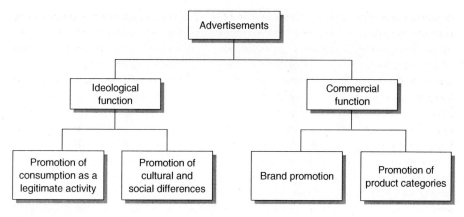

Figure 6.2 The functions of advertisements

available and easily expressible. Through advertising's translation, the symbolic forms which come from everyday cultures, the arts and even scientific imagery become codified in particular ways: adverts tend to transform even the crudest images from real life into a 'type', cleaning off all that might create confusion or contradiction. However, the metaphoric nature and the instrumental mission of advertising makes it potentially open to a host of different values, tendencies and suggestions. In other words, advertisements may come to deploy all that captures the public, while at the same time being inclined to mix everything, reconciling the opposed.

The ideological function of advertising clearly adumbrates a complex *politics of representation*, which mobilizes a variety of social identities. There are two directions in which I may situate the *ideological function* of the commercial advert (see Figure 6.2). The first regards the *relationship between advertising images and social and cultural hierarchies*. Advertising is essentially an *ambivalent* symbolic form: it can both *reproduce* the dominant socio-cultural differences and also, whilst far more rarely, support *new* cultural orientations and innovative social tendencies. This underlying ambivalence may be exemplified by looking at the representation of gender differences. In his *Gender Advertisements* (1979) Erving Goffman showed that advertising images display gender identities providing a 'hyper-ritualized' image of everyday male/female relationships as symbolized by body language, gestures, glances, etc. During the post-war years in the United States men were still represented as taller, in dominant positions, with attitudes of aggression and power; meanwhile women were smaller, in positions of humility and with submissive attitudes. Even the relationship with objects appears unequal: women caress and lightly touch objects; men hold or grasp. In some cases women simply look at an object being used by a man standing at their side. Clearly, in conveying information about commodities, images such as these also suggest the correct gender-specific way of desiring and using them. As such they appear to stabilize hierarchical distinctions between men and women. However advertising has always been host to subversive gender images, and Goffman's study itself reports various examples of 'subversion' of the standard gender codes.

It is especially from the 1970s onwards that advertising rode on the back of the wave of progressive and protest movements such as feminism, as a number of studies extending Goffman's analysis have confirmed (Belknap and Leonard 1991; King 1997; Klassen et al. 1993). While gender differences remain quite noticable, today advertising increasingly proposes innovative images: 'new men' and 'new lads' on the one hand, and, on the other, new femininities – women who play sport, who keep up with men and overtake them, strong women deeply engaged with their work, sexually active women, aggressive women who fight between themselves, and so on. Female emancipation made it necessary for advertising people to package different and non-traditional visions of femininity, and to construct women as independent and strong consumers (Wernick 1991). As suggested, especially in the 1990s new gender cultures within advertising agencies themselves have contributed to the development of new visions of masculinity (Nixon 1996; 2003). All in all, alongside hegemonic masculinity and femininity, ads have thus conveyed non-traditional images of gender to the wider public, even if only to attract the attention of a distracted spectator or to bestow the thrill of the forbidden onto a brand. These may be subversive, often marginal images, showing deviant masculinity and femininity, playing with sexual ambiguity, homosexuality, drag imagery and camp culture (Bergman 1993; Lewis and Rolley 1997).

Of course, in the final analysis even the most eccentric campaign wants to sell commodities. Therefore, different authors such as Goldman (1992) and Lasch (1991) have condemned the use of feminist images in advertising because they consider that this form of communication spoils feminism[9] as it is inherently linked to the growth in demand, considered as the single principal factor of the development of the capitalist economy. According to Lasch (1991, 74):

> The logic of demand creation requires that women smoke and drink in public, move about freely, and assert their right to happiness instead of living for others. The advertising industry thus encourages the pseudo-emancipation of women, flattering them ... and disguising the freedom as genuine autonomy. Similarly it flatters and glorifies youth in the hope of elevating young people to the status of full-fledged consumers in their own right, each with a telephone, a television set, and a hi-fi in his own room .... [This] has altered the balance of forces within the family, weakening the authority of the husband in relation to the wife and parents in relation to their children. It emancipates women and children from patriarchal authority, however, only to subject them to the new paternalism of the advertising industry, the industrial corporation, and the state.

Lasch's claims contain a barely concealed nostalgia for a traditional and patriarchal society in which only men had the possibility to consume in a righteous and blameless fashion. He likewise leaves little space for women and youth – their alternative apparently is to be either slaves of commodities, or slaves of adult men. In spite of their moralistic flamboyance, similar claims may well help us introduce the second ideological function of commercial advertising: *the promotion of consumption as a meaningful and legitimate social activity*. If today advertising messages contain contradictory images of gender, race, age, class, and so on, taken as a whole, advertising naturalizes the role of the 'consumer' as a social identity by addressing individuals as consumers and taking a consumption angle. Even if the intentions of producers and advertisers may not actually be so wide-ranging, advertising, as Lasch (*ibid*, 72) writes, 'promote[s] consumption as a way of life' and 'upholds consumption as the answer to the age-old discontents of loneliness, sickness, weariness, lack of sexual satisfaction'. It is no coincidence that a perfume of the American designer Calvin Klein was given the name Eternity.

However, this doesn't mean that advertising automatically 'produces', as Lasch argues, a consumer who is 'perpetually unsatisfied, restless, anxious and bored'. Dissatisfaction, anxiousness and boredom more often come out of real life, out of work in particular, rather than from the glossy patina presented by mass media, whose surrealist slant may be recognized quite easily. Advertising may produce frustration if taken literally because self-realization, happiness and status cannot be obtained from a billboard and buying the goods doesn't gain you access to the worlds presented as surrounding them. While the promises of ads are perhaps its greatest strength, the impossibility of advertising actually fulfilling its promises is probably its greatest weakness. The consumer is arguably increasingly aware of this fragility. Contemporary advertisements' growing resort to indirect ways of conveying a message – such as humour, irony and paradox – may be considered evidence of this. Certainly, as suggested, consumers' capacity to appreciate more complex and allusive messages may be somehow colonized by advertising. The development of 'postmodern' image-led advertising where the products disappear behind the image (as in many Benetton campaigns) has likewise being interpreted as the acknowledgement of consumers' interpretive powers and the attempt to put these powers to work for commercial ends (Morris 2005). Still, the critique of such campaigns as opportunist forms of commoditization should be placed against a wider picture. A study of the US discourse on the Benetton 'We on the death row' campaign in the so-called prestigious press, shows that this campaign was a site where ideological differences between the US and Europe were played out (Kraidy and Goeddertz 2003). The political potential of such advertisements can be seen in that the US press eagerly deployed 'commodification' as a power-ful 'frame of othering' in order to portray Benetton as the foreign 'other' and push the issue of capital punishment which was bought up by the campaign to the mar-gin of public discourse.

Finally, we must ask ourselves whether the promotion of consumption as a meaningful social activity always implies the promotion of acquisitive individ-ualism as an alternative to political action. This is what really troubles authors like Lasch (*ibid*, 73): that commercial advertising is able to commend consump-tion as an alternative to protest or political rebellion, so that '[t]he tired worker, instead of attempting to change the conditions of his work, seeks renewal in brightening his immediate surroundings with new goods and services'. Similar claims fit with the critical theory tradition which denied that the sphere of consumption can also constitute itself as a space for (different) forms of politi-cal action. Of course, commercial advertising teaches us that through commod-ity consumption (often an individualized or private activity) we can solve all problems (even social ones). In this sense, it doesn't favour traditional forms of political mobilization (linked to the factory, the party or to street protests).

Consumption however is by no means just the exercise of private egotism. A growing body of research on the new forms of political participation is documenting the political uses of a variety of consumers' actions (see Micheletti 2003; Micheletti et al. 2004; Sassatelli 2006 and Chapter 8). Increasingly, advertising has thus to take account of the development of alternative forms of consumption, such as the 'green', 'ethical' and even 'critical' varieties which characterize the consumer as a political actor. In doing so ads may come to put to work consumers' ethical and political sentiments, revealing yet again that even the image of a powerful politically-oriented consumer may be quite ambivalent.

Summary

This chapter has looked at the *cultural representation* of consumption. It has considered the opposite rhetorical tropes, both *anti-consumerist* and *pro-consumerist* which have been deployed to portray consumption. On the one hand, *apocalyptic views* remove consumption from the web of social relations only to criticize its social impact. **Lasch**'s idea that through advertising consumer culture fosters a *narcissistic* personality and **Bordo**'s idea of a *bulimic* personality which becomes the norm within consumer culture offer a one-sided, abstract reading of consumers and their practices. On the other hand, *apologetic views* of consumption are blind to the social limits of consumption, including the fact that increased expenditure does not necessarily lead to well-being and happiness. Still, the swing of the pendulum between apology and criticism appears to have a *generative* role within consumer culture, as may be seen when referring to the ambivalent position and function of advertising. Against *textual determinism*, there is an increasing awareness that by getting and using commodities consumers do not simply realize the symbolic associations suggested by advertisements. At the same time, advertising 'creatives' should not be seen against the model of the 'genius' or the 'brainwasher'. A perspective on the inner workings of the advertisements' world shows that *advertising cultures* are embedded in social relations. It offers a more sophisticated image of the *politics of representation* by rendering less opaque the relation between production and consumption. Because they are mediated by a variety of contexts of retail and use, both the *commercial function* of advertising and its *ideological function* are difficult to assess in general terms. Still, advertisements circulate cultural classifications, and they do so in a particular language. **Barthes** showed that advertising uses *metaphoric* language and symbolic associations so that it accommodates a variety of different contents, which might otherwise be conflicting. Advertising is an ambivalent phenomenon: it both reflects social hierarchies and draws on subversive images. It both promotes consumption as a way of life and comes to reflect the contested nature of commercialization.

Notes

1 Glickman (1999) considers that consumption and its political aspects are pivotal in the formation of American identities and ideologies; see also Cohen (2003), and for a comparative perspective Strasser et al. (1998). More broadly on the interface between the social identities of the citizen and the consumer see Daunton and Hilton (2001); Trentmann (2006) and Chapter 2 and 7.

2 Related issues are the referential meanings historically taken up by the word 'consumption' – which, as shown by Roy Porter (1993), especially in the 18th and 19th centuries mainly evoked the much-dreaded disease of tuberculosis – and its etymological roots. Indeed, the Latin etymology of the word 'consumption' is ambiguous and can be traced back, on the one hand, to *cum* and *sumere*, meaning 'wasting away' and, on the other, to *cum* and *summa*, meaning 'summing up', indicating either a destructive end or an augmenting completion (see Williams 1982).

3 For a discussion of anorexia as part of a long history of the secularization and medicalization of the (female) body, see Bell (1985) and Spitzack (1990).

4 Obviously there are also forms of social advertising (those which advertise public services and goods or which endorse a particular social issue), as well as political advertising. Alongside these there are also forms of counter-publicity promoted by organizations including *Adbusters*, which publishes an anti-consumerist magazine and has created ironic and desecrating campaigns against McDonald's, Calvin Klein, Benetton, and other global brands. The target of similar symbolic campaigns may be the product itself (coming clean on the process of production or stressing various externalities, from environmental effects to costs in terms of human or animal rights), the advertising imaginary which surrounds it or, more widely, consumer culture as a way of life. Overall, they promote an imagery of brand subversion which is the counterpart of the phenomenal development of branding and which deploys irony, pastiche and the carnivalesque to contest the lifestyles associated with global brands that often encode sexism, racism, homophobia, disrespect for environment and so on. For a critical perspective on *Adbusters* magazine see Littler (2005) and Rumbo (2002) and more broadly see Chapter 8.

5 Although brands have a long history, reaching as far back as the 18th century, their position as central elements of the social and economic fabric was established much more recently. Recent research suggests that it is especially from the 1980s that brands, as symbols rather than products, have become widespread cultural resources that people relate to, often dialectically, as significant components of their identities (Holt 2002). Legally, a brand is a propertied logo, and what brand owners own is the exclusive right to use the logo. Logos, in turn, are much more than visual conventions, they are 'virtual goods' and each of them may be seen as providing a cognitive and affective frame to action that 'anticipates the object that it brings into focus' (Lury 2004).

6 Further studies have confirmed and nuanced this finding, showing a great deal of variation in the reading of *Dallas* across countries (Liebes and Katz 1990).

7 The strategy of the Body Shop is also characterized by its means of communication: instead of television and women's magazines it uses its outlets, filling them with posters, cards, magazines, leaflets, etc. It has developed a well-structured website, published books on natural beauty, even managing to link publications to one of Britain's most important newspapers. The Body Shop is a good example of so-called 'ethical business', an ambiguous phenomenon for both consumers and producers (Salmon 2000). In this specific case, the emphasis on ethics has been an important marketing tool, and at the same time has made the business a favourite objective of environmentalist associations who feel it is their right to demand ever greater levels of transparency (see also Chapter 8). Labelling schemes have here a crucial and contradictory role: see Kolk and van Tulder (2002) and Micheletti et al. (2004).

8 Those who write critically about advertising stress that we consume the meanings of products more than the products themselves; instead those who sell products tend to mix what is symbolic with what is material. According to the *marketing mix* formula (Kotler 2000), adverts are only part of a larger promotion strategy which also includes public relations and institutional websites. Along with promotion strategy there is also a product strategy (packaging, for instance), a price strategy (special offers) and a place strategy (such as incentives for the seller).

9 Robert Goldman has severely judged the effect this has had on feminism. According to Goldman (1992, 131), advertising has transformed feminism into a 'fetish': it becomes 'a look' with 'object-signs' literally 'substituting' feminist aims. Whilst it may be true that advertisers may not have political intentions and that the kind of feminism (or chauvinism) which we find in some adverts is mainly a style which expresses itself through a collection of goods, it is clearly problematic to maintain that such style can 'substitute' for real life. To this point, we should notice that de-coding of advertisments' gender codes varies across countries. In Italy for example, women seem less offended by female nudity in ads than they appear to be in the American world, and more concerned with the posture and position of women relative to men (see Harper and Faccioli 2000). More broadly on feminism and consumer culture, see also Nava (1991).

7 Commodities and Consumers

Amongst the critiques of consumption the condemnation of the commodity form and the process of commoditization has probably been the most influential. The word 'commoditization' denotes a particular social construction of things: it is the social process through which things are produced and exchanged as commodities. The commoditization process is often described as enlarging: in fact, there are very few things or services that can never be sold under any circumstances. Even with those 'priceless' objects which are not for sale, such as particularly significant art works symbolizing the identity of a museum (such as Leonardo's *Mona Lisa* in the Louvre, Botticelli's *The Birth of Venus* in the Uffizi), or sacred relics (from the Turin Shroud to the Black Stone of Mecca), there is always the possibility that they could be transformed into commodities, to be ceded in a moment of absolute necessity for an enormous amount of money. Even that which at first sight seems to have no value for anyone may become a commodity. Such process of value creation has appeared so pervasive and paradoxical that literature has often dabbled in it. In his short story 'Les Repoussoirs', Emile Zola tells of a wily salesman who was able to transform ugliness into a commodity by a 'rental' service of very ugly girls who were hired for a stroll by girls who were not so ugly but not with much charm either, in order to pass themselves off as 'beauties' (Bowlby 1985). This case appeared not only grotesque but also morally dubious, as our culture rests on the antinomy between intimate or personal relations and the cash nexus, people and things. Still, what Zola does not say is that for this commercial service to be successful, the hired person had to inspire confidence and that in strolling the Parisian streets the two girls would probably end up developing a relationship which was irreducible to the monetary exchange between them.

As I shall suggest, consumption often consists in reframing the meaning and uses of material culture by translating the purely commercial value of goods into other forms of value: affection, relationships, symbolism, status, normality, etc. Contemporary consumer practices can be seen as practices of de-commoditization: diverse and varied, they all nevertheless inevitably engage with the process of commoditization which they are built upon. Likewise, as an increasingly central social identity, the 'consumer' takes up the object/subject dialectic which characterizes the constitution of modern subjectivity as normatively defined in opposition to objects, even though these serve to fix various aspects of identity itself.

Commoditization and de-commoditization

Amongst the most influential perspectives on the character of commodities, Marx's (1973, 1974) still stands out. As suggested (see Chapter 4), in Marxist theory commodities have an exchange value (price) which is the product of a situation of dominance crystallized in the capitalist means of production. Prices thus render commodities equivalent and perfectly interchangeable, subjecting them to an abstract calculation which 'masks' their real value. In this perspective, it is not by exchanging commodities nor by consuming them that people can really make the world their own: only through transforming materiality with their creative work, unconstrained by the imperatives of capitalist production, can they effectively produce real values. Thus the Marxist view not only tends to propose radically binary visions of work and consumption, but it also tends to conceive of commoditization as a totalizing form of *abstraction* from human relations and it denies that the consumer contributes to the realization of objects' values and diversity.

As Simmel (1990, 175 ff.) noted, the equivalence of commodities is due to the form of exchange, that is, money, which presents itself as a universal equivalent to be used without the inertia inherent in barter. According to Simmel, monetary exchange is associated with impersonal relationships, but these in turn function through relations of trust which are generalized and consolidated in specific institutions: for instance, the value of money is guaranteed in time and space in the central banks of various nation states. Marx's notion was that money 'masks' an underlying reality, but Simmel views money as a social relation itself, one that like credit creates a liability rather than liquidating it. Monetary transactions between individuals may appear as private affairs, purely economic and interest-driven only because the obligation of the creditor is assumed by the public which is called into being as the constituency of large financial institutions (Sassatelli 2000a).[1] From Simmel's perspective then, even in market economies economic exchange is founded on *networks of tacit agreement and trust* between buyers and sellers. Each properly conducted transaction contributes to the stabilisation of these networks.

In this perspective, no matter how much market exchanges try to shut themselves off from particularistic and subjective differences, they are, as contemporary sociology emphasizes by taking on a term of Karl Polanyi's (1957), '*embedded*' in social networks and are never reducible to the logic of price alone (see Abolafia 1998; Appadurai 1986b; Carrier 1997; Carrier and Miller 1998; Zelizer 1994).[2] Those who stigmatize commoditization often speak of markets in which people disappear, and those who celebrate them underline that the market promotes impartiality and frees individuals from personal reciprocity. However, the spread of the market simply laminates personal attachments and the tendency to trust and deploy social networks of friendship and kinship, above all to make important purchases. This is true not only in recently modernized societies like Taiwan (Lai 2001), but also in a society strongly characterized by the free market like that of the United States. As Paul Di Maggio and Hugh Louch (1998) have demonstrated, nearly 50 per cent of Americans prefer to buy their houses and cars from relations or friends, and more than 60 per cent prefer to resort to such networks in the case of legal services and domestic maintenance. Robin Leidner's (1993) study of the routinization of service work in fast food outlets shows that, despite the rigorous bureaucratization of the transaction setting, the minutie of actual interaction between serving personnel and costumers are all but irrelevant. Drawing on her fieldwork in a US McDonald's outlet, Leidner reveals not only the importance of organizational scripting of work routines and consumer transactions, but also the creative role of personal involvement which variously shades even the most fleeting encounter, obstructing or facilitating service. Indeed, rather than viewing personal involvement and social relations as 'irrational' residues, economic sociology now considers that they enable economic transactions, they may be the reason why transactions happen in the first place, and they may facilitate trust and counter risks; they may also be appropriated for exploitation or gain in market exchanges (Biggart and Castanias 2001). In broader terms, borrowing Viviana Zelizer's (2004b) words, not only may we purchase friendship and intimacy, but intimacy and personal relations too have a purchase on market relations, because the latter often both presupposes and generates the former. Likewise, the spread and professionalization of various service jobs which commercialize emotionally thick and ill-bounded caring functions (from the hostess to the nanny) do not mean that feelings are expunged from economic transactions; on the contrary they are put to work in a continuous and unstable balance between personal involvement and commercialized detachment (Hochschild 2003a and b).

Production and *exchange* are clearly less impersonal phenomena than they may appear when the market is ideologically either advocated or rejected. Even more so, to keep the wheels of commerce turning, it is absolutely vital that *consumption* be conducted as far from an impersonal and indifferent affair, that different goods make a difference for consumers. As Igor Kopytoff (1986) has emphasized, it is obvious that even whilst being reducible to a single scale of value on the market (i.e. price), once acquired commodities enter different social spheres and take on other values. Considered from the point of view of consumption, and thus from their symbolically rich contexts of use, commodities are irreducible to the logic of production and monetary exchange. Appadurai (1986b, 41, my emphasis) has clarified this point very well:

> Commodities represent very complex social forms and distributions of knowledge. In the first place, and crudely, such knowledge can be of two sorts: the knowledge (technical, social, aesthetic, and so forth) that goes into the production of the commodity; and the knowledge that goes into appropriately consuming the commodity. The *production knowledge* that is read *into* a commodity is quite different from the *consumption knowledge* that is read *from* the commodity.

Now, 'production knowledge' and 'consumption knowledge' are clearly *asymmetrical*: they mark different stand points with respect to commodities and commoditization. In particular, Appadurai underlines that, as modernity becomes consolidated, the social actors' knowledge as consumers generally becomes infinitely more varied than and different from their knowledge as producers. This is in fact a characteristic trait of the progressive affirmation of the capitalist system which escaped Marx. Today it has become increasingly clear that, as anticipated by Simmel (1990; see also Miller 1987 and Sassatelli 2000a), the process of homogenization which accompanies commoditized production is, in its turn, accompanied by an explosion of variety in consumer practices which de-commoditize goods. Such variety requires quite a bit of work on the part of consumers, thus opening up a space for new social differences. All in all, the storing up of consumption knowledge is a serious affair which may be demanding both on time-pressured elites and on the money-short working classes.

We should thus be wary of a heroic picture of *de-commoditization*. To capture the kind of practical and symbolic translation which occurs with de-commoditization we may draw on Goffman's (1974, 41 ff.) work on *framing*. In particular, we may resort to the notion of '*keying*'. Keying is a form of re-framing, a 'transcription or transposition', a 'transformation in the geometrical sense', which 'laminates' or 'adds a layer' to the original practical and symbolic configuration of an activity or object. It often happens in 'contexts' which offer 'conventions by which a given activity, one already meaningful in terms of some primary framework is transformed into something patterned on this activity but seen by the participants to be something quite else' (*ibid*, 43–4). As a geometrical translation it does not replace the original framework, without which the keying would indeed be meaningless, but it blocks its relevance and systematically transforms it so that participants in the activity 'are meant to know and to openly acknowledge that a systematic alteration is involved, one that will radically reconstitute what it is for them that is going on'. De-commoditization is provided by contexts, spatially and temporally defined, within which people transform commodities but do not overturn the commoditization process as such. In other words, contexts of consumption exist as *relatively separated fields of practice* against the background of commoditization (see Chapter 5). Contexts of consumption are made through rituals and practices of embodiment, marking, sharing, sacralization, etc. which personalize commodities, code them through lived experiences, socialize them via social gatherings of various kinds, restrict their possibility of being exchanged on the market, attach them to specific settings, and so forth. Different contexts of consumption may add different layers or laminations to the product or the practice, and going back to the commodity frame may always occur.

Given this configuration, we may address two 'features' of consumer contexts: '(o)ne is the innermost layering, wherein the dramatic activity can be at play to engross the participant. The other is the outermost lamination, the rim of the frame, as it were, which tells us what sort of status in the real world the activity has whatever the complexity of the inner laminations' (*ibid*, 82; see also Goffman 1961). This adumbrates the fact that what I have called consumer capital – or the locally sustained consumer capacities, knowledge and hierarchies – may not be easily transferable across fields, as it is evident in the case of subcultural capital or marginal amateur practices (see Chapter 5). Indeed there may a gap between internal meanings (i.e. satisfaction, creativity, identities) and external rewards of consumption (i.e. social status, recognition and mobility). Likewise external effects on the broad commoditization process are all but automatic, the wider economic significance and political reach of consumer practices being itself mediated by business cultures (see Chapters 6 and 8).

Considered in their socially embedded trajectories, commodities have their own 'social life', a 'biography' (Appadurai 1986a; Mintz 1985) which cuts across contexts of commoditization and of de-commoditization in a string of laminations. To illustrate this point we can take as an example a particular mass-produced commodity available worldwide, such as the 'Billy' bookshelf sold by Ikea, the Scandinavian giant of low-cost furnishing and design, whose catalogue is currently the most widely distributed volume in the world. This bookshelf is clearly a mass product for a mass public located in five continents. The wood-shavings composite from which it is made has been obtained from the commoditization of a natural resource. It is an extremely standardized commodity, only varying slightly in the colours that are made available from season to season. If however we follow the route through which an anonymous cardboard box containing the various elements of a bookshelf becomes a part of the home, we can better understand what de-commoditization may actually mean and ponder on its scope. A first move in this direction is carried out by Ikea's own catalogue, which is formulated as a particular kind of commercial message – a hybrid between an advert, sales catalogue and lifestyle magazine – orientated to displaying the commodity in use, associating it with practices and meanings which take it out of its commercial context and insert it as an object with meaning in various daily contexts. This commercial representation, which works as a bridge between the context of commoditization and that of de-commoditization, is but the pallid and typified reflection of what can happen in real life. Someone buying Billy has to marshal good doses of practical knowledge: they have to take it home, if it fits in their car, they then have to carry it to the right room, unpack it, read the assembly instructions and then try to carry them out. Ikea has effectively offloaded on to the consumer some of its production costs, which are normally directly met by smaller businesses dealing with furnishings, and it has done so by promoting a taste for 'Do-It-Yourself' which goes well beyond saving money alone, being intertwined, among other things, with the creation of a masculine space within the home (Gebler 1997; Williams 2004). More generally, a widespread phenomenon among the Western public – a quarter of the British population is involved in it according to Watson and Shove (2005) – DIY is indeed a vibrant expression of how consumers try and create a de-commoditized sphere around them, made by themselves for themselves; in other words, a genuinely personal sphere (Miller 1997b).

In the example above, assembly and finishing (using coloured paints, wall fixing, inserting lights, etc.) are but the beginning of an ongoing embodied process of re-framing which makes an anonymous Billy into an integral part of the domestic environment. As we saw earlier, every new object or furnishing, even the most banal bit of furniture, in fact has to go through what Grant McCracken (1988) calls a 'ritual of possession' (see also Belk et al. 1989; Holt 1995; Miller 1987 and 1998; Rook 1985). In the case of the simplest of commodities these rituals consist, for example, in taking off price labels and reorganizing, even if only minimally, domestic geography. In the case of our Billy, one has to decide what to put on the bookshelf and how to organize the objects and books within it. In the long run, embodied routines, and household necessities, the incorporation of more consumer goods and the coupling with other practices of consumption will inscribe difference and indeed uniqueness in it, both materially and symbolically. Ordering objects in space and mixing them with each other is one way in which the subject can create a personalized domestic environment; in this way the actor bestows different and new values on objects, which are expressed in the different positions they occupy in space (Csikszentmihalyi and Rochberg-Halton 1981; Gell 1986; Pink 2004; Riggins 1990; Wilk 1989). This is obviously also true for technology: against technological determinism, many studies have shown that when technologies of communication and representation enter the home (radio, television, DVD-players, hi-fi, but also computers, cameras, camcorders) they are mediated by family and gender structures and by the politics of domestic management (McKay 1997; Silverstone and Hirsch 1994). Whilst being less rich in technological content, bookshelves are nevertheless objects which acquire their full meaning when they are filled with books, CDs, photographs, ceramics, etc., which attest to the lives lived by their owners. As *Histoires de lecteurs*, life-history research conducted in France on reading practices demonstrates (Mauger et al. 1999), books are purposively arranged and displayed in domestic spaces as identity toolkits. Bookshelves in particular are often organized with care by readers, reflecting their personal and literary biographies, providing a tangible space in which to organize their knowledge of the world and of themselves. Thus, following the social trajectory of a mass-produced bookshelf, we may penetrate a succession of laminations which, in more or less reflexive ways and coupled with the reframing of other goods, are the blood and bones of everyday consumption.

The organization of books on a bookshelf may appear to be a rather sophisticated form of de-commoditization, a practice that may not stand as standard consumption for the 'masses'. Still, we can also refer to lots of more banal and ordinary routines which show that consumption is essentially a process of reframing, which laminates commodities with new meanings. For example, let us think of the periodic necessity of arranging purchased products (from the mini-market, supermarket, market or corner shop) in the domestic fridge or freezer. Of course, these are banal practices, but they are also fully social, continuously accomplished as the embodied and practical work of product integration in a material context thick with historically specific meanings and associated with visions of comfort and convenience, identity and the body, the home and cohabitation (Hoy 1997; Shove 2003; Shove and Southerton 2000). The refurbishing of a fridge in a kitchen is coterminous with household composition and organization, reflecting, for example, the chaos of a students' house or the scrupulous organization of a middle-class housewife and the forms of practical knowledge which go with them. In particular, fridge practices in the West have historically been placed on the normative benchmark of a host of discourses on hygiene and the organization of the kitchen which accompanied the consolidation of the figure of the housewife and the frozen goods industry. Broadly speaking, the encounter between food, durables and people in fridge practices allows for a mutual adjustment of objective and subjective worlds: whether or not to put coffee, eggs, or marmalade in the fridge, using cling-film, plastic or glass containers to conserve leftovers, whether to separate meat from vegetables or from milk-products; these are not purely idiosyncratic choices, nor are they simply required by the nature of the food or the equipment, they are rather expressions of an ongoing negotiation of taste and necessity which testify to and reproduce gender, generational, class, religious and national differences.

While home routines surrounding consumption are best understood as material and symbolic processes of commodity reframing, most of them are not self-reflexively understood as de-commoditization. However, alongside perfunctory routines, there are also some contexts of consumption where de-commoditization is institutionally organized end explicitly coded. *Explicit forms of de-commoditization* are important in contemporary societies and they range from gift-giving to collecting. These are all forms of re-framing sustained by contexts of consumption which quite explicitly work on commoditization, in a continuous dialectic which is perhaps best reflected in contemporary art.

By and large, we are accustomed to think that the *logic of the gift* characterizes exchange in the so-called tribal societies (Mauss 1954 orig. 1924; Sahlins 1972). Exchange in these societies is thus seen in the organization of 'reciprocal total services', through which individuals as members of a group (family, clan, tribe) renew the social order. There are various gifting occasions, from marriages to births and deaths, and the motives are not only economic: as Marcel Mauss wrote in his classic essay on the gift (1954, 5), exchanges are above all else acts of courtesy: 'the passing on of wealth is only one feature of a much more general and enduring contract' which signals alliances on one side and warfare and rivalries on the other. In all cases, the rationale of the gift is reciprocity: the gift links two units through rivalry (to be able to reciprocate adequately) or through alliance (because he who gives can always expect to receive adequate acknowledgement of his link with the receiver) (Berking 1999; Cheal 1987; Polanyi 1957). As an ideal-typical logic, that of the gift may be considered as opposed to the calculability, universality and abstraction which are attributed to commodity exchange, for it entails the use and creation of links requiring a reciprocity of unpredictable personal contributions. However, as suggested before, reciprocity has not disappeared from the market (Carrier 1995; Zelizer 1994; 2004a, 2004b). Gift elements – such as social networks, pre-contractual trust, and unspecified obligations – are still strongly intertwined with the cash nexus and they account for much routine de-commoditization in everyday life.

More to the point though, *gift-giving* is an important social phenomenon in contemporary societies: commodities are explicitly reframed as 'gifts' or 'presents' in specific, spatially and temporally bounded occasions, from Christmas to dinner parties. Thus, a highly commercialized occasion, such as contemporary Western Christmas, bears witness to the fact that it is precisely in a continuous productive tension with market values, that the gift-giving works to transfigure commodities into catalysers of personal bonds, removing them from commercial circuits and refilling them with sentimental and personal meanings (Miller 1993). All in all, gift-giving tells us once more that consumer practices are reducible neither to a single, instrumental logic, nor to advertising-induced status emulation (see Chapter 3): in gift-giving practices, we are asked to work on the backdrop of the commodity frame while monitoring its boundaries (it would be crass to intentionally remind the recipient of the cost of the present); in other words we must be stepping in and out of the gift framing, keeping a double eye, both instrumental and expressive, on overall expenditures (as through presents one may be judged 'lavish' or a 'scrooge') (Khalil 2004).

Another particular context of consumption which can be read as reflexively playing with de-commoditization is that of *collecting* (see Belk 1995b; Bianchi 1997; Leonini 1988; Steward 1993). The kind of relationship put into action in this case isn't inspired by reciprocity, even if collectors often organize themselves as communities where barter rules as a privileged form of exchange. While a strongly 'passionate' form of consumption (Belk 1995b, 66), a collection provides a particular pleasure which, according to Baudrillard (1996, 88 ff., orig. 1968) is just as that of a harem: the pleasure of an 'intimate series' and of a 'serial intimacy' which evokes the thrill of a strongly passionate mode of relation differing from the symmetrical and exclusive Western ideal of romantic love. The organization of series of infinitesimal modulations indeed reframes goods and translates them as part of new circuits of value, circuits for the initiated and the connoisseurs which are neither coterminous nor reducible to prices in the wider market. We can take the collection of stickers as an example, a practice that is widespread amongst children in many countries. The stickers are purchased as commodities, but then they become individual, sacred objects, no longer equivalent to every other through money to the point that they are exchanged between collectors only for other stickers. In collecting stickers children take them out of their commercial context and at the same time create an inclusive/exclusive world, in which specific competences rule and strong personal ties are reinforced.

Indeed, many amateur practices involving the collection or the use of marginal objects – from sewing to mushroom collecting – may be seen as ways of building relatively separate cultures and universes of value alternative to dominant cultural hierarchies expressed in monetary terms (Bromberger 1998; Burman 1999; Fine 1998). More generally, this is also the reason for collecting commoditization by-products or 'rubbish' like beer cans: these collections (which require an ongoing effort and a never-ending erudition) may help in the building of a relatively separate culture, and can be used to stage an ideal and ordered world where collectors' aspirations are represented. The sacralization of objects as items for collection, their separation from the circulation of commodities *tout court*, does however mean that they may (re)acquire a monetary value: 'as one makes them more singular and worthy of being collected, one makes them valuable; and if they are valuable, they acquire a price and become a commodity and their singularity is to that extent undermined' (Kopytoff 1986, 81). In such cases, as with second-hand dresses or farmers' markets, commoditization indeed follows routes different from that of industrial production, and may become an important economic resource for marginal groups (Gregson and Crewe 2003; Williams and Paddock 2003).

Considering a variety of daily practices of consumption, we may see that the *commodity form* is only one guise, albeit the dominant and most general, under which goods can appear in contemporary culture: *rather than an essence it is a hegemonic framing*. Objects themselves are typically classified according to how easily they can be treated and identified as commodities or how much they resist such framing, in a complex puzzle of contrast and analogy. Value is thus created both through the commoditization process, and as a difference from the commodity form. *Art* clearly testifies to this. As modern Western society consolidated, art and the commodity market were historically bound in a web of antinomies (Baxandall 1972). Bourdieu (1993) considers that the 'field of cultural production' is like a 'reversed economic world', trying to institutionalize the expressive principle of 'art for art's sake' as against other fields of production. While working as a fundamental normative and regulative principle, the opposition between art and commodities is not absolute and never fully realized, both because of the contiguity between art production and other fields of cultural production such as popular music, fashion, media entertainment, etc. (see Hesmondhalgh 2006) and because of the historical parallel development of art worlds and market relations. On the one side, the birth of a modern art sphere is linked to the spread of the market economy which enabled artists (or at least some of them) to overcome their dependence on particular and well-off patrons; on the other side, the attributes which have been culturally associated with art (originality, authenticity, uniqueness) are opposed to those associated with the commodity form.

This configuration shapes contemporary art worlds. Distance from commercial music, for example, was a prime classificatory device among 'jazz' musicians in Becker's (1963) classic study. Musicians classified themselves according to how much they surrendered to outsiders' demands, in a continuum which oscillated between the extreme 'jazz' musician and the commercial 'square' musician (see also Thornton 1995 for dance music, and Chapter 4). This configuration also produces quite a bit of cultural dynamism within art worlds. By and large, we can consider art as a particular 'key' for goods, which with increasing reflexivity works on the commodity framing.[3] A can of tomato soup is an ordinary commodity; a painting by Warhol reproducing a can of tomato soup is a particular commodity, an art object which reflexively engages with the commodity form, and which is sold at a high price and by auction to stress its exclusivity despite the intentions of the artist. Pop art may indeed be seen as a symbolic form which articulates a more general dialectic between commoditization and de-commoditization. In broader terms, the manifold practical articulation of such dialectic configures the relationships between objects and subjects in contemporary societies.

Goods, values and the boundaries of commoditization

In his *Philosophy of Money*, Georg Simmel (1990, orig. 1907) had already suggested considering consumption as a process of *appropriation* unfolding against the background of an increasingly commoditized world. One of the central theses of this work is the idea that the modern monetary economy heralds a new season in the relationship between human subjects and material objects, favouring particular visions of what it is to be a subject, and what it should be. According to Simmel, social actors move from a situation in which their identity is, as it were, imposed by the things which they happen to possess (i.e. their actions are determined by bundles of objects corresponding to a traditional and rigid distribution of roles and resources), to a situation of 'absolute potentiality'. Thanks to the diffusion of the monetary economy and commoditization, the subject is freed from the structural links with goods that 'enslave' him or her: 'possessions are no longer classified according to the category of a specific life-content, that inner bond … in no way develops which, though it restricts the personality, nonetheless gives support and content to it' (*ibid*, 403). In a mature monetary economy, precisely because objects have become commodities, everything can be bought and sold, and subjects are not able to fuse or coincide with things; all objects remain in their hands for a limited period only or are always encumbered with their potential convertibility into money.

The most immediate consequence of such a phenomenon is the neutralization of the power of things to determine people, their lives, their actions. However, the 'absolute dominion over things' and 'the potentiality of doing' gained by social actors have mixed consequences. The freedom that money confers paves the way to indeterminacy, it is a freedom 'without any directive, without any definite and determining content. Such freedom favours that emptiness and instability that allows one to give full rein to every accidental, whimsical and tempting impulse' (*ibid*, 402). The process described by Simmel doesn't imply an intensification of power relations; on the contrary, it actually seems to augment 'negative freedom', meaning freedom *from* external bonds, including restrictions (linked to tradition, religion and magic, etc.) on what to consume and how. Tensions derive from the fact that this process doesn't lead to a growth in 'positive freedom', namely freedom *to* do things. In fact, negative freedom does not provide indications for the constitution of individual identities consistent through time; in this way, Simmel explains, people's lives become dominated by a 'deep nostalgic desire to confer new meaning on things' and with this by a constant uneasiness with respect to the rationale of their consumption (*ibid*, 283–354).

This perspective is resolutely opposed to the idea that commoditization, and with it the multiplication of images and objects, accompanies the dissolution of the subject and the collapse of available space for appropriating, decoding and de-commoditizing objects and images. On the contrary, the space available for the subject increases, but paradoxically it is precisely for this reason that he can find himself paralysed, incapable of giving personal value to things. In other words, according to Simmel, in modern societies the constitution of the subject through goods is an active but inconclusive process, a never-ending endeavour which cannot provide once and for all a stable identity. Still, it is precisely because of this inconclusiveness that consumption is a creative and dynamic process, an ongoing emancipation from the constraints implicit in the possession of any particular good: what was once natural or taken for granted becomes, in one way or another, an ongoing concern and an increasingly reflexive pursuit. The heteronomy of the modern subject is to be traced back to the fact that he or she is pushed to self-construction. If we are heteronymous, this is so not because 'we live the rhythm of objects' as Baudrillard (1998) maintains, but because, having freed ourselves from them, we are forced to live day by day, in different spheres and environments, by our rhythm. The obligation to live by our own rhythm expresses itself also in playfulness and aestheticization which, at first glance, may appear as the triumph of the subject. In reality, making oneself 'a work of art', the logic of self-experimentation or imaginary hedonisms which Featherstone (1991) and Campbell (1987) associate with the modern consumer, should be considered the result of a cultural obligation to produce oneself as the source of value of commodities. Modern practices of consumption are, like modernity itself, ambivalent phenomena which, placing emphasis on subjectivism, do not free human beings from their own being (Foucault 1983, 1988). Expressed in wider social-theoretical terms, we may say that contemporary consumer practices allow for a maximum of individual specificity. This may well correspond to what Erving Goffman (1959) described as 'bureaucratization of the spirit': the fragmentary condition of the modern subject who has to manage a highly specific set of different roles while projecting a unitary and coherent self. Conceived as a whole, material culture corresponds to a public domain of *indifference* which becomes meaningful only in the *difference* made by subjective valuation (Sassatelli 2000a). However, consumer practices with their necessary plasticity do not secure ultimate support for individual self-constitution. The multiplication and differentiation of objects, their organization into different hierarchies and contexts of consumption make global logics of social distinction more blurred and less efficient. Subject to an ongoing keying process, modern material culture testifies to the relativity of value and no longer bestows a difference on the individual.

All in all, modern consumers are asked to actively participate in the process of de-commoditization, *producing themselves as the source of value*. Put differently, consumption is a sphere of social action regulated according to the cultural principle of individual expression. Obviously, this is not to say that the actor is absolutely free; on the contrary, the subjectivity required by consumption is, in some ways, a binding individuality. To adequately perform their social roles as consumers, actors must thus find a point of balance between indifference to commodities and the search for difference as an end in itself. The pressure on subjects is such that they sometimes seek refuge in eccentricity precisely so as to demonstrate (to others and themselves) that they know how to give personal value to things; on the other hand one way to defend oneself emotionally from this irksome duty is to become blasé or cynical (Simmel 1971a). By embracing cynicism and eccentricity, however, one is not carrying out one's role as a consumer properly. In his play *Lady Windermere's Fan* (1892, Act 3), Oscar Wilde suggested that a cynic 'knows the price of everything and the value of nothing'. Wilde was an aesthete, a refined connoisseur of the world of things, one who dictated fashion. Nevertheless, his phrase attests to a fundamental feature of contemporary culture: the price of an object is a 'public' framing; the value of an object (which serves to sustain its price over an extended period, and ultimately sustains the entire market economy) is a 'private' keying. As such it is posited, so we are asked to believe, as linked to the expression of our deepest and most peculiar subjectivity.[4] For this reason we cannot content ourselves with the other-directed and shallow difference of the eccentric, or with the bored indifference of the cynic.

As a *normative cultural identity*, the 'consumer' appears in striking continuity with hegemonic modern views of subjectivity. The dominant modern ideal of subjectivity depicts a unique and autonomous subject, independent of social contexts and material possessions which are in fact fundamental to the construction of identity. Liberal political thought has, from Locke onward, placed the subject's autonomy at the root of its theorization along with the right of private property seen as a guarantee of such autonomy (Brewer and Staves 1995). In contemporary societies, inasmuch as they are subjects, people have to ground their own humanity in their *being different from the 'objectivity'* of things, namely the passivity, docility and transience of the many objects that surround them. As I shall show, this has important effects on the *boundaries of commoditization*.

Amongst the many boundaries which structure our daily life the strongest, even if one of the most contested, is that which separates humans from commodities. In contemporary Western societies *human beings* should not become *commodities*, something to be bought and sold on the market. Although widespread in many societies, slavery has been abolished, at least formally, and this was argued against the backdrop of a moral discourse which considered objects and subjects as radically different – just recall that Kantian morals forbid treating people as objects (Taylor 1989). All commodities are not only potentially equivalent, but also alienable: a perfect commodity can be exchanged *ad infinitum* and without limits, its owner can thus get rid of it as he pleases, giving it to anyone at any time in exchange for money. Alienability and equivalence are clearly at odds with the qualities we attribute to human beings. As Richard Sennett (1976) and Charles Taylor (1989) have shown, the development of capitalist society has consolidated and made popular a notion of the subject which is actually quite particular: this is the autonomous actor, accomplished in himself, in a growing distance from things. Things are increasingly seen as radically different from humans, and this growing distance between the nature or substance of people on one side, and that of objects on the other, accompanies the idea that objects can compromise people's humanity rather than complete, or better, it. Helga Dittmar (1992) provides a similar view by maintaining that there is a fundamental contradiction in the way we conceive modern identity: a paradox between idealism and materialism, which predominantly touches consumption. Briefly, such paradox requires that subjects perform their identity *through commodities as difference from commodities*. Idealism thus stimulates materialism: in fact, as Daniel Miller (1987) has noted, in contrast to many 'tribal' societies where people become the objects through which the values of a culture are fixed, in our culture things, and not people, have been given the fundamental role of objectifying cultural categories, of tangibly fixing meanings and values.

To be sure, in different cultures people may find different ways to come to terms with materialism. Analyzing accounts of consumption in Romania, Turkey, Western Europe and the US, Güliz Ger and Russell Belk (1999) have shown the different cultural repertoires which are mobilized to reconcile the discrepancy between the belief that materialism is bad and the existence of increased consumption. Materialism was either re-coded as something else ('connoisseurship', 'instrumentalism' or 'altruism'), or excused as either 'compensation' for prior deprivation, external pressure, or just the way things are in the 'modern world'. All in all, Western Europeans seemed to make greater use of the connoisseurship narrative, stressing aestheticized consumption; while Americans were more inclined to resort to instrumentalism, stressing that material consumption may just be a means to other, non-material goals. Altruistic narratives, considering that shared material consumption contributes to warm and loving relationship with friends and family, were present in all cultures, but particularly so in Turkish and Western European accounts. While Turks and Romanians often used the compensation narrative to excuse materialism, Americans were willing to acknowledge their powerlessness in the face of it, excusing their behaviour by reference to societal or media pressures. In this study, a divide and a contraposition emerges between European and American accounts: 'Western European informants stress that materialism is American ... By contrast in America anti-aristocratic individualism, Puritan perspective and less class awareness along with the egalitarian myth of a classless society are paramount' (*ibid*, 198). The characterization of materialism as American is supported by both Europeans and Americans in different ways: since the 19th century, the former have perceived themselves as pursuing an aestheticized form of consumption superior to American vulgar mass-consumerism, whilst the latter have strongly associated their national culture with the consumption of mass-produced luxuries and their public front with a reflection on the illnesses of individualizing markets and consumerism (for an historical perspective see Horowitz 1985 on the US; Searle 1998 on Great Britain and Williams 1982 on France).

Not only must consumers evaluate consumption by drawing on specific cultural repertoires of justification, they must also evaluate themselves as moral beings who consume, and do so against the commodity form. This paradoxical configuration of modern identity helps explain the efforts of legal and political boundary-marking that the expansion of the market into the biological realm has brought about. While salaried labour itself has demanded a plethora of legal and political regulation, fiery contestation still accompanies the application of a commodity frame to human-like materials (Scheper-Hughes and Waquant 2001). For example, although they do happen, practices like surrogate motherhood and the purchase of an unwanted newborn are not only morally condemned but also often legally banned (Radin 1996). The fear is that if babies become mere commodities, all of their personal attributes (from their IQ to their sex and eye colour) will become commoditized. There would thus be babies of superior and inferior quality with different prices: a white male perhaps costing more than a black female, whilst a baby with a stigmatized gene would run the risk of being unmarketable. Even this, though, is contested territory: one of the toughest challenges for today's political institutions is that of controlling and managing the commercialization of biological material, from the body to its parts, cells or genes. So, while the donation of organs is possible and even encouraged in many societies, the commercialization of human body parts is illegal or at least stigmatized everywhere and the trafficking of them is severely punished in many countries (Lock 2002). More generally, the application of genetic manipulation techniques to humans (to embryos, stem-cells, etc.) is extremely controversial, largely because it prefigures an extension of commoditization to domains considered inalienable and sacred (Steinberg 1997). For similar reasons prostitution remains challenging and contradictory: on the one hand, absolute sovereignty over one's own body on the model of modern private property is thought of as a precondition of individual autonomy; on the other hand, the sale of the intimate capabilities of the body comes to be seen as a subjugation of the deepest part of the subject to market circulation. Liberal democracies have typically solved such difficulties with some form of partial commoditization (Radin 1996). In fact, in many Western countries those who buy sexual services are not prosecuted, and even selling these services is not itself illegal, though soliciting and profiting from it is. In this ambiguous way, such norms try to leave it up to people (normally women) to choose whether to sell these services, and try to guard against the degrading effects which can derive from the sale.

All in all, the rise and expansion of consumer culture has been punctuated by *political and legal boundary-marking*. The functional difference between politics and the economy, which is taken for granted in 'liberal market' societies, is historically grounded on a series of tacit agreements of collaboration and coupling – as vividly demonstrated by the history of colonial commercial companies which unified political and economic power in controlling a territory (Pomeranz 2000) or by the reconstruction of how US politics has mobilized the consumer as a viable political actor (Cohen 2003). Let's take a step back and consider commoditization, focusing more explicitly on the interface between politics and the market. In abstract terms, we can certainly imagine a world that is totally commoditized in which everything can be exchanged and put on sale, in which there are no protected or separate circuits of exchange, and every object is exchangeable with another without any difference or further regulation. We can also imagine a diametrically opposed world, a un-commoditized world in which everything is individual, unique and non-exchangeable. But these are of course entirely hypothetical situations. As a matter of fact, every society has its (more or less formalized) regulations over what can and cannot be exchanged, rules that determine between whom, when and how particular exchanges can occur. Such regulations are always the object of contention and conflict. In Western capitalist soicieities political conflicts over deciding what can enter into the commodity circuit and what must remain outside are important in catalysing the formation of influential social groups and the articulation of social problems, just recall the key role that free trade debates and policies had in defining the development of British culture and economy in Victorian times (Kroen 2004; Trentmann 2003).

By and large, even in so-called 'liberal market' societies, political institutions do *regulate the circulation of goods* (Daunton and Hilton 2001; Hilton 2002; Wickham 1997; Wilska 2001). For example, a champion of liberalism like the United States has been profoundly marked by the temperance movement and a prohibitionist era banning alcohol consumption, though leaving space for a flourishing illegal trade (Rumbarger 1989). Price watchdogs played an important role in the US during the Second World War (Jacobs 1997; see also Cohen 2003). Indeed, in times of war, the state appears to exercise a stronger control on the population and on economic resources via the restriction and rationing of consumption – and this is true both of authoritarian regimes such as Fascism in Italy (Helstosky 2004) and liberal states such as Britain during the Second World War and the post-war reconstruction (Zweiniger-Bargielowska 2000). More broadly, even in times of peace, legal prohibitions (or incentives) do exist, and in some cases they differently regulate the use of a commodity across the population, signalling and reinforcing different social identities. In contemporary liberal democracies, age restrictions have survived the general demise of sumptuary laws, and they often mark the exclusion of children from that which might be defined as *full consumership*, the entitlement to act freely as consumers within the general rules provided by market institutions and sustained by wider political settings. While explicit recognition and use of the notion of 'consumer' has come late to law (Everson 2006), this emphasizes that, as with the right to vote, there are certain risky commodities to be used only when one is adult and therefore, one hopes, in full control of oneself.[5] Furthermore, as the history of cigarettes and tobacco shows, through the creation of innocent victims and reference to apparently universalistic notions of the 'healthy body', state interference in individual consumption decisions and in the broader social regulation of consumption is legitimized (Hilton 2002). Broadly speaking, Western countries all have their history of food scares and food regulations. By and large, contemporary food policies and food safety measures seem to abandon a distinction between 'rich' and 'poor' stomachs in favour of 'consumer policies' inspired by a medicalized vision of the social order embodied by the notion of 'public health' (Ferrières 2002). Indeed, in democratic market societies which rely on consumer choice for the masses, medicalization may appear the most legitimate route to the regulation of consumption.

The interplay between political institutions and market institutions is crucial to macro socio-dynamics and it clearly goes beyond restrictions and negative regulation. Besides their regulatory functions, modern states have also *intervened directly* in consumption. What Michel Foucault (1978; 1988) has called 'biopolitics' (namely the power to govern life rather than take it away, to make individual bodies and populations acquire capacities in prescribed forms) and 'governmentality' (the governing of conduct by intervening in people's understanding of the alternatives from which they must choose) has much to do with consumption. To be sure, state-planned production and distribution of goods was a key feature of the Communist regimes: it consolidated an autarchic regime of consumption which provided generalized access to a distinctive and highly codified set of luxuries (i.e caviare) and transformed mass items from the West (i.e. nylon panties) into highly desired but forbidden luxury goods (Gronow 1997; Merkel 2006).[6] Even in advanced capitalist societies, state provision or collective consumption (from roads to libraries, from street lights to natural parks) plays an important role. Today, with Keynesian measures out of fashion, it is often forgotten that government welfarism was, and is, a politics of consumption as a well as a politics of redistribution which set minimum standards of quality of life (see Keat et al. 1994, part III; see also Chapter 6). In the West, the state has also provided direct incentives for consumption or credit – from incentives to facilitate credit for young people's education as public provision of education declined, to incentives for destroying old cars or restructuring property. Clearly, there are different national traditions of state/market articulation as related to consumption both in public discourse and public policy (Bevir and Trentmann 2004; Carrier 1997; Daunton and Hilton 2001; Strasser et al. 1998). Since the Second World War, selective incentives to boost private consumption notably in the car and housing sectors, have been a feature of Italy, France and West Germany, countries with strong interventionist traditions.[7] These incentives not only denote precise politico-economic choices, selectively helping some national industries, but they also justify private consumption of certain goods as a sign of progress and promote certain lifestyles as 'normal'. Bourgeois comforts, the car and the house, are seen as indispensable necessities, as means for consuming other commendable things (tourism, television, electrical appliances, furniture, etc.), and as signs of belonging to a modern democratic community.

If public provision of goods and services or consumers' incentives has a normalizing function, the privatization of public services, which is very much the order of the day in many Western societies, has likewise normalizing results. Still a contested issue, privatization of certain key services (health, education) may spill over the entire pattern of consumption of large fractions of a whole population, nurturing feelings of decline even in the face of stable income and demanding a readjustment of family priorities. It may also touch more directly a small group within a population, perhaps a particularly weak or stigmatized group, with ambiguous effects on its social circumstances, as when psychiatric patients and ex-patients are faced with consumers' options rather than public provision (McLean 2000). Above all, the privatization of public service is predicated on a particular normative vision of the subject-consumer, entrusted with freedom and power. A vision which often conjoins the citizen and the consumer.

A number of authors have stressed that after the Second World War, 'consumption and democratic citizenship became increasingly intertwined in official and popular ideologies' (Strasser et al. 1998, 5; see also Mort 2006) and that *citizenship* is increasingly conceived in *market terms* as the 'free exercise of personal choice among a variety of marketed options' (Rose 1999, 230). National and party politics in liberal democracies have often been concerned with consumer issues, both directly and indirectly by associating with or promoting consumer protection organizations as viable political partners. For example, looking at the development of consumer defence in the UK, we may clearly see linkages between New Labour and the social democratic goals of consumer activists like Michael Young, the founder of the Consumers' Association which aimed at offering a third way for the British political system and to contribute to establish consumers' organization as a third political force (Hilton 2003, see also Chapter 8). Drawing on the historical development of the figure of the consumer on the US public scene, Lizabeth Cohen (2003, 214) has proposed that we are now living with a 'a new post-war ideal of the consumer as citizen who simultaneously fulfils personal desires and civic obligation by consuming'. Leaving the intricacies and nuances of historical detail aside, we may notice that in such configuration, much depends on the definition of consumership, namely consumers' identities and capacities, rights and duties. Like citizenship, consumership places value on liberty and normatively qualifies it. Indeed, now as in the course of the development of modern consumer culture, there are continuous attempts to draw consumer choice back to a particular normative model of subjectivity.

The normalization of consumption

Just as commoditization is bounded, so *de-commoditization is normalized.* Notions of the 'consumer' are important instruments and effects of this. While the qualities and capacities attributed to the consumer are contested and vary across nations with different political traditions and economic structures, we may try to pin down some of its dominant features. As suggested, in everyday life people spend a huge quantity of energy trying to live up to the expectation that they are able to govern the world of things and avert the doubt that they are slaves to mass-produced objects and their rhythms. Considering the different discourses through which consumption has been celebrated or denigrated, it appears that all of them hinge on a notion that occupies a hegemonic position in modern Western culture, namely, *individual autonomous choice.* Rather than describing how consumption takes place in practice, the notion of autonomous choice works as a *hegemonic normative frame,* which has both been sustained by expert knowledge and deployed through a myriad of local norms and particularities to evaluate consumer practices, their worth, moral adequacy and normality (Sassatelli 2001a, 2001b; see also Chapters 2 and 3). Choosing things just for a try or just for fun, for present physical enjoyment or for sophisticated aesthetic pleasure is fine so long as it is the self who is playing the game. As such, choice relies on specific anthropological presuppositions: invited to think of themselves as choosers, individuals are asked to promote their desires and pleasures as the ultimate source of value while keeping mastery over them.

Going back at least to Smith's portrayal of the consumer as a rational, self-interested, forward-looking and autonomous hedonist who orchestrates immediate pleasures visualizing a long-term project of well-being, this solicits a particular picture of 'normality' which normalizes consumption: to consume properly, people must be masters of their will. In other words, consumers are *sovereigns of the market* in so far as they are *sovereigns of themselves*. The consumer's sovereignty is a double-edged sovereignty: hedonism, the search for pleasure, must thus be tempered by various forms of detachment which stress the subject's capacity to guide that search, to govern pleasures, to avoid addiction, to be, in a word, recognizable as someone who autonomously chooses. To this we may add that, especially from the late 19th century, *commodity standardization* has been perceived as a *potential threat to individuality*, thus stressing various forms of personalization and refinement which keep at bay the spectre of herd-like behaviour engulfing the sovereign individual (Hilton 2004). As I shall show, awareness of the double-edged nature of consumer sovereignty reveals that the universal character attributed to individual autonomous choice is only apparent. Autonomous choice is clearly coded by gender, class and race, in so far as certain categories of people (women, the poor and racial minorities in particular) are perceived as closer to bodily desires and nature, thus being considered as less able to display a self-possessed self.

If renouncing the material world has been one way that many cultures have used to signal a spiritual calling (early Christian anchorites, Buddhist monks, medieval saints refusing food, etc.), our world, both idealist and materialist, calls on us all to *positively* demonstrate our capacity to choose. In this situation, even the fact that our desires may discover different objects, and that these objects are continuously changing, may help in sustaining the game of having a self-possessed self. The development of the so-called post-Fordist economy may be seen in this light: the ceaseless innovation of consumer goods, the merry-go-round of fashion, the endless combination of styles appear to grant consumers constant liberation from the specific objects they have chosen, allowing for the renewed exercise of choice. Still, the possibility of choosing *not to choose* a particular good remains a powerful means of guaranteeing that what links us to it is indeed *our* choice. This obviously doesn't imply a return to asceticism; rather, that the emphasis must remain on the subject and their ability to govern the world and themselves, on the right of the subject to satisfy their own desires with objects, and not on the objects and their pleasures. Individuals who are sovereigns of themselves and of their will have not only the capacity to continue willing what they once chose because it corresponded to their desires, they can also exit that choice, should the conditions of choice be altered, the initial wants remain unsatisfied, or indeed their capacity for autonomous choice be put into question, as happens when the spectre of 'addiction' is evoked.

The cult of individual autonomy and the theme of the control of desires are crucial to Western consumer culture. On such premises, authors such as Roy Porter (1992, 1993) and Eve Sedgewick (1992, 1994) have considered that the *paradigm of 'addiction'* helps in explaining the anxieties associated with consumption: as fixed social hierarchies of goods and people recede, the fears that commodities will consume the self rather than the opposite occupy an increasingly central place in the cultural repertoire used to understand and govern consumer practices.

'Addiction' – conceived as a disease of the will induced by a substance or an object – articulates concerns with disorder and works as 'the other' of autonomous choice with various 'addict identities' providing a dystopic image of the consumer. Thus, while it amounts to a tiny fraction of consumer behaviour, compulsive consumption draws much attention because it stands for the boundary which consumers must not overstep if they want to appear convincing in their role as sovereigns of the market. Consolidated across history as distinctive types of deviant identity, the kleptomaniac (Abelson 1989), the immoderate gambler (Collins 1996) and the alcoholic (Valverde 1998) were often coded as the outcome of the encounter between specific objects and contexts and dangerous social groups (women, working-class people, migrants). Indeed, products are still differentiated according to how much they support the image of consumer sovereignty. For example, alcoholic drinks still have an ambiguous status because their consumption can be easily medicalized as pathological dependency. Even more so with 'drugs' – a category created to define certain discredited substances, risky and powerful, which end up taking on a quasi-mythic status as generators of addiction.[8] Therefore while the boundaries of what is an addictive 'drug' and what is not are subject to an ongoing negotiation, 'addiction' itself is one of the most powerful ways of stigmatizing all and every kind of consumption. The spectre of addiction can be invoked not only with respect to alcohol and drugs; every commodity can be described as causing dependence. The experiences of 'addictive consumers' are increasingly singled out and placed under scrutiny, being associated with consumerism or materialism, with modernity or postmodernity, in a proliferation of consumer pathologies which has been branded as 'epidemics of the will' (Sedgewick 1992; see also Eccles 2002; Elliott 1994; Hirschmann 1992). What is more, in current medical practice addict identities has come to be defined in terms of subjective evaluations of a loss of control (Reith 2004). In this way otherwise healthy practices like dieting or physical exercise can become 'excessive', and when they spin out of an individual's control, they appear abnormal or maniacal. Precisely because consumption *must* be constituted as a place for the expression of individual free will, preoccupation grows regarding the effective capacity of consumers to exercise their will in all circumstances.

Considering autonomous choice and its 'other', addiction, we find ourselves right on the boundary between what appears to be 'normal' and what is 'deviant'. Consumer practices can be stigmatized as corrupting mostly through a denunciation of excess and addiction, which is nothing but a suspicion regarding the ability of the self to gain distance from his or her desires and – stretching the point – to get along without them.[9] In all consumption there is therefore the necessity to govern desires through forms of detachment from objects and their pleasures, so that a convincing and strong image of the self can be projected. Model consumers have to busily enjoy the commodities they have chosen and at the same time they must know that their deepest selves lie somewhere else. Hedonism must thereby be domesticated or tamed to work as the hegemonic legitimizing narrative in consumer culture (Campbell 1987; Featherstone 1991). Articulated in various contexts and by different people to account for consumption practices, *tamed hedonism* might be succinctly expressed in the paradoxical formula: 'consumers must be after pleasure only when pleasure is after them' (Sassatelli 2001a, 100). No matter how different they may be, consumer practices considered as 'normal' all have in common the fact they are viewed as both the realization of desires and their containment: they are presented and regulated as moral worlds responding to autonomous and self-possessed selves. The commoditization of dieting or of low-fat food – goods which articulate self-control within choice or offer pleasure without excess – may be taken as an attempt at overturning the anxieties about the corrosive nature of consumption (Bordo 1993; Schwartz 1986). Likewise, the development of a market for body care and maintenance provides a telling example of how immediate gratifications and longer-term projects of well-being which stress an autonomous self are normatively articulated (Sassatelli 2000b).

As a hegemonic narrative, tamed hedonism can be stirred up by various marginal groups to legitimize a host of practices at the fringes of consumer culture as well as goods of ambiguous, even illegal, status. In this case, reference is often made to *self-experimentation*, that is, the idea that consuming dangerous goods is only a way of testing oneself, that the intense pleasure derived from consumption is just 'fun', an inconsequential involvement in the present which does not jeopardize the self and can always be given up (Sassatelli 2001a). If successfully portrayed as entirely circumstantial (i.e. confined to a phase in one's life, a specific place, for a limited period), even the excess and intoxication associated with drugs may appear compatible with individual autonomy. This form of domestication of pleasure is often found in contemporary films, songs and books which deal with marginal youth experience. For example, the 1995 film *Trainspotting*, based on the eponymous cult novel by Irvine Welsh, follows the experiences of poverty, drugs and sex in a group of young unemployed Scots. The leading character is different from his friends, being disenchanted, a working-class champion of that ironic focalization on the present which has been associated with dandyism: he extols the pleasures of consuming heroin but ends up demonstrating that he hasn't in fact been seduced by the substance, thus normalizing the pleasure he derives from it. Instead, his friends are depicted as real deviants: they are compulsive users escaping pain, or thoroughly embrace drugs as a philosophy of life – either way they cannot detach themselves from the habit. In the end, the leading character chooses a different life, epitomized by a different list of pleasures, normal ones this time: the pleasures of bourgeois domesticity, from television to toasters. These are pleasures which, in the film's plot, were previously denied him by his low social position. Yet, the spectators are brought to appreciate him not so much for this choice of his, as for the distance and sarcasm with which, once again, he refers to his new preferences.

Drugs are still considered dangerous by the medical profession and the majority of the Western population, yet a significant minority of this same population sees them as acceptable recreational forms, distinguishing 'soft' from 'hard' drugs. This is particularly true for middle- and upper-middle-class youth, who live in a phase of their lives in which they can, indeed must, as suggested earlier, dedicate themselves almost exclusively to consumption. A number of studies on contemporary youth cultures have underlined that a significant share of European youngsters consider the consumption of certain drugs – from cannabis to ecstasy – something innocuous, innocent and even normal, something connected to a particular phase of life (Parker et al. 1998; Shiner and Newburn 1997; South 1998). Drug consumption is experienced as a momentary parenthesis before the seriousness and responsibility that is said to accompany adult life. Independently of what happens later in life, when young people account for their drug consumption by maintaining that they can quit it and know how to govern pleasure, they are doing nothing more than finding the narrow line which may allow them to act outside 'normality' without losing their selves and being excluded once and for all from dominant culture. So this is not a legendary, heroic and rebellious youth culture; it is a protected period of pleasure, where the necessity of showing responsibility and planning is simply bracketed off, to then be recognized as relevant through the idea that what one is living through is only a limited and particular period.

Similar legitimizing styles are not only found in films, nor does their success only depend on people's ability to articulate a narrative. The provision of specific spaces for the consumption of risky commodities has been, in effect, one of the most important strategies for their social containment and, at the same time, for their translation into a normalized format which may be described as legitimate. The development of pubs in Great Britain and Nordic countries, for example, coincided with the institutionalization of a series of regulations and habits that didn't just make consuming alcohol easier, but also controlled its consumption in prescribed forms. Such places enable customers to account for their drinking practices, making reference to experiences and ideas, like conviviality, which pre-figure forms of domestication and qualification of individual desires (Alasuutari 1992). These are places of 'ordered disorder', where practices which would be embarrassing, excessive or even dangerous elsewhere can and must be carried out (Elias and Dunning, 1986; Turner 1969; Urry 1990). Here 'normal' consumers can experiment with swinging between being in and out of control which, if prop-erly controlled, seems to offer a pleasurable reassurance.

To provide a normalized picture of consumption with reference to altruism, sociability and collective goods as well as to the individual's capacity to take care of herself and plan her future is perhaps even more crucial. These codifications consolidate a picture of the self through time. They are close to the Smithian plot anchoring individual pleasures to *long-term projects of well-being* which embody a vision of social order. They harmonize personal and social benefit, translating individual self-realization into a wider perspective. Reference to these may be found in a number of discourses which reclassify the repeated use of a good as part of an overall design, a promise of the self to the self corresponding to an orig-inal and autonomous will to archieve certain socially commendable states of hap-piness, prosperity, welfare, etc. Discourses on regime, regulation and nature associated with visions of both personal and social order have indeed become important to provide legitimizing grounds for routine and ordinary practices. However, goods which are coded as equivocal, marginal or deviant, such as alco-hol and drugs, may also be justified by seizing some moralizing rhetoric stressing the strength, the authenticity and even the rationality of the choosing self (Sassatelli 2001a). Doubtful as it may appear to the moralist, reference to a pro-ject of well-being is often implicated in the way cannabis consumption is por-trayed as legitimate. Despite a number of legal restrictions, in many European countries the consumption of home-produced cannabis appears to be on the increase. *Weedworld* – a magazine for the self-producer initiated over a decade ago in the Netherlands but now largely available across Europe – opens with the hope 'to educate the worlds' population as to the many and varied uses of Cannabis Hemp and teach how it can be used to save our increasingly unstable environment'. Its pages, together with factual advertising for seeds and growing paraphernalia and detailed farming tips, feature editorials and readers' letters on issues such as the traditional uses of marijuana, the disinformation about hemp, support networks for misuse, etc. The emerging picture is that cannabis, when grown at home for self-consumption, is to be understood as a well-managed pleasure: it is politically correct as it does not finance the Mafia, it is a social activity with ordinary rhythms dictated by growing and harvesting and facilitating occasions for sharing, and it favours personal wellness by being absolutely natural.

Just as the cut-off line between 'good' commodities and 'bad' ones is the object of an ongoing social and political conflict, so the fears of social disorder associated with those goods and practices classified as 'deviant' do not bother all social actors equally. It is mostly the consumption (deviant, but not only) of disadvantaged groups which happens to be stigmatized, whilst privileged groups are better able to present even their most disputable preferences as innocuous forms of recreation. In this they are helped by the possibility of using their economic, cultural and social resources to consolidate institutions and rituals through which consumption can be framed as a separated sphere of action responding to specific norms and rules. A card table, for example, has totally different meanings if it is located in a rich bourgeois living-room, or an underground underworld gambling den (Reith 1999). Indeed, gambling offers a perspective on the social articulation of tamed hedonism. From the Middle Ages to the 19th century, gambling was considered the epitome of vice, a symptom of excess, contrary to the competitive work ethic which was canonized in the teachings of Protestantism (Muntin 1996). During the 18th century, in a period of increasing control of the working classes, card and dice games became taxed, with the clear objective of making them so costly that only the most affluent could use them as a pastime, thereby marking social distinction too. However, along with the development of the scientific theory of probability which codified and rationalized causality, gambling gradually came to be seen less as a source of social disorder and more as an economic opportunity. During the 19th century, an industry of risk developed which commoditized gambling for the masses (McMillan 1997).[10] Alongside it, medical discourse created a distinct 'type' of person with distinctive, stable personality traits whose nature is to consume to excess and whose only cure is to give up consumption altogether (Collins 1996; Reith 1999). The creation of a distinct diseased personality to be medically treated has allowed for the normalization of gambling in other specialized settings: in casinos gamblers were redefined as subjects who know how to play with 'risk', that is, they are capable of evaluating options and remain in control even in extreme circumstances (Goffman 1967). And it is in the success of this reclassification of the gambler that gambling has become a widely acceptable activity, legitimized and promoted by the state, often in the bureaucratic form of a lottery. Still, as shown by a recent study of lottery practices in the UK, working-class women may be under particular pressure to make their gambling practices, which do not sit comfortably with norms of budgeting in a situation of scarcity, 'respectable' (Casey 2003).

All in all, the politics of consumption largely takes the shape of a *politics of normality* which works through the subject in a dispersed and yet deep manner (Foucault 1988, 1991): consumers are governed and govern themselves through the articulation of a normative and institutionally sustained vision of choice, which shapes the possibility of self-realization as consumers. Still, as a hegemonic normative subjectivity and a set of cultural entitlements, consumership is not available to all on equal terms. Let us take a classic, everyday practice such as supermarket shopping and let us read it, yet again, in the context of gender differences. Shopping practices are structured through unequal gender relations: if men and women today often go to the supermarket together, men often act as sanctioning choices, while women try to anticipate the desires of others (Miller 1998; see also Chapter 8). These practices are also represented as more or less autonomous and normalized practices according to what we expect from different actors. Indeed, women are supposed to be self-abnegating consumers and, as Miller (*ibid*, 96) states clearly, 'despite feminism, the transgressive element (attributed to shopping) is extended by the idea of the pure profligate shopper being female, precisely because the female remains the gender which bears the mantle of responsibility for actual or potential households'. In sum, not all social actors are seen as convincing in performing a normal consumer role, not all of them are asked to police their desires equally strictly in their consumer activities, nor are all commodities or contexts of consumption uncontroversial and indeed successfully encompassed by normalizing narratives. As suggested, normalization, social differences and representation all contribute to the politics of consumption: social actors are not only called upon to de-commoditize what is offered on the market, but they also have to do so by negotiating a normative and yet unevenly assertable narrative of normality.

Summary

In this chapter we have addressed *commoditization* and *de-commoditization* as two fundamental processes within contemporary consumer culture. The word 'commoditization' denotes a particular social and economic construction of things: it is the process through which things are produced and exchanged as commodities. It refers to market devices for the promotion of abstract and impersonal relationships. As suggested by **Kopytoff**, commoditization is a contested, unfinished and reversible social process. Consumption in its turn may be seen as a process of de-commoditization. Both *perfunctory routines* in everyday life and *reflexive forms* of de-commoditization are considered (in particular, gift-giving, collecting and arts). Through the notion of *embeddedness*, economic sociology has shown that production and exchange are less impersonal phenomena than they may appear. Through the notion of *appropriation*, cultural sociology has demonstrated that consumption is grounded in personal relationships and social institutions which transform commodities and their meanings. Playing these notions one against the other, the chapter provides an understanding of the *social, political* and *moral boundaries* of both commoditization and de-commoditization. It looks at how *political* and *market actors* have interacted to shape the contexts of consumption, considering that the

(Continued)

functional difference between politics and the economy, which is taken for granted in many contemporary societies, is historically grounded on tacit agreement and explicit coupling. Just as commoditization is *bounded*, so de-commoditization is *normalized*. In particular consumers are asked to be active and participate in the process of de-commoditization, producing themselves as the source of value. Consumption is a sphere of social action regulated according to the *cultural principle of individual expression*. This is not to say that the subject is absolutely free; on the contrary, the subjectivity required by consumption is a binding individuality. To consume in appropriate ways people must be masters of their will and signal their difference from commodities. In other words, consumers may be legitimate *sovereigns of the market* in so far as they are *sovereigns of themselves*. The spectre of *addiction* is often used to condemn consumption and regulate it through medicalization.

Notes

1 See Zelizer (1994) for a wider discussion of social relations associated with monetary exchange and Leyshon and Thrift (1997) for a discussion of the institutional dimension of a global cultural geography of monetary fluxes.

2 Contemporary economic sociology has placed great emphasis on the notion of the 'embeddedness' of the economy in society (Granovetter 1985; Swedberg 1987) and in culture (Di Maggio 1990), even if until very recently it has given its attention almost exclusively to the processes of production and exchange. However, see Zelizer (2004a) for a recent review of consumption from an economic sociology perspective and Zukin and Maguire (2004) for an attempt at charting the intersection between the cultural and economic sociology of consumption.

3 Contemporary art often works on the reframing of objects, and on the juxtaposition of different framings: at this level artefacts 'make meanings of any sort possible. That a urinal can be assumed to be for peeing, full stop, is a bedrock social agreement that Duchamp trades on to do his mischief' in his famous museum installation (Molotch 2003, 11).

4 In this light, it can be argued that the market mechanism needs an articulation of the public/private divide, whereby contexts of consumption work as (private) spaces of and for subjectivity, coalescing desires that can be revealed (publicly) in individual purchases (Sassatelli 2000b).

5 More generally, those who find themselves at the poles of life – children and the old – seem to be in a contradictory position with regard to consumption. On the one side, they don't yet work or no longer do so, and they thus can act economically mainly in their capacity as consumers. On the other side, they are strongly limited by fixed budgets and dependence on public services or the family, and thus find it difficult to affirm themselves fully as consumers. For further reflections on the relationship between consumption and the life course see Featherstone (1991).

6 After being dismissed as illiberal in the enthusiastic embracing of Western commodities which followed the disillusionment that accompanied the fall of the Soviet regime

(Humphrey 1995), these Communist luxuries are now the object of considerable *nostalgia*: see Merkel (2006).

7 This may be seen in the context of an international political economy. Historians of the Marshall Plan largely agree that a distinctly political transformation was attempted in Europe in the post-war period, with the citizen being reconfigured as a consumer, whose individual prosperity was witness to the triumph of democracy (De Grazia 2005; Kroen 2004). See also Chapters 2 and 8.

8 The social history of opium in England and the United States shows that the notion of 'drug' was constructed during the 19th century by the new medical organizations, the philanthropic movement, and state institutions which managed to outlaw a substance that had previously been widely and legally available (Berridge and Edwards 1987; Parssinen 1983).

9 Utopias of total self-sufficiency are always lurking behind the pressure for becoming self-calculating and calculable and, coupled with body–mind dualism, foster the perception of the body as an instrument of the self. As a master of his or her body, the self could, if necessary, keep his or her originality by renouncing everything, even his or her own body (see Bordo, 1993).

10 Gambling is only one of many examples of the commercialization of risk, from the growing popularity of adventure holidays to ski-alpinism; all 'extreme' activities in which actors play with their capacity to risk and to control risk (Le Breton 2002a).

Contexts of
Ⓑ Consumption

Consumption is surely a matter of taste, but tastes are not the only thing that counts in understanding our desires: the institutions and occasions, places and times of consumption are social structures in relation to which tastes become translated into practice. Just as production has been distilled and organized in specific institutions (the factory, the office), so consumption is often concentrated in institutions typically coded as places of 'leisure' and which have their own rules, sanctioning certain forms of interaction while stigmatizing others. Thus the home, the space for private consumption *par excellence*, goes hand in hand with a number of public commercial spaces such as shopping centres, health clubs, restaurants, theme parks and tourist villages. For all their differences, the practices organized by these settings demonstrate how inadequate it is to reduce consumption either to absolute freedom or to total determination. A group of friends in a tourist village, as much as a family in front of the television, take advantage of the activities and programmes offered through articulating the frames and resources made available on each of these social occasions: ideals of friendship or family, notions of gender identity, formal or informal types of interaction, rigid or flexible organization of time and space, gendered division of domestic labour, a variety of emotional codes, and so on.

Whilst global chains and franchised outlets which have helped spread global brands everywhere have been touted as McDonaldization (Ritzer 1993) or the triumph of 'non-places' (that is, hyper-real places detached from the territory in which the individual lives in a provisional and solitary state: see Augé 1995), we are now aware that the world has not become a globalized, de-humanized theme park. Even fast-food chains have adapted to the cultural diversity of local contexts. McDonald's itself is at the same time both a cultural icon and a target of criticism: back in Woody Allen's 1973 film *Sleeper* the hero wakes up in a future in which everything has been commoditized, technologized and standardized, finding himself in front of a McDonald's. Of course, social radicalism in both Europe and the US has always considered a highly industrialized diet the symptom and metaphor of the evils of capitalism ('We may find in the long run that tinned food is a deadlier weapon than the machine gun,' wrote George Orwell in *The Road to Wigan Pier* in 1937). Still, today resistance to multinationals has tended to become more prevalent, self-aware and explicit. Thus, alongside the spread of global brands, a variety of social movements, which question the limits of the market and the relationship between production and consumption, are growing, suggesting alternative forms of consumption and putting into question the separation between private and public, local and global realities that the split between production and consumption helped consolidate.

Leisure, commercial institutions and public places

Consumption takes place in a variety of *institutions* and *settings* which are often coded as 'leisure' spaces and times. The transformation of retailing has frequently been indicated as a pivotal factor in the development of contemporary Western consumer culture (see Chapters 1 and 2). As Rudi Laermans (1993, 94) writes, '(t)he early department stores pioneered the transformation of traditional customers into modern consumers and of "just merchandise" into spectacular "commodity signs" or "symbolic goods". Thus they laid the cornerstones of a culture we still inhabit'. So, the first shopping arcades, world exhibitions and then department stores embody a shift from buying to going shopping: especially for the female consumer, 'shopping' gets coded as a pastime no longer made up of haggling with the seller but of the ability to dream with one's eyes open, to gaze at commodities and enjoy their sensory spectacle. With the development of large out of town malls especially after the Second World War (Kowinski 1985) and, more recently, thematic sales outlets in central high streets (i.e. 'concept stores', franchise outlets which express the philosophy of the company down to the smallest detail), shopping places are becoming hybrid spaces mixing goods and leisure in varied proportions.

Large shopping centres have increasingly come to characterize contemporary Western retail, above all in North America, where they already represented 50 per cent of sales at the beginning of the 1990s (Goss 1993). However, they have not simply replaced previous forms of retail and distribution. To be sure, a *composite* and *differentiated* retail system characterizes contemporary Western experiences of shopping – dispersed and personalized retailing such as street markets, second-hand shops, charity shops, high street boutiques go hand in hand with different (more or less de-personalized) forms of concentration, from consumer cooperatives to shopping malls; classic forms of directs sales, from door-to-door to sales parties, coexist with various forms of indirect sales, from mail order to telemarketing, and with the development of e-commerce.[1] In practice, thus, shopping is an assorted activity, differently coded according to the specific retail site and the shopper's social identity, conducted as much with the principle of saving in mind as of hedonistic consumption, of personal gratification as much as of sacrifice or the expression of social attachments (Falk and Campbell 1997). Still, the fact that modern shopping places have historically been characterized by the so-called 'principle of free entry' has some important consequences. Free entry epitomizes the ambivalence of the contemporary sphere of consumption: it is not the mark of absolute freedom (because the shopper has to learn to behave according to specific norms and manners), nor of growing oppression (because free entry is correlated with a democratization of access to leisure and luxury). However, discussing 19th century department stores in France, Richard Sennett (1976,

Chapter 10) in his well-known book *The Fall of Public Man* has maintained that it was precisely fixed price and free entry which conspired against the consumer. In his view, free entry has made passivity the norm because the consumer is no longer able, nor indeed obliged, to negotiate. Sennett considers that these public spaces epitomized the particular cultural opposition between private and public domains which has come to characterize contemporary societies: on the one hand, private, secret expression of sentiments in the home and, on the other, public silent watching in the department store. Still, he considers that, as commodities were made more spectacular in the *comédie* of the commercial cities of modernity, the vast majority just played the role of onlooker. Sennett's insistence on the passivity of the consumer, which essentially rests on the fact that price negotiation is no longer required, has been challenged by a variety of works which stress that the spectacle of the commodities mobilizes new capacities and offers new possibilities to the wandering shoppers. Indeed, the pleasures, meanings and competences which consumers put to work in shopping centres and department stores are far broader than their ability to bargain on price and purchase objects: in these spaces people do not just buy things, they keep up with the world of things, spending time with friends in a polished environment filled with both fantasy and information.[2] In fact, around a third of those who enter a shopping centre leave without having bought anything (Shields 1992). Because of this, John Fiske (1989, 13 ff.) stressed that malls have the potential to become a 'site of resistance' for marginalized groups in society: women socialize and the unemployed youth allay boredom and engage in various tactics aimed at teasing the security guards. With less confidence in their subversive potential, we may say that shopping centres are essentially spaces for socializing people to consumption: between the windows and the commodities on display one compares not only what is on offer in the shops, but also what other consumers do, their styles, their ways of dressing and using goods.[3]

Shopping is neither passive, nor a pure space of freedom. Market transactions and merchant–costumer relations may be sites for dramatizing social conflict, in terms of class, gender and ethnic clashes (Campbell 1997b; De Grazia and Cohen 1999; Lee 2002; Nava 1997). They are perhaps even more visibly sites for mobilizing hegemonic views of social identities and social relations. Going shopping may thus be represented as a *legitimate and disciplined form of leisure* in so far as it exemplifies the distant but polite encounter between free moneyed individuals, which corresponds with the ideal of the free market and the dominant tendencies of capitalist culture. As much as there has been a cultural pressure to codify it as disciplined leisure, shoppers are keen to present shopping as a regulated social practice. A study conducted in Great Britain by the two social psychologists Peter Lunt and Sonia Livingstone (1992) shows that the majority of people formulate a series of rules or strategies to organize their shopping practices. Amongst the most important strategies, we find the capacity to make 'appropriate social comparisons' (avoiding thinking, for example, that an object is a necessity just because someone else has it) and to 'follow guiding principles' (that is, to have certain rules which can be applied to uncertain situations so that one doesn't have to decide only on the basis of the individual case). Although these are expressions of aspirations and fears as much as real events, they are patently important in coming to terms with commodity culture, underlining individual autonomy, self-control and fears of stigmatization through 'excessive' behaviour (see Chapter 7). If retail works on people's desires, offering direct forms of consumer credit as well as a cornucopia of goods, people are asked to respond adequately as consumers by disciplining their desires and by negotiating the tension intrinsic in consumer freedom between pleasure and social order, liberty and responsibility, possibility and danger scarcity and abundance. Such negotiation works through different visions of social identity, in particular through visions of masculinity and femininity which qualify the codification of shopping as leisure.

While both men and women are involved in shopping, shopping takes on different meanings according to gender. Of course, a number of studies have shown that men increasingly participate in leisure shopping, and that a leisured involvement in fashion shopping marks new forms of masculinity (Edwards 1997; Mort 1996; Nixon 1996; for an historical perspective see Kutcha 1996). Still, looking into shopping attitudes among British men and women in the early 1990s, Colin Campbell (1997b) has shown that shopping is a *gender battlefield* for dominant masculinities and femininities. Indeed, in Campbell's study, women were more enthusiastic about shopping and men appeared more annoyed and distant. But these different expressions were sustained by different shopping practices (women in this study associated shopping more often with fashion and men with technology) and different definitions of efficiency and cost-benefit computation (women tended to consider the time spent wandering around shops as necessary and important, men instead aimed to minimize shopping time, giving their own time a higher value). Through these two different conflicting '*ideologies of shopping*', both gender relations and shopping were reciprocally defined: thus, as champions of dominant masculinity men appeared to women as simply 'poor' shoppers, while women were described by men as 'irrational' shoppers. In particular, the dominant association between leisure and shopping emerged as contested and qualified by gender. Women described shopping using frames of meanings borrowed from discourses on leisure (sociability, fantasy). Men, for their part, more often resorted to frames borrowed from work (efficiency, rationality), to the point that they sometimes denied that their practices could actually be described as shopping.

We should be wary of thinking that *technological innovation* in the retail sector, such as that related to information technology, will put a stop to shopping being the terrain of an ongoing negotiation of meaning embedded in social relations and coded by power differences. Electronic commerce has not simply opened up the possibility of navigating freely between commodities (perhaps assuming a different gender identity) or of concentrating only on the meaning of objects freed from the temptations of their materiality. Nor, on the other hand, does it just make consumers more easily prey to impulse purchases, captured by the Net in the total solitude of a sleepless night armed only with their credit cards. The Internet is a morally structured space which has its elaborate moral rules, even when the object of exchange appears to challenge standard morality like pornography (Slater 1998). As such, electronic commerce requires consumers to be much more active than anticipated by apocalyptic views. Thus, for example, the virtual bookstore Amazon asks its clients to send in their reviews and opinions on books they have bought, subsequently to appear on the website. In this way, on the one hand consumers may contribute to the wider circulation of some commodities rather than others, supporting certain meanings rather than others. On the other, however, they are charged with the labour previously accomplished by the promotional system, having the onus of classifying as well as reviewing the books, so that those who express positive opinions may be exploited as unpaid public relations staff (Ritzer 1999). Still, e-commerce does not entirely automate the retail process: in particular, customer service costs are not eliminated as buyers still have questions and these may be much more demanding, requiring more rather than less investment by the company (Zelizer 2004a). By and large, e-commerce can be a way for the buyers to free themselves from some traditional social networks while binding them to new ones; an opportunity to save time and, at the same time, an invitation to infinitely enlarge the time dedicated to the selection of products, in the constant hope of gaining all the information necessary to make the wisest choice.

If time dedicated to consumption is productive time, producing and reproducing meanings and identity, it is nevertheless time spent and used up, no longer available for other uses. Perhaps it is for this reason that – following the logic of efficient use of time which, from Weber to Foucault, has been associated with the development of modernity – the time of consumption is both contrasted with that of production, and shares with it bureaucratic principles of organization.[4] Studying the relationship between *leisure time, consumption* and *modernity*, Gary Cross (1993, 5) has maintained that consumer society 'emerged in the often unacknowledged social decision to direct industrial innovation toward producing unlimited quantities of goods rather than leisure'. In fact, idleness and 'killing time' are not considered contemporary leisure activities. Leisure time itself is increasingly organized and structured by the leisure and tourism industries (Rojek 1985; Urry 1990). Alongside the development of an articulated, leisure-coded retail system, a succession of dedicated *commercial institutions* have developed in the course of modernity providing specialized and well-organized *settings for consumption*. Traditional cinemas, stadiums, restaurants and museums are now accompanied by a countless variety of new commercial spaces, from theme parks to tourist villages. Theme parks, Disneyland above all, have sparked the curiosity of many scholars of consumption because they are commercial institutions offering complex experiences, part play and part shopping, all brought together through a 'theming' of the environment, relations, activity and so on (Bryman 1999; Watts 1998; Zukin 1991). The possibility of entering into a fantasy world is favoured, in this case, by the 'emotional labour' (Hochschild 2003a, orig. 1983) of those who work in these places. The animators of theme parks and tourist villages are much like gym trainers in that they have to get consumers to partake in a meaningful experience by furnishing them with a series of practical cognitive and emotive instruments to read and enjoy the scene they are entering. Places which could otherwise be too rationalized and standardized may thereby be framed as free, self-gratifying, personalized, amusing, and creative. These motivational professionals are also fundamental in speeding up peoples' involvement in these worlds of consumption, something which may be of importance for time-pressured consumers and contributes to their commercial success.

The different sectors of the leisure industry provide spaces, frames and experiences which, as idealized as they might be, do resound with each other. For example, the leisure industries, and in particular the commercialization of travel and the development of tourism as a specialized industry have relied also on the consolidation of cultural and emotional repertoires for the reading of distant, different or marginal people, places and goods (Azarya 2004; Baranowski and Furlough 2001; Corbin 1995). The development of a global consumer culture, and in particular the development of cinema as a leisure industry, has contributed to this. Especially after the Second World War, cinema has been an ambassador of consumer lifestyles, as well as a commoditized form of art and entertainment to be consumed in itself (Bruzzi 1997; De Grazia 2005). Thus, for example, Hollywood films have cast Mediterranean identity in a particular light, offering a blurred, romanticized picture of the southern regions of Europe as an orientalized 'other' in continuity with the needs and frames of the tourist industry. While sustaining economic development, such idealization may end up leaving the 'other' mute, as has been noted for *Captain Corelli's Mandolin*, which works as an advert for tourism in the Mediterreanean, romanticizing the landscape and reducing local culture and history to it (Tzanelli 2003).

To a large extent, the hold of leisure and consumption institutions on consumers is that they offer situated, embodied *experiences* of locally relevant *structured variety*, drawing people into *relatively separated realities* where they can engage with a different, specific set of goods, activities, manners and identities. They offer, as it were, the possibility of getting into organized contexts of involvement which arrange a world of internal rewards that is partly disjoined from broader social rules of relevance. They thus provide for learning experiences which may mobilize identities quite profoundly. Of course, different institutions deploy different ways of framing and structuring the disciplining of the consuming subject, putting more or less emphasis on pleasure and internal rewards. This is partly a function of the institutional goals defining the context of consumption. For example, the spread of factory canteens from the first half of the 20th century (Trentmann 2004) was largely due to the attempt to manage the workforce by supplying specific controlled spaces for consumption, thereby stressing functionality rather than pleasure.

Fitness centres are excellent examples of how subjects are shaped through pleasure and self-discipline in commercial institutions rather than only through work or public institutions with political ends (Sassatelli 2000b). Gymnastics was for a long time an expression of public health concerns or the military objectives of nation states. Following the Second World War things changed. With the development of body-building, aerobics, and more generally fitness, physical training has been firmly grounded by reference to consumers' desires, aspirations and needs. While fitness centres are encoded as a means of self-expression for the individual consumer who knows and must realize his or her most fundamental needs, training in gyms implies concentration, discipline, the ability to follow rather strict rules, to know one's place, to get into the right mood, and so on. Of course, dealing with subjects who pay and can always decide they no longer need the gym, fitness centres must emphasize the personal dimension, playing up fun elements and subverting daily routines (Sassatelli 1999). However, leisure time is not 'free time' (Rojek 1985). As a recreational commercial phenomenon, fitness training demonstrates the ambiguity of the idea of free time. Training in the gym is time which may subvert daily body constrictions as prescribed by people's different roles in everyday life, particularly the workplace. However, it is far less time spent free of all rules; on the contrary it is based on shared rules and rigidly codified practices. It is time which is organized through elements which derive from the world of work (discipline, bureaucracy), but re-coded in opposition to work itself. As stated by Callan Pickney, the creator of 'Callanetics', a popular way of training and an exercise handbook of the 1980s, 'physical exercise is not a second, unpaid job, or unrewarded effort. Time is money. Energy is precious. Why waste it doing something which is of no use? … Make sure the time you spend working on your body is actually working for you.' For many participants, exercise is experienced as being time dedicated to themselves. However, this is based on what clients have learned in the gym: in other words, they view training as being aimed at balancing and improving their own behaviour in relation to their own nature, as it is experienced through structured exercising. Even the informality that qualifies interaction during physical activity is managed by trainers and is marshalled as a resource to permit clients to continue exercising. In the same way, although it can express self-assertion in opposition to the sacrifices of maternity and marriage, the soaring participation of women in fitness as opposed to competitive sports shows that, when physically active, women still prefer to spend their spare time in making themselves physically desirable.

Restaurants provide a similar structuring of the experience. Restaurants are, indeed, key institutions of consumption, and eating out is one of the most popular of contemporary leisure activities. While the pleasures of eating in taverns and inns has been recognized since early modernity and is certainly a feature of urban living (Mennell 1996), restaurants and the cultural economy (TV programmes, magazines, guides, gastronomic tourism) which they generate is a distinctive characteristic of the contemporary period. Restaurants are emblematic of the post-Fordist service industry, generalizing a mode of food provision which removes eating from the domestic sphere and transforms it into a public event. Despite being largely conceived as a pleasurable matter of choice, dining out is anything but a free practice. It requires command of manners and ceremonies, the deployment of knowledge and demeanour which are differentiated amongst consumers as much as restaurants and continuously in the making in the coming together of people and places. There is a set of widely recognized, institutionalized procedures for conduct which are the product of both the intentional design of specific sites (Finkelstein 1989) and a generally diffused, but highly differentiated, notion of the conventions of the practice (Warde 1997). To be sure, eating out involves spending time and money on a discretionary basis, choosing among places, menus, ambiences, staff, and so on. However, it also entails an elaborate code of conduct, sociability and aesthetic appreciation, which is institutionally sustained and enforced as well as subjectively learned through a lifelong self-disciplining process. As is the case with amateur practices, such as wine-tasting and collecting or playing and listening to music (Hennion and Teil 2004), the continuous, often strenuous, and never-ending disciplining of a taste *vis-à-vis* the physical and symbolic engagement with objects and places is intrinsic to the pleasures of consumption, rather than its opponent.

While all consumption is situated, not all consumption takes places in commercial institutions, or with the direct help of various professional intermediaries (such as trainers or tourist guides) and their skilled management of emotions and involvement. A notable share of consumption now takes place in *individualized form* in public places, such as public transport, squares, streets, parks and so on. While take-aways are becoming gentrified, a new etiquette for the display of solitary consumption in public places is taking shape, whereby eating, drinking or listening to music are becoming more widely accepted. The spread of various technological supports for the private consumption of cultural goods – from books, to CD players, to iPods – has significantly increased the possibility of consuming privately in public. Michael Bull's *Sounding Out the City* (2000) shows the role that personal stereos fulfil in the management of everyday life, often challenging the functional and spatial differentiation of work and consumption, play and politics (see also Du Gay et al. 1997). While, for example, the Sony Walkman was put on the market without anticipating any definitive desire for a portable cassette recorder, once the new instrument met consumers a new, portable 'aural culture' was generated which threatened previous embodied ways of managing rituals of deference and demeanour in public spaces. During its release conference the Walkman was described as just a 'smallish stereo-headphone cassette-player', but in its diffusion phase it began to be coded as entertainment, as youthful, symbolizing Japanese technology and urban nomadic mobility. For cultural critics the Walkman represented alienation, anomie and atomization. Yet, for users it meant 'escape', which was defined both as a 'heightened experience' and as 'resistance' – and in the case of Chinese youth distressed by urban loudspeakers, this took on a clearly political slant.

The home, the commercialization of feelings and cultural consumption

Just as goods refer to each other and get their meanings only in relation to each other, so the contexts of consumption, private and public, are mutually constituted. The shaping of the home as a private space of consumption is part of the larger historical architecture which gave rise to contemporary consumer culture (see Chapters 1 and 2). Domestic environments probably are the most intricate settings, in which daily consumption, of both material and cultural goods, takes place (Bell and Valentine 1997; Cowan 1983; Csikszentmihalyi and Rochberg-Halton 1981; Jackson and Moores 1995; Parr 1999; Riggins 1990; Silverstone and Hirsch 1994; Wilk 1989). Even a cursory glance at the domestic sphere demonstrates quite clearly that we cannot understand the complex web of interdependences, pleasures and duties which are sustained through consumer practices in the home by reference to the freedom/oppression dichotomy. Consumption at home entails some form of commodity appropriation which is regulated by rules of informality or by reference to emotional authenticity. Still, the home itself is not the safe haven for individual self-realization in total freedom or equality. In today's Western societies household spending is still heavily gendered (Pahl 2000) showing that as private as it might be, the domestic sphere is also a site of power relations (Cowan 1983; Jackson and Moores 1995). More broadly, the domestic sphere is ideally constituted in opposition to that of production as a space of consumption and leisure; yet much of what passes for consumption is in fact mediated by the unpaid work of women and, increasingly, by their paid domestic services.

Although difficult to pin down, housework practices are an integral part of the domestic environment and are deeply intertwined with domestic consumption, its routines and pleasures as well as its gendered structure (Pink 2004; Shove 2003). This is still evident today even in the smallest habits: an evening spent as a family watching television will often involve women, mothers and wives, getting up to replenish their younger and older spectators with something to drink or snack on; they will rush to the kitchen in a commercial break to finish washing the dishes, or they will watch distractedly, putting down the shopping list for the weekly visit to the supermarket, and so on. Likewise, a weekend at home will often entail some DIY, cleaning or decorating – practices which continuously re-organize the spatiality of the home and its capacity to facilitate consumption. We must thus regard those practices which have conventionally been singled out as domestic consumption (such as food or media consumption) as contextual and structured alongside contiguous practices: there may be little sense in considering the meanings drawn from a programme or the preferences expressed at the table if we do not account for how these are practically co-constituted – i.e. managed, distributed, sequenced, cross-referenced – in the domestic space.

Domestic spaces, and their maintenance, are thus of the essence. Kitchen deco-ration, for example, can tell us much of class aspirations and how this may shape consumption (Miller 1997b). It can also tell us of distinctively different national domestic cultures and of their different, typically gendered, ways of coming to terms with leisure and consumer culture, as suggested by Sarah Pink (2004) in a comparative work on British and Spanish homes (on ethnicity, family relations and domestic consumption, see also Pleck 2000). Strikingly different from Spanish kitchens, even the tiniest English kitchen is a 'room to be lived in', per-sonalized with ornaments, photographs and drawings. Also, while food tends to be placed out of sight in Spain, in England food and drink are used as 'expressive objects'. Such different spatialities prefigure different ways of organizing house work. In Pink's study, English women rejected the idea of following a housewifely domestic routine, insisting that their own spur for doing housework was a more 'embodied, emotional need': when in the mood, they found cleaning 'therapeu-tic'. Spanish women displayed a different attitude to routine, seeing structured routine as positive, bringing 'natural balance' between different areas of their life. All in all, in this study all women differed from men because they refused tradi-tional housewife identities but saw housework as part of their alternative embod-ied femininity; while men tried hard to use traditional masculinity to reframe their housework practices as 'hard work'. Such study shows not only that housework is coded by gender, but also that different gendered codes draw on different reper-toires which bring housework closer to consumption and leisure, or to work and discipline.

Housework distribution and framing is slowly changing, although there is a marked diversity and unevenness of change across professional groups and nations. In particular, especially among the upper-middle and upper strata of the US and European population, there seems to be a trend for the commercialization of care and home services. Clearly there is a structural and global dimension to the gendered commercialization of care, as stressed by Arlie Russell Hochschild (2003b). Care (for children, the old, the sick) is not rewarded as much as market success, yet it is necessary and is being increasingly transformed into paid work, bringing commercialization into intimate life. Care jobs in the home are typically carried out by female migrants, who are often portrayed as essentially more 'caring' than Western women: '(t)he way some employers describe it, a nanny's love of her employer's child is a natural product of her more loving Third World culture, with its warm family ties, strong community life, and long tradition of patient maternal love of children. In hiring a nanny ... they import the benefits of Third World family values' (*ibid*, 191). Latinas and Filipinas are portrayed as knowing how to 'love a child better than the middle-class white parents'; the latter must look at the former so that they can really 'learn how to love'. Western professional women are thus exposed as pressured for time, oriented towards their kids' achievement and incapable of being relaxed, patient and joyful. While the global flux of care workers clearly has mixed effects (on adults and children, both in developed and Third World countries), these discourses testify to what extent the commercialization of domestic work, emotions and intimate life is a contested issue. In particular, in spite of the fact that nannies are clearly paid to love and that, as a result, they may have acquired considerable expertise in doing so, their capacity for love is constructed as the natural outcome of some pre-commercial cultural endowment, opposed to commercial culture. This may reinforce sharp dualities which are inadequate in describing rather more blurred social relations (within both the market and the family) and cultural traditions (both Western and non-Western), preserving an ideology of pure loving parenthood which has gone hand in hand with the transformation of the nuclear family into a very particular unit of consumption in contemporary Western culture (see also Zelizer 2004b).

   The commercialization of feelings concurs with the spread of cultural goods putting emotions and bodily processes which had been privatized (such as eroticism, love and intimacy) back on to the front stage. The press, radio and television have opened up a space for the public display of intimacy, and they have brought it back, right inside the home. While food consumption and food provisioning, with all the changes they have undergone in post-Fordist economies, remain key domestic activities through which family, gender and generation are structured (Lupton 1996; see also Chapter 4), the home is increasingly described as a place of 'cultural' consumption: the TV, stereo, computer and DVD-player/recorder sit alongside more traditional bookshelves, stamp collections, prints, photograph albums, etc. The different domestic practices of cultural consumption are all, each in their own way, profoundly influenced by the structure and asymmetry which characterize the social institution of the family. The meaning which subjects derive from a text and the way this is consumed are riddled with power relations, not only in large rationalized institutions but also in private, relationally dense environments such as the home. For example, ethnographic studies of the way television is used have become central to research on TV publics, because of the evident limitations of semiotic approaches which, grounded on textual determinism, concentrated on the formal analysis of programmes' content to infer how they were interpreted by consumers (Moores 1993). Media consumption implies something more and different from individual spectators providing particular interpretations of specific programmes. As David Morley (1992) has emphasized, 'watching TV' is a common expression which masks what consumers actually do with TV and while watching it: this practice is to be understood less as a series of cognitive acts than as a form of domestic consumption, in which the domestic context is 'constitutive' of the meaning of television programmes. It is this context which renders the process of de-codification both possible and necessary, while at the same time guiding it.

Of course, 'watching TV' is a multifaceted activity, in no way uniform. It has no constant meaning or importance, it can be defined and experienced in different ways according to the time of day, specific family relationships, programmes, etc. (Morley 1992; Silverstone 1994). However, in the London families that Morley interviewed, two distinct modes of watching TV did present themselves: a female and a male one. Domestic responsibilities and women's self-perception as the guardians of the well-being of the family meant that they rarely watched television, including their favourite programmes, with full concentration. The way television is consumed thus reinforces the perception that for women, even for those who are in full-time paid employment, the home remains a place of work, whereas for men it essentially remains a place of rest and detachment from the responsibilities of work. Indeed, other forms of typically female cultural consumption are to be seen against the background of the gender structure of household work. A study on female magazines, for example, has shown that their attractiveness wasn't in the meanings they conveyed, but in the way in which they could be read: above all they are 'easy' to read, not only because they are simply written, but because they are in 'bite-size' formats which can be easily abandoned and then taken up again during household chores (Hermes 1995).

In contrast to the critique which stigmatizes TV as a source of social isolation, TV consumption is an activity that can be used both to isolate oneself and to spend time with others. In fact, programmes often offer the occasion and content to stimulate conversation, both within and without the family. It is the most popular programmes like soap operas and sit-coms which provide themes for discussion and even slogans that may be used in daily life, with friends as much as strangers (Ang 1985; Geraghty 1991). More to the point, organized fan clubs are an extreme example of the possibility of creating a common language through the consumption of popular culture. In *Textual Poachers*, an important study of television fans, Henry Jenkins (1992) illustrates the inadequacy of the stereotypical image of the fan as a weak subject, passive and other-directed. In fact, the fans Jenkins consulted watched and re-watched their favourite series, developing truly 'critical' perspectives (becoming, for example, ever more attentive to 'how things happened' rather than 'what happens') and giving way to well-organized communities. From this point of view, 'fan cultures' are cultures of communication and circulation of meanings. Fans of a television series or a literary genre tend to develop genuine communities which develop heated debates enabling them to extend the experience of the text way beyond its initial reading. Organized groups of fans can thus be considered as 'an institution of criticism', a 'semi-structured space where competing interpretations and evaluations of common texts are proposed, debated, negotiated and where readers speculate about the nature of the mass media and their own relationship to it' (*ibid*, 86).

Even the readers of pulp romances studied by Janice Radway (1987) in her fundamental study *Reading the Romance* are configured as 'interpretative communities' linked to a particular bookshop which worked as a cultural catalyst and a meeting place. The women studied by Radway describe reading as a 'special gift' which they allow themselves from time to time. Even in this case, to understand the experience of consumption, Radway had to consider the strong gender asymmetry which still characterizes Western families. Whilst men are supported emotionally by women, women often have to find for themselves relaxation and reassurance: reading pulp romances is an important contribution to emotional reproduction for many of them, offering a 'temporary but literal refusal' of the demands made on them as loving wives and mothers, providing pleasures that are perhaps 'vicarious', but are undoubtedly 'real'. It is thus precisely in the difference from ordinary life that reading has its significance: finding time for oneself in a moment when the home is quiet, in a particular room, is thus not only 'a relaxing release from the tension produced by daily problems and responsibilities', but also creates 'a time or a space within which a woman can be entirely on her own, preoccupied with her personal needs, desires, and pleasure' (*ibid*, 61).

Of course, Radway correctly emphasizes how difficult it is to determine whether these pleasures are effectively instruments of liberation and social change or whether instead they reproduce the structures of gender inequality. Certainly female reading practices, and reading groups in particular, have the potential to construct a space for public awareness inside the private space of the home, and conversely, provide a platform for allegedly private issues to find public resonance (Hartley 2001; Long 2003). This is part of what Elizabeth Long (2003) has noticed in her study of women's reading groups in Houston, Texas. Starting from a critical discussion of the ideological image of the solitary reader as expressed in visual representations of reading in European and American art, Long considers both the historical importance of white women's reading groups following the American Civil War and their contemporary reality. Historically, women's reading groups catalysed organizational, literary and 'sisterly' practices that gave them the confidence to re-imagine themselves, transforming a literary movement into a movement for social reform, a development which they attributed directly to the influence of the books they studied as well as to the ways that self-organization acquainted them with the skills of the public sphere. While continuing a tradition of exclusivity along class and racial lines, contemporary reading groups in Houston also encouraged members towards a critical appraisal of the social order: books became both the language through which women narrated their own experience and the catalyst for serious conversation, full of innovative understanding and personal insights, encouraging social relationships and political participation.

Localized consumption in McDonaldized settings

The ambivalent potentialities of consumption seem clear enough when we analyse the domestic sphere and cultural consumption. When we consider institutions of global consumption like fast-food chains, or strongly standardized commodities seen as expressions of American imperialism like Coca-Cola, it is easier to fall into that rhetoric which opposes consumption with 'Culture' intended as the highest expression of being human. It was above all the popular book, *The*

McDonaldization of Society by the American sociologist George Ritzer (1993) which offered a critical reading of consumption and globalization. Ritzer maintains that 'consumer culture' has a 'dehumanizing' effect because it is the final globalized expression of the process of rationalization begun with the birth of modernity and magisterially described by Weber at the dawn of the 20th century. McDonald's is taken up as a paradigmatic case of a new type of venture.[5] This chain of cheap and 'fast' restaurants is presented as the tip of the iceberg and the model of a process of 'McDonaldization' which informs numerous other businesses: it thus marks (much like Ford, who inaugurated Fordism at the beginning of the 20th century) a new period in the organization of production. McDonaldized production is based on the articulation of four principles: *efficiency, predictability, calculability* and *control* through the substitution of human labour with that of machines (Ritzer 1993, 1999).

Efficiency implies an emphasis on saving time and thus individuating the most rapid and economic means to obtain these ends. Calculability needs quantification and substitutes quantity for quality. Predictability requires the search for reproducibility and standardization of products, which is guaranteed by an increasing control of the various phases of production and distribution, mainly through the substitution of human labour with technology. These are bureaucratic principles of organization which should put people in a condition of knowing what to expect in every moment and place. According to Ritzer (1999, 84–5), in fact:

> In a rational society consumers want to know what to expect in all settings and at all times. They neither want nor expect surprises. They want to know that the 'big Mac' they order today is going to be identical to the one which they ate yesterday and they will eat tomorrow. The fast-food industry has perfected things such as replicated settings, scripted interactions with customers, predictable employee behaviour and predictable products.

Ritzer notes, obviously, that these characteristics have spread far beyond McDonald's and may be found in other chains, even in rather upmarket ones like the Hard Rock Café as well as non-American ones such as the Body Shop and Benetton. In his view, contemporary 'means of consumption' – from large shopping centres to slot machines, from mail-order catalogues to electronic commerce – are essentially *de-humanized, rationalized* and thus *efficient means* of rapid supply. According to Ritzer (1993), the result is a form of consumption that no longer offers surprises. Continuing to draw on Weberian terminology, Ritzer maintains that the rationalization of the 'means of consumption' leads to their 'disenchantment': systems inspired by efficiency don't allow for casual, vague or aimless elements, they systematically attempt to eliminate all that is magic or mysterious from their functioning because it will produce inefficiencies (Ritzer 1999). To continue to 'attract', 'control' and 'exploit' consumers, a kind of rationalized form of 're-enchantment' is created, like the 'cold and utilitarian fantasy' provided by shopping centres ceaselessly presenting themselves as offering 'huge bargains'. The rationalization of the means of consumption, their efficiency and, where it fails, technology, has thus 'substituted the old witchcraft', fully socializing consumers into a McDonaldized world, global and predictable.

Whilst recognizing that McDonald's is in fact experiencing a number of difficulties, Ritzer (2001; 2004) believes that McDonaldization as a process that will continue to spread, being carried ahead by other businesses. In his provocative phrasing, we are moving from 'something' to 'nothing' – from that which is 'indigenously conceived', 'locally controlled' and 'rich in distinctive content', to that which is 'centrally controlled and conceived', and relatively 'devoid of distinctive substance'. Small businesses don't represent a serious threat to this process, and with time they will only just survive by trying to fill the smallest interstices left by large multinationals. Even the rising trend of revaluing local traditions will be inconsequential: traditional and local products are said to be doomed to either marginality or incorporation into McDonaldized production. Successful local products, Ritzer (2001, 49) affirms, 'will probably suffer the fate of Colonel Sanders' original Kentucky Fried Chicken and many other products that at first were highly original and distinctive, but over time were turned into pale, McDonaldized imitations of what they once were'. In the end, as 'time passes and the older generations die off, we can expect a more uniform propensity toward McDonaldized settings across generations' (*ibid*, 68).

Ritzer's apocalyptic affirmations paint a picture of the rationalization process which is too one-sided and totalitarian (Smart 1999).[6] They are likewise biased with regard to the current trends in the retail system. Personal relations and involvement are still important in McDonaldized settings and transactions (Leidner 1993). Furthermore, global chains don't simply follow the logic of McDonaldization. To borrow from Weber's well-known terminology, we may instead say that they mix rationalized forms with charismatic and traditional elements. An interesting example is that of the Body Shop, the British cosmetics chain which, as already touched upon, has made environmentalism, transparency and ethics its selling point (see Chapter 6). For Ritzer (1993) this chain is essentially characterized by efficiency, calculability, predictability and control, but anyone who enters one of their shops immediately notices different aspects, too. If the process of production is one of standardization, mechanization and bureaucratization, the Body Shop does all it can to rehumanize the product, insisting, for example, that the primary materials are procured ethically. Calculability is, at least in part, counterbalanced by the strong emphasis on quality; predictability by the fact that consumers can purchase different essential oils that they can mix themselves; efficiency by the fact that consumers are invited not only to recycle their containers by refilling them in the shop, but also to spend quite a bit of time through reading thick brochures. In this sense the Body Shop appears as one of those marketplaces devised to fulfil the desire for personal and intimate spaces which precisely the spread of global and impersonal retailing – from supermarkets and discount stores to McDonald's – has elicited. Indeed, we can trace two directions of development in the contemporary retail sector which both diverge and reinforce one another: on the one hand the spread of outlets and discount stores emphasizing price and standardization, on the other speciality shops and niche chains with a renewed emphasis on quality, difference and variety (Lee 1993).

To give a different, more accurate image of the practices of getting and using goods and services one doesn't need to turn Ritzer's plot on its head, claiming that today's consumers are 'uncontrollable' or 'mercurial' figures (see Gabriel and Lang 1995). It is enough to emphasize that he falls into the productivist fallacy against which not only scholars of consumption have rallied, but also a significant part of contemporary social theory. This is apparent in his idea that today's consumer practices are determined by rationalized 'means of consumption' – i.e. commodity circuits and retail organizations which are 'too dependent on control to meet their own needs for efficiency and profit to allow consumers to escape from the boxes in which the system places them' (Ritzer 2001, 63). As suggested (see Chapter 4), we cannot derive the meanings of consumer practices directly from the intentions of the commodity retailers and producers, nor can we take for granted that those who control the production of an object or provide a service also control its consumption. Commercial institutions are far from being compulsive institutions. In fact, consumer culture is based on institutions which place the emphasis on individuality and work on people's capacity to choose. This tendency has become increasingly evident with the post-Fordist enterprise which tries to respond to the growing request on the part of the public for authenticity, originality, personalization with flexible production, the serialization of made-to-measure, niche marketing and so on.

It is true that McDonald's offers more of a pre-packaged consumer experience than a single commodity might do. However, the way in which this experience is articulated by different consumers in the same place and by similar consumers in different nations cannot be reduced to the culture of production and service originally promoted by McDonald's. A collection of papers on McDonald's in East Asia put together by James Watson (1997) has shown that not only were the menus altered to take account of the tastes of the youth of Taipei, Shanghai, Seoul, but also that they use these spaces differently from their peers in the United States. In Asia, McDonald's are seen less as fast-food outlets than as meeting places where youngsters will spend entire afternoons: here McDonald's are the equivalent of leisure centres where one can chat, study and snack on something. Of course, none of this runs against the existence of complex networks of power: these youngsters, for instance, make the spaces and meanings of McDonald's their own, often relying on traditionalist visions of class, gender and generation difference. As suggested by Rick Fantasia's (1994) study of the spread of the fast-food industry in France, this may entail the spread of indigenous fast food chains which mix and mingle McDonaldized elements with national and local ones. Melissa Caldwell's (2004) study of McDonald's in Russia shows that fast-foods were 'domesticated' and put to use to elaborate new nationalistic identities. Thus, we do not find ourselves facing a split between a free and active consumer and a McDonaldized one: for example, in response to global commodities, consumers can either negotiate standardization through propping up local cultural repertories and traditional hierarchies, or they can embrace the elements of universalism which mass culture always contains to unhinge the inequalities embedded in their traditions.

We can use Ritzer's observations as a springboard for discussing the complex relationship which runs between consumption and globalization, offering a perspective on the *politics of effects* which consumption as a form of appropriation, or in this case domestication, brings forth. As a start, we should notice that the spread of global chains like McDonald's is only one of many aspects of globalization. Globalization is a complex phenomenon which involves *national, supranational* and *local* actors and which doesn't resolve itself in an unstoppable and purely economic dynamic, but has important and contested political and cultural aspects, including various levels of *governance*. In the field of food consumption, for example, it is precisely in response to the needs of global commerce that the provision of safety and regulatory norms for foodstuffs has increasingly been transferred to supranational bodies (from the Codex Alimentarius, to the World Trade Organization (WTO), to the European Union and so on); the harmonization of different traditions has, however, been fraught with conflicts. Let us consider the case of genetically modified (GM) food, namely the application of genetic engineering to the production of foodstuffs (Adam 2000). In Europe a number of food scares, especially the so-called 'Mad Cow Disease', prepared the terrain for a vibrant politicization of food consumption, the adoption of a vocabulary of risk on the part of (most) political institutions, vociferous criticism on the part of consumers and commercial opportunities for green products well beyond niche marketing. Mediating between the different interests of its member states, the European Union has adopted a politics of 'precautionality' which differs markedly from the deregulatory position taken by the US. While there are important national differences between European states with respect to GM food, the differences between Europe and the United States are probably greater. They respond to different conditions at different levels: economic (the US is the principal producer of genetically modified foodstuffs and the master of this technology), cultural (in Europe greater weight is given to food safety and gastronomy, and environmentalism is more widely spread), and political (the centralised agricultural policies of the European Union and its subsidies have safeguarded, at least in some regions, small scale agricultural traditions) (Sassatelli and Scott 2001).

The process of globalization doesn't imply that *states* have abdicated their function of regulating the circulation of commodities (Robertson 1992; Scott 1997). The history of modernity has often been accompanied by battles and wars undertaken in the name of protectionism and anti-protectionism. One only needs to recall that the very birth of the United States was principally due to the continually frustrated requests of American colonists to trade freely, without having to be subject to the heavy English taxes on sugar, molasses, tobacco, cod, etc. and that at the time of the American Revolution sympathizers of the American cause would refuse to buy English goods (Breen 2004; Glickman 1997; see also Chapters 2 and 7). Common belief has it that this same nation, following its own decolonization, is now guiding the global colonization of markets. To be sure, the United States is not only the promoter of the free global market: staying with the food sector for example, after the European Union had prohibited trading hormone-treated meat and milk, the US responded by raising punitive taxes on typically European cheeses like Roquefort and Parmigiano Reggiano, and on high quality traditional products like *foie gras* and Parma ham. However, the process of globalization itself is something more than, and different from, Americanization in disguise.

While it would be foolish to deny that American lifestyles (for certain commodities and certain people in specific times and places) have come to play a hegemonic role, in the course of the 20th century America has not worked alone as the harbinger of an irresistible empire of taste (De Grazia 2005; see also Chapter 2). There are undoubtedly certain brands that are genuine global icons, but not all of these brands come from the US: alongside the paradigmatically American

Coca-Cola, Nike, Apple and McDonald's, we can place the Japanese Toyota, the Finnish Nokia, the Swedish Ikea, the British Body Shop, the Italian Benetton, the Dutch Heineken, the Austrian Red Bull, the Swiss Swatch, and so on. In turn, rationalized forms of provision such as McDonald's are anything but exclusively American in origin. Against the vices of diffusionism, we may recall that, precisely in the case of fast-food, the first instance of a rationalized chain has occurred in Germany. Exploiting the advantages of mass production and reaching impressive levels of predictability, as early as the beginning of the 20th century the Aschinger brothers had established the fast-food model with their chain of eateries, serving low-cost, ready-to-eat and indeed pre-fabricated food such as white bread break-fast rolls (including the popular *Hackepeter*, with minced raw meat and onions), *Bockwurst*, cold potato salad and beer (Allen 2002).

Furthermore, while 'America' and the 'West' are (unevenly) hegemonic, there are various, more or less powerful, versions of them. Various national and local cultures construct particular visions of America, American consumer lifestyles and American business procedures (Howes 1996; Zeitlin and Herrigel 2000). Nicholas Thomas (1991) has demonstrated the pivotal role played in the colonies of the South Pacific by the construction of narratives around European trade goods which indigenized them in accordance with local cultural schemes. Eastern countries, such as India, Japan and China, which have national traditions often much longer than those of Western countries, clearly offer their own picture of the West and America (Brewer and Trentmann 2006). For example, it is through the marking of certain foods and clothes in public presentational arenas as 'Western' that contemporary 'Japanese' menus and dress styles are re-invented and canonized in an increasing market for nostalgic goods (Goldstein-Gidoni 2001). More broadly, as Richard Wilk (1998) has shown, it is difficult to maintain that developing countries simply imitate Western models of consumption, following in their footsteps. Instead, they construct their own vision of Western modernity. All in all, both West and East, as well as otherness and similarity, are continuously reframed in the cultural circuit of the commodity: they are played upon both in the commoditization process and in the various local practices of appropriation across the globe (Howes 1996). A final cautionary tale should be mentioned here: nationality of origin or spatial coding is not always primarily relevant for the consumption of global products. More important is how they manage to embed themselves in different local cultures, mixing with different commodities and being translated into new, particular meanings by their local practical uses which are often primarily coded by gender, generation, profession or status.

All in all, the notion of globalization adopted by Ritzer places an excessive emphasis *on homogeneity* and *American imperialism*. On the contrary, the most important studies in this field have shown that *standardization* is accompanied by *heterogenization*, and *globalization* by *localization* (Appadurai 1996 García Canclini 2001; Featherstone 1990; Robertson 1992). Concepts such as 'hybridization', 'creolization', 'domestication' all point to the fact that goods, as well as market transactions, have to be contextualized in local realities, and are thus transformed in the process. As we have already seen (see Chapter 1), globalization is a process that stretches over a long period, with its origins at the end of the medieval era and coeval with the development of modernity. In this light, it is clearer that the economic and cultural interconnection of the entire globe was and still is accompanied by the localization of the concrete forms in which it occurs. Studying consumption in Caribbean cultures, Daniel Miller (1997a) has shown, for instance, that the inhabitants of Trinidad have made Coca-Cola their own, modifying its uses and meanings: for them this is not so much a soft drink as a drink for evenings of entertainment, to be drunk along with rum, the preferred local tipple (see also Howes 1996, introduction). Like Coca-Cola, McDonald's adapts to local conditions, tastes and habits: in Israel Big Macs are sold without cheese so as not to contravene the kosher norms of Jewish cuisine which require the separation of meat and milk-products; in India the Maharajah Mac made with mutton is the most popular burger, being consumed by both Muslims prohibited from eating pork and Hindus prohibited from eating beef (Watson 1997). In almost all countries something has been inserted from local traditions into McDonald's menus: Würstel and beer in Germany, salmon sandwiches in Norway, and pasta salad in Italy.

These phenomena cannot simply be reduced to marketing strategies or superficial concessions to local traditions, as Ritzer would have it. Trying to qualify Ritzer's claims, Uri Ram (2004) has proposed that homogenization occurs at the structural-institutional level, and heterogenization at the expressive-symbolic level. Ram looks at the spread of McDonald's in Israel and at the development of the indigenous 'falafel' fast-foods, which provide locals with an ethnic alternative within the wider paradigm of McDonaldization. His contention is that global technological, organizational and commercial flows need not destroy local habits; on the contrary they feed on them, 'subsuming and appropriating the local, to the extent that the seemingly local, symbolically, becomes a specimen of the global, structurally' (ibid, 11). Such a perspective implies that production and consumption are asymmetrical. Still, it displays some of the vices of technological determinism, suggesting yet again that modern, rationalized technology is 'real' and local, indigenous meanings are purely cosmetic. Whatever is touched by global retail and production techniques, involving economies of scale, standardization and rationalization, is posited as losing its deep specificity and not making a difference. This presumes that indigenous forms are mere instruments in the hands of a monolithic global trend rather than addressing how, in actual practice, the local cultures of production and retail have negotiated global business techniques. It thus offers a partial reading not only of consumption, but also of production and retail, all of which are embedded in particular shared cultural understandings, social relations and political contexts. In fact, the process of globalization pulls in two different directions: it implies a change of the local culture of consumption but also an adjustment of the operating standards of the business in a given territory (Brewer and Trentmann 2006; Howes 1996; Jackson 2004; Zeitlin and Herrigel 2000).

All in all, the spread of instrumental rationality which Ritzer conveniently sums up with the term McDonaldization does not exhaust the global dynamics of consumption (see Figure 8.1). Just as globalization is accompanied by localization, so de-territorialization and universalism are matched by an emphasis on the territory and cultural specificity. Likewise, Mcdonaldization (the efficiency, predictability, calculability and control which increasingly characterize global commodity

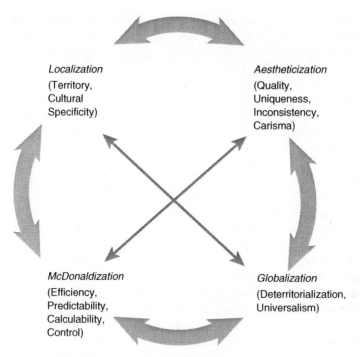

Figure 8.1   The global dynamics of consumption

production and circulation) is countered by aestheticization. The latter takes the form of local quality-oriented business and retail, of various kinds of associations which promote taste refinement, tradition and territorial awareness and, above all, of consumer practices which stress quality and uniqueness, and may pursue irregularity as a trace of charismatic elements.

In the final analysis, globalization is not just homogenization, but also hetero-genization: it exposes local realities to the numerous fluxes of global commodities so that each local reality ends up closer to a greater variety of changes as well as dangers. In conceptual terms, a complete globalization of culture would probably implicate a shared but hyper-differentiated field of tastes, values, styles and opportunities uprooted from their places of provenance (Appadurai 1996). In such a field, power differences and power relations will not disappear, but will become more complex and finely tuned. In actual fact, processes which are cur-rently collected under the banner of globalization tend to make clear that tradi-tions are continually invented rather than the response of a homogeneous culture, that they are not neutral and often favour hierarchies and inequalities. Even in traditional and tribal societies, the members of a group don't share a single and uniform set of understandings: culture is not something that social actors inherit as an undifferentiated block from their forebears. Culture, including the culture of consumption, is a social practice which is continually accomplished in various ways by social actors who thereby overcome some differences and create others. Facing globalization, local cultures of consumption offer both possibilities of empowerment and development, and occasions for the reproduction or creation of exclusion and disadvantage.[7]

Ethnic differences in particular tend to consolidate themselves reflexively through consumption, especially when migrants encounter commodities and commercial contexts different from those taken for granted by tradition. By and large, international migration is an important feature of globalization, which the McDonaldization thesis leaves largely unexplored. International migration spurs transnational economic links through family networks (i.e. the growing phenomenon of remittances) and implies that the same people may manage consumption in quite different ways across different cultures (i.e. migrants' periodic returns to the country of origin being an occasion for conspicuous consumption which is otherwise negated in the hosting country) (see Salih 2003). Moreover, in Western multicultural societies consumption has come to be coded by ethnicity both in the private sphere, through family rituals celebrating the family (Pleck 2000), and on the commercial scene, through marketing and advertising addressing ethnic identities (Davila 2001).

A much-studied phenomenon is that of ethnic cuisine (Belasco and Scranton 2002). Also in this case we must acknowledge the ambivalence of consumption. Refugees and immigrants certainly use food to remain anchored to their traditions, but in doing so they reproduce them in their destinations, often becoming important agents of change in the eating habits of their host society (Cook and Crang 1996). Gastronomic traditions have thus not simply been pushed out by the food industry. On the contrary, at present we are witnessing a genuine boom in ethnic cuisine, which is the result both of migrants' self-promotion and entrepreneurship and of marketing needs for 'themes' and 'types' adjusted to multicultural markets (Ferrero 2002; Girardelli 2004; Van der Berghe 1984; Warde 2000). In her book *We Are What We Eat* the American historian Donna Gabaccia (1998) has shown how the development of a national canned food industry in that crucible of mass multiculturalism that is the United States hasn't meant the negation of every form of ethnic association. Instead, ethnic traditions have been put into play and re-invented through a process of creolization. No matter how much they may be constructed and tenuously connected to local culture and environment, the various ethnic or regional cuisines of the US represent a code which helps consumers choose their meals. Moreover, these have an ambivalent role with respect to the different ethnicities themselves: on the one hand, they contribute to fixing pretty clear images, even stereotypes, of these differences; on the other, they provide a territory in which respective boundaries can be overcome without serious risks.

Alternative consumption and social movements

McDonaldization has had, and may well continue to have, its moment of popularity, but it is difficult to agree with Ritzer's (1993) warning that this has become indisputable as 'a value in and of itself'. It is beyond doubt that through its brands and lifestyles the US in particular promotes itself and its dominant model of development on a global scale, claiming both economic and moral leadership. However, the globalized rationalization bound to American cultural hegemony tends to raise local hackles, provoking resistance in many different forms, including fundamentalist ones. Following what has been called the 'global paradox' (Naisbitt 1994), we may say that globalization underlines the market's effects because it makes the production chain more complex, but also more visible. It therefore spurs the development of new global dimensions of inequality as well as helping the diffusion of tools of industrial regulation, highlighting the environmental and social effects of economic processes and creating the conditions for market contestation. Focusing once again on the food sector by way of example, we can see that the diffusion of low-cost fast-food based on minced meat has done much to promote a request for health, authenticity and taste. Thus, vegetarianism, especially when predicated on an ethics of respect for animals, can take shape as a kind of resistance, itself global and even universalistic, to some aspects of the spread of McDonald's (Tester 1999). Likewise, while the different European nations have responded differently to the question of the promotion and safeguarding of their culinary traditions, food scares associated with heavily industrialized farming have often directed the attention of European consumers towards products which are 'natural', 'local', 'traditional' and from sources that adopt sustainable agricultural practices (Sassatelli and Scott 2001).

According to this logic, some consumers, some cultural intermediaries and some (small) producers have allied through various forms of association against standardization and globalization, promoting *alternative consumption* in the form of local, traditional and sustainable produce (Sassatelli 2004). For example, thanks to an initiative to save traditional bread, the majority of bread consumed in France still comes from small neighbourhood bakeries; in England, on the other hand, the campaign for traditional beer produced directly by pubs, the Real Ale Campaign, has spurred a genuine renaissance in local brewing. Movements for the safeguarding of local produce and territories have emerged both in the Western and the Eastern world. A well-known example is Navdanya ('nine seeds'), founded in India in 1987 by economist and social ecologist Vandana Shiva. In Europe, Italy has given birth to Slowfood, a movement specifically dedicated to the safeguarding of typical local produce and gastronomy. Demonstrating the strength of the local/ global dialectic, Slowfood has quickly become an international actor for the global promotion of the local.[8] The initial idea of this movement was to favour a gastronomic association which could connect food culture to local traditions and the biodiversity of territory. Of course, a significant portion of the Slowfood initiative – from the International *Salone del Gusto* (Hall of Taste) which takes place in Turin, to their gastronomic guides translated into many languages – concerns middle-class consumers who like good cooking; but the movement also has different ambitions. In the name of what one of its founders has defined as an 'eco-gastronomic vocation', Slowfood has extended its action from consumers to producers, filling the space between production and consumption which characterizes modernity, and promoting gastronomic diversity as an intrinsic part of biological, environmental and cultural diversity.

Consumers' resistance to multinationals and standardization may also be found in a number of grass-roots movements which have organized not only boycotts of particular products, but also powerful symbolic protests. While consumer boycotts have a long history, especially in the Anglo-American world (Friedman 1999; Smith 1990), as globalization proceeds it is especially large multinationals that have become the targets of growing critical attention, both from environmentalist organizations and from the 'new global' movement. If we return again to McDonald's, it is evident that the fact that it is a global business with a pervasive territorial presence makes it an accessible target for international and local protest movements alike. A rather eloquent argument against the idea that globalization is simply a form of McDonaldization is that the spread of McDonald's on the world scale has stimulated numerous hotbeds of resistance which have often taken on global dimensions but press for local control of resources. In particular, since 1985 the London-based group of the international environmental movement Greenpeace has promoted an anti McDonald's campaign, a boycott day which is held every autumn in a growing number of countries.[9] Internationally, protests against McDonald's have generally been non-violent but none the less emblematic: for example, in France, McDonald's were filled with apples, occupied by farmers with chickens, ducks and geese, covered with dung, and so on.[10]

The anti-McDonald's movement is an example of a politics of consumption which clearly goes beyond standard consumer defence, such as that represented by the consumerist and product-testing organizations, which developed especially after the Second World War and became consolidated with the adoption by various international organizations of a body of 'consumer rights' (Aaker and Day 1982; Mayer 1989; and for a legal perspective see Everson 2006). This body is composed of four rights: the 'right to safety', to be protected from dangerous products; the 'right to information', to be protected against misleading advertising; the 'right to choose', to have access to a vast assortment of products competing for price and quality; and the 'right to be heard', that is the recognition of the importance of the consumer in the economic process. Especially in the 1980s and 1990s consumer defence has come to coincide with the provision of commoditized information-type measures which follow an instrumental 'best-buy' logic – from hunting down fraud, to the control of prices and the correctness of information. Such a consumerist approach is inspired by the idea that the sovereignty of the consumer simply goes hand in hand with the growth of product alternatives, so that consumer organizations cannot complain if the choice of products has become almost overwhelming (Sassatelli 1995). This approach responded clearly to a situation of perceived, steady 'affluence' and to the increased professionalization of consumer activists and their incorporation within marketing expert discourse (Hilton 2003). All in all, it adopts the atomistic vision of choice promoted by neo-liberal ideologies, thus individualizing consumption both in terms of effect and, paradoxically enough, representations. In fact, the vision of the consumer promoted by product-testing consumerist magazines – such as the British *Which?* or the French *Que Choisir?* – tends to translate the instrumental and calculating mentality typical of private capitalist businesses into the domestic sphere (Aldridge 1994; Pinto 1990; see also Chapters 3 and 6). Conventional product-testing consumerism constructs an allegedly isolated and powerless consumer in order to carve a particular role for itself, namely that of making sure that what powerful producers say is correct. Thus constructed, consumer choice is severed from a host of relevant issues, such as the social and environmental effects of choice, or the rights of those who are excluded from access to the variety of options available on Western markets. In doing so, conventional consumer defence has tended to externalize all factors in consumption but individualistic cos- tumer satisfaction, and to produce a defendable consumer which, corresponding to the neo-classical vision of the economic actor, may be unviable as a political agent.

While largely dominant in the course of recent history, this blend of con- sumerism is clearly not the only way for consumers to associate and for activists to represent consumers. Historically, and in particular at the beginning of the 20th century, in times of scarcity and war, consumer concerns and movements did not seem to be so severed from labour interests as they later became. In the US, for example, the National Consumer Leagues appeared just before the turn of the 20th century in large cities such as Boston, Philadelphia and Chicago. They were mostly concerned with using protests and boycotts on the part of con- sumers to exert pressure on specific enterprises denounced as both producers and employers. Founded by Florence Kelley and inspired by the Progressive Movement, social justice was their utmost purpose, i.e. they published 'white lists' of manufacturers who treated their workers fairly (Glickman 1999; Strasser et al. 1998). As suggested by Cohen (2003), the master narrative in American culture at the time was indeed that of the 'citizen consumer' rather than of the 'consumer- customer' which developed after the Second World War (see also Daunton and Hilton 2001; Strasser et al. 1998; Trentmann 2006b). Similar ethical and politi- cal concerns anticipated the sequence of mobilizations against the rising cost of living which sprang up around the First World War and which were often led by housewives' organizations (Frank 1985): they spread across myriad consumer initiatives in many Western countries, from France to Italy, from Germany to Holland. The French *Ligue Sociale d'Acheteurs*, for example, was influenced by its American counterpart and was likewise created for the ethical education of consumers, with the aim of bringing about changes in working conditions by developing a sense of responsibility in customers for the treatment of workers: 'insisting on their duties (as consumers) they posed, in fact, as citizens who had rights, in particular, the right to intervene in capitalism' (Chessel 2006, 139). While it still remains difficult to evaluate the importance and scope of such movements, as well as that of consumer cooperatives which also appeared at the beginning of the 20th century (Furlough and Strikwerda 1999), they clearly demonstrate that consumption may be coded as a politically consequential action. Broadly speaking, these movements were successful in inspiring real changes in legislation regarding work or price control, and they effectively offered women a possibility to speak out and act in the public sphere. In their capacity as 'con- sumers' women claimed the responsibility and right to intervene in masculine territories such as work, trade unionism and local and national politics (see Hilton 2002; Micheletti et al. 2004).

Such claims may be traced rather further back in history. For example, as early as the late 18th century, English women used their consumer power to support abolitionism (Davies 2000). Indeed, we may consider the political framing of the consumer a marginal but nonetheless influential stream across modern history which has appeared, in different moments and guises, to counter the dominant instrumental economic view of consumption (see Kroen 2004; Trentmann, ed. 2006b). We are now witnessing one such moment, and probably one with peculiar features (Chessel and Cochoy 2004; Micheletti 2003; Sassatelli 2006).

Indeed, as suggested, globalization has highlighted a number of external diseconomies which derive from market expansion as currently managed (such as pollution, inequality between consumers, the widening gap between North and South, food scares, etc.). In introducing innovations which alter the routines of consumption, expanding the relevant human community and promoting transnational economic flows, globalization creates a space to bring into question the naturalized boundaries of the market. Just as it becomes clear that there is nowhere else to go outside of the market, the market itself appears, on the one hand, less natural and neutral, less open and efficient, less able to guarantee alternatives to everyone's advantage; and, on the other, a site of politics to which consumers may actively contribute using their purchasing power. While traditional consumerist organizations are now trying to move on to these more systemic and political issues (see Hilton 2003), other social actors (from NGOs to environmental groups to Fair Trade organizations) are already quite active and are equipped with a framing of the consumer which better fits the task.

The growth of 'alternative' or 'ethical', 'critical' or 'political' modes of consumer action is found not only in the successful boycotting of global brands and the flourishing of symbolic initiatives against multinational companies, but also in ethical finance, the rising demand for local or organic produce, the development of Fair Trade initiatives. Such phenomena are often taken as an example of what is widely portrayed as a bottom-up cultural revolution, touching upon both everyday lifestyles and the nature of political participation. 'Negative' and 'positive' forms of 'political consumerism', as Michele Micheletti (2003) has branded them, now seem to concern a wide sector of the population in developed countries. While boycotts draw on consumers' ability to refuse certain goods, alternative consumption choices or 'buycotts' critically address contemporary consumer culture from within. For all their diversity, alternative products – green and Fair trade goods for example – are commodities which embody a critical dialogue with many aspects of commoditization as we know it (from rationalization to standardization, from lengthy commodity chains to the externalization of environmental and human costs). While they are still to be considered niche products, they score remarkable annual rates of growth and, what is more, their symbolic impact should not be underestimated. Indeed, the greening of even a tiny fraction of our daily consumption routines as well as successful boycotting combined with media campaigns of 'naming & blaming' may sometimes induce large multinationals to modify their strategies or adopt codes of best practice to recuperate a positive image with customers (Micheletti et al. 2004).

It is not easy to draw an inclusive map of the issues contained within the boundaries of critical and alternative consumption. However, the starting point of these initiatives is that consumer choice is *not universally good* and it certainly is *not a private issue* (Sassatelli 2004; 2006). Most forms of alternative consumption share some kind of interest in environmental values and address both re-distribution issues and the problems generated by the increased separation and disentanglement of production and consumption. People are typically invited to consider that over-consumption might be the root of global disasters such as climate change, and to consume better rather than to give up consumption altogether. In other words, the dominant attitude is not that of the renunciation of consumption, as Douglas (1996) wrote about green consumption, but that of a re-evaluation of what it is to consume. Consumer choice is not taken for granted as necessarily good or as a private question. Rather it is framed as a consequential and momentous practice, capable of expressing consumer sovereignty only if consumers take full responsibility for the environmental, social and political effects of their choices. Despite their diversity, many forms of alternative and critical consumption articulate a distinct notion of consumer sovereignty. Consumer sovereignty is something other than consumer choice as predicated on the variables singled out by neoclassical economics and free-market ideologies alike (i.e. price and quantity). The value-for-money logic does not hold when the target is not only individual satisfaction, but (also) a set of public goods. In the discourses surrounding alternative and critical consumer practices, consumer choice becomes action in the strong sense, i.e. consequential action. Choice as power and therefore duty is also a key theme in discourses surrounding Fairtrade initiatives: we can 'make a difference with every cup' of coffee, says Canadian Fairtrade Activist Laure Waridel in her *Coffee with Pleasure*, a well-known book on sustainable consumption. Furthermore, in many forms of alternative consumption there is, to different degrees, an attempt to re-establish a direct relation to goods, de-fetishizing commodities. Such attempts may be aimed at countering 'risk' and the perception that one is no longer controlling one's material world, as an expanding material culture has led to a separation between the spheres of production and consumption. However, they also signal that the symbolic boundaries which define the 'consumer' as a specific economic identity that lives in a private world removed from production are being destabilized.

Ethical shopping guides offer an insight into the moral and political problematization of the consumer. In the case of food, ethical shopping guides entail a shift in the way food is classified as 'good to eat': issues most conventionally related to food quality, such as safety, health, taste and aesthetic pleasure are very marginal while the environment, human rights or workers' labour conditions become primary concerns (Sassatelli 2004). Ethical shopping guides provide a set of specific criteria of choice drawing on political and ethical codes and principles. The discourses surrounding ethical shopping have to do with 'orders of justifications' (Boltanski and Thévenot 1991) which have been pushed outside the dominant mode of legitimizing markets in Western culture, i.e. the redistribution of resources and the role of demand. They promote a particular image of the consumer as truthful and right. Reference to the conditions of labour in general and child labour in particular as well as to the North/South divide are the main codifications marshalled for reframing the role of the consumer. Considered as a normative frame, critical consumerism engages directly with the hegemonic legitimizing rhetoric which emerged in the 18th century to justify market societies. As suggested (see Chapter 2), such rhetoric entailed a particular political morality, epitomized not so much by the de-moralization of luxury, as by the entrenchment of a consumption as a new sphere of action with its own rules of propriety and its own order of justification. Consumption became a matter of choice, it was constructed in opposition to production and politics as the pursuit of private happiness that would, through the invisible hand of the market, give way to public benefits.

As a frame, critical consumerism takes issue with the idea that consumers are and should be private economic hedonists, preoccupied with individual pleasures, and proposes, for the good of both the consumer and society, that the former be virtuous so as to offset the vices of both the market and politics. The identity thus bestowed on consumers draws on themes that cut across the different symbolic boundaries which have consolidated in the course of modernity (Sassatelli 2006). Themes prevalently associated with the promotion of consumption as legitimized spheres of action *per se* – 'taste', 'good taste', 'pleasure', 'fantasy', 'comfort', 'distinction', 'happiness', 'refinement', and so on – are substituted by themes prevalently associated with the definition of a democratic public sphere and production. The political and moral discourses informing critical consumerism, in Italy, Great Britain and the United States portray the consumer as essentially active. They often resort to a vocabulary which draws either on social and political activism (to purchase is to 'vote', 'protest', 'make oneself heard', 'change the world', 'help the community', 'mobilize for a better future', and so on) or on production (to purchase here becomes 'work you do for the community', 'effort done for yourself and the other', 'creative', 'productive', and so on). It might be too early to say whether this prefigures a viable shift in the notion of consumer choice itself. Yet, it emphasizes choice as a public, other-related, and therefore political, action, rather than a self-interested, private and therefore apolitical affair.

A number of voices have thus been raised in celebration of the political persona of the consumer. Political sociologists and political scientists working on new social movements have addressed these developments as essentially new forms of political participation which have supplanted and can supplant previous, traditional ones. Ulrich Beck (1997) has famously argued that if modernity is a democracy oriented towards producers, late modernity is a democracy oriented towards consumers: a pragmatic and cosmopolitan democracy where the sleepy giant of the 'sovereign citizen-consumer' is becoming a counterweight to big transnational corporations. Fuelled by the combined processes of 'individualization' and 'subpoliticization', he considers that today 'citizens discover the act of shopping as one in which they can always cast their ballot – on a world scale, no less' (Beck and Gernsheim 2001, 44). The enthusiastic tone of such ideas notwithstanding, it would be mistaken to attribute an intrinsic and deliberately political finality to consumer choice or to consider it equivalent to more traditional forms of political action. As suggested, practices of getting and using are often not construed as consumption by social actors who self-reflexively constitute themselves as consumers, let alone 'political' ones. Many of the practices which come under the umbrella of political consumerism might indeed be conducted by consumers who have in mind meanings and objectives other than the strictly political. What they are doing, both in form and content, cannot be easily equated with the expression of a 'vote' on collective goods such as justice, equality, nature, etc. For one thing, for example, while each citizen has one vote in contemporary democracies, consumers are notably different in terms of purchasing power and may thus have rather different degrees of influence.

We must thus open up the equation between political consumerism and political action. Only in this way can we better understand the ambivalent role of critical consumption. Today's politically charged consumer action often articulates the local/global dynamic. Humanitarian justice and respect for local tradition may run into conflict in Fairtrade protocols. Fairtrade protocols may themselves work as instruments of cultural hegemony and economic domination in an ever-competitive global market. A global humanitarian consumer-citizenship may also require further economic disentanglement, as it commands growth rates and volumes for green and ethical products which are at odds with small-scale local production. It may therefore run against the re-embedment of economic action in local environments, which is one of the aspirations of alternative and critical consumer practices. Furthermore, while the different practices which contribute to the field of alternative consumption do signal a political problematization of consumer culture, they are nonetheless fragmented and potentially conflicting, rendering the formation of viable collective identities rather difficult. For example, alternative distribution networks (from second-hand shops to farmers' markets to box schemes) not only respond to a politically conscious middle-class consumer, but also attract urban disadvantaged groups which might not be able to afford shopping via formal channels (Williams and Paddock 2003). Likewise, the demand for organically grown vegetables typically mixes private health concerns with some degree of environmental consciousness and emerges from diverse sources, from a large vegetarian movement as well as health-conscious or gourmet carnivores (Lockie and Kristen 2002). Indeed, different practices and issues may converge or not – just as green consumers may or may not sympathize with the re-distributive concerns which inspire Fairtrade.

Contradictions of this kind might be acknowledged, and yet they are not easy to tackle for activists themselves. In particular, engaging with global markets, may imply an emphasis on efficiency and promotion which can transform green and Fairtrade products into fetishes (Hudson and Hudson 2003; Levi and Linton 2003), especially as the marketing and advertising industries are well aware of the interests in ecological, ethical and political themes among certain strata of Western populations and have long started to promote their own versions of the 'greening of demand' (Micheletti et al. 2004; Zinkhan and Carlson 1995). The institutionalization of a dialogue between consumerist and environmental organizations and large multinational commercial companies may also have ambivalent effects (Doubleday 2004). This does not mean that ethical claims can be easily used in a pure instrumental fashion, as ethically oriented consumers may demand proof of standards and may exert much greater pressure on companies than expected. But it does suggest that while Ritzer's apocalyptic description of McDonaldization is largely one-sided, it would likewise be mistaken to suppose that the consumer now translates on a global scale the duties and capacities of the citizen as Beck would have it. Political consumerism, in other words, does not simply realize a new 'global citizenship', working on pure universalistic, cosmopolitan and humanitarian grounds as suggested by Lance Bennett (2004).[11] It is unrealistic to imagine that there is a clear-cut, direct and symmetrical demand/ supply relation between consumers and producers which can immediately translate awareness of effects into a politics of justice. We are perhaps still a long way from being able to evaluate whether a political view of consumer choice will have appreciable effects on the way we consume, and on the dynamics of inclusion and exclusion which run through them. However, the current framing of the consumer as a political actor suggests that consumers today, perhaps more than ever, are continuously turned into key social figures via symbolic processes which cut across some of our firmest cultural boundaries, thus making consumption an important and contested terrain of social change.

Summary

Consumption happens in space and takes time. This chapter considers consumption as a situated social activity and addresses institutions and occasions, places and times of consumption as social settings which facilitate the translation of consumers' taste into practice. In contemporary society consumption is often organized in specific *commercial institutions* typically coded as places of 'leisure' (restaurants, gyms, theme parks, malls, etc.). These *public spaces* of consumption have their own rules, sanctioning certain behaviours and identities while stigmatizing others. They go hand in hand with the organization of the *home* as a *private space* of consumption opposed to production. The coding of consumption as *leisure*, both within public and private spaces, is an ambivalent phenomenon which overlooks the fact that consumption and work, pleasure and discipline are closely intertwined. Consumption is also shown to be ambivalent in that it both produces genuine personal involvement and meanings and works on commercial codes and social hierarchies, which it partly reproduces and partly overturns. Furthermore, the chapter addresses the *disarticulation* of production and consumption in time and space which has been enhanced by *globalization*. Globalization and consumption have been read together by **George Ritzer** through the lenses of *McDonaldization*. Modelled on to McDonald's, this process signals the global diffusion of business which organizes contexts of consumption through efficiency, predictability, calculability and the substitution of human labour with that of machines. McDonaldization paints a picture which is excessively characterized by homogeneity and American imperialism and does not account for the local domestication of global trends. On the contrary, the most important studies in this field have shown that *standardization* is accompanied by *heterogeneity*, and *globalization* by *localism*. Finally, the chapter deals with the spread of *social movements* which question the limits of the market and the relationship between production and consumption. *Alternative consumption* critically address globalization as de-territorialization, the disarticulation of production and consumption, and the separation of politics and the market. This opens the question whether awareness of systemic, unintended effects may translate consumption into a genuine politics of justice.

Notes

1 Worth mentioning is the organization of direct sales at home through involving and putting to work housewives' networks, such as in the case of Avon, Stanhome or Tupperware. Initiated in the 1950s, the 'Tupperware party' retail strategy-whereby the dealers went to a volunteer 'hostess' home, first demonstrating and then selling their products to gatherings of friends and neighbours-has been highly successful (Clark 1997).

2 The possibility of exploiting the spectacle of commodities without actual purchase is a fundamental characteristic of the new shopping places, as evidenced in the ubiquitous use of the phrase 'I'm just looking' to justify one's presence in shops (Bowlby 1993; Williams 1982). Obviously the shopper's gaze is a codified gaze which, for example, cannot express itself in touch ('look but don't touch') and has to be contained, at least openly, by various forms of respect for others, including Goffman's 'civil inattention'. In other words, rather than a solitary practice, shopping may be an interactive dance in which consumers frequently play the role of the apprentice in disguise: they have to learn new styles and tastes without letting this be openly understood.

3 Liz Cohen (2003) also stresses the ambivalence of shopping centres in providing genuine public spaces. She counters the image of shopping as an activity which increasingly privatizes and isolates the American public, showing that shopping malls have provided their costumers with a whole range of community activities including city fairs and concerts. However, she shows that shopping malls have become much more exclusive than city streets and that market segmentation has become the guiding principle of their mix of commercial and civic activities.

4 To be sure, the 'liberation' of time from work is not an evenly distributed phenomenon; moreover amongst the new middle classes there is a growing conception of work as a hobby, in which work takes on some of the characteriztics of leisure and consumption (Gershuny 2000).

5 McDonald's is present in 115 countries around the world: there are more than 2,800 McDonald's in Japan, more than a thousand in Canada, almost a thousand in Germany and 680 in traditionalist Italy. For an illuminating discussion of the global fast-food industry and the food sector in general which, albeit critical, differs from Ritzer's, see Fine (2002b).

6 For example, Ritzer uses the Weberian metaphor of the 'iron cage' (*stalhartes Gehause*) in a one-sided manner, when in fact it implies a fundamental ambivalence: it is a shell that protects and provides opportunity to the actor even as it limits action: (see Smart 1999).

7 Such a position provides an entry into the debate about the protection of local and marginal culture and the opportunity to close off cultures from the market. An informed discussion of this topic which offers an analysis of policy making and law regulation is provided by David Howes's (1996) study of the situation of the Hopi Indians in Arizona.

8 Slowfood was started in the middle of the 1980s by a group of cooks and gastronomes following the protests that accompanied the opening of the first McDonald's in Rome. The movement intended to promote traditional Italian *osterie* and *trattorie* (i.e. traditional eateries) threatened by the appearance of chains of cheap restaurants. The organization has spread to 83 countries around the world. The magazine *Slow* is distributed to 40,000 members in Italy, and more than 70,000 globally, is produced in five languages and presents articles on culinary traditions around the world; see also Miele and Murdoch (2002) and Pietrykowski (2004).

9 The growing success of this initiative is also due to the massive public resonance of the libel case that McDonald's brought against two Greenpeace activists, for their distribution of protest leaflets. The leaflet maintained that the American giant exploited children in its advertising and its employees with low pay, promoted unhealthy eating, damaged the environment through encouraging the deforestation of Amazonia to produce low-cost forage, and treated animals in an inhumane fashion. The so-called 'McLibel case', still the longest running case in English legal history (from 1994 to 1997), was a public relations disaster for McDonald's (see Vidal 1997).

10 Some of these actions were guided by the farmer and trade-unionist Joseph Bové, who reached international fame by destroying a barrel of his precious Roquefort cheese in front of a McDonald's during the anti-globalization protest in Seattle in 1999. Bové's actions can be seen as part of the French tradition which, has given a patriotic cast to agricultural policy and ties gastronomy to the safeguarding of the national territory

(Mennell 1996), and yet transcend this to promote local and sustainable agriculture at the international level. In the logic behind Bové's protest, production and consumption are not separated: both are political questions since the counterpart to exploited workers is said to be the consumers, who find it ever harder to locate genuine products (see Bové 1999).

11 Certainly in post-colonial times such as ours, overt nationalistic uses of goods may come under attack, but this does not mean that our consumer identities are truly cosmopolitan. Politically charged consumer actions often have a national orientation (see Micheletti 2003; Trentmann 2006b), being entangled in national public debates, rather than representing a real form of transnational citizenship embedded in a global public discourse.

Epilogue:
Consumers, Consumer Culture(s) and the Practices of Consumption

This book has set itself an ambitious goal: offering a critical view of the phenomena gathered under the aegis of consumption, a view which both gives the practices of getting and using goods their due and sets them in wider social and economic, cultural and political contexts. To a large extent, to talk about consumer culture today is to talk about modernity or late modernity. Such an epochal reading has helped to establish consumption as a legitimate and important field of enquiry. Yet, if it remains at an abstract level, an engagement with modernity may jeopardize our capacity to read consumption in everyday life.

To be sure, consumer culture is constantly used as a hybrid concept, referring sometimes exclusively to advertising and the commercialization of goods, sometimes to the web of practices which make up everyday consumption. Just as well, the notion of consumption covers different meanings – from purchase, to use, to waste – which are equally inscribed in ordinary language and expert discourse. Finally, people are described as consumers because they buy and use, store and maintain, manage and fantasize commodities, yet we rarely ask ourselves to what extent people actually conceive themselves as consumers while they perform these assorted activities. Awareness of these issues should sensitize us to the multiplicity of meanings, images, practices, institutions and identities which fill in the arena of consumption. We all consume, but we all do it differently, and certainly we think of it differently. While conventionally we speak of 'consumer culture' in the singular, there are a variety of different, situated, institutionalized consumer cultures in the plural. Likewise, while we speak of 'consumer choice' in the singular, there are multiple, often conflicting reasons for choosing goods, as well as a variety of ways of both representing the 'consumer' and claiming such a role for oneself.

This should not mean that we ought to throw away notions such as consumer culture or the consumer. Yes, they are indeed both imprecise and analytically wanting. Still, they are used in everyday life and public discourse, and increasingly so. They are, as it were, key elements of 'folk language' in contemporary culture whose wide currency is partly due to the fact that they are greatly contested and go right to the heart of our ways of being and living together. They are called forth by market actors to sell goods as well as being deployed by social and political actors to mobilize people towards more collective ends. Analytical clarification within scholarly language should thus be pursued by problematizing these notions with reference to historically and socially situated processes of cultural classification and representation.

Consumer culture is made of both individual and collective actors, commodities and institutions, representations and actual patterns of actions. For consumption as for other social arenas, we may say with Foucault (1980) that 'nothing happens exactly as forecast', even though it happens within a determined field of possibilities and through cultural repertoires, whose anticipated rewards and losses contribute to structure. Being themselves the result of situated practices assembled in specific contexts (advertising cultures, consumerist groups, commercial spaces, etc.), representations reflect, to varying degrees, the consumer practices they are meant to portray or call forth, and the consumer identities they wish to mobilize. Still, as repertoires for mutual understanding and justification, images and discourses cannot be reduced to patterns of actions. Hirschman (1977) has taught us that not all the elements of a historical transformation coincide perfectly: there is always a gap between discourse and intentions, intended and unintended effects. Awareness of this potential gap helps account for the dynamics through which certain themes emerged and became hegemonic throughout history: that is how power and history shape the conditions for mutual understanding. It allows us to address the contested nature of representation, considering people in different institutional positions and their different capacities to fix powerful images of consumption in the public domain. It also draws our attention to the elusive and multiform nature of the interlocking of representations and actual events. People may use certain goods and readily embrace the encoded commercial images, such as when they perform gender identities using goods in accordance with commercial scripts of more or less hegemonic masculinity or femininity. People may also use goods in oppositional ways, such as when the mainstream is turned upside down in sub-cultural styles; or they may make use of goods out of necessity and with a degree of distance, such as when the poor half-willing recur to welfare provision trying to shut themselves off its disciplinary effects. People may also find themselves using goods which are encoded through meanings contradictory to actual events, such as when working women do not have time to cook but prefer pre-cooked food coded through traditional images of femininity; or they may be unable to carry out the actions which a variety of unused items help them fantasize, such as when time-pressured businessmen purchase expensive camping equipment which will be used only to dream of more leisured styles of fatherhood. The disarticulation in time and space of production, exchange and consumption probably helps widen the gap between patterns of actions and representations, thus making commodity circuits contested and contradictory, but also dynamic and creative, arenas.

While they may be presented as neutral and objective, processes of cultural classification and representation always entail some measure of moralization. As cultural analysts we better leave moral criticism to the philosophers. Yet we can and indeed should scrutinize very closely the ways in which commodities are considered superior or inferior, consumers' actions are deemed appropriate and legitimate or inappropriate and deviant, consumers themselves are portrayed as moral beings or as depraved souls. Certainly, there is ample evidence that, no matter how much markets try to shut themselves off from other spheres of life, they are, to quote Polanyi (1957), 'embedded' in social networks. Likewise, we witness daily the extent to which the instrumental picture of the consumer is institutionally reinforced, and frankly hegemonic, in a number of key institutional contexts. Much more research is needed on how these competing views of the consumer and consumption are promoted by institutional actors and are being mixed and mingled in daily practices, taking on a distinctive moral character which accounts for much of their compelling force. Consumer culture is constituted as a culture both *for* consumers and *of* consumers: both a set of commodities for people to consume and a set of representations of people as consumers. Just as the notion of consumer sovereignty has worked as a normative claim which helped construct the market as specialized sphere of action, so the current political framing of consumers, which builds on and mobilizes their capacity to resist market disentanglement, constructs an ideal image of the consumer. As shown, the negotiation of the boundaries of the commodity form and the normalization of consumption as premised on visions of the subject-consumer may tell us much of what is cooking in contemporary consumer culture. The seductive charm of the consumer as a free autonomous chooser – whether as a self-interested forward-looking hedonist or a politically engaged responsible actor – is all but gone, yet its many practical renditions and symbolic nuances means that it can be dragged into service for a variety of different pursuits, contributing to the continuous shifting of the repertoires for representing and accomplishing consumer practices.

As suggested throughout the book, everyday consumption should be seen as a territory neither for the domination of the masses nor for the freedom of the self. While the separation between production and consumption informs much of our thinking, ordinary life and large scale social process are equally based on their combination. Likewise, consumption cannot be seen as either instrumentally rational behaviour or as irrational expressive behaviour. The pleasures and tyrannies of consumption are not islands of indigenous local traditions in a frigid sea of centrally controlled technologies and standardization. All in all, consumption need not be a dichotomous phenomenon; it may involve dichotomy but it also includes other patterns of relations, more complex, nuanced and opaque. Yet, consumption is often understood through dichotomies. To say that images, representations and vocabularies are structured through chains of binary oppositions while reality may not be, does not mean that we have to blind ourselves to the fact that cultural processes do happen through the negotiation, qualification, and challenging of dichotomies. In this sense, while we may be convinced that dichotomies are fallacies of Western thinking, a host of dichotomous oppositions such as public/private, local/global, individualization/mobilization, etc. are productive cultural devices. They are confronted and qualified through meaningful and complex social relations which pervade economic relations, including production, acquisition and the use of goods and services.

The cultural repertoires for understanding consumption are as rich and varied as the material circumstances in which consumption occurs. An awareness of the diverse material, historical and cultural scripting of consumption may help us consider the specificity of contemporary consumer culture. In particular, through the first part of the book I have shown that goods have always had symbolic value, but they have not always been, nor indeed always are, commodities. Likewise, people have always used and consumed goods, but they have not always been, nor always are, consumers. The commoditization process appears to be enlarging, intermingling with intimate relations. Still, in this book the commodity form has been considered as a hegemonic framing of goods which is not co-extensive with the symbolic values and the material practices through which people consume, and indeed produce and distribute, goods. In particular, as suggested in the second and third parts of the book, through consumption people negotiate in everyday life the symbolic values which have been inscribed in the goods by commercial processes, the identities which are implicit in promotional images, and the very ways of using which are organized by commercial institutions. Following authors such as Simmel, Sahlins, De Certeau and Miller, the book has pursued the idea that consumption is a form of value production which realizes the object as lived culture: it engages with commoditization, works on it and sometimes subverts it. Part of this value production has a routine character and happens without much intended attention to the commodity form; part of it is more reflexively related to the commodity form, such as gift-giving and collecting; finally, part of it, such as recycling or political consumption, tries to redress the commoditization process as we know it. Yet, even the choice of alternative Fairtrade goods or consumers' boycotts is not guaranteed to alter political economic structure or to shape consumption into political action as such.

In other words, by appropriating goods in everyday life consumers de-commoditize them, but this does not mean that they overturn the commoditization process. We should be wary of an heroic picture of de-commoditization. It is wrong to suppose that consuming Coke in a particular way creates communities, but does not create a new product. Indeed, products exist as culture through the practices which entangle them in lived social relationships. Yet, the economic value of a commodity is, to a degree, independent of the particular meanings which may be given to it, or the specific uses it may be put to in everyday life. To capture such value articulation and the asymmetry between production and consumption, I have looked at consumption through Goffman's (1974) notion of 'keying' – a form of re-framing which, like geometrical translation, does not substitute the original framework, but blocks its relevance and systematically transforms it so that participants in the activity may reconstitute what is going on. In this perspective, consumption takes place in institutional contexts which exist as relatively separated fields of practice against the background of commoditization. These fields consolidate around the reception of goods, their de-commoditization and the production of consumers. Fields of practical activities are of the essence: it is fields of practical activity which generate wants, rather than vice versa. Differentiation within such fields is also, at least partly, a function of their internal history and of our involvement in it, rather than being directly determined by larger processes such as the social structure, transferable dispositions, production or commercialization. Following this line of thought, I have proposed that contexts of consumption – from subcultures, to amateur circles, to homes and families, to commercial institutions – are also arenas for the consolidation of consumer capital, namely locally sustained consumer capacities, knowledge and hierarchies. Such a notion, however, does not simply vindicate consumption as a creative pursuit. It may be used to show that the accumulation of consumer capital requires time and resources, and that each instance of consumption competes with other consumption as well as other social activities. It may be deployed to show that consumption contributes to producing and orientating further consumption by providing people with specific abilities, manners and knowledge. It allows us to think that genuine experiences of involvement and pleasure are organized and patterned and that they may be more or less conducive to creativity depending on the organization of context. Therefore, it should also alert us to the fact that contexts of consumption are different. These differences, in turn, shed light on the fact that there may be a gap, and even a trade-off, between internal meanings in terms of satisfaction and creativity and external rewards in terms of status and recognition. Consumer capital may not be easily transferable across fields, as it is evident in the case of sub-cultural capital.

A similar line of thought can be pursued at the macro level. While they are relatively autonomous from production, consumers' activities may not have the intended effects. There is no simple relation between the consolidation of a specific field or culture of consumption, and its external effects on production and retail. As suggested, volumes of sale do not describe what consumers do, yet they are pretty much what producers are professionally asked to be looking for. Still, rather than being untouched by de-commoditization, the processes of production of economic value need to draw on the active work done by consumers. And just as the effect of production on consumption is mediated through consumer rituals and practices, the effect of consumption on production is mediated through the cultures of the business world. This picture gives rise to countless questions which have largely to do with how cultures of production, commercialization and consumption interface. Much of what is now going on in scholarship about consumption indeed addresses such questions. It problematizes the reification of the boundary between economy and culture, which the disciplinary specialization of those who study economic processes and those who study cultural processes has sustained.

The book has pointed out the remarkable richness and diversity of contemporary consumption and the difficulty of accommodating such variety within scholarly research. An excessive emphasis on the differences between consumption and production may exclude from view the patterns of difference among consumers. A focus on the different goods which are used by people of different sorts may blind us to the fact that different people give different meanings to the same goods or that the same people give different meanings to goods according to context. Emphasis on commercial institutions as shaped by standardized scripts of provision may blind us to the fact that they are also sites for the consumption of goods enriched by personal relations. A perspective on commodities as a set of cross-referencing symbols may jeopardize our understanding of consumer cultures as ongoing social networks bringing these goods to life. Emphasis on consumption as performing crucial relational work and on the relatively separated worlds which are sustained through consumption may blind us to the fact that the external rewards for engaging in different consumer activities may vary quite dramatically. To do justice to consumption and its plenitude, I have called for an awareness of its ambivalence and of the power relations through which it unfolds. This is facilitated by an integration of theory and empirical research and recommends a degree of methodological and disciplinary pluralism.

An apparently simple catch-phrase such as 'consumer culture' may be used as a fetish to ignore the contested genealogy of the subject-consumer and the complex economic and cultural processes which underpin consumption. Studies of consumption appear to have reached such maturity as to open up and problematize this notion. Reference to consumer culture can thus be put to use to reveal that in contemporary culture subjects change commodities through consumption, and are likewise changed in the process. This is what my book has attended to, offering a taste of the many trajectories though which cultures of consumption are constituted as ongoing, creative and dynamic fields of power relations.

Further Reading and Resources

The reader may find here a selective guide for further reading and resources from the vast scholarship on consumption and consumer cultures in the English language. Full references are given only for works which do not appear in the bibliographic references.

As consumption is now a consolidated field of study, there are a number of recent edited collections which work well to provide **overviews** of the theories, themes, disciplines and methodologies available. In particular, Juliet Schor and Douglas Holt (eds) *The Consumer Society Reader* (New York: The New York Press, 2000) gathers together key contemporary contributions to the field and includes chapters from the classics on consumer culture (Veblen, Simmel, Adorno, Bourdieu, Baudrillard, etc). Daniel Miller's monumental four volumes of *Consumption: Critical Concepts in the Social Sciences* (ed. London: Routledge, 2001) provide an exhaustive interdisciplinary overview, ranging from classic theoretical discussion within sociology to recent empirical studies coming from different disciplines.

In varying proportions, a measure of **interdisciplinarity** is a feature of much contemporary writing on consumption. For a fundamental interdisciplinary collection, covering consumer behaviour studies, sociology, political economy, social psychology, anthropology and communication studies, the reader may refer to Daniel Miller's *Acknowledging Consumption* (ed., 1995). *Consumers*, a marketing textbook and reader edited by Eric Arnould, Linda Pince and George Zinkhan (2002) provides a wide ranging and critical introduction to marketing scholarship sensitive to the debates in the social sciences and humanities. *The Consumption Reader* edited by geographers David B. Clarke, Marcus A. Doel and Kate M. L. Housinaux (London: Routledge, 2003) furnishes an updated overview which approaches issues of places and spatiality. For economics, especially political economy and critical economics, a useful collection has been edited by Neva R. Goodwin, Frank Ackerman and David Kiron, *The Consumer Society. Frontier Issues in Economic Thought* (Washington DC: Island Press, 1996). Situating itself at the crossroads of history, anthropology and marketing, Grant McCracken's (1988) *Culture and Consumption* is a classic read which provides a perspective on consumer rituals.

Itself largely interdisciplinary, the **material culture** tradition is reflected in two recent readers which offer a critical survey of the field: *The Material Culture Reader* edited by Victor Buchli (London: Berg, 2002) and the *Handbook of*

Material Culture edited by Chris Tilley, Webb Keane, Susanne Kuechler, Mike Rowlands and Patricia Spyer (London: Routledge, 2005). Victor Buchli's three-volume set on *Material Culture* (London: Routlege, 2004) supplies a broad overview of the studies and approaches within this perspective. A fundamental read is Appadurai's influential collection *The Social Life of Things* (1986) which bridges anthropology and history in the study of global commodity flows. The reader should also refer to Miller's (1987) *Material Culture and Mass Consumption*, which provides a theoretical discussion of material culture and an influential perspective on consumption as appropriation. A useful text, more grounded in sociology, is Tim Dant's (1999) *Material Culture and the Social World*. Coming from a social psychological perspective Helga Dittmar's (1992) *The Social Psychology of Material Possession* may also be useful to chart the relationship between people and objects in contemporary cultures.

There are a number of other important volumes which collect detailed studies of consumer cultures across time, nations and markets. John Brewer and Roy Porter have distinctively contributed to summing up the **history of consumption** with their edited collection *Consumption and the World of Goods* (1993). Other useful collections are Bermingham and Brewer's (1995) *The Consumption of Culture* and Strasser, McGovern and Judd's (1998) *Getting and Spending: European and American Consumer Societies in the Twentieth Century*. To appreciate the role of both materialistic values and hedonistic ethics in the long-term development of consumer culture, the reader should consult the influential works by two historical sociologists: Chandra Mukerji's (1983) *From Graven Images* and Colin Campbell's (1987) *The Romantic Ethic and the Spirit of Modern Consumerism*. These may be usefully complemented by works on the conceptualization of luxuries through history such as Berry's (1994) *The Idea of Luxury*; on moral attitudes towards consumption such as Williams's (1982) *Dream Worlds* and Horowitz's (1985) *The Morality of Spending*. For the rise of market culture, its many manifestations across time and space, and its working the reader may also refer to Carrier's (ed. 1997) *Meanings of the Market* and Bevir and Trentmann's (eds, 2004) *Markets in Historical Contexts*. A theoretical discussion of markets sensitive to history may be found in *The Laws of the Market*, an important collection of essays edited by Michel Callon (1998) and in Don Slater and Fran Tonkiss's (2001) *Market Society* (Cambridge: Polity Press).

Consumer cultures are sites for the consolidation of **social** and **cultural boundaries**. The classic works by Pierre Bourdieu (1984), *Distinction*, and Mary Douglas and Baron Isherwood (1979) *The World of Goods* are a must here. There are a number of recent collections and contributions which chart the creative interplay between social differences and consumption across time and space. An entry into gender and consumption is provided by J. Scanlon (ed.) *The Gender and Consumer Culture Reader* (New York: New York University Press, 2002) and by *The Sex of Things*, an influential collection of historical works on gender edited by Victoria de Grazia and Elizabeth Furlough (1996). For class differences the reader may refer to the special issue of *International Labour and Working-Class History* on 'Class and Consumption' edited by De Grazia and Cohen (1999) and to the still useful sociological outlook provided by Burrows and Marsh (1992) *Consumption and Class*. Arlene Davila's (2001) *Latinos Inc.*

and Marilyn Halter's (2000) *Shopping for Identity* offer a perspective on ethnicity and marketing/advertising and Elizabeth Pleck's (2000) *Celebrating the Family* provides a theoretically informed study of ethnicity, family rituals and consumption. Consumption also works as a catalyst for social groups and in particular for sub-cultural groups. On sub-cultures and consumption, the reader may refer to Paul Willis' (1978) classic study of motorbikers and hippies and to *Club Cultures*, an important study by Sarah Thornton (1995). More broadly on popular culture and consumption the reader may find useful material in *Popular Culture: Production and Consumption*, a recent collection edited by C. Lee Harrington and D.D. Bielby (Oxford: Blackwell, 2000).

The **private sphere**, the family and intimate relationships are also important sites of consumption and labour where emotions and economic rationality intermingle. For families, the market and intimate relationships see Arlie Russel Hochschild (2003) *The Commercialization of Intimate Life* and Viviana Zelizer (2004) *The Purchase of Intimacy*. The management of domestic environments often entails routine, inconspicuous and ordinary consumption: see the second volume of *The Practice of Everyday Life* on living and cooking by Michel De Certeau, Luce Giard and Paul Mayo (Minneapolis: University of Minnesota Press, 1998) as well as Elizabeth Shove's (2003) *Comfort, Cleanliness and Convenience* which focuses on the routinized normality of consumption in the home by addressing personal cleanliness, domestic laundering and air conditioning. For a broader perspective on the routine aspect of consumption, both within and without the domestic sphere, see the collection on *Ordinary Consumption* edited by Yukka Gronow and Alan Warde (2001).

In the literature on consumer culture there is a growing awareness that consumption and production should be seen as interrelated spheres of actions. For a cultural studies perspective on such interplay the reader may refer to the important volume edited by Paul du Gay et al. (1997) *Doing Cultural Studies*. For political economy, Ben Fine's (2002) *The World of Consumption* provides an outline and application of the 'system of provision' approach. **Cultural industries** and cultural intermediaries play a key role in the interaction between production and consumption. In particular, for advertising the reader may refer to *Buy this Book*, a collection of essays edited by Mica Nava et al. (1997) while Thomas Frank's (1997) *The Conquest of Cool* offers a telling case study of the interplay between business culture and counterculture in America. For fashion, a useful compilation of contributions is supplied by J. Ash and E. Wilson, (eds) *Chic Thrills: A Fashion Reader* (London: Pandora Press, 1992) while Diana Crane's (2000) *Fashion and its Social Agenda* proposes an institutional look at the fashion world sensitive to gender issues.

A visible and institutionally consolidated phenomenon, **shopping** is much studied within both the humanities and the social sciences. Important recent studies include Erika Rappaport's (2000) *Shopping for Pleasure* on women and shopping in 18th century London; Rachel Bowlby's (2000) *Carried Away* which bridges literature, history and cultural studies; Sharon Zukin's (2004) *Point of Purchase* which offers an empirically grounded sociological perspective on contemporary American shopping cultures; and Pasi Falk and Colin Campbell's (1997) *The Shopping Experience*, which provides a useful collection of sociological studies with a more European perspective. The reader may also refer to Miller's (1998) *A Theory of Shopping*, which proposes an elaborate theoretical argument for reading shopping as a ritual.

Issues of **globalization** and **localization** have been addressed though the lenses of consumer culture. George Ritzer's (1993) *The McDonaldization of Society* contains the original formulation of the McDonaldization thesis and Victoria De Grazia's *Irresistible Empire* (2005) offers a perspective on the hegemony exercised by American culture through consumption. Arjun Appadurai's (1996) *Modernity at Large* and Nestor García Canclini's (2001) *Consumers and Citizens* put forward strong arguments for the key role of local cultures in elaborating notions of hybridization and creolization. A few collections, such as David Howes's (1996) *Cross-cultural Consumption* and Daniel Miller's (ed. 1995) *Worlds Apart* offer further detailed studies on cross-cultural consumption while the collection edited by Jonathan Zeitlin and Gary Herrigel (2000) *Americanization and its Limits* provides essays which nuance the Americanization thesis focusing on the domestication of American technologies and business procedures. Finally, for a recent global topography of consumer culture informed by historical scholarship see John Brewer and Frank Trentmann's (2006) *Consuming Cultures, Global Perspectives*.

National cultures and consumption are also important topics. England and Great Britain are probably the most documented. Many studies considered in this book indeed look at this area – from McKendrick et al. 1982, to Warde and Martens 2001, to Zweniniger-Bargielowska 2000, to cite a few. For American consumer culture see *Consumer Society in American History: A Reader*, ed. Lawrence B. Glickman (Cornell University Press, 1999) and Elizabeth Chin's (2001) *Purchasing Power*, a recent study of African American kids and their practices of getting and using goods. For consumption in the Asian continent see Beng-Huat's (2000) *Consumption in Asia* and James Watson's (ed. 1997) *Golden Arches East*. Tony Bennett, Michael Emmison and John Frow's (1999) *Accounting for Tastes* provides a useful empirical study of Australian tastes and lifestyles. Adam Arvidsson's (2002) *Marketing Modernity* and Carol Helstosky's (2004) *Garlic and Oil* address respectively the development of advertising in Italy and Italian food culture and politics; Tiersten's (2001) *Marianne in the Market* presents an outline of consumer culture in *fin-de-siècle* France, whilst Lamant (1992) compares contemporary France and US.

More recent scholarship has tried to address explicitly the **political mobilization** of consumers. Elizabeth Cohen's (2003) *A Consumers' Republic* deals with the politics of consumption in post-war America. Matthew Daunton and Matthew Hilton's (2001) *The Politics of Consumption* offers a broad historical perspective on the interface between consumers and citizens, while the collection on *Politics, Products and Markets* edited by Michele Micheletti et al. (2004) includes a variety of contributions on contemporary forms of political consumerism.

A vast **bibliography** in English is available at the website of the 'Cultures of Consumption research programme' (*http://www.consume.bbk.ac.uk/word documents/consumption%20biblio.doc*). Also useful is the annotated bibliography and selected list of websites contained in Douglas Goodman and Mirelle Cohen's *Consumer Culture. A Reference Handbook* (Oxford: ABC-Clio, 2004). A large bibliography on market cultures and the social science understanding of markets has been provided by Don Slater at the website 'New Cultures and Economies' (*http://homepages.gold.ac.uk/slater/markets/marketbiblioa.htm*). The bibliographical essay at the end of De Grazia (2005) offers useful indications as to American politics, consumption and globalization.

A number of **journals** are also currently dedicated to the study of consumption from different perspectives: both the *Journal of Material Culture*, which offers an anthropological angle on the relationship between persons and things, and the *Journal of Consumer Culture*, which, albeit grounded in sociology, provides an interdisciplinary space for discussion. There are also several marketing journals which offer wide ranging discussion, both empirical and theoretical, of consumption, and in particular the *Journal of Consumer Research and Advances in Consumer Research*. Finally a number of journals are concerned with consumer policy and education, in particular, *Consumer Issues*, the *International Journal of Consumer Studies* and the *Journal of Consumers' Affairs*.

References

Aaker D. and Day G. S. (1982) *Consumerism: Search for the Consumer Interest*, New York: Macmillan.

Aaker, D. A. and Karman, J. M. (1982) 'Are you overadvertising? A review of advertising-sales studies', *Journal of Advertising Research*, 22: 57–70.

Abelson, E. (1989) *When Ladies go A-Thieving: Middle Class Shoplifters in the Victorian Department Stores*, Oxford: Oxford University Press.

Abolafia, M. Y. (1998) 'Markets as cultures: an ethnographic approach', in M. Callon (ed.) *The Laws of the Market*, Oxford: Basil Blackwell.

Adam, B. (2000) 'The temporal gaze: the challenge for social theory in the context of GM food', *British Journal of Sociology*, 51 (1): 125–42.

Adams, R. D. and McCormick, K. (1992) 'Fashion dynamics and the economic theory of clubs', *Review of Social Economy*, 50 (1): 24–39.

Adorno, T. (1941) 'On popular music', *Studies in Philosophy and Social Sciences*, 9 (1): 17–48.

Akerlof, G. A. (1970) 'The market for "Lemons": quality uncertainty and the market mechanism', *Quarterly Journal of Economics*, 84 (August): 488–500.

Alasuutari, P. (1992) *Desire and Craving. A Cultural Theory of Alcoholism*, Albany: Suny Press.

Alberoni, F. and Baglioni, G. (1965) *L'integrazione dell'immigrato nella società industriale*, Bologna: Il Mulino.

Aldrigde, A. (1994) 'The construction of rational consumption in *Which?* magazine: the more blobs the better?', *Sociology*, 28 (4): 899–912.

Allen, K. (2002) 'Berlin in the Belle Epoque: a fast food history', in W. Belasco and P. Scranton (eds) *Food Nations*, New York: Routledge.

Ames, K. and Martinez, K. (eds) (1996) *The Material Culture of Gender/The Gender of Material Culture*, Ann Arbor: University of Michigan Press.

Ang, I. (1985) *Watching Dallas: Soap Opera and the Melodramatic Imagination*, London: Methuen.

Appadurai, A. (ed.) (1986a) *The Social Life of Things. Commodities in Cultural Perspectives*, Cambridge: Cambridge University Press.

Appadurai, A. (1986b) 'Introduction: commodities and the politics of value', in A. Appadurai (ed.) *The Social Life of Things. Commodities in Cultural Perspectives*, Cambridge: Cambridge University Press.

Appadurai, A. (1988) 'How to make a national cuisine: cookbooks in contemporary India', *Comparative Studies in Society and History*, 30: 3–24.

Appadurai, A. (1996) *Modernity at Large. Cultural Dimensions of Globalization*, Minneapolis: University of Minnesota Press.

Appleby, J. O. (1978) *Economic Thought in Seventeenth-Century England*, Princeton: Princeton University Press.

Appleby, J. O. (1993) 'Consumption in early modern social thought', in J. Brewer and R. Porter (eds), *Consumption and the World of Goods*, London: Routledge.

Arnould, E. J. and Wilk, R. (1984) 'Why do the natives wear Adidas?', *Advances of Consumer Research*, 15: 139–68.

Arnould, E. J., Pince, Linda and Zinkhan, George (eds.) (2002) *Consumers*, Boston: McGraw Hill.

Arvidsson, A. (2001) 'From counterculture to consumer culture: Vespa and the Italian youth market, 1958–78', *Journal of Consumer Culture*, 1 (1): 47–71.

Arvidsson, A. (2002) *Marketing Modernity. Italian Advertising from Fascism to Postmodernity*, London: Routledge.

Augé, M. (1995) *Nonplaces: Introduction to an Anthropology of Supermodernity*, London: Verso (1995).

Azarya, V. (2004) 'Globalization and international tourism in developing countries. Marginality as a commercial commodity', *Current Sociology*, 52 (6): 949–67.

Badgett, M. V. L. (2001) *Money, Myths and Change: The Economic Lives of Lesbians and Gay Men*, Chigago: University of Chicago Press.

Baker, A. (ed.) (2000) *Serious Shopping. Essays in Psychotherapy and Consumerism*, London: Free Association Books.

Baranowski, S. and Furlough, E. (eds) (2001) *Being Elsewhere. Tourism, Consumer Culture and Identity in Modern Europe*, Ann Arbor: University of Michigan Press.

Barry, A. and Slater, D. (2002) 'Introduction. The technological economy', *Economy and Society*, 2: 175–93.

Barthes, R. (1972) *Mythologies*, New York: Hill and Wang [1957].

Bataille, G. (1988) *The Accursed Share, Vol. 1*, New York: Zone Books [1949].

Baudrillard, J. (1981) *For a Critique of the Political Economy of the Sign*, London: Telos Press, [1972].

Baudrillard, J. (1983) *Simulations*, New York: Semiotexte [1981].

Baudrillard, J. (1996) *System of Objects*, London: Verso [1968].

Baudrillard, J. (1997) *Objects, Images and the Possibilities of Illusion*, in M. Zurbrugg (ed.) *Jean Baudrillard. Art and Artefact*, London: Sage.

Baudrillard, J. (1998) *The Consumer Society: Myths and Structures*, London: Sage [1970].

Bauman, Z. (1992) *Intimations of Post-modernity*, London: Routledge.

Baxandall, M. (1972) *Painting and Experience in Fifteenth Century Italy*, Oxford University Press, Oxford.

Beardsworth, A. and Keil, T. (1992) 'The vegetarian option. Varieties, conversions, motives and careers', *The Sociological Review*, 40 (2): 253–93.

Beck, U. (1992) *Risk Society: Towards a New Modernity*, London: Sage [1986].

Beck, U. (1997) *The Reinvention of Politics: Rethinking Modernity in the Global Social Order*, Cambridge: Polity Press.

Beck, U. and Gernsheim, E. (2001) *Individualisation*, London: Sage.

Becker, Gary S. (1996) *Accounting for Tastes*, Cambridge, Mass.: Harvard University Press.

Becker, Howard S. (1963) *Outsiders. Studies in the Sociology of Deviance*, New York: The Free Press.

Belasco, W. and Scranton, P. (eds) (2002) *Food Nations. Selling Taste in Consumer Societies*, London: Routledge.

Belk, R. W. (1995a) 'Studies in the new consumer behaviour', in D. Miller (ed.) *Acknowledging Consumption*, London: Routledge.

Belk, R. W. (1995b) *Collecting in a Consumer Society*, London: Routledge.

Belk, R. W., Wallendorf, M. and Sherry, J. (1989) 'The sacred and the profane in consumer behaviour', *Journal of Consumer Research*, 16: 1–38.

Belknap, P. and Leonard, W. M. (1991) 'A conceptual replication and extension of Erving Goffman's study of gender advertisements', *Sex Roles*, 25 (314): 103–18.

Bell, D. (1976) *The Cultural Contradictions of Capitalism*, London: Heinemann.

Bell, D. and Valentine, G. (1997) *Consuming Geographies*, London: Routledge.

Bell, R. (1985) *Holy Anorexia*. Chicago: University of Chicago Press.

Beng-Huat, C. (ed.) (2000) *Consumption in Asia: Lifestyles and Identities*, London: Routledge.

Benjamin, W. (1968) 'The work of art in the age of mechanical reproduction', in *Illuminations: Essays and Reflections*, New York: Harcourt, Brace and World [1936].

Benjamin, W. (1999) *The Arcades Project*. Cambridge, Mass.: Belknap Press [1981].

Bennett, L. B. (2004) 'Branded political communication: lifestyle politics, logo campaigns and the rise of global citizenship', in Micheletti et al. (eds) (2004) *Politics, Products and Markets Exploring Political Consumerism Post and Present*, New Brunswick: Transaction Publishers.

Bennett, T., Emmison, M. and Frow, J. (1999) *Accounting for Tastes. Australian Everyday Culture*, Cambridge: Cambridge University Press.

Benson, S. P. (1986) *Counter Cultures: Saleswomen, Managers and Costumers in American Department Stores*, Urbana: University of Illinois Press.

Bergman, D. (ed.) (1993) *Camp Grounds: Style and Homosexuality*, Amherst: University of Massachusetts Press.

Berking, H. (1999) *The Sociology of Giving*, London: Sage.

Bermingham, A. and Brewer J. (eds) (1995) *The Consumption of Culture, 1600–1800, Image, Object, Text*, London: Routledge.

Berridge, V. and Edwards, G. (1987) *Opium and the People: Opiate Use in Nineteenth Century England*, London: Allen Lane.

Berry, C. J. (1994) *The Idea of Luxury*, Cambridge: Cambridge University Press.

Bevir, M. and Trentmann, F. (eds) (2004) *Markets in Historical Contexts. Ideas and Politics in the Modern World*, Cambridge: Cambridge University Press.

Bianchi, M. (1997) 'Collecting as a paradigm of consumption', *Journal of Cultural Economics*, 21: 275–89.

Bianchi, M. (1999) 'In the name of the tulip. Why speculation?', in M. Berg and H. Clifford (eds) *Consumers and Luxury*, Manchester: Manchester University Press.

Bianchi, M. (2003) 'A questioning economist: Tibor Scitovsky's attempt to bring joy into economics', *Journal of Economic Psychology*, 24: 391–407.

Biggart, N. W. and Castanias, R. P. (2001) 'Collateralized social relations. The social in economic calculation', *American Journal of Economics and Sociology*, 60: 471–500.

Blumer, H. (1969) 'Fashion: from class differentiation to collective selection', *Sociological Quarterly*, 10: 275–91.

Boltanski, L. (1971) 'Les Usages sociaux du corps', *Annales ESC*, 26 (1): 205–33.

Boltanski, L. and Thévenot, L. (1991) *De La Justification. Les économies de la grandeur*, Paris: Gallimard.

Bordo, S. (1993) *Unbearable Weight. Feminism, Western Culture and the Body*, Berkeley: University of California Press.

Borsay, P. (1989) *The English Urban Reinassance, 1660–1770*, Oxford: Clarendon Press.

Bourdieu, P. (1977) *Outline of a Theory of Practice*, Cambridge: Cambridge University Press [1972].

Bourdieu, P. (1978) 'Sport and social class', *Social Science Information*, 17 (6): 819–40.

Bourdieu, P. (1984) *Distinction: A Social Critique of the Judgement of Taste*, London: Routledge [1979].

Bourdieu, P. (1990) *The Logic of Practice*, Cambridge: Polity Press [1980].

Bourdieu, P. (1993) *The Field of Cultural Production: Essays on Art and Literature*, New York Columbia University Press.

Bourdieu, P. and Delsaut, Y. (1975) 'Le Couturier et sa griffe: contribution à une théorie de la magie', *Actes de la Recherche en Sciences Sociales*, 1 (1): 7–35.

Bové, J. (1999) 'Yankee (Food) go Home!', *Micromega*, 5: 165–70.

Bowlby, R. (1985) *Just Looking*, New York: Methuen.

Bowlby, R. (1993) *Shopping with Freud*, London: Routledge.

Bowlby, R. (2000) *Carried Away. The Invention of Modern Shopping*, New York: Columbia University Press.

Braham, P. (1997) 'Fashion: unpacking cultural production', in P. du Gay (ed.) *Production of Culture, Cultures of Production*, London: Sage.

Braudel, F. (1979) *Civilization matérielle, économie et capitalisme (XV–XVIII). Le structure du quotidien*, Paris: Librarie Armand Colin.

Breen, T. H. (2004) *The Marketplace of Revolution: How Consumer Politics Shaped American Independence*, New York: Oxford University Press.

Breward, C. (1994) 'Femininity and consumption. The problem of the late nineteenth century fashion journal', *Journal of Design History*, 7 (2): 71–89.

Brewer, J. and Porter, R. (eds) (1993) *Consumption and the World of Goods*, London: Routledge.

Brewer, J. and Staves, S. (1995) *Early Modern Conceptions of Property*, London: Routledge.

Brewer, J. and Trentmann, F. (2006) *Consuming Cultures, Global Perspectives. Historical Trajectories, Transnational Exchanges*, Oxford: Berg.

Broadbent, S. and Coleman, S. (1986) 'Advertising effectiveness across brands', *Journal of the Market Research Society*, 28: 15–24.

Bromberger, C. (ed.) (1998) *Passions ordinaires*, Paris: Bayard.

Bruzzi, S. (1997) *Undressing Cinema*, London: Routledge.

Bryman, A. (1999) 'Theme parks and McDonaldization', in B. Smart (ed.) *Resisting McDonaldization*, London: Sage.

Bull, M. (2000) *Sounding Out the City: Personal Stereos and the Management of Everyday Life*, Oxford: Berg.

Burke, P. (1978) *Popular Culture in Early Modern Europe*, London: Temple Smith.

Burke, P. (1993) 'Res et verba. Consumption in the early modern world', in J. Brewer and R. Porter, (eds), *Consumption and the World of Goods*, London: Routledge.

Burman, B. (ed.) (1999) *The Culture of Sewing: Gender, Consumption and Home Dress-making*, Oxford: Berg.

Burrows, R. and Marsh, C. (1992) *Consumption and Class. Divisions and Change*, New York: St. Martin's Press.

Caldwell, M. (2004) 'Domesticating the French fry! McDonald's and consumerism in Russia', *Journal of Consumer Culture*, 4: 5–26.

Callon, M. (ed.) (1998) *The Laws of the Market*, Oxford: Blackwell.

Campbell, C. (1987) *The Romantic Ethic and the Spirit of Modern Consumerism*, Oxford: Basil Blackwell.

Campbell, C. (1994) 'Capitalism, consumption and the problem of motives', in J. Friedman (ed.) *Consumption and Identity,* Chur: Harwood Academic Publishers.

Campbell, C. (1995) 'The sociology of consumption', in D. Miller (ed.) *Acknowledging Consumption*, London: Routledge.

Campbell, C. (1997a) 'When the meaning is not a message', in M. Nava, A. Blake, I. MacRury and B. Richards (eds) *Buy this Book. Studies in Advertising and Consumption*, London: Routledge.

Campbell, C. (1997b) 'Shopping, pleasure and the sex war', in P. Falk and C. Campbell (eds). *The Shopping Experience*, London: Sage.

Camporesi, P. (1994) *Indian Broth, Exotic Brew: Art of Living in the Age of Enlightenment*, Cambridge: Polity Press [1990].

Capuzzo, P. (2001) 'Youth cultures and consumption in contemporary Europe', *Contemporary European History*, 1: 155–70.

Carrier, J. (1995) *Gifts and Commodities. Exchange and Western Capitalism since 1700*, London: Routledge.

Carrier, J. (ed.) (1997) *Meanings of the Market*, Oxford: Berg.

Carrier, J. and Miller, D. (eds) (1998) *Virtualism: A New Political Economy*, Oxford: Berg.

Casey, E. (2003) 'Gambling and consumption: working-class women and UK national lottery play', *Journal of Consumer Culture*, 3 (2): 245–63.

Castells, M. (1977) *The Urban Question*, London: Edward Arnold (1972).

Chaney, D. (1996) *Lifestyles*, London: Routledge.

Cheal, D. (1987) 'Showing them you love them. Gift-giving and the dialectic of intimacy', *The Sociological Review*, 35: 151–69.

Chessel, M. -E. (2006) 'Women and the ethics of consumption in France at the turn of the twentieth century', in F. Trentmann (ed.) *The Making of the Consumer: Knowledge, Power and Identity in the Modern World*, Oxford: Berg.

Chessel, M. -E. and Cochoy, F. (2004) 'Marché et politique: autour de la consommation engagée', *Sciences de la societé*, 62: 45–67.

Chin, E. (2001) *Purchasing Power. Black Kids and American Consumer Culture*, Minneapolis: University of Minnesota Press.

Clark, A. (1997) 'Tupperware in the 1950s. Gender and consumption', in R. Silverstone (ed.) *Visions of Suburbia*, London: Routledge.

Clunas, C. (1999) 'Modernity global and local. Consumption and the rise of the West', *American Historical Review*, 104: 1497–511.

Cochoy, F. (1999) *Une Histoire du marketing. Discipliner l'économie du marché*, Paris: La Découverte.

Cochoy, F. (2002) *Une Sociologie du packaging, ou l'âne de Buridan face au marché*, Paris: Presses Universitaires de France.

Cohen E. (2003) *A Consumers' Republic. The Politics of Mass Consumption in Postwar America*, New York: Knopf.

Cohen, S. (1972) *Folk Devils and Moral Panics: The Creation of the Mods and Rockers*, London: McGibbon and Kee.

Collins, A. F. (1996) 'The pathological gambler and the government of gambling', *History of the Human Sciences*, 9 (3): 69–100.

Cook, D. T. (2004) *The Commodification of Childhood: The Children's Clothing Industry and the Rise of the Child Consumer*, Durham, NC and London: Duke University Press.

Cook, I. and Crang, P. (1996) 'The world on a plate: culinary culture, displacement and geographical knowledge', *Journal of Material Culture*, 1 (2): 131–53.

Corbin, A. (ed.) (1995) *L'Avènement du loisirs, 1850–1960*, Paris: Aubier.

Cowan, R. S. (1983) *More Work for Mother: The Ironies of Household Technology*, New York: Basic Books.

Crainz, G. (1996) *Storia del miracolo italiano. Cultura, identità, trasformazioni tra anni Cinquanta e Sessanta*, Roma: Donzelli.

Crane, D. (2000) *Fashion and its Social Agenda. Class, Gender and Identity in Clothing*, Chicago: University of Chicago Press.

Crompton, R. (1996) 'Consumption and class analysis', in S. Edgell, K. Hetherington and A. Warde (eds) *Consumption Matters*, Oxford: Blackwell.

Cronin, A. M. (2004) 'Currencies of commercial exchange. Advertising agencies and the promotional imperative', *Journal of Consumer Cultures*, 4 (3): 339–60.

Cross, G. (1993) *Time and Money. The Making of Consumer Culture*, London: Routledge.

Cross, G. (2000) *An All-Consuming Century: Why Commercialism Won in Modern America*, New York: Columbia University Press.

Cruise, J. (1999) *Governing Consumption. Needs and Wants, Suspended Characters and the 'Origins' of the Eighteenth-Century English Novel*, Oxford: Basil Blackwell.

Csikszentmihalyi, M. and Rochberg-Halton, E. (1981) *The Meaning of Things: Domestic Symbols and the Self*, Cambridge: Cambridge University Press.

Curtin, P. (1984) *Cross-cultural Trade in World History*, Cambridge: Cambridge University Press.

Dant, T. (1999) *Material Culture and the Social World*, Buckingham: Open University Press.

Daunton, M. and Hilton, M. (eds) (2001) *The Politics of Consumption*, Oxford: Berg.

Davies, K. 2000 'A moral purchase: femininity, commerce, abolition, 1788–1792', in E. Eger and C. Grant (eds) *Women and the Public Sphere. Writing and Representation, 1660–1800*, Cambridge: Cambridge University Press.

Davila, A. (2001) *Latinos Inc. The Marketing and Making of a People*, Berkeley: University of California Press.

Davis, F. (1992) *Fashion, Culture and Identity*, Chicago: University of Chicago Press.

De Certeau, M. (1984) *The Practice of Everyday Life*, Berkeley: University of California Press [1980]

De Grazia, V. (1998) 'Changing consumption regimes in Europe, 1930–1970,' in Strasser et al. (eds) *Getting and Spending: European and American Consumer Societies in the Twentieth Century.* Cambridge: Cambridge University Press.

De Grazia, V. (2005) *Irresistible Empire: America's Advance through 20th-Century Europe,* Cambridge, Mass.: Belknap Press.

De Grazia, V. and Cohen, L. (eds) (1999) 'Class and consumption', special issue of *International Labour and Working-Class History,* 55, spring.

De Grazia, V. and Furlough, E. (eds) (1996) *The Sex of Things: Gender and Consumption in Historical Perspective,* Berkeley: University of California Press.

De Marchi, N. (1999) 'Adam Smith's accommodation of "altogether endless" desires', in M. Berg and H. Clifford (eds) *Consumers and Luxury,* Manchester: Manchester University Press.

DeVault, M. (1991) *Feeding the Family,* Chicago: University of Chicago Press.

De Vries, J. (1975) 'Peasant demand patterns and economic development: Friesland, 1550–1750', in W.N. Parker and E.L. Jones (eds) *European Peasants and their Markets: Essays in Agrarian Economic History,* Princeton: Princeton University Press.

De Vries, J. (1993) 'Between purchasing and the world of goods', in J. Brewer and R. Porter (eds) *Consumption and the World of Goods,* London: Routledge.

Di Maggio, P. (1982) 'Cultural entrepreneurship in nineteenth century Boston. The creation of an organizational base for high culture in America', *Media, Culture and Society,* 4: 33–50.

Di Maggio, P. (1987) 'Classification in arts', *American Sociological Review,* 52: 440–55.

Di Maggio, P. (1990) 'Cultural aspects of economic action', in R. Friedland and A. F. Robertson (eds) *Beyond the Marketplace,* Chicago: Aldine.

Di Maggio, P. and Louch, H. (1998) 'Socially embedded consumer transactions', *American Sociological Review,* 63: 619–37.

Dittmar, H. (1992) *The Social Psychology of Material Possession,* Hemel Hempstead: Harvester Wheatsheaf.

Dolfsma, W. (2002) 'Mediated preferrences – how institutions affect consumption', *Journal of Economic Issues,* 36 (2): 449–57.

Doubleday, R. (2004) 'Institutionalizing non-governmental organization dialogue at Unilever: Framing the public as "consumer-citizens" ', *Science and Public Policy,* 31 (2): 117–26.

Douglas, M. (1966) *Purity and Danger,* London: Routledge.

Douglas, M. (1978) *Cultural Bias,* London: Royal Anthropological Institute, Occasional Paper no. 35.

Douglas, M. (1982) 'Introduction to grid/group analysis', in M. Douglas (ed.) *Essays in the Sociology of Perception,* London: Routledge.

Douglas, M. (1992) 'Wants', in *Risk and Blame: Essays in Cultural Theory,* London: Routledge.

Douglas, M. (1996) *Thought Styles,* London: Sage.

Douglas, M. and Isherwood, B. (1979) *The World of Goods. Towards an Anthropology of Consumption,* New York: Basic Books.

Drumright, M. E. (1994) 'Socially responsible organizational buying', *Journal of Marketing,* 58: 1–19.

Duesenberry, J. S. (1949) *Income, Saving and the Theory of Consumer Behaviour,* Cambridge, Mass.: Harvard University Press.

Du Gay, P., Hall S., Janes, L. Mckay, H. and Negus, K. (1997) *Doing Cultural Studies. The Story of the Sony Walkman*, Milton Keynes: Open University Press.

Eccles, S. (2002) 'The lived experiences of additive consumers', *Journal of Research for Consumer Issues*, 4: 1–17.

Eco, U. (1994) *Apocalypse Postponed*, Bloomington: Indiana University Press [1964].

Edwards, T. (1997) *Men in the Mirror: Men's Fashion and Consumer Society*, London: Cassell.

Ekstrøm, K. M and Brembeck, H. (eds) (2004) *Elusive Consumption*, Oxford: Berg.

Elias, N. (1978/82) The Civilizing Process, Oxford: Basil Blackwell, 2 vols [1936/9].

Elias, N. and Dunning, E. (1986) *The Quest for Excitement: Sport and Leisure in the Civilizing Process*, Oxford: Basil Blackwell.

Elliott, R. (1994) 'Addictive consumption. Function and fragmentation in post-modernity', *Journal of Consumer Policy*, 17: 159–79.

Ellwood, D. (2001) 'Italian modernization and the propaganda of the Marshall Plan', in L. Cheles and L. Sponza (eds) *The Art of Persuasion. Political Communication in Italy from 1945 to the 1990s*, Manchester: Manchester University Press.

Entwistle, J. (2000) *The Fashioned Body*, Cambridge: Polity Press.

Etzioni, A. (1998) 'Volutary simplicity: characterization, select psychological implications, and societal consequences', *Journal of Economic Psychology*, 19 (5): 619–43.

Evans, C. and Thornton, M. (1989) *Women and Fashion*, London: Quartet Books.

Everson, M. (2006) 'Legal constructions of the consumer', in F. Trentmann (ed.) *The Making of the Consumer: Knowledge, Power and Identity in the Modern World*, Oxford: Berg.

Ewen, S. (1976) *Captains of Consciousness. Advertising and the Social Root of Consumer Culture*, New York: McGraw-Hill.

Ewen, S. (1988) *All Consuming Images. The Politics of Style in Contemporary Culture*, New York: Basic Books.

Fairchilds, C. (1998) 'Consumption in early modern Europe. A review article', *Comparative Studies in Society and History*, 35: 850–58.

Falk, P. and Campbell, C. (eds) (1997) *The Shopping Experience*, London: Sage.

Fantasia, R. (1994) 'Fast food in France', *Theory and Society*, 24 (2): 201–43.

Fawcett, T. (1990) 'Eighteenth-century shops and the luxury trade', *Bath History*, 3: 49–75.

Featherstone, M. (ed.) (1990) *Global Culture. Nationalism, Globalization, and Modernity*, London: Sage.

Featherstone, M. (1991) *Consumer Culture and Postmodernism*, London: Sage.

Ferrero, S. (2002) '*Comida sin par*. Consumption of Mexican food in Los Angeles', in W. Belasco and P. Scranton (eds) *Food Nations. Selling Taste in Consumer Societies*, London: Routledge.

Ferrières, M. (2002) *Histoire des peurs alimentaires du Moyen Age à l'aube du XX siècle*, Paris: Seuil.

Findlen, P. (1998) 'Possessing the past: the material world of the Italian Renaissance', *American Historical Review*, 103: 83–114.

Fine, B. (1999) 'A question of economics: is it colonizing the social sciences?', *Economy and Society*, 28 (3): 403–25.

Fine, B. (2002a) 'Callonistics: a disentanglement', *Economy and Society*, 32 (3): 478–84.

Fine, B. (2002b) *The World of Consumption. The Material and the Cultural Revisited*, 2nd edn, London: Routledge [1992 with E. Leopold].

Fine, G. A. (1998) *Morel Tales. The Culture of Mushrooming*, Cambridge, Mass.: Harvard University Press.

Finkelstein, J. (1989) *Dining Out: A Sociology of Modern Manners*, Cambridge: Polity Press.

Finnegan, M. (1999) *Selling Suffrage: Consumer Culture and Votes for Women*, New York: Columbia University Press.

Fish, S. (1980) *Is there a Text in this Class? The Authority of Interpretative Communities*, Cambridge, Mass.: Harvard University Press.

Fiske, J. (1989) 'Shopping for pleasure', in J. Fiske, *Reading the Popular*, Boston: Unwin Hyman.

Flink, J. (1988) *The Automobile Age*, Cambridge, Mass.: MIT Press.

Forty, A. (1986) *Objects of Desire*, London: Thames and Hudson.

Foucault, M. (1978) *History of Sexuality. Vol. 1*, Harmondsworth: Penguin [1976].

Foucault, M. (1980) 'Débat avec les historiens', in M. Perrot (ed.) *L'impossible prison*, Paris: Seuil.

Foucault, M. (1983) 'The subject and power', in H. L. Dreyfus and P. Rabinow (eds) *Michel Foucault: Beyond Structuralism and Hermeneutics*, Chicago: University of Chicago Press.

Foucault, M. (1988) 'Techniques of the self', in L. H. Martin et al. (eds) *Technologies of the Self. A Seminar with Michel Foucault*, London: Tavistock.

Foucault, M. (1991) 'Governmentality', in C. Burchell, C. Gordon and P. Miller (eds) *The Foucault Effect*, Chicago: University of Chicago Press.

Frank, D. (1985) 'Housewives, socialists, and the politics of food: the 1917 New York cost-of-living protests', in *Feminist Studies*, 11: 255–85.

Frank, T. (1997) *The Conquest of Cool. Business Culture, Counter Culture and the Rise of Hip Consumerism*, Chicago: University of Chicago Press.

Fraser, H. W. (1981) *The Coming of Mass Market, 1850–1914*, Amden: Anchor Books.

Friedman, J. (1991) 'Consuming desires: strategies of selfhood and appropriation', *Cultural Anthropology*, 6 (2): 154–64.

Friedman, J. (ed.) (1994) *Consumption and Identity*, Chur: Harwood Academic Publishers.

Friedman, M. (1999) *Consumer Boycotts. Effecting Change through the Marketplace and the Media*, New York: Routledge.

Fromm, E. (1976) *To Have or To Be?* London: Abacus.

Frost, B. (1983) 'Machine liberation. Inventing housewives and home appliances in interwar France', *French Historical Studies*, 18 (1): 109–30.

Frow, J. (1991) 'Michel de Certeau and the practice of representation', *Cultural Studies*, 5 (1): 52–60.

Frow, J. (1995) *Cultural Studies and Cultural Value*, Oxford: Clarendon Press.

Furlough, E. and Strikwerda, C. (eds) (1999) *Consumers Against Capitalism? Consumer Cooperation in Europe, North America and Japan, 1840–1990*, Oxford: Rowman & Littlefield.

Gabaccia, D. (1998) *We Are What We Eat. Ethnic Foods and the Making of America*, Cambridge, Mass.: Harvard University Press.

Gabriel, Y. and Lang, T. (1995) *The Unmanageable Consumer: Contemporary Consumption and its Fragmentation*, London: Sage.

Galbraith, J. K. (1958) *The Affluent Society*, London: André Deutsch.

Galbraith, J. K. (1971) *The New Industrial State*, London: André Deutsch, [1967].

Galilee, J. (2002) 'Class consumption: understanding middle-class young men and their fashion choices', *Man and Masculinities*, 5 (1): 32–52.

Gans, H. J. (1974) *Popular Culture and High Culture. An Analysis and Evaluation of Taste*, New York: Basic Books.

Garber, M. P. (1989) 'Tulipmania', *Journal of Political Economy*, 97 (3): 353–80.

García Canclini, N. (2001) *Consumers and Citizens. Globalization and Multicultural Conflicts*, Minneapolis: University of Minnesota Press [1999].

Garfinkel, H. (1984) *Studies in Ethnomethodology*, Cambridge: Polity Press [1967].

Garnham, N. and Williams, R. (1980) 'Pierre Bourdieu and the sociology of culture', *Media, Culture and Society*, 2: 209–23.

Garon, S. (2006) 'Japan's post-war "consumer revolution", or striking a "Balance" between consumption and savings', in J. Brewer and F. Trentmann (eds) *Consuming Cultures, Global Perspectives. Historical Trajectories, transnational Exchanges*, Oxford: Berg.

Gebler, S. (1997) 'Do-it-yourself: constructing, repairing and maintaining domestic masculinity', *American Quarterly*, 49 (1): 66–112.

Gell, A. (1986) 'Newcomers to the world of goods: consumption among the Nuria Gonds', in A. Appadurai (ed.) *The Social Life of Things. Commodities in Cultural Perspectives*, Cambridge: Cambridge University Press.

Gell, A. (1988) 'Anthropology, material culture and consumerism', *Journal of the Anthropological Society*, 19 (1): 43–8.

Ger, G. and Belk, R. W. (1999) 'Accounting for materialism in four cultures', *Journal of Material Cultures*, 4 (2): 183–204.

Geraghty, C. (1991) *Women and Soap Opera*, Cambridge: Polity Press.

Geras, N. (1983) *Marx and Human Nature*, London: Verso.

Gershuny, J. (2000) *Changing Times*, Oxford: Oxford University Press.

Giddens, A. (1990) *The Consequences of Modernity*, Stanford: Stanford University Press.

Girardelli, D. (2004) 'Commodified identities: the myth of Italian food in the United States', *Journal of Communication Enquiry*, 28(4): 307–24.

Glennie, P. (1995) 'Consumption within historical studies', in D. Miller (ed.) *Acknowledging Consumption. A Review of New Studies*, London: Routledge.

Glickman, L. B. (1999) 'Born to shop? Consumer history and American history' in L. B. Glickman (ed.) *Consumer Society in American History. A Reader*, Ithaca, NY: Cornell University Press.

Goffman, E. (1959) *The Presentation of the Self in Everyday Life*, New York: Doubleday.

Goffman, E. (1961) *Encounters. Two Studies in the Sociology of Interaction*, London: Penguin.

Goffman, E. (1967) *Where the Action Is*, in *Interaction Ritual*, New York: Doubleday.

Goffman, E. (1974) *Frame Analysis: An Essay on the Organization of Experience*, New York: Harper and Row.

Goffman, E. (1979) *Gender Advertisements*, London: MacMillan.

Goldman, R. (1992) *Reading Ads Socially*, London: Routledge.

Goldman, R. and Papson, S. (1996) *Sign Wars*, New York: Guildford.

Goldman, R. and Papson, S. (1998) *Nike Culture*, London: Sage.

Goldstein-Gidoni, O. (2001) 'The making and marking of the "Japanese" and the "Western" in Japanese contemporary material culture', *Journal of Material Culture*, 6 (1): 67–90.

Goss, J. (1993) 'The magic of the mall: an analysis of form, function and meaning in the contemporary retail built environment', *Annals of the Association of American Geographers*, 83 (1): 18–47.

Gottdiener, M. (1997) *The Theming of America: Dreams, Visions and Commercial Spaces*, Boulder: Westview Press.

Granovetter, M. (1985) 'Economic action and social structure: the problem of embeddedness', *American Journal of Sociology*, 91: 481–510.

Greenhalgh, P. (1988) *Ephemeral Vistas. A History of the Expositions Universelles, Great Exhibitions and World Fairs, 1951–1939*, Manchester: Manchester University Press.

Gregson, N. and Crewe, L. (2003) *Second Hand Cultures*, Oxford: Berg.

Gronow, Y. (1997) *The Sociology of Taste*, London: Routledge.

Gronow, Y. and Warde, A. (eds) (2001) *Ordinary Consumption*, London: Routledge.

Grundmann, R. and Stehr, N. (2001) 'Why is Werner Sombart not part of the core of classical sociology?', *Journal of Classical Sociology*, 1 (2): 257–87.

Gunter, B. (1998) *Understanding the Older Consumer. The Grey Market*, London: Routledge.

Gunter, B. and Furnham A. (1998) *Children as Consumers. A Psychological Analysis of the Young People Market*, London: Routledge.

Guttman, A. (1991) *Women's Sport*, New York: Columbia University Press.

Habermas, J. (1992) *The Structural Transformation of the Public Sphere: An Inquiry into a Category of Bourgeois Society*, Cambridge: Polity Press [1962].

Halkier, B. (2001) 'Routinization or reflexivity? Consumers and normative claims for environmental consideration', in J. Gronow and A. Warde (eds) *Ordinary Consumption*, London: Routledge.

Hall, S. (1980) 'Encoding/decoding', in S. Hall, D. Hobson, A. Lowe and P. Willis (eds) *Culture, Media, Language*, London: Hutchinson.

Hall, S. and Jefferson, T. (eds) (1976) *Resistance through Rituals: Youth Subcultures in Post-war Britain*, London: Hutchinson.

Halter, M. (2000) *Shopping for Identity. The Marketing of Ethnicity*, New York: Schocken Books.

Hargreaves Heap, S. (1989) *Rationality in Economics*, Oxford: Basil Blackwell.

Harker, R., Mahar, C. and Wilkes, C. (eds) (1990) *An Introduction to the Work of Pierre Bourdieu. The Practice of Theory*, London: MacMillan.

Harper, D. and Faccioli, P. (2000) '"Small Silly Insults" Mutual seduction and misogyny: the interpretation of Italian advertising signs', *Visual Sociology*, 15: 23–49.

Hartley, J. (2001) *Reading Groups*, Oxford: Oxford University Press.

Haug, W. F. (1986) *Critique of Commodity Aesthetics*, Cambridge: Polity Press.

Haupt, H. G. (2002) *Konsum und Handel. Europa im 19 und 20 Jahrhundert*, Göttingen, Vandenhoeck und Ruprecht.

Hayek, F. A. (1961) 'The *"non sequitur"* of the dependence effect', *Southern Economic Journal*, 27: 346–8.

Hebdige, D. (1979) *Subculture. The Meaning of Style*, London: Methuen.

Hebdige, D. (1988) *Hiding in the Light: On Images and Things*, London: Comedia.

Helstosky, C. (2004) *Garlic and Oil. Food and Politics in Italy*, Oxford: Berg.

Hennion, A. and Meadel, C. (1989) 'The artisans of desire: the mediation of advertising between product and consumer', *Sociological Theory*, 7 (2): 191–209.

Hennion, A. and Teil, G. (2004) 'L'attività riflessiva dell'amatore. Un approccio pragmatico al gusto', *Rassegna Italiana di Sociologia*, 45 (4): 519–42.

Hermes, J. (1995) *Reading Women's Magazines*, Cambridge: Polity Press.

Hesmondhalgh, D. (2006) 'Bourdieu, the media and cultural production', *Media, Culture and Society*, 28 (2): 211–31.

Hilton, M. (2002) 'The female consumer and the politics of consumption in twentieth-century Britain', *The Historical Journal*, 45 (1): 103–28.

Hilton, M. (2003) *Consumerism in Twentieth-Century Britain*, Cambridge: Cambridge University Press.

Hilton, M. (2004) 'The legacy of luxury: moralities of consumption since the eighteenth century', *Journal of Consumer Culture*, 4 (1): 101–23.

Hirsch, F. (1977) *The Social Limits of Growth*, London: Routledge.

Hirsch, P. (1972) 'Processing fads and fashions: an organization-set analysis of cultural industry systems', *American Journal of Sociology*, 77: 639–59.

Hirschman, A. O. (1977) *The Passions and the Interests: Political Arguments for Capitalism before its Triumph*, Princeton: Princeton University Press.

Hirschman, A. O. (1982a) *Shifting Involvements. Private Interests and Public Action*, Princeton: Princeton University Press.

Hirschman, A. O. (1982b) 'Rival interpretations of market society: civilizing, destructive or feeble', *Journal of Economic Literature*, 20: 1463–84.

Hirschman, A. O. (1985) 'Against parsimony: three easy ways of complicating some categories of economic discourse', *Economics and Philosophy*, 1: 7–21.

Hirschmann, E. C. (1992) 'The consciousness of addiction. Towards a general theory of compulsive consumption', *Journal of Consumer Research*, 19: 155–79.

Hobhouse, H. (1985) *Seeds of Change. Five Plants that Transformed Mankind*, New York: Harper and Row.

Hobsbawm, E. and Ranger, T. (1983) *The Invention of Tradition*, Cambridge: Cambridge University Press.

Hochschild, A. R. (2003a) *The Managed Heart. Commercialization of Human Feelings*, Berkeley: University of California Press [1983].

Hochschild, A. R. (2003b) *The Commercialization of Intimate Life*, Berkeley: University of California Press.

Holt, D. B. (1995) 'How consumers consume: a typology of consumption practices', *Journal of Consumer Research*, 22: 1–16.

Holt, D. B. (1997) 'Poststructuralist lifestyle analysis: conceptualizing the social patterning of consumption in post-modernity', *Journal of Consumer Research*, 23: 326–50.

Holt, D. B. (2002) 'Why do brands cause troubles? A dialectical theory of culture and branding', *Journal of Consumer Research*, 29 (1): 70–96.

Horkheimer, M. and Adorno, T. W. (1973) *Dialectic of Enlightenment*, London: Allen Lane [1947].

Horowitz, D. (1985) *The Morality of Spending*, Baltimore: Johns Hopkins University Press.

Howes, D. (ed.) (1996) *Cross-Cultural Consumption. Global Markets, Local Realities*, London: Routledge.

Hoy, S. (1997) *Chasing Dirt: The American Pursuit of Cleanliness*, Oxford: Oxford University Press.

Hudson, I. and Hudson, M. (2003) 'Removing the veil?', *Organization & Environment*, 16 (4): 423–30.

Hughes, J. (2003) *Learning to Smoke. Tobacco Use in the West*, Chicago: University of Chicago Press.

Hume, D. (1993) 'Of refinement in the arts', in *Selected Essays*, Oxford: Oxford University Press [1760].

Humphrey, C. (1995) 'Creating culture of disillusionment: consumption in Moscow, a chronicle of changing times', in D. Miller (ed.) *Worlds Apart: Modernity through the Prism of the Local*, London: Routledge.

Hundert, E. G. (1994) *The Enlightenment's Fable*, Cambridge: Cambridge University Press.

Huyssen, A. (1986) 'Mass culture as woman: modernism's Other', in *After the Great Divide: Modernism, Mass Culture and Postmodernism*, Basingstoke: MacMillan.

Ilmonen, K. (2001) 'Sociology, consumption and routine', in J. Gronow and A. Warde (eds) *Ordinary Consumption*, London: Routledge.

Jackson, P. (2004) 'Local consumption cultures in a globalizing world', *Transactions. Institute of British Geographers*, 29 (2): 165–78.

Jackson, P., Stevenson, N. and Brooks, K. (2001) *Making Sense of Men's Magazines*, Cambridge: Polity Press.

Jackson, S. and Moores, S. (eds) (1995) *The Politics of Domestic Consumption*, London: Prentice-Hall.

Jacobs, M. (1997) 'How about some meat? The office of price administration, consumption politics and the state building from the bottom-up, 1941–46', *Journal of American History*, 84: 910–41.

James, A. (1993) 'Eating green(s): discourses of organic food', in K. Milton (ed.) *Environmentalism*, London: Routledge.

Jameson, F. (1989) *Postmodernism, or the Cultural Logic of Late Capitalism*, London: Verso.

Jay, M. (1973) *The Dialectic Imagination*, London: Heinemann.

Jenkins, H. (1992) *Textual Poachers. Television Fans and Participatory Culture*, London: Routledge.

Jhally, S. (1987) *The Codes of Advertising*, New York: Frances Pinter.

Jones, E. L. (1968) 'The agricultural origins of industry', *Past and Present*, 11: 58–71.

Kates, S. M. and Belk, R. W. (2001) 'The meanings of Lesbian and Gay Pride Day: resistance through consumption and resistance to consumption', *Journal of Contemporary Ethnography*, 30 (4): 392–429.

Katona, G. (1960) *Psychological Economics*, New York: Elsevier.

Katz, E. (1959) 'Mass communication research and the study of culture', *Studies in Public Communication*, 2: 1–6.

Kawashima, N. (2006) 'Advertising agencies media and consumer market: The changing quality of TV advertising in Japan', *Media, Culture and Society*, 28 (3): 393–410.

Keat, R., Whiteley, N. and Abercrombie, N. (eds) (1994) *The Authority of the Consumer*, London: Routledge.

Kellner, D. (1989) *Jean Baudrillard: From Marxism to Postmodernism and Beyond*, Oxford: Basil Blackwell.

Khalil, E. L. (2004) 'The gift paradox: complex selves and symbolic good', *Review of Social Economy*, 62 (3): 379–92.

Kidd, A. and Nicholls, D. (eds) (1999) *Gender, Civic Culture and Consumerism: Middle-class Identity in Britain, 1800–1940*, Manchester: Manchester University Press.

King, M. E. (1997) 'The portrayal of women's images in magazine advertisements: Goffman's gender analysis revisited', *Sex Roles*, 37 (11/12): 979–96.

Kirkham, P. (ed.) (1996) *The Gendered Object*, Manchester: Manchester University Press.

Klassen, M. L., Jasper, C. R. and Schwartz, A. M. (1993) 'Men and women. Images of their relationship in magazine advertisements', *Journal of Advertising Research*, 33 (2): 30–9.

Klein, N. (2001) *No Logo*, London: HarperCollins.

Kline, S. (1995) 'The play of the market: on the internationalization of children's culture', *Theory, Culture and Society*, 12 (2): 103–29.

Kline, S. (2006) 'Becoming subject: consumer socialization in the mediated marketplace', in F. Trentmann (ed.) *The Making of the Consumer: Knowledge, Power and Identity in the Modern World*, Oxford: Berg.

Kolk, A. and van Tulder, R. (2002) 'Child labour and multinational conduct: a comparison of international business and stakeholder codes', *Journal of Business Ethics*, 36: 291–301.

König, R. (1973) *The Restless Image: A Sociology of Fashion*, London: Allen and Unwin [1971].

Kopytoff, I. (1986) 'The cultural biography of things: commoditization as process', in A. Appadurai (ed.) *The Social Life of Things. Commodities in Cultural Perspectives*, Cambridge: Cambridge University Press.

Kotler, P. (2000) *Marketing Management*, (Millenium ed.) Upper Saddle River, NY: Prentice-Hall International.

Kowinski, W. S. (1985) *The Malling of America*, New York: William Morrow.

Kraidy, M. M. and Goeddertz, T. (2003) 'Transnational advertising and international relations. US press discourses on the Benetton "we on death row" campaign', *Media, Culture and Society*, 25: 147–65.

Kroen, S. (2004) 'A political history of the consumer', *The Historical Journal*, 47 (3): 709–36.

Kutcha, D. (1996) 'Making of the self-made man, class, clothing and English masculinity, 1688–1832', in V. De Grazia and E. Furlough (eds). *The Sex of Things: Gender and Consumption in Historical Perspective*, Berkeley: University of California Press.

Laermans, R. (1993) 'Learning to consume: early department stores and the shaping of the modern consumer culture, 1896–1914', *Theory, Culture and Society*, 10 (4): 79–102.

Lahire, B. (2004) *La Culture des individus. Dissonances culturelles et distinction de soi*, Paris: La Découverte.

Lai, S. C. (2001) 'Extra-ordinary and ordinary consumption. Making sense of acquisition in modern Taiwan', in J. Gronow and A. Warde (eds) *Ordinary Consumption*, London: Routledge.

Lamont, M. (1992) *Money, Morals and Manners*, Chicago: University of Chicago Press.

Lamont, M. and Molnar, V. (2001) 'How Blacks use consumption to shape their collective identities', *Journal of Consumer Culture*, 1 (1): 31–46.

Lancaster, K. (1991) *Modern Consumer Theory*, Aldershot: Edward Elgar.

Lasch, C. (1991) *The Culture of Narcissism*, New York: Norton [1979].

Lash, S. and Urry, J. (1987) *The End of Organized Capitalism*, Cambridge: Polity Press.

Lash, S. and Urry, J. (1994) *Economies of Sign and Space*, London: Sage.

Leach, W. (1993) *Land of Desire. Merchants, Power and the Rise of a New American Culture*, New York: Pantheon.

Lears, T. J. J. (1983) 'From salvation to self-realization: advertising and the therapeutic roots of the consumer culture, 1880–1930', in R.W. Fox and T.J. Lears (eds) *The Culture of Consumption: Critical Essays in American History, 1880–1980*, New York: Pantheon Books.

Lears, T. J. J. (1994) *Fables of Abundance. A Cultural History of Advertising in America*, New York: Basic Books.

Le Breton, D. (2002a) 'Il corpo in pericolo. Antropologia delle attività fisiche e sportive a rischio', *Rassegna Italiana di Sociologia*, 3: 407–28.

Le Breton, D. (2002b) *Signes d'identité. Tatouages, piercings et autres marques corporelles*, Paris: Métailié.

Lee, J. (2002) 'From civil relations to racial conflict. Merchant–costumer interaction in urban America', *American Sociological Review*, 67: 77–98.

Lee, M. (1993) *Consumer Culture Reborn: The Cultural Politics of Consumption*, London: Routledge.

Leibenstein, H. (1950) 'Bandwagon, snob and Veblen effects in the theory of consumers' demand', *Quarterly Journal of Economics*, 64: 183–207.

Leidner, R. (1993) *Fast Food, Fast Talk. Service Work and the Routinization of Every Day Life*, Berkeley: University of California Press.

Leiss, W., Kline, S. and Jhally, S. (1991) *Social Communication as Advertising: Persons, Products and Images of Well-being*, New York: MacMillan.

Lenman, B. P. (1990) 'The English and Dutch East India companies and the birth of consumerism in the Augustan World', *Eighteenth-Century Life*, 14: 47–65.

Leonard-Barton, D. (1981) 'Voluntary simplicity lifestyles and energy conservation', *Journal of Consumer Research*, 8: 243–52.

Leonini, L. (1988) *L'identità smarrita. Il ruolo degli oggetti nella vita quotidiana*, Bologna: Il Mulino.

Leslie, D. (1995) 'Global scan: the globalization of advertising agencies, concepts and campaigns', *Economic Geography*, 71 (4): 402–26.

Levi, M. and Linton, A. (2003) 'Fair Trade, a cup at a time?', *Politics & Society*, 31 (3): 407–32.

Levine, L. W. (1988) *Highbrow/Lowbrow. The Emergence of Cultural Hierarchy in America*, Cambridge, Mass.: Harvard University Press.

Lewis, R. and Rolley, K. (1997) '(Ad)dressing the dyke: lesbian looks and lesbian looking', in M. Nava et al. (eds) *Buy this Book. Contemporary Issues in Advertising and Consumption*, London: Routledge.

Leyshon, A. and Thrift, N. (1997) *Money/Space. Geographies of Monetary Transformation*, London: Routledge.

Liebes, T. and Katz, E. (1990) *The Export of Meaning: Cross-Cultural Readings of Dallas*, New York: Oxford University Press.

Littler, J. (2005) 'Beyond the boycott. Anti-consumerism, cultural change and the limits of reflexivity', *Cultural Studies*, 19 (2): 227–52.

Lock, M. (2002) *Twice Dead – Organ Transplants and the Reinvention of Death*, Berkeley: University of California Press.

Lockie, S. and Kristen, L. (2002) 'Eating green', *Sociologia Ruralis*, 42 (1): 23–40.

Long, E. (2003) *Book Clubs. Women and the Uses of Reading in Everyday Life*, Chicago: University of Chicago Press.

Lukács, G. (1971) *History and Class Consciousness: Studies in Marxist Dialectics*, London: Merlin [1923].

Lunt, P. (1995) 'Psychological approaches to consumption', in D. Miller (ed.) *Acknowledging Consumption*, London: Routledge.

Lunt, P. and Livingstone, S. (1992) *Mass Consumption and Personal Identity*, Buckingham: Open University Press.

Lupton, D. (1996) *Food, the Body and the Self,* London and Thousands Oaks: Sage.

Lury, C. (1996) *Consumer Cultures*, Cambridge: Polity Press.

Lury, C. (2004) *Brands. The Logos of the Global Economy*, London: Routledge.

Maclachlan, P. and Trentmann, F. (2004) 'Civilizing markets: traditions of consumer politics in twentieth-century Japan, Britain and America', in M. Bevir and F. Trentmann (eds) *Markets in Historical Contexts. Ideas and Politics in the Modern World*, Cambridge: Cambridge University Press.

Malbon, B. (1997) 'Clubbing. Consumption, identity and the spatial practices of every-night life', in T. Skelton and G. Valentine (eds) *Cool Places*, London: Routledge.

Malthus, T. R. (1951) *Principles of Political Economy*, New York: Kelley [1820].

Mandeville, B. (1924) *The Fable of the Bees, or Private Vices, Publick Benefits*, vol. 1, ed. F. B. Kaye, Oxford: The Clarendon Press [1714].

Marchand, R. (1985) *Advertising the American Dream. Making Way for Modernity, 1920–1940*, Berkeley: University of California Press.

Marcoux, J. -S. (2001) 'The *casser-maison* ritual. Constructing the self by emptying the home', *Journal of Material Culture*, 6 (6): 213–35.

Marcuse, H. (1964) *One-dimensional Man*, Boston, Beacon Press.

Margolis, J. (1999) 'Pierre Bourdieu. Habitus and the logic of practice', in M. Shusterman (ed.) *Bourdieu. A Critical Reader*, Cambridge: Polity Press.

Marx, K. (1973) *Grundrisse: Foundations of the Critique of Political Economy*, London: Penguin [1857].

Marx, K. (1974) *Capital*, Vol. I, London: Allen and Unwin [1867].

Mauger, G., Poliak, C. F. and Pudal, B. (1999) *Histoires de lecteurs*, Paris: Nathan.

Mauss, M. (1954) *Gift. Forms and Functions of Exchange in Archaic Societies*, London: Cohen and West [1924].

Mayer, R. N. (1989) *The Consumer Movement: Guardians of the Marketplace*, Boston: Twayne.

Mazzanti, D. (2004) *Vespa. Style in Motion*, San Francisco: Chronicle Books.

McCracken, G. (1988) *Culture and Consumption: New Approaches to the Symbolic Character of Consumer Goods and Activities*, Bloomington: Indiana University Press.

McKay, H. (1997) 'Consuming communication technologies at home', in H. McKay (ed.) *Consumption and Everyday Life*, Buckingham: Open University Press.

McKendrick, N. (1982) 'Commercialization and the economy', in N. McKendrick, J. Brewer and J. M. Plumb (eds) *The Birth of a Consumer Society: The Commercialization of Eighteenth-Century England*, Bloomington: Indiana University Press.

McKendrick, N., Brewer, J. and Plumb, J. M. (eds) (1982) *The Birth of a Consumer Society: The Commercialization of Eighteenth-Century England*, Bloomington: Indiana University Press.

McLean, A. H. (2000) 'From ex-patient alternatives to consumer options: consequences of consumerism for psychiatric consumers and the ex-patient movement', *International Journal of Health Services*, 30 (4): 821–47.

McLuhan, M. (1967) *The Mechanical Bride. Folklore of Industrial Man*, Boston: Beacon Press.

McMillan, J. (ed.) (1997) *Gambling Cultures*, London: Routledge.

McNay, N. (1999) 'Gender, *habitus* and the field: Pierre Bourdieu and the limits of reflexivity', *Theory, Culture and Society*, 16 (1): 95–117.

Mendels, F. (1981) 'Les Temps de l'industrie et le temps de proto-industrialisations', *Revue du Nord*, 18: 21–34.

Mennell, S. (1996) *All Manners of Food. Eating and Taste in England and France from the Middle Ages to the Present*, Urbana: University of Illinois Press.

Merkel, I. (2006) 'From stigma to cult. Changing meanings in East German consumer culture,' in F. Trentmann (ed.) *The Making of the Consumer: Knowledge, Power and Identity in the Modern World*, Oxford: Berg.

Micheletti M. (2003) *Political Virtue and Shopping. Individuals, Consumerism and Collective Action*, London: Palgrave.

Micheletti M., Follesdal, A. and Stolle, D. (eds) (2004) *Politics, Products and Markets. Exploring Political Consumerism Past and Present*, New Brunswick: Transaction Publishers.

Miele, M. and Murdoch, J. (2002) 'Fast food, Slowfood: standardizing and differentiating cultures of food', in R. Almas and G. Lawrence (eds) *Globalization, Localization and Sustainable Livelihoods*, Cambridge, Mass.: Kluwer.

Miller, D. (1987) *Material Culture and Mass Consumption*, Oxford: Basil Blackwell.

Miller, D. (1993) *Unwrapping Christmas*, Oxford: Oxford University Press.

Miller, D. (ed.) (1995) *Acknowledging Consumption. A Review of New Studies*, London: Routledge.

Miller, D. (1997a) 'Coca-Cola: a black sweet drink from Trinidad', in D. Miller (ed.) *Material Cultures*, London: University College London Press.

Miller, D. (1997b) 'Consumption and its consequences', in H. Mackay (ed.) *Consumption and Everyday Life*, London: Sage and the Open University.

Miller, D. (1998) *A Theory of Shopping*, Cambridge: Polity Press.

Miller, D. (2001) 'The poverty of morality', *Journal of Consumer Culture*, 1 (2): 225–44.

Miller, D. (2002) 'Turning Callon the right way up', *Economy and Society*, 31 (2): 218–33.

Miller, D. (2004) 'The little black dress is the solution, but what is the problem?' in K.M. Ekstrøm, and H. Brembeck (eds) *Elusive Consumption*, Oxford: Berg.

Miller, D. et al. (eds) (1998) *Shopping, Place and Identity*, London: Routledge.

Miller, M. B. (1981) *The Bon Marché. Bourgeois Culture and the Department Store, 1869–1920*, London: Allen and Unwin.

Miller, N. and Rose, N. (1997) 'Mobilizing the consumer. Assembling the object of desire', in *Theory, Culture and Society*, 14 (1): 1–36.

Mintz, S. W. (1985) *Sweetness and Power*, New York: Viking.

Mintz, S. W. (1993) 'The changing roles of food in the study of consumption', in J. Brewer and R. Porter (eds) *Consumption and the World of Goods*, London: Routledge.

Molotch, H. (2003) *Where the Stuff Comes From*, New York: Routledge.

Moores, S. (1993) *Interpreting Audiences*, London and Thousand Oaks: Sage.

Morley, D. (1992) *Television, Audience and Cultural Studies*, London: Routledge.

Morris, M. (2005) 'Interpretability and social power, or why postmodern advertising works', *Media, Culture and Society*, 27 (5): 697–718.

Mort, F. (1996) *Cultures of Consumption. Masculinities and Social Space in Late Twentieth-Century Britain*, London: Routledge.

Mort, F. (2006) 'Competing domains: democratic subjects and consuming subjects in Britain and the United States since 1945', in F. Trentmann (ed.) *The Making of the Consumer: Knowledge, Power and Identity in the Modern World*, Oxford: Berg.

Mukerji, C. (1983) *From Graven Images: Patterns of Modern Materialism*, New York: Columbia University Press.

Muller, J. Z. (1993) *Adam Smith in his Time and Ours: Designing the Decent Society*, New York: The Free Press.

Muntin, R. (1996) *An Economic and Social History of Gambling in Britain and the USA*, Manchester: Manchester University Press.

Naisbitt J. (1994) *Global Paradox*, New York: Avon Books.

Nava, M. (1991) *Changing Cultures: Feminism, Youth and Consumerism*, London: Sage.

Nava, M. (1997) 'Women, the city and the department store', in P. Falk and C. Campbell (eds) *The Shopping Experience*, London: Sage.

Nava, M., Blake, A., MacRury, I. and Richards, B. (eds) (1997) *Buy this Book. Contemporary Issues in Advertising and Consumption*, London: Routledge.

Nedelmann, B. (1991) 'Individualization, exaggeration and paralysation: Simmel's three problems of culture', *Theory, Culture and Society*, 8: 69–94.

Nixon, S. (1996) *Hard Looks. Masculinities, Spectatorship and Contemporary Consumption*, London: University College London Press.

Nixon, S. (2003) *Advertising Cultures*, London: Sage.

Nussbaum, M. and Sen, A. (eds) (1993) *The Quality of Life*, Oxford: Clarendon Press.

Packard, V. (1958) *The Hidden Persuaders*, New York: McKay.

Pahl, J. (2000) 'The gendering of spending within the household', *Radical Statistics*, 75: 38–48.

Parker, H., Aldridge, J. and Measham, F. (1998) *Illegal Leisure. The Normalization of Adolescent Recreational Drug Use*, London: Routledge.

Parr, J. (1999) *Domestic Goods. The Material, the Moral and the Economic in Postwar Years*, Toronto: University of Toronto Press.

Parssinen, T. (1983) *Secret Passions, Secret Remedies: Narcotic Drugs in British Society 1820–1930*, Manchester: Manchester University Press.

Pateman, C. (1988) *The Sexual Contract*, Stanford: Stanford University Press.

Peiss, K. L. (1998) *Hope in a Jar. The Making of America's Beauty Culture*, New York: Metropolitan Books.

Perrot, M. (1985) *Le Mode de vie des familles bourgeoises*, Paris: Presses de la Fondation Nationale des Sciences Politiques.

Perrot, Ph. (1987) 'Pour un Généalogie de l'austérité des apparences', *Communication*, 46: 157–80.

Peterson, R. (1992) 'Understanding audience segmentation: from elite and mass to omnivore and univore', *Poetics*, 21: 243–58.

Peterson, R. and Kern, R. (1996) 'Changing highbrow taste: from snob to omnivore', *American Sociological Review*, 61: 900–7.

Pietrykowski, B. (2004) 'You are what you eat: the social economy of the Slow Food movement', *Review of Social Economy*, 62 (3): 307–21.

Pink, S. (2004) *Home Truths. Gender, Domestic Objects and Everyday Life*, Oxford: Berg.

Pinto, L. (1990) 'Le Consommateur: agent économique et acteur politique', *Revue Française de Sociologie*, 31: 79–98.

Pleck, E. H. (2000) *Celebrating the Family: Ethnicity, Consumer Culture and Family Rituals*, Cambridge, Mass.: Harvard University Press.

Pocock, J. G. A. (1985) *Virtue, Commerce, History*, Cambridge: Cambridge University Press.

Polanyi, K. (1957) *The Great Transformation*, New York: Rinehart.

Polhemus, T. (1994) *Streetstyles. From Sidewalks to Catwalks*, London: Thames and Hudson.

Pomeranz, K. (2000) *The Great Divergence: China, Europe, and the Making of the Modern World Economy*, Princeton: Princeton University Press.

Porter, R. (1992) 'Addicted to modernity. Nervousness in early consumer society', in J. Melling and J. Barry (eds) *Culture in History: Production, Consumption, and Values in Historical Perspective*, Exeter: University of Exeter Press.

Porter, R. (1993) 'Consumption: disease of the consumer society?' in J. Brewer and R. Porter (eds) *Consumption and the World of Goods*, London: Routledge.

Poster, M. (ed.) (1988) *Jean Baudrillard: Selected Writings*, Cambridge: Polity Press.

Radin, M. J. (1996) *Contested Commodities*, Cambridge, Mass.: Harvard University Press.

Radway, J. (1987) *Reading the Romance: Women, Patriarchy and Popular Literature*, London: Verso.

Ram, U. (2004) 'Glocommodification: how the global consumes the local–McDonald's in Israel', *Current Sociology*, 52 (1): 11–31.

Rappaport, E. D. (2000) *Shopping for Pleasure: Women in the Making of London's West End*, Princeton: Princeton University Press.

Rappaport, E. D. (2006) 'Packaging China. Foreign articles and dangerous tastes in mid-Victorian tea party' in F. Trentmann (ed.) *The Making of the Consumer: Knowledge, Power and Identity in the Modern World*, Oxford: Berg.

Reddy, W. M. (1984) *The Rise of Market Culture*, Cambridge: Cambridge University Press.

Reith, G. (1999) *The Age of Chance: Gambling in Western Culture*, London: Routledge.

Reith, G. (2004) 'Consumption and its discontents: addiction, identity and the problems of freedom', *The British Journal of Sociology*, 55 (2): 283–300.

Riesman, D. (1961) *The Lonely Crowd. A Study of the Changing American Character*, New Haven: Yale University Press.

Riggins, S. H. (1990) 'The power of things: the role of domestic objects in the presentation of the self', in S. H. Riggins (ed.) *Beyond Goffman. Studies on Communication, Institution and Social Interaction*, Berlin: Mouton de Gruyter.

Ritson, M. and Elliot, R. (1999) 'The social uses of advertising. An ethnographic study of adolescent advertising audiences', *Journal of Consumer Research*, 26: 260–77.

Ritzer, G. (1993) *The McDonaldization of Society*, Newbury Park, Calif.: Pine Forge Press.

Ritzer, G. (1999) *Enchanting a Disenchanted World. Revolutionizing the Mean of Consumption*, London: Pine Forge Press.

Ritzer, G. (2001) *Explorations in the Sociology of Consumption*, London: Sage.

Ritzer, G. (2004) *The Globalization of Nothing*, Thousand Oaks: Pine Forge Press.

Roberts, M. L. (1998) 'Gender, consumption and commodity culture', *American Historical Review*, 103 (3): 817–44.

Robertson, R. (1992) *Globalization. Social Theory and Global Culture*, London: Sage.

Roche, M. (1981) *Le Peuple de Paris*, Paris: Aubier.

Rogers, M. F. (1999) *Barbie Culture*, London: Sage.

Rojek, C. (1985) *Capitalism and Leisure Theory*, London: Routledge.

Rook, D. (1985) 'The ritual dimension of consumer behaviour', *Journal of Consumer Research*, 12: 251–64.

Rose, N. (1999) *Governing the Soul: The Shaping of the Private Self*. 2nd edn, London: Free Associations Books [1989].

Rubin, I. (1972) *Essays on Marx's Theory of Value*, Detroit: Black and Red.

Rumbarger, J. (1989) *Profits, Power and Prohibition. Alcohol Reform and the Industrializing of America, 1800–1930*, Albany: State University of New York Press.

Rumbo, J. D. (2002) 'Consumer resistance in a world of advertising clutter. The case of Adbusters', *Psychology and Marketing*, 19 (2): 127–48.

Sahlins, M. (1972) *Stone Age Economics*, Chicago: Aldine.

Sahlins, M. (1974) *Culture and Practical Reason*, Chicago: University of Chicago Press.

Sahlins, M. (2000) *Culture in Practice*, New York: Zone Books.

Salih, R. (2003) *Gender in Transnationalism. Home, Longing and Belonging among Moroccan Migrant Women*, London: Routledge.

Salmon, A. (2000) 'Le Réveil du souci étique dans les enterprises. Un nouvel esprit du capitalisme?' *Revue du MAUSS*, special issue on *Etique et économie*, 15 (1): 296–319.

Santoro, M. (2002) 'What is a "cantautore"? Distinction and authorship in Italian (popular) music', *Poetics*, 30 (1–2): 111–32.

Santoro, M. and Sassatelli, R. (2001) 'La voce del padrino', *Il Mulino*, 50 (395): 505–13.

Sassatelli, R. (1995) *Power Balance in the Consumption Sphere. Reconsidering Consumer Protection Organizations*, EUI Social and Political Sciences Working Papers, no. 5, pp. 1–74, European University Institute.

Sassatelli, R. (1997) 'Consuming ambivalence: eighteenth century public discourse on consumption and Mandeville's legacy', *Journal of Material Culture*, 2 (3): 339–60.

Sassatelli, R. (1999) 'Interaction order and beyond. A field analysis of body culture within fitness gyms', *Body and Society*, 5 (2–3): 227–48.

Sassatelli, R. (2000a) 'From value to consumption. A social-theoretical perspective on Simmel's Philosophie des Geldes', *Acta Sociologica*, 43 (3): 207–18.

Sassatelli, R. (2000b) 'The commercialization of discipline. Keep-fit culture and its values', *Journal of Modern Italian Studies*, 5 (3): 396–411.

Sassatelli, R. (2001a) 'Tamed hedonism: choice, desires and deviant pleasures', in J. Gronow and A. Warde (eds) *Ordinary Consumption*, London: Routledge.

Sassatelli, R. (2001b) 'Trust, choice and routine: putting the consumer on trial', *Critical Review of International Social and Political Philosophy*, 4 (4): 84–105.

Sassatelli, R. (2004) 'The political morality of food. Discourses, contestation and alternative consumption', in M. Harvey et al. (eds) *Qualities of Food*, Manchester: Manchester University Press.

Sassatelli, R. (2006) 'Virtue, responsibility and consumer choice. Framing critical consumerism', in J. Brewer, and F. Trentmann (eds) *Consuming Cultures, Global Perspectives. Historical Trajectories, Transnational Exchanges*, Oxford: Berg.

Sassatelli, R. and Scott, A. (2001) 'Trust regimes, wider markets, novel foods', *European Societies*, 3 (2): 211–42.

Savage, J. (1997) 'What's so new about the new man? Three decades of advertising to men', in D. Jones (ed.) *Sex, Power and Travel: Ten Years of Arena*, London: Virgin.

Schama, S. (1987) *The Embarrassment of Riches. An Interpretation of Dutch Culture in the Golden Age*, New York: Knopf.

Schatzki, T. (2001) *The Practice Turn in Contemporary Theory*, London: Routledge.

Scheper-Huges, N. and Wacquant, L. (eds) (2001) 'Commodifying bodies', special issue of *Body and Society*, 7: 2–3.

Schivelbusch, W. (1988) *Disenchanted Light: The Industrialization of Light in the Nineteenth Century*, Berkeley: University of California Press [1983].

Schivelbusch, W. (1992) *Tastes of Paradise: A Social History of Spices, Stimulants and Intoxicants*, New York: Pantheon Books, (1980).

Schor, J. B. (1999) *The Overspent American*, New York: HarperCollins.

Schudson, M. (1984) *Advertising, the Uneasy Persuasion. Its Dubious Impact on American Society*, New York: Basic Books.

Schumpeter, J. A. (1955) *History of Economic Analysis*, New York: Oxford University Press.

Schwartz, H. (1986) *Never Satisfied: A Cultural History of Diets, Fantasies and Fat*, New York: Free Press.

Schwartz, H. (1996) 'Hearing aids. Sweet nothing, or an ear for a ear', in P. Kirkham (ed.) *The Gendered Object*, Manchester: Manchester University Press.

Scitovsky, T. (1992) *The Joyless Economy*, New York: Oxford University Press [2nd revised edn, 1976].

Scott, A. (ed.) (1997) *The Limits of Globalization*, London: Routledge.

Searle, G. (1998) *Morality and the Market in Victorian Britain*, Oxford: Clarendon.

Sedgewick, E. K. (1992) 'Epidemics of the will', in J. Crary and S. Kwinter (eds) *Incorporations*, New York: Zone.

Sedgewick, E. K. (1994) *Tendencies*, London: Routledge.

Seiter, E. (1993) *Sold Separately: Parents and Children in Consumer Culture*, New Brunswick: Rutgers University Press.

Sekora, J. (1985) *Luxury: The Concept in Western Thought, Eden to Smollet*, Baltimore: Johns Hopkins University Press.

Sen, A. K. (1977) 'Rational fools: a critique of the behavioural foundations of economic theory', *Philosophy and Public Affairs*, 6 (4): 317–44.

Sen, A. K. (1985) *Commodities and Capabilities*, Amsterdam: Elsevier.

Sennett, R. (1976) *The Fall of Public Man*, Cambridge: Cambridge University Press.

Shammas, C. (1990) *The Preindustrial Consumer in England and America*, Oxford: Basil Blackwell.

Shields, R. (ed.) (1992) *Lifestyle Shopping: The Subject of Consumption*, London: Routledge.

Shiner, M. and Newburn, T. (1997) 'Definitely, maybe not? The normalization of recreational drug use among young people', *Sociology*, 31 (3): 511–29.

Shove, E. (2003) *Comfort, Cleanliness and Convenience: The Social Organization of Normality*, Oxford: Berg.

Shove, E. and Southerton, D. (2000) 'Defrosting the freezer: from novelty to convenience', *Journal of Material Culture*, 5 (3): 301–20.

Silverstone, R. (1994) *Television and Everyday Life*, London: Routledge.

Silverstone, R. and Hirsch, E. (eds) (1994) *Consuming Technologies: Media and Information in Domestic Spaces*, London: Routledge.

Simmel, G. (1890) *Uber sociale Differenzierung. Sociologische und psychologische Untersuchungen*, Leipzig: Duncker & Humblot.

Simmel, G. (1971a) 'The metropolis and mental life', in *On Individuality and Social Forms*, Chicago: Chicago University Press, pp. 324–39 [1903].

Simmel, G. (1971b) 'Fashion', in *On Individuality and Social Forms*, Chicago: Chicago University Press, pp. 294–323 [1904].

Simmel, G. (1990) *Philosophy of Money*, 2nd edn, London: Routledge [orig. 2nd edn 1907].

Simmel, G. (1991) 'The problem of style', *Theory, Culture and Society*, 8: 63–71 [1908].

Skov, L. (2005) 'The return of the fur coat: a commodity chain perspective', *Current Sociology*, 53 (1): 9–32.

Slater, D. (1997) *Consumer Culture and Modernity*, Cambridge: Polity Press.

Slater, D. (1998) 'Trading sexpics on IRC: embodiment and authenticity on the Internet', *Body and Society*, 4 (4): 90–118.

Smart, B. (ed.) (1999) *Resisting McDonaldization*, London: Sage.

Smith, Adam (1981) *An Enquiry into the Nature and Causes of the Wealth of Nations*, ed. A. Skinner and R. Meek, Indianapolis: Liberty Classics [1776].

Smith, Adam (1982) *Lectures on Jurisprudence*, ed. R. Meek, D. Raphael and P. Stein Indianapolis: Liberty Classics [1762–6].

Smith, C. W. (1989) *Auctions: The Social Construction of Value*, London: Harvester Wheatsheaf.

Smith, Nancy C. (1990) *Morality and the Market. Consumer Pressure for Corporate Accountability*, London: Routledge.

Soar, M. (2000) 'Encoding advertisements. Ideology and meaning in advertising production', *Mass Communication and Society*, 3 (4): 425–37.

Sombart, W. (1928) *Der moderne Kapitalismus: historisch-systematische Darstellung des gesamteuropäischen Wirtschaftslebens von seinen Anfangen bis zur Gegenwart*, Munchen: Dunker & Humblot.

Sombart, W. (1967) *Luxury and Capitalism*, Ann Arbor: University of Michigan Press [1913].

South, N. (ed.) (1998) *Drugs. Cultures, Controls and Everyday Life*, London: Sage.

Spitzack, C. (1990) *Confessing Excess: Women and the Politics of Body Reduction*, Albany: University of New York Press.

Spooner, B. (1986) 'Weavers and dealers: the authenticity of an oriental carpet', in A. Appadurai (ed.) *The Social Life of Things. Commodities in Cultural Perspectives*, Cambridge: Cambridge University Press.

Stearns, P. (2001) *Consumerism in World History. The Global Transformation of Desire*, London: Routledge.

Steedman, I. (2001) *Consumption Takes Time. Implications for Economic Theory*, London: Routledge.

Steele, V. (1997) 'Anti-fashion. The 1970s', *Fashion Theory*, 1 (3): 279–95.

Steele, V. (2003) *Fashion. Italian Style*, New Haven: Yale University Press.

Steinberg, D. L. (1997) *Bodies in Glass: Genetics, Eugenics, Embryo Ethics*, Manchester: Manchester University Press.

Steward, S. (1993) *On Longing. Narratives of the Miniature, the Gigantic, the Souvenir, the Collection*, Durham, NC: Duke University Press.

Strasser, S. (1989) *Satisfaction Guaranteed. The Making of the American Mass Market*, New York: Pantheon Books.

Strasser, S., McGovern, C. and Judd, M. (eds) (1998) *Getting and Spending: European and American Consumer Societies in the Twentieth Century*, Cambridge: Cambridge University Press.

Sullivan, O. and Gershuny, J. (2004) 'Inconspicuous consumption. Work-rich, time-poor in the liberal market economy', *Journal of Consumer Culture*, 4 (1): 79–100.

Swann, P. (2002) 'There's more to the economics of consumption than (almost) unconstrained utility maximization', in A. McMeekin et al. (eds) *Innovation by Demand: An Interdisciplinary Approach*, Manchester: Manchester University Press.

Swedberg, R. (1987) 'Economic sociology', *Current Sociology*, 35: 1–21.

Taylor, C. (1989) *The Sources of the Self. The Making of Modern Identity*, Cambridge: Cambridge University Press.

Tester, K. (1999) 'The moral malaise of McDonaldization. The values of vegetarianism', in B. Smart (ed.) *Resisting McDonaldization*, London: Sage.

Thomas, N. (1991) *Entangled Objects. Exchange, Entangled Objects and Colonialism in the South Pacific*, Cambridge: Mass.: Harvard University Press.

Thompson, M. and Ellis, R. J. (1997) 'Introduction', in R. J. Ellis and M. Thompson (eds) *Culture Matters*, Boulder: Westview Press.

Thornton, S. (1995) *Club Cultures. Music, Media and Subcultural Capital*, Cambridge: Polity Press.

Thrisk, J. (1978) *Economic Policy and Projects. The Development of a Consumer Society in Early Modern England*, Oxford: Clarendon Press.

Tiersten, L. (2001) *Marianne in the Market. Envisioning Consumer Society in Fin-de-Siècle France*, Berkeley: University of California Press.

Tilman, R. (1996) *The Intellectual Legacy of Thorstein Veblen*, Westport, Conn.: Greenwood.

Tomlinson, M. (2003) 'Lifestyle and social class', *European Sociological Review*, 19 (1): 97–111.

Trentmann, F. (2003) 'Civil society, commerce and the "citizen consumer": Popular meanings of free trade in modern Britain', in F. Trentmann (ed.) *Paradoxes of Civil Society: New Perspectives on Modern German and British History*, New York: Berghahn Books.

Trentmann, F. (2004) 'Beyond consumerism: new historical perspectives on consumption', *Journal of Contemporary History*, 39 (3): 373–401.

Trentmann, F. (2006a) 'The modern genealogy of the consumer. Meanings, identities and political synapses', in J. Brewer and F. Trentmann (eds) *Consuming Cultures, Global Perspectives. Historical Trajectories, Transnational Exchanges*, Oxford: Berg.

Trentmann, F. (ed.) (2006b) *The Making of the Consumer: Knowledge, Power and Identity in the Modern World*, Oxford: Berg.

Trigg, A. B. (2001) 'Veblen, Bourdieu and conspicuous consumption', *Journal of Economic Issues*, 35 (1): 99–115.

Turner, V. (1969) *The Ritual Process: Structure and Anti-structure*, London: Routledge.

Tzanelli, R. (2003) 'Casting the Neohellenic "Other": tourism, the culture industry and contemporary orientalism in *Captain Corelli's Mandolin* (2001)', *Journal of Consumer Culture*, 3 (2): 217–44.

Urry, J. (1990) *The Tourist Gaze*, London: Sage.

Valverde, M. (1998) *Diseases of the Will. Alcohol and the Dilemma of Freedom*, New York: Cambridge University Press.

Van der Berghe, P. (1984) 'Ethnic cuisine: culture in nature', *Ethnic and Racial Studies*, 7 (3): 387–97.

Van Eijck, K. (2000) 'Richard A. Peterson and the culture of consumption', *Poetics*, 28: 207–24.

Veblen, T. (1994) *The Theory of the Leisure Class*, London: MacMillan [1899].

Vidal, J. (1997) *Mclibel: Burger Culture on Trial*, New York: The New York Press.

Warde, A. (1994) 'Consumption, identity formation and uncertainty', *Sociology*, 28 (4): 877–98.

Warde, A. (1997) *Consumption, Food and Taste*, London: Sage.

Warde, A. (2000) 'Eating globally: cultural flows and the spread of ethnic restaurants', in D. Kalb et al. (eds) *The End of Globalization*: Boulder: Rowman and Littlefield.

Warde, A. (2005) 'Consumption and theories of practice', *Journal of Consumer Culture*, 5 (2): 131–53.

Warde, A. and Martens, L. (2001) *Eating Out. Social Differentiation, Consumption and Pleasure*, Cambridge: Cambridge University Press.

Warde, A., Martens, L. and Wendy, O. (1998) 'Consumption and the problem of variety. Cultural omnivorousness, social distinciton and eating out', *Sociology*, 33 (1): 105–27.

Wardlow, D. L. (1996) *Gay, Lesbians and Consumer Behavior*, New York: Haworth Press.

Waters, M. (1990) *Ethnic Options: Choosing Identities in America*, Berkeley: University of California Press.

Watson, J. (ed.) (1997) *Golden Arches East. McDonald's in East Asia*, Stanford: Stanford University Press.

Watson, M. and Shove, E. (2005) 'Doing it yourself? Products, competence and meaning in the practices of DIY', paper presented to the ESA meeting in Torun, Poland, September.

Watts, S. (1998) *The Magic Kingdom: Walt Disney and the American Way of Life*, New York: Houghton Mifflin.

Weatherhill, L. (1988) *Consumer Behaviour and Material Culture, 1660–1760*, London: Routledge.

Weber, M. (1930) *The Protestant Ethic and the Spirit of Capitalism*, London: Allen and Unwin [1904–5].

Weber, M. (1980) *General Economic History*, New Brunswick: Transaction Books [1920].

Wernick, A. (1991) *Promotional Culture: Advertising, Ideology and Symbolic Expression*, London: Sage.

Wheaton, B. and Tomlinson, A. (1998) 'The changing gender order in sport? The case of windsurfing sub-cultures', *Journal of Sport and Social Issues*, 22: 252–74.

White, N. (2000) *Reconstructing Italian Fashion. America and the Development of the Italian Fashion Industry*, Oxford: Berg.

Wickham, G. (1997) 'Governance of consumption', in P. Sulkunen, J. Holwood, H. Radner and G. Schulze (eds) *Constructing the New Consumer Society*, London: MacMillan.

Wiggershaus, R. (1995) *The Frankfurt School: Its History, Theories and Political Significance*, Cambridge: Polity Press [1986].

Wilk, R. (1989) 'Houses as consumer goods', in H. Rutz and B. Orlove (eds) *The Social Economy of Consumption*, Lanham: University Press of America, pp. 297–322.

Wilk, R. (1998) 'Emulation, imitation and global consumerism', *Organization and Environment*, 11 (3): 314–33.

Wilk, R. (2004) 'Morals and metaphors. The meaning of consumption', in K. M. Ekstrøm, and H. Brembeck (eds) *Elusive Consumption*, Oxford: Berg.

Williams, C. (2004) 'A lifestyle choice? Evaluating the motives of do-it-yourself (DIY) consumers', *International Journal of Retail and Distribution Management*, 32 (5): 270–78.

Williams, C. C. and Paddock, C. (2003) 'The meaning of alternative consumption practices', *Cities*, 20 (5): 311–19.

Williams, R. H. (1982) *Dream Worlds. Mass Consumption in Late Nineteenth Century France*, Berkeley: University of California Press.

Williamson, J. (1978) *Decoding Advertisements*, London: Marion Boyars.

Willis, J. (1993) 'European consumption and Asian production in the seventeenth and eighteenth centuries', in J. Brewer and R. Porter (eds) *Consumption and the World of Goods*, London: Routledge.

Willis, P. (1978) *Profane Culture*, London: Routledge.

Willis, P. (1990) *Common Culture*, Milton Keynes: Open University Press.

Wilska, T. (2001) 'The role of states in the creation of consumption norms' in J. Gronow and A. Warde (eds) *Ordinary Consumption*, London: Routledge.

Wilson, E. (1985) *Adorned in Dreams: Fashion and Modernity*, London: Virago.

Winch, D. (2006) 'The problematic status of the consumer in orthodox economic thought', in F. Trentmann (ed.) *The Making of the Consumer: Knowledge, Power and Identity in the Modern World*, Oxford: Berg.

Winship, J. (1987) *Inside Women's Magazines*, London: Pandora.

Zahidieh, N. (1994) 'London and the colonial consumer in the late seventeenth century', *Economic History Review*, 47: 239–61.

Zamagni, V. (1992) 'The Italian economic miracle revisited. New markets and American technology', in E. Di Nolfo (ed.) *Power in Europe?* vol. 2, Berlin: De Gruyter.

Zeitlin, J. and Herrigel, G. (eds) (2000) *Americanization and its Limits. Reworking US Technology and Management in Post-war Europe and Japan*, Oxford: Oxford University Press.

Zelizer, V. (1994) *The Social Meaning of Money*, New York: Basic Books.

Zelizer, V. (2004a) 'Culture and consumption', in N. Smelsner and R. Swedberg (eds) *Handbook of Economic Sociology*, Princeton: Princeton University Press.

Zelizer, V. (2004b) *The Purchase of Intimacy*, Princeton: Princeton University Press.

Zinkhan, M. G. and Carlson, L. (1995) 'Green advertising and the reluctant consumer', *Journal of Advertising*, 24 (2): 1–16.

Zukin, L. A. (1991) *Landscapes of Power. From Detroit to Disneyworld*, Berkeley: University of California Press.

Zukin, S. (2004) *Point of Purchase: How Shopping Changed American Culture*, New York: Routledge.

Zukin, S. and Maguire, J. S. (2004) 'Consumers and consumption', *Annual Review of Sociology*, 30: 173–97.

Zweiniger-Bargielowska, I. (2000) *Austerity in Britain: Rationing, Controls, and Consumption, 1939–1955*, Oxford: Oxford University Press.

Index